Serious Violations of Human Rights

On the Emergence of a New Special Regime

ILIA SIATITSA

OXFORD
UNIVERSITY PRESS

OXFORD
UNIVERSITY PRESS

Great Clarendon Street, Oxford, OX2 6DP,
United Kingdom

Oxford University Press is a department of the University of Oxford.
It furthers the University's objective of excellence in research, scholarship,
and education by publishing worldwide. Oxford is a registered trade mark of
Oxford University Press in the UK and in certain other countries

First Edition published in 2022

Impression: 1

Published in the United States of America by Oxford University Press
198 Madison Avenue, New York, NY 10016, United States of America

British Library Cataloguing in Publication Data

Data available

Library of Congress Control Number: 2022930025

ISBN 978–0–19–286304–1

DOI: 10.1093/oso/9780192863041.001.0001

Printed and bound in the UK by
Clays Ltd, Elcograf S.p.A.

Στον Πασχάλη

Foreword

In recent decades, reference to serious or gross violations of human rights has mushroomed in diplomatic settings, case law, international instruments, and legal scholarship. However, international lawyers have refrained from engaging thoroughly with the contours of the notion and the question of whether it involves legal consequences making up a specific legal regime.

This book brilliantly fills the gap. It persuasively demonstrates that labelling a violation of international human rights law as serious is not just a rhetorical device used to signal gravity and condemnation, but rather that there is an emergent legal regime attached to it. To this end, the book identifies the criteria apt to describing violations of international rules protecting human rights as serious. It then moves on exploring the institutional mechanisms set up for monitoring these violations and those geared to their enforcement. Finally, it delves into the issue of the international right of the victims to reparation. By pointing at the emergence of a new regime attached to serious violations of international law protecting human rights, the author thus persuasively provides the reader with a comprehensive picture of its key components—namely the substantive, monitoring, enforcement, and remedial components.

The research underpinning this book is rigorous and rich. It is also particularly valuable for the systematization of the practice of a variety of international bodies, such as human rights monitoring bodies, the UN Security Council, and the UN General Assembly. This is in itself a considerable achievement, in light of the sparse nature of the primary sources taken into account.

There is a pressing need to strengthen the regime of international responsibility for serious violations of human rights and this book highlights it in the best possible way. Therefore, this book constitutes an indispensable reference for international law scholars and practitioners in the field of the protection of human rights. It will also be of a great value to scholars and researchers of disciplines other than international law who want to enhance their legal understanding of the current international legal frameworks and practices related to serious violations of international human rights law.

The author of the book is particularly qualified to write a monograph on the emerging legal regime attached to serious violations of international rules on human rights, being a human rights expert with a strong and solid background in public international law. She specialized in international humanitarian law and human rights at the Geneva Academy of International Humanitarian Law and Human Rights and worked there as a Research Fellow leading the research on human rights in the digital age. She carried out her PhD research at the Law Faculty of the University of Geneva under the supervision of myself and Professor Linos-Alexander Sicilianos (as external co-supervisor), who is a renowned expert in international human rights law currently serving as judge at the European Court of Human Rights. This book is based on her PhD thesis and I am particularly delighted to see it published as a pioneering book in the field.

Paola Gaeta
Professor of International Law
Graduate Institute of International and Development Studies
Geneva, 8 February 2022

Brief summary

This book analyses the use of the expression 'serious violations of human rights'—and similar ones—in international practice, highlighting some of the recurring responses and consequences to such violations, and suggests that a new special regime—eponymous with the above-mentioned expression—was formed. This special regime is understood as substantively limited to a very specific issue-area of human rights violations; where a series of monitoring mechanisms and procedures is in place to predominantly highlight, document, and record such violations; where specific measures are taken, aimed at enforcing compliance; where certain consequences arise, focusing primarily on affording the victims of such violations a remedy. As such, this special regime is arguably comprised of at least four thinly interconnected components: the substantive, the monitoring, the enforcement, and the remedial ones.

The first component of this special regime is the specific subject-matter itself, namely, the serious violations of human rights. This is the substantive component. Seriousness is understood qualitatively as a combination of different elements present in a specific context that determines the gravity of the violation. It describes a category of human rights violations rather than a list of human rights. The substantive component is the one around which all the other components of the regime operate. There are arguably at least three distinct components operating around the subject matter that occasionally function in conjunction with each other. The monitoring component of the special regime is a diverse network of special monitoring and inquiry processes. It contains various procedures and mechanisms, such as country-specific resolutions and commissions of inquiry, that are set up or triggered following the occurrence of serious violations of human rights. Beyond their material scope, their formal institutional character and their means of operation, constituting primarily promotional and declaratory processes, bring them together. The enforcement component includes measures taken as a response to serious violations of human rights within both the UN sanctions regime and the inter-state countermeasures framework aiming at coercing the wrongdoers to cease such violations. The last component of the special regime around serious violations of human rights is the remedial component. It comprises both adjudicative procedures, facilitating access to redress, and remedial awards, reflecting the gravity of the violations. On the one hand, several *ad hoc* mass claims processes have been established as a response to serious violations of human rights. On the other hand, the human rights courts increasingly recognise serious violations of human rights in their jurisprudence as a separate category of violations giving rise to specific procedures and remedies. The primary aim of the remedial component is to ensure that victims of such violations receive some form of remedy for the harm they suffered. It is not intended to punish the responsible state.

This book constitutes a first step towards the recognition of the existence of such a regime, allowing for far more constructive and coherent elaboration in the future. Of course, future practice may dictate alternative interpretations of the role of this category of violations occupies in the international legal order. However, what becomes apparent from this work is that the concept of serious violations of human rights is a key notion, as it allows the international community to pinpoint those factual situations requiring its attention and action.

Acknowledgements

Nessie, the monster residing in the deep waters of Loch Ness, made people feel its presence without ever revealing its image; similarly to that mythical creature, the writing of the doctoral thesis—that is now converted to a book—was always present in my mind throughout the whole process, even during the times I was not working on it. Solitary but not alone in the process, many people have been beside me, supporting me and assisting me to reach the surface.

First and foremost, I am forever grateful to the two people without whose guidance and support this work would not have been possible. The discussions I have had with each of them will follow me into my future endeavours. I would like to thank Professor Paola Gaeta for inspiring me and pushing me forward to become a better scholar and writer. By challenging my ideas, she encouraged me to reflect critically on my arguments and enabled me to develop a more nuanced reflection on the topic. I would also like to thank Professor Linos-Alexander Sicilianos for always patiently and carefully guiding me throughout the process from early on in my career. He encouraged me to move forward, to become more assertive and to explore the positive side of international legal affairs.

I am grateful to the libraries of the Faculty of Law of the University of Geneva and the Graduate Institute of International and Development Studies for providing, in combination, one of the largest collections of books worldwide; and to the staff of the United Nations Library of Geneva for their utmost dedication. I will always remember the CERN library, which surprisingly became my sanctuary and where the final draft of the thesis that has now become a book was written.

I would like to thank the Swiss National Science Foundation (SNSF) for trusting me with a one-year fellowship that allowed me to complete my work, as well as the Faculty of Law at the University of Nottingham and the Irish Centre for Human Rights of the University of Galway for hosting me during that year. Particularly, I would like to thank Professor Aoife Nolan and Professor Shane Darcy. I am especially grateful to Professor Nehal Bhuta, for constructively challenging my work, for his thought-provoking questions, and for his encouragement to publish it.

There is an endless list of people with whom I have shared my thoughts and ideas, and who have helped me progress. I am grateful to all, even if they are not individually mentioned. Particularly, I would like to thank Professor Andrew Clapham for his support and encouragement; Nelleke van Amstel for cheering me on throughout and for reading the very first draft of the first chapter; Iris van der Heijden for pushing me to complete this work from the beginning until the end; Marie Wilke for our enriching conversations; Stella Kelemouridou for bearing with me throughout the process. Many thanks to Helen Cecilia Obregón, Dave Tuck, Firouzeh Mitchell, Ezequiel Heffes, Ellen Policinski, Mina Radončić, and Catherine Minahan for their help. I would also like to thank my colleagues and friends at Privacy International, who have been a constant factor of cheer and support as I transformed my thesis into this book.

Special thanks to my friend Dr Sandra Krähenmann for lending me her mind so often to advance my thoughts, and for providing me with brilliant insights and moral support. Behind the scenes, Valentina Cadelo has been patiently and relentlessly pushing me towards every finish line. She has lent me her ears not only for academic discussions, but also for every moment of doubt I had. She also read almost every new version of each outline and each chapter up until the end.

No words can describe the never-ending support from Paschalis Vichoudis, to whom this work is dedicated.

Contents

Table of cases

INTERNATIONAL COURT OF JUSTICE

PERMANENT COURT OF INTERNATIONAL JUSTICE

EUROPEAN COURT OF HUMAN RIGHTS

INTER-AMERICAN COURT OF HUMAN RIGHTS

AFRICAN COURT ON HUMAN AND PEOPLES' RIGHTS

INTERNATIONAL CRIMINAL COURT

INTERNATIONAL CRIMINAL TRIBUNAL FOR THE FORMER YUGOSLAVIA

INTERNATIONAL CRIMINAL TRIBUNAL FOR RWANDA

OTHER JUDGMENTS

Table of other instruments

UNITED NATIONS DOCUMENTS

UNITED NATIONS RESOLUTIONS

UN General Assembly

UN ECOSOC

UN Human Rights Council

UN Commission on Human Rights

UN Sub-Commission on Prevention of Discrimination and Protection of Minorities

OTHER UN DOCUMENTS

CCPR Committee General Comments

CCPR Committee Views

CCPR Committee Concluding Observations

CESCR Committee Concluding Observations

CESCR Committee General Comment

CERD Committee Decisions

CERD Committee Letters and Statements

CERD Committee other documents

CAT Committee Reports and Summary Accounts

CEDAW Committee Reports

CRC Committee Reports

CRPD Committee Reports

UN Secretary General Reports

OHCHR Reports

International Law Commission Reports

Other independent experts reports (special rapporteurs, commissions of inquiry)

UN organs Verbatim records

Other UN Documents

Online sources

'UNHRC: List of HRC-Mandated Commissions of Inquiries / Fact-Finding Missions & Other Bodies (as of October 2019)' <http://www.ohchr.org/EN/HRBodies/HRC/Pages/ListHRCMandat.aspx> accessed 9 August 2021 . . . . 80n.86

'UNHRC: Sessions' <http://www.ohchr.org/EN/HRBodies/HRC/Pages/Sessions.aspx> accessed 9 August 2021 . . . . 68n.11, 72n.36

'UNHRC: Special sessions' <https://www.ohchr.org/EN/HRBodies/HRC/SpecialSessions/Pages/SpecialSessions.aspx> accessed 9 August 2021 . . . . 72n.35, 72n.39

'UNSC Sanctions' <https://www.un.org/securitycouncil/sanctions/information> accessed 18 August 2021 . . . . 114n.76

CCPR Committee, 'Early-warning measures and urgent procedures, Working Methods' <http://www.ohchr.org/EN/HRBodies/CCPR/Pages/WorkingMethods.aspx> accessed 11 August 2021 . . . . 90n.145

CCPR Committee, 'The Committee's procedures in dealing with emergency situations' (1994) A/49/40 (Vol I)) 9 . . . . 90n.145

CERD decisions since 2003: CERD Committee, 'Early-Warning Measures and Urgent Procedures' <http://www.ohchr.org/EN/HRBodies/CERD/Pages/EarlyWarningProcedure.aspx> accessed 11 August 2021 . . . . . 90n.150, 91n.154

UNCC, 'Category B' <http://www.uncc.ch/category-b> accessed 20 September 2021 . . . . 155–56n.35

UNCC, 'The Claims' <http://www.uncc.ch/claims> accessed 20 September 2021 . . . . 155n.34

UNGA: 74th Session (2019-2020)' <https://research.un.org/en/docs/ga/quick/regular/74> accessed 9 August 2021 . . . . 73n.44

Institut de Droit International Resolutions and reports

Institut de Droit International, Resolution on the obligations and rights *erga omnes* in international law, IDI, Krakow Session (27 August 2005) 9n.41, 9n.44

Institut de Droit International, Resolution on the protection of human rights and the principle of non-intervention in internal affairs of states (13 September 1989) [1989] 63 AIDI 338 . . . . 18n.96, 126n.142

Giorgio Gaja, 'First Report on Obligations *Erga Omnes* in International Law' [2005] 71 AIDI 119 . . . . 132n.180

Giorgio Gaja, 'Second Report on Obligations *Erga Omnes* in International Law' [2005] 71 AIDI 189 . . . . 130n.175

ICISS Report

ICISS, 'The responsibility to Protect: Report of the International Commission on Intervention and State Sovereignty', IDRC (2001) <https://www.idrc.ca/en/book/responsibility-protect-report-international-commission-intervention-and-state-sovereignty> accessed 20 August 2021 . . . . 140–41, 140n.229, 142n.242

AMERICAN REGION

Inter-American Commission on Human Rights Decisions

IAComHR, *Abu-Ali Abdur' Rahman v US* (Merits), Case 21422, Report No 13/14, 2 April 2014 . . . . 35n.43

IAComHR, *Franklin Guillermo Aisalla Molina (Ecuador v Colombia)*, Case 12.779, Decision to archive, Report No 96/13, 4 November 2013 . . . . 168n.107

IAComHR, *Jeffrey Timothy Landrigan v US* (Merits), Case 12776, Report No 81/11, 21 July 2011 . . . . 35n.43

IAComHR, *Manoel Leal De Oliveira v Brazil*, Case No 12308 (17 March 2010) Report No 37/10 . . . . 31n.23

IAComHR, *Nicaragua v Costa Rica*, Inter-state Case 01/06, Report No 11/07 (8 March 2007). 168n.107

Inter-American Commission on Human Rights Reports

IAComHR, 'Report on Gross Human Rights Violations in the Context of

AFRICAN REGION

African Commission on Human and Peoples' Rights Decisions

League of Arab States Resolution

European region

COUNCIL OF EUROPE

European Commission of Human Rights Decisions

Committee of Ministers Resolutions

Committee of Ministers Annual Reports

Commissioner for Human Rights, Reports

Secretary-General, Reports

European Court of Human Rights documents

EUROPEAN UNION

EU Regulations

European Council Decisions

Other EU documents and sources online

NATIONAL LEGISLATION AND OTHER DOCUMENTS

National legislation

National commissions of inquiry and truth commissions reports

Other sources online

Other countries documents

Other sources online

Table of treaties

List of abbreviations

ACHPR	African Charter on Human and Peoples' Rights
ACHR	American Convention on Human Rights
AComHPR	African Commission on Human and Peoples' Rights
ACtHPR	African Court on Human and Peoples' Rights
AIDI	Annuaire de l'Institut de droit international
AJIL	American Journal of International Law
ARSIWA	Articles on Responsibility of States for Internationally Wrongful Acts
ASILP	American Society of International Law Proceedings
ATT	Arms Trade Treaty
AU	African Union
AUILR	American University International Law Review
Aust YBIL	Australian Yearbook of International Law
BJIL	Berkeley Journal of International Law
BYIL	British Yearbook of International Law
CAH	Crimes against humanity
Cal W Intl LJ	California Western International Law Journal
CAR	Central African Republic
CAT	Convention against Torture and Other Cruel, Inhuman or Degrading Treatment or Punishment
CAVR	Commission for Reception, Truth and Reconciliation in East Timor
CCPR	Human Rights Committee
CDDH	Steering Committee for Human Rights
CED	International Convention for the Protection of All Persons from Enforced Disappearance
CEDAW	Convention on the Elimination of All Forms of Discrimination against Women
CERD	International Convention on the Elimination of All Forms of Racial Discrimination
CETS	Council of Europe Treaty Series
CFSP	Common Foreign and Security Policy
CIA	Central Intelligence Agency
CIJ	Commission Internationale des Juristes
CJIL	Chinese Journal of International Law
CoE	Council of Europe
COHRE	Centre on Housing Rights and Evictions
CoM	Committee of Ministers
ComHR	Commission on Human Rights

CONADEP	National Commission on the Disappeared (Comisión Nacional sobre la Desaparición de Personas)
CRC	Convention on the Rights of the Child
CRPD	Convention on the Rights of Persons with Disabilities
CUP	Cambridge University Press
CYIL	Canadian Yearbook of International Law
BJIL	Berkeley Journal of International Law
DPRK	Democratic People's Republic of Korea
DRC	Democratic Republic of Congo
EC	European Community
ECHR	European Convention of Human Rights
EComHR	European Commission of Human Rights
ECOSOC	Economic and Social Council
ECOWAS	Economic Community of West African States
ECtHR	European Court of Human Rights
ed/eds	editor/editors
edn	edition
EEC	European Economic Community
EJHR	European Journal of Human Rights
EJIL	European Journal of International Law
Eth & Int A	Ethics & International Affairs
ETS	European Treaty Series
EU	European Union
EWA	Early Warning and Urgent Action Procedure
FILJ	Fordham International Law Journal
FRY	Socialist Federal Republic of Yugoslavia
GaJ Intl & Comp L	Georgia Journal of International & Comparative Law
GC	Grand Chamber
HR Dev CYB	Human Rights in Developing Countries Yearbook
HRJ	Revue des droits de l'homme/Human Rights Journal
HRL Rev	Human Rights Law Review
HRQ	Human Rights Quarterly
IAComHR	Inter-American Commission on Human Rights
IACtHR	Inter-American Court of Human Rights
ICC	International Criminal Court
ICCPR	International Covenant on Civil and Political Rights
ICESCR	International Covenant on Economic, Social and Cultural Rights
ICISS	International Commission on Intervention and State Sovereignty
ICJ	International Court of Justice
ICLQ	International & Comparative Law Quarterly
ICON	International Journal of Constitutional Law
ICRC	International Committee of the Red Cross
ICTR	International Criminal Tribunal for Rwanda

ICTY	International Criminal Tribunal for the former Yugoslavia
IDI	Institute de Droit International/Institute of International Law
IDRC	International Development Research Centre
IJHR	International Journal of Human Rights
ILC	International Law Commission
IRRC	International Review of the Red Cross
IS/ISIS	Islamic State/Islamic State of Iraq and Syria/Islamic State of Iraq and the Levant/Islamic State of Iraq and al-Sham
JC & SL	Journal of Conflict and Security Law
J Contemp Hist	Journal of Contemporary History
JIHLS	Journal of International Humanitarian Legal Studies
J Intl Rel Dev	Journal of International Relations and Development
KIC	Kyrgyzstant Inquiry Commission
LGDJ	Librairie Générale de Droit et de Jurisprudence
LJIL	Leiden Journal of International Law
LNTS	League of Nations Treaty Series
Mich L Rev	Michigan Law Review
MINUSCA	Multidimensional Integrated Stabilization Mission in the Central African Republic
MINUSMA	United Nations Multidimensional Integrated Stabilization Mission in Mali
MISCA	African Union Support Mission to the Central African Republic
MONUC	United Nations Organisation Mission in the Democratic Republic of the Congo
MONUSCO	United Nations Organisation Stabilisation Mission in the Democratic Republic of the Congo
n/nn	footnote(s)
NATO	North Atlantic Treaty Organization
NILR	Netherlands International Law Review
Nordic JIL	Nordic Journal of International Law
NQHR	Netherlands Quarterly of Human Rights
NYUJILP	New York University Journal of International Law and Politics
OAS	Organization of American States
OAU	Organisation of African Unity
OHCHR	Office of the United Nations High Commissioner for Human Rights
OJEU	Official Journal of the European Union
OP-CEDAW	Optional Protocol to the Convention on the Elimination of all Forms of Discrimination Against Women
OP-CRC-IC	Optional Protocol to the Convention on the Rights of the Child on a communications procedure
OP-CRPD	Optional Protocol to the Convention on the Rights of Persons with Disabilities
OP-ICESCR	Optional Protocol to the International Covenant on Economic, Social and Cultural Rights

OSCE	Organization for Security and Co-operation in Europe
OUP	Oxford University Press
p/pp	page/pages
PACE	Parliamentary Assembly of the Council of Europe
para/paras	paragraph/paragraphs
PCIJ	Permanent Court of International Justice
PUF	Presses Universitaires de France
QIL	Questions of International Law
R2P	Responsibility to Protect
RBDI	Revue belge de droit international
RCADI	Recueil des cours de l'Académie de droit international de La Haye/ Collected Courses of the Hague Academy of International Law
Res	resolution
Rev Intl Stud	Review of International Studies
RGDIP	Revue générale de droit international public
RIAA	Reports of International Arbitral Awards
RTDH	Revue trimestrielle des droits de l`homme
SAJHR	South African Journal on Human Rights
SFDI	Société Française pour le Droit International
SSRN	Social Science Research Network
svhr	serious violation(s) of human rights
TFEU	Treaty on the Functioning of the European Union
TILJ	Texas International Law Journal
TMCP	Transnational Mass Claim Processes
UK	United Kingdom
UN	United Nations
UN Doc	UN Document
UNCC	United Nations Compensation Commission
UNGA	General Assembly
UNHRC	Human Rights Council
UNISFA	United Nations Interim Security Force for Abyei
UNMISS	United Nations Mission in the Republic of South Sudan
UNSC	United Nations Security Council
UNSG	United Nations Secretary General
UNTAET	United Nations Transitional Administration in East Timor
UNTS	United Nations Treaty Series
UPR	Universal Periodic Review
US	United States of America
Va J Intl L	Virginia Journal of International Law
VCLT	Vienna Convention on the Law of Treaties
vol/s	volume(s)
Yale J L Fem	Yale Journal of Law & Feminism
Yb ILC	Yearbook of the International Law Commission
ZaöRV	Zeitschrift für ausländisches öffentliches Recht und Völkerrecht

Introduction: The origins of the regime

International law discourse (particularly since 1945) has been marked by persistent attempts to give expression to what have been referred to as communitarian values.[1] The rise and systematic overview of the special regime around serious violations of human rights forms part of these discussions. Following the Second World War, treaties were signed and institutions were put in place, at both universal and regional levels, to ensure that the horrific events of the War would never occur again.[2] Yet events like the apartheid regime in South Africa; the brutal dictatorships in Chile and Argentina, and also in Greece and Portugal; the Khmer Rouge in Cambodia; the Rohingya genocide in Myanmar; as well as the atrocities during the wars in the former Yugoslavia, Rwanda, Libya, and Syria, to name but a few, keep mobilising the international community to a greater or lesser extent.

The increasing engagement with community interests in international law marks the transformation of international law from a legal system primarily based upon bilateral legal relations among states to a system where respect for certain common fundamental values is brought to the forefront.[3] Nevertheless, voluntarism and consent are deeply engraved on the 'international community's' modus operandi.[4] The traditional international legal order is one defined by states, whose relations are governed by the principles of equal sovereignty and non-intervention in their domestic affairs.[5] The lack of a central higher authority prevents the outright and complete development of

[1] For a brief account of the development of the international community from 1945 onwards, see Robert Kolb, 'La structure constitutionnelle du droit international public' (2001) 39 CYIL 69, 71–73 (hereinafter Kolb, 'La structure constitutionnelle').

[2] Maya Hertig Randall, 'The History of International Human Rights Law' in Robert Kolb and Gloria Gaggioli (eds), *Research Handbook on Human Rights and Humanitarian Law* (Edward Elgar Publishing 2013) 17–20.

[3] See Giorgio Gaja, 'The Protection of General Interests in the International Community: General Course on Public International Law' (2013) 364 RCADI 9 (hereinafter Gaja, 'The Protection of General Interests'); Bruno Simma, 'From Bilateralism to Community Interest in International Law' (1994) 254 RCADI 217, 244 (hereinafter Simma, 'From Bilateralism to Community Interest').

[4] Prosper Weil, 'Towards Relative Normativity in International Law' (1983) 77 AJIL 413.

[5] Declaration on Principles of International Law concerning Friendly Relations and Co-operation among States in accordance with the Charter of the United Nations, UNGA Res 2625(XXV) (24 October 1970) (hereinafter UNGA Res 2625(XXV)).

Serious Violations of Human Rights. Ilia Siatitsa, Oxford University Press. © Ilia Siatitsa 2022.
DOI: 10.1093/oso/9780192863041.003.0001

any legal construct at international level. Due to these pitfalls, the emergence of community values has proved to be a complicated matter.

Numerous legal structures have been developed to allow the international community to step in, put pressure on those responsible, and assist societies to recover from traumatic experiences. Among others, the notion of *erga omnes* obligations emerged to describe certain obligations that 'are of concern to all states' due to the 'importance of the rights involved'.[6] Equally, developments in the field of international criminal law, including the emergence of new international crimes such as the crime of genocide and crimes against humanity, allowed for the prosecution at the international level (as well as at the national level) of individuals liable for crimes that directly attack the values of the international community.[7] These notions are all partial expressions of the fundamental interests of the international community.[8]

Serious violations of human rights as a category of violations of international human rights law also incorporates some of these community values. Starting in the early 1970s, a wide array of rules and procedures has been developing around this specific category of human rights violations. Among the more recent examples is Article 11 of the 2008 Optional Protocol to the International Covenant on Economic, Social and Cultural Rights, which refers to 'grave *or* systematic violations' of the Covenant as a condition allowing the monitoring Committee to initiate an accelerated inquiry procedure.[9] Often uncoordinated and relying on the exceptional nature of circumstances, this set of rules, procedures, and consequences—some permanent, others temporal; some exclusive, others not; some legally binding, others not—has formed a new special regime around serious violations of human rights.

1. The *ad hoc* evolution of a legal regime

The international human rights system that was set up in 1945 and in the years that followed has been continuously evolving, incorporating new experiences and adjusting to the needs specific to a period. The regime described below

[6] ICJ, *Barcelona Traction, Light and Power Company, Limited (Belgium v Spain) (New Application: 1962)*, 5 February 1970, para 33 (hereinafter *Barcelona Traction* case).

[7] Antonio Cassese and Paola Gaeta, *Cassese's International Criminal Law* (3rd edn, OUP 2013)20 (hereinafter Cassese and Gaeta, *Cassese's International Criminal Law*).

[8] On these three notions, as formal expressions of the values of the international community, see Santiago Villalpando, *L'émergence de la communauté internationale dans la responsabilité des états* (PUF 2005) 75–123.

[9] UNGA Res 63/117 (10 December 2008) (emphasis added). See further Chapter 2.

has generally arisen out of responses to urgent situations on the basis of already available tools, with gradual adjustments, as well as exceptional one-off measures that eventually may or may not evolve into permanent ones. One of the first instances was the response of the UN Economic and Social Council (ECOSOC) to the apartheid regime in South Africa. It eventually led to the establishment of a permanent complaints procedure before the then UN Commission of Human Rights (replaced by the UN Human Rights Council), examining situations that reveal 'a consistent pattern of gross violations of human rights'.[10]

This regime has not been the result of careful planning and organisation. Its emergence and formation have been slow, gradual, and often unintentional. Many of the processes and mechanisms found hereinafter are the outcome of practical considerations and compromise. Seldom has any attention been given to serious violations of human rights as a separate category of human rights violations that encapsulates some of the core community values. On the contrary, other closely related notions—namely, *jus cogens* norms, *erga omnes* obligations, and international crimes—have been extensively analysed.

2. Connection of serious violations of human rights to other notions

2.1 Peremptory norms and serious violations of human rights

Jus cogens norms (or peremptory norms)[11] are often understood as corresponding primarily to human rights norms.[12] It is this conflation that makes the present comparison compelling. The two may be closely related and overlapping but are not identical—neither substantively nor functionally.

[10] Institution-building of the United Nations Human Rights Council, UNHRC Res 5/1 (18 June 2007) paras 85–109. The procedure was first established by the resolution on Procedure for dealing with communications relating to violations of human rights and fundamental freedoms, ECOSOC Res 1503(XLVIII) (27 May 1970). Howard Tolley, 'The Concealed Crack in the Citadel: The United Nations Commission on Human Rights' Response to Confidential Communications' (1984) 6 HRQ 420, 420–62. See further Chapter 3.

[11] The two terms are used interchangeably hereinafter.

[12] Sandesh Sivakumaran, 'Impact on the Structure of International Obligations' in Menno T Kamminga and Martin Scheinin (eds), *The Impact of Human Rights Law on General International Law* (OUP 2009) 143ff, 133–50 (hereinafter Sivakumaran, 'Impact on the Structure'); Andrea Bianchi, 'Human Rights and the Magic of *Jus Cogens*' (2008) 19 EJIL 491, 506 (hereinafter Bianchi, 'Human Rights and the Magic of *Jus Cogens*').

2.1.1 Peremptory norms as a substantively narrower notion

As with every aspect of *jus cogens*, there is little agreement regarding its substantive definition or the method for identifying a peremptory norm.[13] Based on the 1969 Vienna Convention on the Law of Treaties[14]—where they made their debut—the main criterion for identifying a peremptory norm is its non-derogable nature.[15] However, the notion has evolved since then. The predominant school today maintains that the notion of *jus cogens* norms comprises a series of specific norms that are vital to the international community and as a result non-derogable.[16] Starting from this general definition, a short list of norms manages by 'consensus' to acquire *jus cogens* status, including: the prohibition on the use of force, the ban on genocide, the right to self-determination, as well as the prohibition of slavery and the slave-trade, racial discrimination, apartheid, and torture.[17] Depending on each author's approach to *jus cogens* and serious violations of human rights (svhr), the two circles could overlap to a greater (Figure 2) or lesser (Figure 1) extent. Still, they would never be identical.

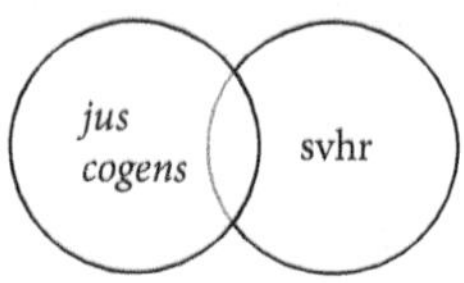

Figure 1 Relationship between svhr and *jus cogens* norms

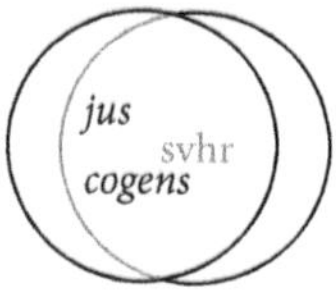

Figure 2 Closer relationship between svhr and *jus cogens* norms

[13] ILC, Articles on Responsibility of States for Internationally Wrongful Acts, with commentaries (2001) Yb ILC, Vol II, Part Two (hereinafter 'ARSIWA with commentaries') 113; ILC, 'Draft Articles on the Law of Treaties with commentary, Report of the ILC on the Work of its 15th session' (6 May–12 July 1963) A/CN4/154, 198–99.

[14] Article 53, Vienna Convention on the Law of Treaties (adopted 23 May 1969) 1155 UNTS 331 (hereinafter VLCT).

[15] On the Article 53 definition, see Kirsten Schmalenbach, 'Article 53, Treaties Conflicting with a Peremptory Norm of General International Law ("*Jus Cogens*")' in Oliver Dörr and Kirsten Schmalenbach (eds), *Vienna Convention on the Law of Treaties: A Commentary* (Springer 2011) 910–920.

[16] Simma, 'From Bilateralism to Community Interest' (n 3) 288.

[17] Article 40, ARSIWA with commentaries (n 13) 112–13, paras 4–5. On other candidates, see Sivakumaran, 'Impact on the Structure' (n 12) 145–46.

None of the interpretations of *jus cogens* is substantively identical to serious violations of human rights, as delineated in Chapter 1 of this book.[18] *Jus cogens* norms are inextricably linked to their non-derogable nature. However, serious violations of human rights constitute a category of violations determined by a plethora of elements not directly related to the non-derogable nature of the human right rule that was breached. Additionally, rules that have acquired the *jus cogens* status are both broader and narrower than those that qualify as serious violations of human rights. On the one hand, peremptory norms are broader because they may be closely related to but not necessarily limited to international human rights law—for example, the prohibition of the use of force.[19] On the other, taken one by one, not all human rights rules, the violation of which qualifies as serious, have necessarily acquired *jus cogens* status.[20] In that respect, *jus cogens* is a narrower notion.

2.1.2 The distinct consequences of peremptory norms

Beyond their definition, it is also with regard to their consequences in the international legal system that serious violations do not fully coincide with peremptory norms. Customarily, there are at least three distinct consequences attributed to *jus cogens* norms.[21] First, the Vienna Convention on the Law of Treaties (VCLT) stipulates that a treaty that contains a rule contrary to a peremptory norm is null and void (contractual function).[22] Second, in 2001, peremptory norms were included in the Articles on State Responsibility for Internationally Wrongful Acts, providing a few additional (albeit weak) rights and obligations to all states (retributive function).[23] For instance, states have an obligation not to recognise as lawful a situation arising from a serious breach of a peremptory norm.[24] Lastly, it is widely accepted today that *jus cogens* rules are a form of 'constitutional' boundary limiting the Security Council's

[18] The Inter-American Court appears to almost equate serious violations of human rights with *jus cogens*, but this has been a minority view. IACtHR, *Ríos et al v Venezuela* (Preliminary objections, merits, reparations, and costs), 28 January 2009, para 283. See further Bianchi, 'Human Rights and the Magic of *Jus Cogens*' (n 12) 506.

[19] Article 40, ARSIWA with commentaries (n 13) 112–13, paras 4–5.

[20] See Chapter 1.

[21] Giorgio Gaja, '*Jus Cogens* beyond the Vienna Convention' (1981) 172 RCADI 271.

[22] Article 53, VCLT (n 19). See IACtHR, *Aloeboetoe et al v Suriname* (Reparations and costs), 10 November 1993, paras 56–57.

[23] Articles 40–41, ILC, Articles on Responsibility of States for Internationally Wrongful Acts, UNGA Res 56/83 (12 December 2001) (hereinafter 'ARSIWA').

[24] Article 41(2), ARSIWA with commentaries (n 13). See Alexander Orakhelashvili, *Peremptory Norms in International Law* (OUP 2006) 218–23.

measures controlled by international and national courts and tribunals (judicial function).[25]

Beyond the above-mentioned consequences, *jus cogens* status has been attributed 'virtually unlimited special effects' without necessarily any support in practice.[26] All these are consequences that serious violations of human rights do not have unless the primary rules violated have also acquired *jus cogens* status.[27] Irrespective, peremptory norms have seldom been invoked in practice,[28] while serious violations of human rights are widely and frequently put forward.

2.2 Serious violations of human rights and *erga omnes* obligations

The concept of obligations *erga omnes* is the other notion that has fascinated international lawyers ever since the ICJ explicitly recognised their existence in the *Barcelona Traction* case.[29] They also relate to a great extent to human rights.[30] However, despite their close relation, the two notions—*erga omnes* obligations and serious violations of human rights—are not identical and do not perform the same functions in the international legal order.

2.2.1 *Erga omnes* encompassing serious violations of human rights

There is (an almost) universal consensus today that there are certain values and interests that by their very nature are a matter of legitimate concern for the international community as a whole—described as *erga omnes* obligations.[31] Such community values include at the very least: 'the outlawing of

[25] ICTY, *Prosecutor v Tadić*, Judgment, Appeal Chamber, IT-94-1, 15 July 1999, para 296. See Antonios Tzanakopoulos, *Disobeying the Security Council: Countermeasures against Wrongful Sanctions* (OUP 2011).

[26] Borrowed from Carlo Focarelli, 'Promotional *Jus Cogens*: A Critical Appraisal of *Jus Cogens*' Legal Effects' (2008) 77 NJIL 429, 439 (hereinafter Focarelli, 'Promotional *Jus Cogens*'). On *jus cogens* as a 'supernorm', see Antônio Augusto Cançado Trindade, 'International Law for Humankind: Towards a New *Jus Gentium* (I): General Course on Public International Law' (2005) 316 RCADI 9, 336ff. Standing apart from most scholars, Kolb argues that *jus cogens* is 'nothing but a legal technique': Robert Kolb, *Peremptory International Law—*Jus Cogens*: A General Inventory* (Hart Publishing 2015) 9.

[27] See Chapters 2–4.

[28] Brownlie characterised it as a 'vehicle that hardly leaves the garage'. Ian Brownlie, 'Comment' in Antonio Cassese and Joseph Weiler, *Change and Stability in International Law-Making* (Walter de Gruyter 1988) 110.

[29] *Barcelona Traction* case (n 6) 32, para 34.

[30] Christian J Tams, *Enforcing Obligations* Erga Omnes *in International Law* (CUP 2005) xv (hereinafter Tams, *Enforcing Obligations*).

[31] Article 48(1)(b), ARSIWA (n 23); ILC, Article 43(b), Draft articles on the responsibility of international organizations, 2011 (Yb ILC, Vol II, Part Two).

acts of aggression, and of genocide', 'the principles and rules concerning basic rights of the human person, including protection from slavery and racial discrimination',[32] as well as the prohibition of torture,[33] the right of self-determination of peoples[34] and certain international humanitarian law obligations.[35] Following a broader approach, as illustrated in Figure 3, community values could also be designated by identifying subject areas that concern the preservation of humanity and its habitat—the environment, human rights and arms control.[36]

Today it is agreed that 'the promotion and protection of *all* human rights is a legitimate concern of the international community'.[37] As a consequence, it follows that human rights obligations the violation of which may amount to a serious violation constitute *erga omnes* obligations (Figure 4). However, the substantive limits of *erga omnes* obligations encompass and exceed human rights obligations.[38] It is not only human rights that give rise to *erga omnes* obligations; other areas of law, such as environmental law rules, give rise to them too.[39] In that respect, *erga omnes* obligations concern a broader category than those human rights obligations that amount to serious violations of human rights. Irrespective of whether all human rights (Figure 3) or some human rights give rise to *erga omnes* obligations (Figure 4), the latter encompass but are not limited to, serious violations of human rights.

[32] *Barcelona Traction* case (n 6) para 34. Reproduced in ARSIWA with commentaries (n 13) 127.

[33] ICTY, *Prosecutor v Furundžija*, Judgment, Trial Chamber, IT-95-17/1-T, 10 December 1998, para 151 (hereinafter *Prosecutor v Furundžija*).

[34] ICJ, *East Timor (Portugal v Australia)* (Judgment of 30 June 1995) para 29 (hereinafter *East Timor (Portugal v Australia)*); ICJ, *Legal Consequences of the Construction of a Wall in the Occupied Palestinian Territory* (Advisory Opinion of 9 July 2004) paras 88 and 156 (hereinafter *Wall Advisory Opinion*).

[35] International Committee of the Red Cross (ICRC), 'Article 1: Respect for the Convention' in *Commentary on the First Geneva Convention: Convention (I) for the Amelioration of the Condition of the Wounded and Sick in Armed Forces in the Field* (2nd edn, 2016) <https://ihl-databases.icrc.org/ihl/full/GCI-commentary> accessed 11 October 2021. Also *Wall Advisory Opinion* (n 34) para 155. Further, all peremptory norms arguably give rise to *erga omnes* obligations. On the relationship between *erga omnes* and *jus cogens*, see Maurizio Ragazzi, *The Concept of International Obligations* Erga Omnes (OUP 2000) 189–214 (hereinafter Ragazzi, *The Concept of International Obligations*).

[36] James Crawford, 'Responsibility for Breaches of Communitarian Norms: An Appraisal of Article 48 of the ILC Articles on Responsibility of States for Internationally Wrongful Acts' in Ulrich Fastenrath and others (eds), *From Bilateralism to Community Interest: Essays in Honour of Bruno Simma* (OUP 2011) 229, 240 (hereinafter Crawford, 'Responsibility for Breaches of Communitarian Norms').

[37] Vienna Declaration and Programme of Action, adopted by the World Conference on Human Rights in Vienna (25 June 1993) para 4 (emphasis added) (hereinafter Vienna Declaration (1993)). See further Ian Seiderman, *Hierarchy in International Law: The Human Rights Dimension* (Intersentia 2001) 124 (hereinafter Seiderman, *Hierarchy in International Law*); Sivakumaran (n 12) 137.

[38] Ragazzi, *The Concept of International Obligations* (n 35) 135.

[39] Article 48, ARSIWA with commentaries (n 13) 127 (aggression); Ragazzi, *The Concept of International Obligations* (n 35) 145–63 (development law and environment law).

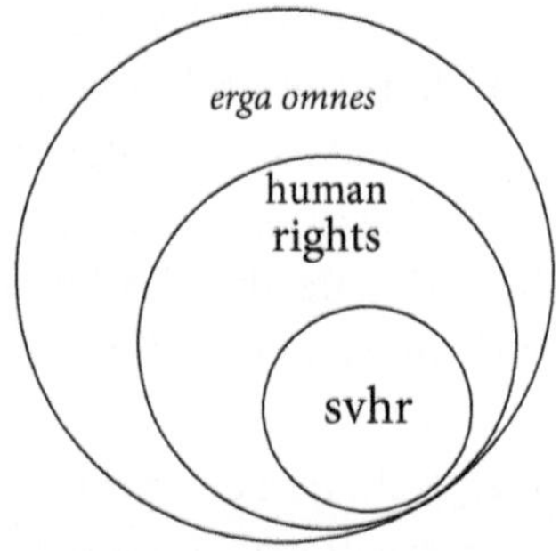

Figure 3 Relationship between svhr and *erga omnes*—option 1

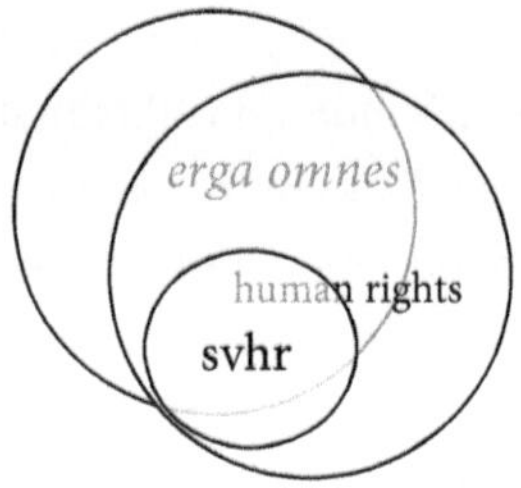

Figure 4 Relationship between svhr and *erga omnes*—option 2

In any event, there is a qualitative difference between *erga omnes* obligations and serious violations of human rights. *Erga omnes* obligations are *erga omnes* irrespective of whether they have been violated. As such, the primary norm gives rise to obligations owed to the international community as a whole, and it logically follows that the lack of respect—that is the violation—is a matter of concern to the international community as a whole. When it comes to serious violations of human rights, it is the violation of a human right that is requalified as serious.

2.2.2 The specific function of *erga omnes* obligations

Erga omnes obligations constitute a well-established part of the reality of international law, but they still have only one widely accepted but restricted function. *Erga omnes* obligations express the legal interest of each state to invoke other states' compliance with them.[40] The International Law Commission (ILC) also endorsed the understanding that states not directly injured are

[40] Crawford, 'Responsibility for Breaches of Communitarian Norms' (n 36) 229.

entitled to invoke the responsibility of another state for breaches of such obligations, including the right to request the cessation of a continuing violation and assurances of non-repetition, and request reparation in the interest of the victim(s).[41] However, the exercise of their function before judicial bodies remains dependent on whether the state concerned has accepted the respective judicial body's jurisdiction.[42] So far, applications that have led to a judicial decision have rather been based on specific treaty provisions, such as the Convention against Torture.[43] It is also increasingly accepted today that when breaches of *erga omnes* obligations occur, states are 'entitled to take non-forcible countermeasures under conditions analogous to those applying to a State specially affected by the breach'.[44]

Undoubtedly, there is a close relationship between *erga omnes* and serious violations of human rights. As a result, some of the responses to serious violations of human rights analysed in the following chapters have evolved due to the *erga omnes* character of the norms breached. For instance, states have been increasingly adopting third-party countermeasures—an enforcement function of *erga omnes* obligations—as a response to serious violations of human rights.[45] However, they remain two distinct notions with distinct functions. A 'serious violations of human rights' is not a substitute expression for *erga omnes* obligations.

On the one hand, the expression 'serious violations of human rights' describes certain violations of just one subcategory of *erga omnes* obligations—human rights obligations—while the latter refers to a broader spectrum of principles and norms in the international legal order. On the other hand, the functions of serious violations of human rights go beyond the recognition of a legal interest of states not directly injured to invoke those violations and the entitlement to take enforcement measures. In addition, similarly to the concept of *jus cogens*, the notion of *erga omnes* has been rarely used in practice in its purest form; most often it relies on its proxies.[46]

[41] Article 48, ARSIWA with commentaries (n 13) 126–27; See also Article 2, Institut de Droit International (IDI), Obligations and rights *erga omnes* in international law, IDI Resolution, Krakow Session (27 August 2005) (hereinafter IDI Resolution 2005).

[42] *Barcelona Traction* case (n 6) para 32; *East Timor (Portugal v Australia)* (n 34) para 29.

[43] Article 7, Convention against Torture and Other Cruel, Inhuman or Degrading Treatment or Punishment (adopted 10 December 1984) 1465 UNTS 85 (hereinafter CAT); ICJ, *Questions relating to the Obligation to Prosecute or Extradite (Belgium v Senegal)*, 20 July 2012, para 68.

[44] Article 5(c), IDI Resolution 2005 (n 41). See Tams, *Enforcing Obligations* (n 30) 311; Martin Dawidowicz, *Third-Party Countermeasures in International Law* (CUP 2017).

[45] Martin Dawidowicz, 'Public Law Enforcement without Public Law Safeguards? An Analysis of State Practice on Third-Party Countermeasures and Their Relationship to the UN Security Council' (2007) 77 BYIL 333. See further Chapter 3.

[46] Hugh Thirlway, 'The Law and Procedure of the International Court of Justice 1960–1989, Part One' (1990) 60 BYIL 1, 102.

2.3 Serious violations of human rights and international crimes

There is a tendency in scholarship to refer to serious violations of human rights as an umbrella term for international crimes.[47] However, the use of serious violations of human rights as an alternative term for the crimes amounting to international crimes is misleading. The two notions may describe similar acts, but they indicate two distinct legal qualifications.

2.3.1 Serious violations of human rights as a broader notion

The expression 'serious violations of human rights' has been used in practice to describe a broader spectrum of human rights violations than those that may also amount to international crimes.[48] Undoubtedly, an act of torture can qualify at the same time as a crime against humanity, a war crime, and a serious violation of human rights.[49] However, the notions are not identical. The Arms Trade Treaty (ATT) maintained the distinction between international crimes and serious violations of human rights. Article 6(3) of the ATT prohibits transfers of arms that will be used to commit international crimes.[50] Complementary Article 7(1)(b)(ii) of the ATT introduces 'a serious violation of human rights' as a distinct violation where an arms transfer might be prohibited.[51] Serious violations of human rights may largely overlap with, but they are not identical to international crimes, as illustrated in Figure 5.

Indeed, '[t]o a large extent many concepts underlying [crimes against humanity] derive from, or overlap with, those of human rights law (the rights to life, not to be tortured, to liberty and security of the person, etc)'.[52] Nonetheless, while any crime against humanity may also amount to a serious violation of human rights, not every serious violation of human rights will amount to a

[47] Juan Carlos Ochoa, *The Rights of Victims in Criminal Justice Proceedings for Serious Human Rights Violations* (Martinus Nijhoff Publishers 2013) (hereinafter Ochoa, *The Rights of Victims*); Anja Seibert-Fohr, *Prosecuting Serious Human Rights Violations* (OUP 2009) (hereinafter Seibert-Fohr, *Prosecuting Serious Human Rights Violations*).

[48] See Chapter 1.

[49] See Youri Rechetov, 'International Responsibility for Violations of Human Rights' in Antonio Cassese (ed), *UN Law Fundamental Rights: Two Topics in International Law* (Sijthoff & Noordhoff 1979), 240.

[50] Arms Trade Treaty (adopted 2 April 2013) UNGA Res 67/234 (hereinafter ATT).

[51] Ilia Maria Siatitsa, '"A Serious Violation of International Human Rights Law"—An Attempt to Clarify a Crucial Provision of the Arms Trade Treaty' (2015) 5 EJHR 606, 609–10.

[52] Cassese and Gaeta, *Cassese's International Criminal Law* (n 7) 92. See also Konstantinos Antonopoulos, 'The Definition of Crimes against Humanity' in Kalliopi Koufa and Fotini Pazartzi (eds), *International Criminal Justice as an Enforcement Mechanism for International Law* (Sakkoulas 2007); Fotini Pazartzi, *Criminal Repression in International Law. International Criminal Justice in Modern Times* (Sakkoulas 2007) (in Greek).

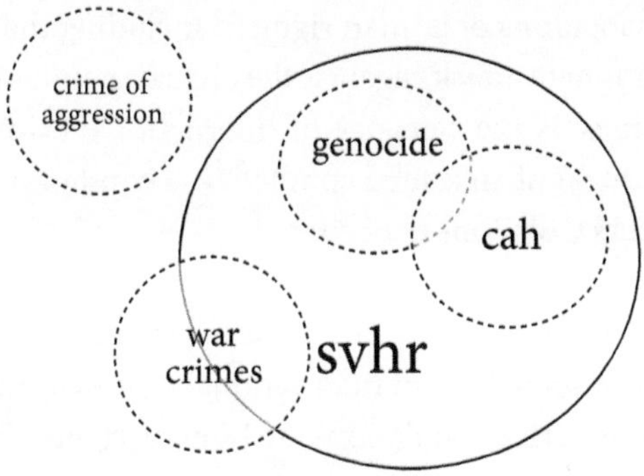

Figure 5 Relationship between svhr and international crimes

crime against humanity. The latter has been defined as a series of enumerated acts, 'committed as part of a widespread or systematic attack directed against any civilian population, with knowledge of the attack'.[53] Crimes against humanity require acts to occur in this specific context,[54] while serious violations of human rights may occur outside and independently of such a context.[55] For instance, an act of arbitrary killing can be considered a serious violation of the right to life, irrespective of whether there is a context of widespread or systematic attack.[56]

Similarly, the acts comprising the crime of genocide would amount, in almost every possible scenario, to serious violations of human rights.[57] However, the reverse is not necessarily true. First, for a case of genocide, it is necessary to prove the special genocidal intent.[58] Second, the material element is restricted to an exhaustive list of acts.[59] Serious violations of human rights neither require special intent, nor are they limited to these specific acts.[60]

Lastly, serious violations of human rights and war crimes do not entirely overlap.[61] Many of the acts amounting to war crimes may at the same time

[53] Article 7(1), Rome Statute of the International Criminal Court (ICC Statute) (adopted 17 July 1998), 2187 UNTS 3 (hereinafter ICC Statute).

[54] ibid.

[55] ibid.

[56] See Chapter 1.

[57] Most recent example: Article 6, ICC Statute (n 53).

[58] On the requirement of 'special intent' see: ICTR, *Prosecutor v Akayesu*, Judgment, Trial Chamber I, ICTR-96-4, 2 September 1998, paras 523–24; Cassese and Gaeta, *Cassese's International Criminal Law* (n 7) 125–27.

[59] Article 6, ICC Statute (n 53).

[60] See Chapter 1.

[61] Vera Gowlland-Debbas and Gloria Gaggioli, 'The Relationship between International Human Rights and Humanitarian Law: An Overview' in Robert Kolb and Gloria Gaggioli (eds), *Research Handbook on Human Rights and Humanitarian Law* (Edward Elgar Publishing 2013)

qualify as serious violations of human rights,[62] including the prohibition of ill treatment, indiscriminate attacks against the civilian population, and others.[63] However, 'war crimes' is the category of international crimes that is conditioned upon the context of an armed conflict[64]—a condition that is not necessary for human rights violations to occur.

2.3.2 The specific consequences of international crimes

The primary legal consequences of international crimes are also distinct from the consequences of serious violations of human rights. Principally, international crimes give rise to individual criminal responsibility, and therefore require specific individual criminal intent. Serious violations of human rights are part of international human rights law which is the branch of international law that was primarily established to protect the individual against the abuse of state power.[65] Its main objective is not to ensure that individuals are held accountable for human rights violations, but to mobilise the state apparatus when abuses against individuals occur.

Over the decades, international human rights law and international criminal law have been influencing and nourishing each other. The point of convergence of the two branches of international law becomes particularly evident in light of the 'fight against impunity'. For instance, it has been established that the effective protection of the right to life and the prohibition of torture requires states to criminalise specific acts.[66] Similarly, the legality of amnesties is a matter that has occupied both human rights and criminal law debates in equal measure.[67]

Nonetheless, there are still valuable arguments for preserving the distinct positions of the two notions in the international legal order. First, international crimes impose very high or different thresholds. The international community does not take measures only once the crimes against humanity's threshold has been reached or when a conflict is taking place.[68] Second, and most

[62] On international human rights law application in armed conflict, see Andrew Clapham, 'The Complex Relationship between the 1949 Geneva Conventions and International Human Rights Law' in Andrew Clapham, Paola Gaeta, and Marco Sassòli (eds), *The 1949 Geneva Conventions: A Commentary* (OUP 2015); Louise Doswald-Beck, 'The Right to Life in Armed Conflict: Does International Humanitarian Law Provide All the Answers?' (2006) 88 IRRC 881.

[63] See Article 8, ICC Statute (n 53).

[64] Paola Gaeta, 'The Interplay Between the Geneva Conventions and International Criminal Law' in Andrew Clapham, Paola Gaeta, and Marco Sassòli (eds), *The 1949 Geneva Conventions: A Commentary* (OUP 2015) (hereinafter Gaeta, 'The Interplay Between').

[65] On serious violations of human rights committed by non-state actors, see Section 3.4, Chapter 1.

[66] ECtHR, *Marguš v Croatia* (GC), App no 4455/10, 27 May 2014.

[67] Notably, IACtHR, *Barrios Altos v Peru* (Merits), 14 May 2001, para 41; *Prosecutor v Furundžija* (n 33) para 155.

[68] See Chapters 2–4.

importantly, international crimes shift the focus on to the individuals responsible for the crimes, which risks reducing the attention paid to the rules of state responsibility.[69] Serious violations of human rights highlight the state's responsibility for violations, which entails a wider set of legal consequences for the responsible state.[70] The two legal regimes act in a complementary manner.[71] What is more, criminal justice dictates that strict standards are maintained in the course of criminal procedures, but the same strict standards will not necessarily apply when taking third-party countermeasures for instance.[72]

2.4 The complementary role of serious violations of human rights

Despite the significant overlap of these notions, 'serious violations of human rights', as a separate category of human rights violations, does not describe exactly the same legal norms as those described or encompassed by *jus cogens*, *erga omnes* obligations, or international crimes. The notion is not identical to any of these others. Depending on the point of departure, the expression can be seen to comprise a set of acts that are at the same time both broader and narrower than each of them.

Undoubtedly, there are certain serious violations of human rights, such as acts of torture, that have acquired *jus cogens* status, give rise to *erga omnes* obligations, amount to an international crime *per se*, and in specific contexts may also amount to international crimes, whether war crimes, crimes against humanity, or genocide. On such occasions, the acts of torture will entail all the consequences that each of these notions may entail, as well as producing all the consequences that any human rights violation (irrespective of its gravity) would have, under both treaty law and customary law. It is beyond this set of already formally recognised functions and consequences that one seeks to hereafter explore. The recurrent invocation of and recourse to the notion of serious violations of human rights in international practice prompts the question whether and to what extent they can today be understood as an autonomous

[69] Andre Nollkaemper, 'Systemic Effects of International Responsibility for International Crimes' (2010) 8 San Cl J Intl L 313, 352.

[70] On the shortcomings of the increasing 'individualisation' of international criminal law at the expense of international humanitarian law, see Gaeta, 'The Interplay Between' (n 64) 751–753.

[71] Andrea Bianchi, 'State Responsibility and Criminal Liability of Individuals' in Antonio Cassese (ed), *The Oxford Companion to International Criminal Justice* (OUP 2009), 24.

[72] On ensuring respect for the principle of legality in criminal matters, see Cassese and Gaeta, *Cassese's International Criminal Law* (n 7) 24ff. On unilateral measures' standards, see Chapter 3.

legal category around which a special regime, composed of decision-making procedures and consequences, is formed.

All these different notions are pieces in the incomplete puzzle that is the international community's legal order.[73] Every one of the notions examined above represents a separate partially and relatively successful attempt to ensure that the international legal order promotes and protects the community values.[74] So far it has been impossible to find the one piece (i.e. one legal notion) that would replace all these partially overlapping/partially distinct notions and perform all the functions they perform, while overcoming all obstacles and constraints of the current state of affairs in the international sphere.[75] Therefore, every one of these pieces remains relevant and necessary for the functioning of the international legal order, as well as complementary to one another.[76] Serious violations of human rights could be understood as another piece of this puzzle, whose relevance and necessity are exemplified in the following pages.

3. Shaping the special regime

It is maintained here that a special regime around serious violations of human rights has been developing within the general international human rights system and broader international legal order, in parallel with the appearance and evolution of the above- discussed legal notions. It is understood as a special regime that is substantively limited to a specific issue-area, namely, the specific category of serious violations of human rights; where there is a series of monitoring mechanisms and procedures that predominantly highlight, document, and record such violations; there are specific measures aiming at enforcing compliance; and there are certain consequences that arise only when serious violations of human rights occur, focusing primarily on remedying the victims. As such, this special regime is arguably comprised of at least four to some extent interconnected components: the substantive, the monitoring, the enforcement, and the remedial ones.

[73] Articles 40, 48(1)(b) and 50(1)(b), ARSIWA (n 23).

[74] See Section 1.

[75] Gaja, 'The Protection of General Interests' (n 3) 32–33.

[76] On the relationship of these different notions, see amongst others, James Crawford, 'Multilateral Rights and Obligations in International Law' (2006) 319 RCADI 325, 452–77.

3.1 What is a special regime?

The ILC extensively analysed the various forms 'special regimes' can take in international law when working on the matter of fragmentation of international law and the relationship between general and special law. In the wider sense, the ILC described a (self-contained) special regime 'to refer to interrelated wholes of primary and secondary rules, sometimes also referred to as "systems" or "subsystems" of rules that cover some particular problem differently from the way it would be covered under general law'.[77] But it also accepted that branches of international law as fields of functional specialisation may be understood as self-contained in the sense that special rules and techniques of interpretation and administration are thought to apply.[78]

Whether one places the special regime of serious violations of human rights closer to the ILC's the wider understanding of a special regime that covers some particular problem differently than general law, or rather opts for the functional understanding of branches of international law, has little consequence here. It is rather the recognition of the development of rule-complexes or regimes in international law as a process that constructs a set of rules, decision-making procedures, and associated consequences around a specific issue-area—here it is serious violations of human rights. The rules of international law are as a result interpreted, understood, and applied dependent on this specific context. As Saul pointed out, while examining a different special regime, 'The existence of a specialized regime is a matter of methodology and appreciation, but also of degree.'[79]

In international relations, an international regime has been defined as 'principles, norms, rules, and decision-making procedures around which actor expectations converge in a given issue-area',[80] or, more narrowly, as 'norms and decision-making procedures accepted by international actors to regulate an issue area'.[81] The regime may not be as unified, centralised, or coherent as some others.[82] Yet it demonstrates the intention of international actors 'to remove

[77] ILC, 'Fragmentation of international law: difficulties arising from the diversification and expansion of international law, Report of the Study Group of the International Law Commission, Finalized by Martti Koskenniemi' (13 April 2006) A/CN4/L682, 68, para 128 (also 81, para 152) (hereinafter ILC, 'Fragmentation Report').

[78] ibid, 68, para 129 (also 81, para 152).

[79] Ben Saul, *Research Handbook on International Law and Terrorism* (Edward Elgar 2014), x (hereinafter Saul, *Research Handbook*).

[80] Stephen D Krasner, 'Structural Causes and Regime Consequences: Regimes as Intervening Variables' (1982) 36 International Organization 185.

[81] Jack Donnelly, 'International Human Rights: A Regime Analysis' (1986) 40 International Organization 599, 602.

[82] Saul, *Research Handbook* (n 79) x–xi.

specific issue-areas of international politics from the sphere of self-help behaviour'.[83] This book reveals a solid and continually evolving accretion of international rules and practice on serious violations of human rights, developed and serviced by institutions and processes.

3.2 Who contributes to the regime?

A broad range of sources and actors contribute to building this special regime around serious violations of human rights. It is not just one single treaty or provision that regulates every aspect related to serious violations of human rights. As Simma and Alston point out, 'reliance upon treaties alone provides an ultimately unsatisfactory patchwork quilt of obligations and still continues to leave many States largely untouched'.[84] The increasing role of international institutions in law-making has reduced the significance of the traditional sources of international law without replacing them.[85]

A wide array of sources of law contribute to the development of this special regime, including: judicial and quasi-judicial bodies' decisions, UN bodies' resolutions (binding and non-binding), ILC reports, and reports of commissions of inquiry and of other independent experts. They all present different degrees of normativity. Their legality is assessed at the level of obligation, precision, and delegation, instead of via a strict traditional division.[86] Accepting that the relevant practice (the practice that counts) for the creation and crystallisation of a regime or system is the behaviour of all subjects of international law—taking into account the legal weight they carry—ensures a holistic understanding of the expression's normative content and the regime developed around it.[87] Higgins understood international law not simply as rules but as a normative system, a decision-making process, whose 'role . . . is to provide an operational system for securing values we all desire'.[88]

[83] Andreas Hasenclever, Peter Mayer, and Volker Rittberger, 'Integrating Theories of International Regimes' (2000) 26 Rev Intl Stud 3.
[84] Bruno Simma and Philip Alston, 'The Sources of Human Rights Law: Custom, *Jus Cogens*, and General Principles' (1988) 12 Aust YB IL 82.
[85] See Kenneth Abbott and Duncan Snidal, 'Hard and Soft Law in International Governance' (2000) 54 International Organization 421, 421–56.
[86] ibid.
[87] Alan Boyle and Christine Chinkin, *The Making of International Law* (OUP 2007), 98ff (hereinafter Boyle and Chinkin, *The Making of International Law*); José E Alvarez, *The Impact of International Organizations on International Law* (Brill/Nijhoff 2016).
[88] Rosalyn Higgins, *Problems and Process: International Law and How We Use It* (Clarendon Press 1994), 1–2.

The competences of the actors involved range from political proclamations merely condemning a serious violation of human rights, to binding judicial decisions ordering remedies to victims of serious violations of human rights.[89] For instance, the response by the UN General Assembly, a political inter-governmental organ with discretionary powers and universal reach, differs from the response of the European Court of Human Rights, a regional judicial organ with a limited scope of application, bound by rigid rules of procedure. Yet the focus hereafter remains on determinations of gravity with a certain legal impact, including assessments that might not be legally binding in the strict sense but that still have normative effects. A determination of gravity impacting decision-making processes, even if not legally binding in the strict sense, still has a certain normative impact.

4. The relationship between the special and the (general) human rights law regimes

The issue of serious violations of human rights engages a very broad spectrum of specialised branches of international law: international human rights law, international criminal law, law on the use of force, state responsibility, international humanitarian law, and the law of the United Nations and international organisations. Certain (if not all) aspects of this regime are also parts of other regimes, especially the special branch of human rights law. For instance, specific provisions on serious violations are found in human rights treaties that form part of the broader international human rights law regime.

Nothing in international law excludes the development of a regime within and next to an already established regime. The phenomenon of fragmentation of international law has been the result of the development of specialised branches of international law within and next to general public international law.[90] There are already specialised fields within international human rights law, including the special legal regimes on torture, enforced disappearances, and others. Rules and procedures can be part of more than one regime at the same time. For instance, the Convention against Torture is at the same time part of the larger international human rights law regime, the UN human rights treaties regime, and the more specialised torture regime.[91]

[89] Boyle and Chinkin, *The Making of International Law* (n 87) 98–162. See also Gaja, 'The Protection of General Interests' (n 3) 32.

[90] See ILC, 'Fragmentation Report' (n 77).

[91] Jack Donnelly, 'The Emerging International Regime Against Torture' (1986) 33 NILR 1.

Also a special regime need not divert entirely from general law or its rules. More often than not, rules applicable in one special regime may actually have developed on the basis of a general rule, complement a regulatory gap, or be interpreted in light of the general rules. All regimes in the international legal system cannot be but interdependent and connected to general international law and to one another. The ILC's description of special regimes as self-contained is misleading in that respect.[92]

The development of the broader regime of international human rights law, of which serious violations of human rights form part, has to a large extent prevented further considerations around the special regime discussed in this book. It appeared unnecessary to explore the practices around a specific category of violations of this body of law separately. The human rights movement struggled to establish 'human rights' as an exception to the matters falling within the exclusive competence of each state. Initially, the treatment of states' own nationals was understood as a matter of the internal affairs of states, and neither the United Nations nor states (other than the injured ones) could intervene in questions concerning such a matter.[93] The serious character of human rights abuses was then used to pressure states to break down this barrier.[94] Eventually, the principle of non-intervention in the internal affairs of states gradually developed to exclude human rights issues, both within the UN[95] and in general public international law.[96] Once this was achieved, there was no need to limit the debate to this category of violations. Any human rights violation became a matter of international concern.[97]

This explains to a great extent the lack of scholarly interest in examining, and even reluctance to examine, serious violations of human rights separately and in a holistic manner. Despite the proliferation of activities at the international

[92] ILC, 'Fragmentation Report' (n 77) 59–101.

[93] The general principle of non-intervention, founded upon the concept of respect for the territorial sovereignty of states, was reaffirmed in ICJ, *Military and Paramilitary Activities in and against Nicaragua (Nicaragua v United States of America)*, Merits, 27 June 1986, para 205. See further Robert Kolb, 'Du domaine reserve—Réflexions sur la théorie du domaine réservé' (2006) 113 RGDIP 597.

[94] On the UN principle of non-intervention in domestic affairs, see Benedetto Conforti and Carlo Focarelli, *The Law and Practice of the United Nations* (5th edn, Brill/Nijhoff 2016), 167–83 (particularly 180–81).

[95] Article 2(7), Charter of the United Nations, San Fransisco (adopted 26 June 1945) 1 UNTS XVI. See also Antônio Augusto Cançado Trindade, 'The Domestic Jurisdiction of States in the Practice of the United Nations and Regional Organisations' (1976) 25 ICLQ 715.

[96] See UNGA Res 2625(XXV) (n 5). See also Article 2, International Law Institute, Resolution on the Protection of Human Rights and the Principle of Non-Intervention in Internal Affairs of States (13 September 1989) [1989] 63 *Institut de Droit International Annuaire* 338. See Georg Nolte, 'Article 2(7)' in Bruno Simma and others (eds), *The Charter of the United Nations: A Commentary* (3rd edn, OUP 2012), 296–99; Menno T Kamminga, *Inter-State Accountability for Violations of Human Rights* (University of Pennsylvania Press 1992) 119, 126 (hereinafter Kamminga, *Inter-State Accountability*).

[97] Vienna Declaration (1993) (n 37), para 4.

level concerning serious violations of human rights, the task of systematically examining the rules and procedures around this category of violations has not been undertaken. The few academic studies focusing on serious violations of human rights and the legal regime that regulates them were published more than twenty years ago.[98] Quiroga's seminal work, for instance, was published in 1988 and mainly concerns the Inter-American human rights system.[99] There have not been, however, any contemporary attempts to examine the category 'serious violations of human rights' and its use in a holistic manner. Most recent academic contributions relating to serious violations of human rights examine only specific legal aspects, mostly pertaining to criminal justice matters[100] or the right to reparation, for instance.[101] The renewed interest in the notion as a result of the adoption of the ATT has concentrated on the interpretation of the expression for the purposes of that treaty.[102]

However, while the legal interest for all human rights has been established, the responses have not been the same for all human rights violations. The type of response is influenced by the degree of gravity of the violation, and certain practices are reserved for a specific set of human rights violations, namely, serious violations of human rights.[103] If there were no separate regime, there would be no need to continue to differentiate between serious and other violations in the various documents, resolutions, and reports. The inclusion of the concept 'serious violations of human rights' in the most recent human rights treaties, such as the 2006 Convention on Enforced Disappearance, indicates that the distinction remains valid.[104]

There is an additional reason that explains the lack of interest in this separate category of human rights. The existence of serious violations of human rights appears to contradict principles of indivisibility, interdependence, and equality of human rights.[105] Similarly, attempts to introduce notions such as

[98] Kamminga, *Inter-State Accountability* (n 96); Cecilia Medina Quiroga, *The Battle of Human Rights: Gross, Systematic Violations and the Inter-American System* (Kluwer 1988) (hereinafter Quiroga, *The Battle of Human Rights*); Flavia Lattanzi, *Garanzie dei diritti dell'uomo nel diritto internazionale generale* (Dott A Giuffrè Editore 1983).

[99] Quiroga, *The Battle of Human Rights* (n 98).

[100] Ochoa, *The Rights of Victims* (n 47); Seibert-Fohr, *Prosecuting Serious Human Rights Violations* (n 47); Lyal Sunga, *Individual Responsibility in International Law for Serious Human Rights Violations* (Martinus Nijhoff Publishers 1992).

[101] Christine Evans, *The Right to Reparation in International Law for Victims of Armed Conflict* (CUP 2012).

[102] Andrew Clapham and others (eds), *The Arms Trade Treaty: A Commentary* (OUP 2016).

[103] Linos-Alexander Sicilianos, *The Human Dimension of International Law; Interplay of General International Law and Human Rights* (Nomiki Bibliothiki Group 2010) (in Greek), 367.

[104] Article 33, International Convention for the Protection of All Persons from Enforced Disappearance (adopted 20 December 2006) 2716 UNTS 3.

[105] Vienna Declaration (1993) (n 37) para 5.

fundamental, basic, or core human rights have mainly been understood as establishing the hierarchical superiority of certain rights.[106] However, the references to serious violations of human rights, as will be discussed below, do not necessarily establish a hierarchy within human rights. Serious violations are not limited to violations of specific human rights; they also incorporate the manner in which violations are committed.[107] Therefore, the violation of any human rights can potentially amount to a serious violation.

5. 'Serious' *versus* 'gross' and other similar expressions

Amongst the most common qualifiers for human rights violations of a certain gravity, one finds: serious, massive, grave, gross, flagrant, widespread, systematic, ongoing, persistent, or continuous. Often, these may be combined to better describe a situation, including: 'serious and systematic', 'gross breach of a fundamental rule', or 'serious, gross and systematic'.[108] These qualifiers do not have exactly the same meaning when used in their literal sense. Some of them concentrate on a specific external characteristic. 'Systematic' underlines the organised character of a violation, while 'massive' indicates the large numbers of victims or the large scale of violations. Meanwhile, other qualifiers are not as specific. 'Grave' or 'gross', for instance, could refer either to a qualitative element (such as the fundamental nature of the rule violated), or to a quantitative external element (such as the number of victims).[109]

All these qualifiers are used to underline the gravity of a human rights violation. The present book integrates the various adjectives that have been used interchangeably to underline that a particular human rights violation is more important than others. To facilitate the analysis, the expression 'serious violations of human rights' has been chosen as the overarching qualifier of gravity in this study and as an umbrella term, encompassing all the different qualifiers.

[106] See Seiderman, *Hierarchy in International Law* (n 37); Koji Teraya, 'Emerging Hierarchy in International Human Rights and Beyond: From the Perspective of Non-Derogable Rights' (2001) 12 EJIL 917; Theodor Meron, 'On a Hierarchy of International Human Rights' (1986) 80 AJIL 1.

[107] See Chapter 1.

[108] Notably, CERD Committee, Decision 1(54) on Yugoslavia (16 March 1999) A/54/18, 6, para 1; Situation of human rights in the Syrian Arab Republic, UNGA Res 70/234 (23 December 2015) para 3.

[109] ARSIWA with commentaries (n 18) 113, para 8; Comment m, Section 702, The American Law Institute, *Restatement of the Law Third, The Foreign Relations Law of the United Nations*, Vol II (American Law Institute Publishers, 1987) 166.

The qualifier 'serious' seems to the present author to be used more frequently.[110] Still, there are further more compelling reasons for this choice.

First, of all the qualifiers used, 'serious' seems to encompass the different adjectives best. It captures all shades of gravity, from the least serious to the most serious. 'Serious' describes 'something significant or worrying because of possible danger or risk; not slight or negligible'.[111] Second, in a similar vein, 'serious' underlines the gravity of a particular violation, irrespective of whether it is considered serious because of the specific rights violated (gross, grave, flagrant) or because of the way the violation was committed (gross, grave, systematic, massive, widespread, or persistent). Third, 'gross', which would be the most likely alternative as it is commonly used, is often associated with large numbers of victims. However, human rights violations can qualify as serious irrespective of the number of victims.[112] Fourth, in practice, the various organs often use the different qualifiers interchangeably. For instance, the UN Human Rights Council, in a resolution on 'Enforced or involuntary disappearances', refers (in the same paragraph) first to gross violations and then to serious violations to describe the same thing.[113]

6. Structuring the special regime

To conclude, it is maintained here that the special regime concerning serious violations of human rights includes the following components: it is substantively limited to a specific-issue area (substantive component, Chapter 1); there is a series of monitoring mechanisms and procedures that predominantly highlight, inquire into, and record such violations (monitoring component, Chapter 2); there are specific measures taken in response to such violations (enforcement component, Chapter 3); and there are certain legal consequences that arise only when serious violations of human rights occur (remedial component, Chapter 4).

The central substantive component of the special regime is the issue-area around which an interrelated but diverse cluster—a regime or subsystem—of

[110] Amongst the most recent examples, see Article 7(1)(b), ATT (n 58); Article 33, International Convention for the Protection of All Persons from Enforced Disappearance (adopted 20 December 2006) 2716 UNTS 3.

[111] 'Definition of Serious by Lexico Produced by Oxford' <https://www.lexico.com/definition/serious> accessed 1 March 2022.

[112] Ochoa, *The Rights of Victims* (n 47) 25.

[113] Enforced or involuntary disappearances, UNHRC Res 21/4 (27 September 2012) para 17. Similarly, see UNHRC, 'First Report of the independent international commission of inquiry on the Syrian Arab Republic' (23 November 2011) A/HRC/S-17/2/Add1, para 112.

rules, decision-making procedures, and consequences revolves—that is here the serious violations of human rights. While the expression is widely used, none of the treaties, decisions, or resolutions using the expression (or similar expressions) defines 'serious violation of human rights'. Also, there has been no attempt so far to develop a common working definition by the various instruments that invoke serious violations. As a result, it appears that there is no uniform understanding regarding the gravity threshold.

Despite an apparent indeterminacy, a careful examination of the relevant practice allows us to deduce a common understanding regarding the human rights violations that would amount to serious violations. The aim is not to create a fixed definition, but rather to understand which human rights violations are perceived as serious by the international community. In order to be able to operate in its subsystem, the expression (or notion) remains flexible. There is no exhaustive list of human rights whose violation amounts to a serious violation, nor are strict thresholds identified beyond which a human rights violation becomes serious. In practice, the character of the violations (their impact and structure) bears more significance than the specific human rights provisions that were breached per se. The shared and diverging elements that seem to influence the determination of a violation as serious are presented one by one in Chapter 1.

All the other components revolve and operate around this substantive component. The second component of this regime is the monitoring component. It incorporates an increasing number of monitoring and inquiry procedures, particularly at the UN level, that focus specifically and more often than not exclusively on serious violations of human rights. It is a multilateral network of procedures that has been progressively emerging and solidifying as a response to serious violations at every level. For instance, specific UN treaty provisions triggering urgent inquiry procedures before UN treaty bodies have been introduced as safeguard clauses to apply only in cases of serious violations of human rights. In parallel, a wide array of extra-conventional international monitoring mechanisms, such as commissions of inquiry, has also been set up to inquire into, document, and report situations of serious violations of human rights. Despite their mostly non-binding character, they play a key role in the system, providing processes for examining and recording serious violations of human rights. They then put pressure to those responsible to cease such violations, and mobilise the international community in the process. They can have a significant impact on the course of events and influence further, stricter measures, such as the imposition of sanctions. These monitoring and inquiry procedures are brought together and examined in Chapter 2.

The second operative component of the special regime encompasses enforcement measures that surpass bilateral inter-state relations. Such mechanisms have increasingly been adopted in response to situations of serious violations of human rights, seeking to compel the perpetrators of such violations to cease them. Such enforcement measures responding to serious violations of human rights have been increasingly imposed by the UN Security Council, but also outside of it. Under the UN Charter, the notion of 'threat to the peace' has been expanded to include serious violations of human rights justifying the taking of certain UN Security Council measures (sanctions, authorisation to use force or peace operations) as a response to such violations, but not to any human rights violation. In parallel, outside the auspices of the UN, international organisations and states other than the state directly injured have been also taking enforcement measures as a response to situations of serious violations of human rights. The UN Security Council measures, as well as third-party countermeasures, that seek to force the perpetrators to cease the commission of serious violations of human rights are examined in Chapter 3.

The last component of the special regime is the remedial one. It is within and not outside of the existing regimes for remedying any violations of human rights that remedial bodies, procedures, as well as remedies and reparations specific to serious violations of human rights, have developed. This is legally the strongest component of the regime, where those who have suffered from serious violations of human rights are awarded reparations to remedy the injustices they have experienced. On the one hand, the international community alone, or in collaboration with the state concerned, has been building *ad hoc* reparation programmes to address exclusively serious violations of human rights and not just any human rights breach. On the other hand, the two regional human rights courts, the European and the Inter-American, have been developing procedures and awarding exceptional awards to victims of serious violations of human rights, as opposed to any human rights violations. The remedial response to serious violations of human rights—both procedures to facilitate access and remedies awarded to victims of such violations—is reviewed in Chapter 4.

The aim in the following pages is to draw a reasonably comprehensive picture (not an exhaustive one) of all of the different components that comprise the special regime applicable to serious violations of human rights. These components bring together the diverse rules and procedures that form part of *ad hoc* but also occasionally systematic efforts of the international community to address serious violations of human rights. Practice invoking serious violations of human rights is abundant. The UN General Assembly adopts on average about four to seven relevant resolutions per year; the UN Human Rights Council about three times that number. Equally, the Inter-American Court of Human Rights has decided hundreds of cases concluding that serious violations of human rights have occurred, and as a result it grants special remedies to the victims of those violations.

Therefore, references to the relevant practice are mostly indicative and not exhaustive. More often than not there will be only a couple of relevant resolutions or judicial decisions referenced as examples of the conclusions reached. The chosen examples are often years apart. For instance there reference may be made to a resolution adopted in 2020, to another in 2007, and to a third in 1995. This is meant to indicate the long period during which these practices have occurred. It does not indicate a gap in practice. In addition, the examples chosen are spread across the globe rather than focusing on one specific instance. The special regime around serious violations of human rights is not unique to one or two specific situations; instead, the practice indicates a recurring set of responses to any situation that presents serious violations of human rights.

By far, these may not be the only components of this regime. Certainly, additional aspects could have been included to draw a complete picture of this special regime. Amongst others, international criminal responsibility should not be overlooked as something distinct from the special regime responding to serious violations of human rights. The evolution and consolidation of international criminal law, including the creation of international criminal law rules and tribunals, are precisely a result of the desire to prosecute some of the most serious of the 'serious violations of human rights'. While recognising the significance of international criminal law, this research focuses primarily on state responsibility rather than individual criminal responsibility. The latter has received much attention since the early 1990s. Also, serious violations of international humanitarian law, both as violations of international criminal law and as violations giving rise to state responsibility, have been left aside, even though a lot of the practice that is analysed could also be construed as a response to serious violations of international humanitarian law as much as to serious violations of international human rights law. Equally, certain more recent trends, such as the discussions on the development of an 'obligation to prevent', have not been examined separately.

While the attempts to theoretically establish specific obligations to prevent or to protect community values, including serious violations of human rights, continue, the development of this special regime and the direction that its structure has been taking seem to shy away from concrete obligations or aggravated consequences for those responsible. There seems already an increasing lack of attention to the state as the power apparatus responsible for the occurrence of serious violations of human rights. The ILC has tried in the past to establish a system of aggravated consequences for the state responsible for serious breaches of international law.[114] The special regime under scrutiny hereafter does not punish the responsible state—responsible either for committing, directing, or tolerating such violations—but rather tries to force it into compliance and ensure that the victims receive some form of reparation.

[114] Article 19(3)(c), ILC, 'Fifth report of the Special Rapporteur, Mr Roberto Ago' (1976) Yb ILC, Vol II, Part Two, 75. See also Eric Wyler, 'From "State Crime" to Responsibility for "Serious Breaches of Obligations under Peremptory Norms of General International Law"' (2002) 13 EJIL 1147, 1157–58.

1

The substantive component—identifying a serious violation of human rights

The central substantive component of the special regime is the issue-area around which an interrelated but diverse cluster—a regime or subsystem—of rules, decision-making procedures, and consequences revolves—here, serious violations of human rights. International practice has recurrently and persistently regarded the seriousness of human rights violations as a distinctive element, that is, an element that marks certain human rights violations as more serious when compared to other human rights violations. Already, in 1970, the 1503 ECOSOC Resolution referred to 'a consistent pattern of gross and reliably attested violations of human rights and fundamental freedoms'.[1] More recently, Article 11 of the 2008 Optional Protocol to the International Covenant on Economic, Social and Cultural Rights requires the occurrence of 'grave or systematic violations … of any of the economic, social and cultural rights' in order to apply.[2]

Despite the extensive use of gravity qualifications, the wider impression remains that there is no uniform understanding regarding which violations of human rights amount to serious violations for the international community. Accordingly, the distinction between serious and other human rights violations 'seems to have been developed only to the extent necessary to achieve certain purposes',[3] on a case-by-case basis. Also, it has not helped that each instrument has been developing its own working 'definition'.[4] Similarly, occasional attention in academia to the gravity of certain human rights violations as opposed to others tends to revolve around specific instruments, mostly written close to the time at which the instrument was promulgated. For example, some

[1] Procedure for dealing with communications relating to violations of human rights and fundamental freedoms, ECOSOC Res 1503 (XLVIII) (27 May 1970) (hereinafter ECOSOC Res 1503 (1970)).

[2] (adopted 10 December 2008) GA Res 63/117.

[3] Cecilia Medina Quiroga, *The Battle of Human Rights: Gross, Systematic Violations and the Inter-American System* (Kluwer 1988) 317 (hereinafter Quiroga, *The Battle of Human Rights*).

[4] Hélène Tigroudja, 'Violations de droits de l'homme et engagement de la "responsabilité aggravée" de l'état: Quelle contribution du droit international des droits de l'homme au droit international de la responsabilité?' in *L'homme et le droit, En hommage au Professeur Jean-François Flauss* (Pedone 2014) 758–761 (hereinafter Tigroudja, 'Violation de droits de l'homme').

Serious Violations of Human Rights. Ilia Siatitsa, Oxford University Press. © Ilia Siatitsa 2022.
DOI: 10.1093/oso/9780192863041.003.0002

studies in the late 1970s focused on the gravity threshold that would trigger the newly established 1503 Complaint Procedure of the United Nations (UN) Commission on Human Rights.[5] More recently, the adoption of the Arms Trade Treaty (ATT) has renewed interest in the notion.[6]

A close scrutiny of the vast array of instances in which gravity is invoked reveals, though, patterns and commonalities that indicate a minimum common understanding regarding the human rights violations that would amount to serious violations for the international community. It is not about providing a closed definition. This would be unhelpful. Occasional attempts to reach a general definition have given generalised and vague statements.[7] For instance, the Basic Principles and Guidelines on the Right to a Remedy and Reparation concluded that gross violations are those that 'by their very grave nature, constitute an affront to human dignity'.[8] A serious violation of human rights is better understood as an accumulation of elements of all kinds (quantitative, situational, and qualitative) that characterise the violation.

The expression 'serious violations of human rights' does not merely describe a closed list of specific rights or specific violations of those rights. Providing a closed list may have been easier and in line with traditional vertical distinctions between human rights. We could attempt to agree on a list where only right-to-life violations are considered as serious, not violations of the right to work.[9] However, such a construction would quickly fall apart. The first Special Rapporteur on basic principles and guidelines, Theo van Boven, included an open-ended list of gross violations of human rights,[10] which was shortly after

[5] Among others, Howard Tolley, 'The Concealed Crack in the Citadel: The United Nations Commission on Human Rights' Response to Confidential Communications' (1984) 6 HRQ 420 (hereinafter Tolley, 'The Concealed Crack'); Felix Ermacora, 'Procedures to Deal with Human Rights Violations: A Hopeful Start in the United Nations?' (1974) 7 HRJ 670 (hereinafter Ermacora, 'Procedures to Deal').

[6] Andrew Clapham and others (eds), *The Arms Trade Treaty: A Commentary* (OUP 2016), 260–71 (hereinafter Clapham and others (eds), *The Arms Trade Treaty*); Ilia Maria Siatitsa, '"A Serious Violation of International Human Rights Law"—An Attempt to Clarify a Crucial Provision of the Arms Trade Treaty' (2015) 5 EJHR 606.

[7] Ellen Desmet, 'The UN Basic Principles and Guidelines on the Right to a Remedy and Reparation: A Landmark or Window-Dressing? An Analysis with Special Attention to the Situation of Indigenous People' (2008) 24 SAJHR 71, 77–79.

[8] Basic Principles and Guidelines on the Right to a Remedy and Reparation for Victims of Gross Violations of International Human Rights Law and Serious Violations of International Humanitarian Law, UNGA Res 60/147 (Annex) (16 December 2005) Preamble, para 6 (hereinafter UNGA, Basic Principles and Guidelines).

[9] Respectively, Article 4, International Covenant on Civil and Political Rights (adopted 16 December 1966) 999 UNTS 171; Article 6, International Covenant on Economic, Social and Cultural Rights (adopted 16 December 1966) 993 UNTS 3.

[10] He included 'genocide; slavery and slavery-like practices; summary or arbitrary executions; torture and cruel, inhuman or degrading treatment or punishment; enforced disappearance; arbitrary and prolonged detention; deportation or forcible transfer of population; and systematic discrimination, in particular based on race or gender'. Principle 1, 'Final report submitted by Mr Theo van Boven, Special

abandoned.[11] For instance, a violation of the obligation to investigate a murder may constitute a violation of the right to life, but it will not necessarily amount to a serious violation of human rights capable of mobilising the international community.[12]

Any such list fails to capture the multi-layered and complex character of serious violations of human rights. There is little difficulty identifying the worst atrocities: there is no question that the crimes of genocide and apartheid describe acts that also amount to serious violations of human rights. Similarly, there is no doubt that having one private letter illegally opened by a state official is not a serious violation, albeit it remains a violation that calls to be remedied. As the Inter-American Court of Human Rights has repeatedly underlined, 'any human rights violation involves a level of severity by its own nature, because it implies a breach of certain State obligations to respect and guarantee the rights and freedoms for people'.[13] The situation becomes more complex, though, when one moves towards the centre of the violation continuum; to identify the lower threshold at which a violation of human rights becomes a serious violation. It is maintained below that in practice, the character of the violations (their impact and structure) bears more significance than the specific human rights provisions that were actually breached. Every element contributing to the elevation of a human rights violation to a serious violation is examined separately below, while paying due regard to their interactions and balances.

1. The elements forming a serious violation of human rights

Inevitably, certain factors should be taken into account while delving into the assessment of international practice. First, the focus on international practice excludes from this equation each victim's self-perception of the harm they suffered. Each victim understands and describes as serious the violations they have endured. What is serious for each person is quite subjective, depending

Rapporteur: Study concerning the right to restitution, compensation and rehabilitation for victims of gross violations of human rights and fundamental freedoms' (2 July 1993) E/CN.4/Sub.2/1993/8.

[11] UNGA, Basic Principles and Guidelines (n 8) Preamble, para 6; 'Revised set of basic principles and guidelines on the right to reparation for victims of gross violations of human rights and humanitarian law prepared by Mr Theo van Boven pursuant to Sub-Commission decision 1995/117 (second draft)' (24 May 1996) E/CN.4/Sub.2/1996/17.

[12] See Section 1.1.

[13] IACtHR, *Vera Vera et al v Ecuador* (Preliminary objections, merits, reparations and costs) 19 May 2011, para 118 (hereinafter *Vera Vera et al v Ecuador*). See Section 1.1.1.3.

on the set of values, previous experience, and position of the observer. The attempt to define serious violations becomes insurmountable. In that sense, '[n]o language-game ... can express every subjectively felt violation'.[14]

Second, the legal nature of the expression 'serious human rights violation' varies, depending on different factors, including, inter alia, the legal basis invoked, the body involved, and the aim. This and similar expressions are equally used by a large variety of actors—political, judicial, and civil society ones. On the one hand, various actors may use the expression in a general way, to underline the importance of a situation deserving particular attention without having a legal impact per se. On the other hand, when the same expression is introduced in a treaty provision, it transforms into a legal notion, entailing a meaning and consequences specific to that treaty.

Lastly, it is often the case that many instances of serious violations of human rights escape the 'radar' of the international monitoring procedures, depending on various factors. For the political organs, any decision to act is the outcome of a careful balance of opposing interests on a global scale. The fact that they do not respond to certain instances of serious violations of human rights should not be taken as an indicator that there is no common understanding regarding which violations qualify as serious.

1.1 The qualitative elements

The qualitative aspect of seriousness are translated into three interconnected elements: (i) the protected value that finds expression in various human rights rules; (ii) the irreparable impact on the victims; and (iii) the vulnerable situation in which the victims are found, which can relate either to the group to which they belong or to the circumstance in which they are found. Each of these elements is inextricably intertwined with the other qualitative elements, making it occasionally difficult to distinguish one from the others. The more vulnerable the position of the victims, the higher the risk of violations having an irreparable impact, and so on.

1.1.1 The 'protected value' element

The protected value here refers to the values a human rights rule protects, which encompasses the integrity and dignity of persons.[15] The connection

[14] Martti Koskenniemi, 'The Pull of the Mainstream' (1989) 88 Mich L Rev 1946, 1946.

[15] Also referred to as the 'nature' or 'type' of rights (Quiroga, *The Battle of Human Rights* (n 3) 13). 'Protected value' seems to create less confusion, as the 'nature of rights' may also refer to other qualities

between seriousness and the protected value is all too present in international law. The International Law Commission (ILC) emphasised that 'the term "gross" ... denotes violations of a flagrant nature, amounting to a direct and outright *assault on the values protected by the rule*'.[16] The value protected has also been a criterion in international criminal law, used to identify those violations of international humanitarian law that have amounted to serious violations.[17] Similarly, in international human rights law practice, the nature of the assaulted value influences the determination of whether a violation is serious. As a result, there are certain rights the violation of which is repeatedly and frequently characterised as serious, while violations of other rights are less frequently so characterised. The qualification of certain rights as serious often appears to be circumstantial, but it should not.

1.1.1.1 Human rights commonly associated with serious violations

In the majority of instances where human rights violations are characterised as serious, at least one of the following human rights is involved: the prohibition of arbitrary deprivation of life (particularly extrajudicial or summary executions and massacres), torture—including rape and other forms of sexual violence (occasionally cases of cruel, inhuman, or degrading treatment), enforced disappearance, arbitrary (mostly prolonged) deprivation of liberty, as well as slavery and forced labour.[18] It is not incidental that special instruments have been adopted to address every one of these rights, or specific practices related to one of these rights.[19] These are the rights that directly protect the integrity

of human rights rules, such as their absolute character. Also 'type' of rights points to a division between specific rights, suggesting that only violations of certain rights would qualify as serious.

[16] ILC, Articles on Responsibility of States for Internationally Wrongful Acts, with commentaries (2001) Yb ILC, Vol II, Part Two, 113, para 8 (emphasis added) (hereinafter ARSIWA with commentaries); Eric Wyler and Alain Papaux, 'The Different Forms of Reparation: Satisfaction' in James Crawford, Alain Pellet, and Simon Olleson (eds), *The Law of International Responsibility* (OUP 2010).

[17] ICTY, *Prosecutor v Tadić*, Decision on the Defence Motion for Interlocutory Appeal on Jurisdiction, Appeal Chamber, IT-94-1, 2 October 1995, para 94 (hereinafter *Prosecutor v Tadić*). See Paola Gaeta, 'The Interplay between the Geneva Conventions and International Criminal Law' in Andrew Clapham, Paola Gaeta, and Marco Sassòli (eds), *The 1949 Geneva Conventions: A Commentary* (OUP 2015).

[18] Thomas Buergenthal, 'Codifications and Implementation of International Human Rights' in Alice Henkin (ed), *Human Dignity, The Internationalization of Human Rights* (Aspen Institute for Humanistic Studies 1979) 17; Manfred Nowak, 'The Right to Reparation of Victims of Gross Human Rights Violations' (2001) 7(1) HR Dev CYB 275, 305.

[19] Slavery Convention (adopted 25 September 1926 and amended 7 December 1953) 212 UNTS 17; Convention against Torture and Other Cruel, Inhuman or Degrading Treatment or Punishment (adopted 10 December 1984) 1465 UNTS 85 (hereinafter CAT); International Convention for the Protection of All Persons from Enforced Disappearance (adopted 20 December 2006) 2716 UNTS 3 (hereinafter CED).

of every right holder.[20] Their violation, in the majority of cases, attacks what is essential for the enjoyment of any other right.[21] This conclusion finds further support in the practice of judicial and quasi-judicial organs examining individual instances of violations, as well as the practice of political organs and other instruments responding to situations of human rights violations.

The Inter-American Court of Human Rights has explicitly invoked the 'nature of the injured rights' as an aggravating element in several enforced disappearance cases that qualified as serious violations of human rights.[22] According to the Court, other offences, such as extrajudicial killings or torture, also harm the essential values and rights of the international community.[23] While the jurisprudence of the European Court of Human Rights (hereinafter the 'European Court') offers similar examples,[24] it has also officially recognised the qualitative difference of those violations that directly threaten the physical integrity and dignity of human beings in its Priority Policy. It gives precedence to allegations that concern one of the 'core rights' of the European Convention on Human Rights (ECHR), meaning those under Articles 2, 3, 4, and 5(1).[25] Likewise, the African Court on Human and Peoples' Rights (hereinafter the 'African Court') has recognised as 'violations of extreme gravity' instances that involved violations of the right to life (extrajudicial killings, massacres) and torture.[26]

[20] On the notion of the 'integrity of persons', encompassing the right to life and the prohibition of torture, inhuman, and degrading treatment, see Nigel Rodley, 'Integrity of the Person' in Daniel Moeckli, Sangeeta Shah, and Sandesh Sivakumaran (eds), *International Human Rights Law* (3rd edn, OUP 2018).

[21] CCPR Committee, General Comment 6, Article 6 (Right to life) (30 April 1982) para 1.

[22] Among others, IACtHR, *Osorio Rivera and Family Members v Peru* (Preliminary objections, merits, reparations and costs) 26 November 2013, para 112; IACtHR, *Goiburú et al v Paraguay* (Merits, reparations and costs) 22 September 2006, para 86.

[23] Among others, IACtHR, *Manuel Cepeda Vargas v Colombia* (Preliminary objections, merits, reparations and costs) 26 May 2010, para 117; IACtHR, *Barrios Altos v Peru* (Merits) 14 May 2001, para 41. See also IAComHR, *Manoel Leal De Oliveira v Brazil*, Case 12308, Report No 37/10, 17 March 2010, para 138.

[24] Notably, on torture, see ECtHR, *Ananyev and others v Russia*, App nos 42525/07 and 60800/08, 10 January 2012, para 236 (hereinafter *Ananyev ao v Russia*); ECtHR, *Aksoy v Turkey* (GC), App no 21987/93, 18 December 1996, para 113 (hereinafter *Aksoy v Turkey*). On enforced disappearance, see ECtHR, *Aslakhanova and others v Russia* (GC), App nos 2944/06, 8300/07, 50184/07, 332/08, and 42509/10, 18 December 2012, para 132 (hereinafter *Aslakhanova ao v Russia*); ECtHR, *Kurt v Turkey* (GC), App no 15/1997/799/1002, 25 May 1998, paras 125, 129.

[25] ECtHR, 'The Court's Priority Policy' (June 2009, as amended 22 May 2017) 2.

[26] Among others, ACtHPR, *African Commission on Human and Peoples' Rights v Great Socialist People's Libyan Arab Jamahiriya*, App No 04/2011, Order for Provisional Measures, 15 March 2011. See also AComHPR, *Organisation Mondiale Contre la Torture and Association Internationale des Juristes Democrates, Commission Internationale des Juristes (CIJ), Union Interafricaine des Droits de l'homme v Rwanda*, Comm 27/89, 46/91, 49/91, 99/93, Decision on Merits, 31 October 2006, 10th ACHPR AAR Annex X (1996–1997).

The practice of UN treaty bodies follows that of regional human rights courts.[27] Numerous cases examined by the Committee on the Elimination of Racial Discrimination (hereinafter the 'CERD Committee') under the Early-Warning and Urgent Action Procedure (which is triggered in cases of 'serious, massive or persistent pattern of racial discrimination') concern violations of the rights to life and physical integrity.[28] The approach at UN political level does not differ either. In all the resolutions where the various UN political organs, including the UN Security Council,[29] the UN General Assembly,[30] and the UN Human Rights Council,[31] have condemned human rights violations as serious, violations of one or (usually) more of the above-mentioned rights have also occurred. Instances in Syria, the Central African Republic (CAR), or the Democratic People's Republic of Korea (DPRK or North Korea) all involve violations of those rights that directly protect the physical integrity of persons, among the wide array of human rights violations that occur therein.[32]

Nonetheless, these instances should not be interpreted as implying that any violation of one of these rights would amount to a serious violation, only that it is most likely that it will be characterised as such. For instance, not every violation of the right to life would amount to a serious violation. In fact, it has tended to be the aggravated forms of violation of these rights that have been

[27] Among others, CCPR Committee, *Bautista d Arellana v Colombia*, Comm No 563/1993, Views, 27 October 1995, para 8.2. See also CCPR Committee, Concluding Observations on Algeria (1 November 2007) CCPR/C/DZA/CO/3, 9, para 7(b)–(c).

[28] Among others, CERD Committee, Decision 1(85) on Iraq, 22 August 2014; CERD Committee, Decision 1(45) on the human rights situation in Rwanda (3 August 1994) A/49/18.

[29] Notably, Reports of the Secretary-General on the Sudan and South Sudan, UNSC Res 2428 (13 July 2018) para 14(d) (hereinafter UNSC Res 2428 (2018)); DRC, UNSC Res 2136 (30 January 2014) Preamble, paras 11–12; Côte d'Ivoire, UNSC Res 2000 (27 July 2011) Preamble, para 13; DRC, UNSC Res 1493 (28 July 2003) para 8 (hereinafter UNSC Res 1493 (2003)). On UNSC practice, see also Daphna Shraga, 'The Security Council and Human Rights—From Discretion to Promote to Obligation to Protect' in Bardo Fassbender (ed), *Securing Human Rights?: Achievements and Challenges of the UN Security Council* (OUP 2011) 19, fn 65.

[30] The UN General Assembly had been condemning as gross, violations of arbitrary arrest, torture, and degrading treatment in detention, as early as 1974. Protection and human rights in Chile, UNGA Res 3219(XXIX) (6 November 1974) Preamble, para 8. More recently, Situation of human rights in the Autonomous Republic of Crimea and the city of Sevastopol, Ukraine, UNGA Res 75/192 (16 December 2020) Preamble, para 29; Situation of human rights in Iran, UNGA Res 68/184 (18 December 2013) para 5(a) (hereinafter UNGA Res 68/184 (2013)); Situation of human rights in Uzbekistan, UNGA Res 60/274 (16 December 2005) para 2.

[31] More recently, among others, Promotion and protection of human rights in Nicaragua, UNHRC Res 43/2 (19 June 2020) para 1; Independent Investigative Mechanism for Myanmar, UNHRC Res 39/2 (27 September 2018) paras 1–2; Ensuring respect for international law in the Occupied Palestinian Territory, including East Jerusalem, UNHRC Res S-21/1 (23 July 2014) Preamble, para 12; Situation of human rights in Belarus, UNHRC Res 20/13 (5 July 2012) para 1 (hereinafter UNHRC Res 20/13 (2012)).

[32] Notably, Situation of human rights in the Syrian Arab Republic, UNGA Res 72/191 (19 December 2017) para 24; CAR, UNSC Res 2134 (28 January 2014) Preamble, paras 5–6, para 38 (hereinafter UNSC Res 2134 (2014)); Situation of human rights in the Democratic People's Republic of Korea, UNHRC Res 40/20 (22 March 2019) para 1 (hereinafter UNHRC Res 40/20 (2019)).

characterised as serious. Summary executions are condemned as serious violations of human rights that constitute violations of the right to life.[33] This conclusion is reinforced when considering that the 'violation of a right' also describes violations of procedural obligations that might not constitute a direct assault on the protected values. A one-time disregard relating to the obligation to investigate under the right to life will not automatically amount to a serious violation, albeit that it will remain a human rights violation.[34] Similarly, a short, even unjustified, delay in bringing a recently arrested person suspected of having committed an offence before the competent judge will not automatically amount to a serious violation of the right to liberty.

1.1.1.2 A serious violation of any human right

The violation of the above-mentioned rights may more often qualify as serious due to the values they protect, but they are not the only rights the violation of which is characterised as serious. Violations of any right—including the rights to a fair trial, privacy, and family life, the freedoms of expression, thought, conscience and religion, assembly and association, but also violations of specific economic, social, and cultural rights (particularly the rights to food, housing, and health)—have been characterised as serious, albeit less frequently. These determinations are an inevitable expression of the realisation that each human right has a minimum core, and a human rights violation involves different nuances.

As Mégret and others pointed out, '[a]ll rights matter equally, and it is rather each right that has a core and a penumbra, where the core is precisely that area in which dignity is at stake'.[35] There is similarly the notion of 'minimum core obligations', as developed by the Committee on Economic, Social and Cultural Rights.[36] It is closely connected to the understanding that the denial of the

[33] Extrajudicial, summary or arbitrary executions, UNGA Res 73/172 (18 December 2018) Preamble, para 25.

[34] IACtHR, *Massacres of El Mozote and nearby Places v El Salvador* (Merits, reparations and costs) 25 October 2012, para 295 (hereinafter *Massacres of El Mozote and nearby Places v El Salvador*); ECtHR, *Tagayeva and others v Russia*, App no 26562/07 and six other applications, 13 April 2017, para 516 (hereinafter *Tagayeva ao v Russia*).

[35] Frédéric Mégret and others, 'Human Dignity: A Special Focus on Vulnerable Groups, Protecting Dignity', Panel on Human Dignity (2014), vii <https://www.graduateinstitute.ch/sites/internet/files/2020-11/HumanDignity_Megret.pdf> accessed 11 October 2021. Theo van Boven has also concluded that 'basic subsistence rights which determine the life, the dignity, and the well-being of individuals and peoples should be considered as core rights': Theo van Boven, 'Categories of Rights' in Daniel Moeckli, Shah Sangeeta, and Sandesh Sivakumaran (eds), *International Human Rights Law* (3rd edn, OUP 2018) 143 (hereinafter van Boven, 'Categories of Rights').

[36] ESCR Committee, General Comment 3, The nature of States parties' obligations (Art 2, para 1), 14 December 1990, para 10. See also Frans Viljoen, *International Human Rights Law in Africa* (2nd edn, OUP 2012) 460–62.

minimum core that is judged essential for each right can have detrimental, irreversible effects on the lives of individuals, such as, for instance, freedom from hunger and access to minimum adequate food.

As an example, prohibiting the publication of an article might be a violation of the freedom of expression, but it will not necessarily be a serious violation of human rights. However, in a case where, in addition to prohibiting publication, those in authority fire the journalist, even prosecute them, and ensure that they will not find a job again in their lifetime, this raises the whole situation to a different level. That person is denied all means of existence. The Inter-American Court has recognised the importance of such violations.[37]

On certain occasions, the classification of other rights as 'serious' may appear purely circumstantial. They are listed as serious in a broader context of violence, where violations of one or more of the rights in the previous section have already occurred. This practice is more frequent when examining situations of human rights violations rather than individual cases. For instance, the UN General Assembly has in more than one situation listed violations of the freedoms of movement, opinion, expression, religion, thought and conscience, the right to privacy, and discrimination against ethnic minorities and women as serious in ongoing situations where at least the right to life and liberty are also violated.[38] These are ongoing situations that perpetuate an environment of abuse and systematic undermining of fundamental freedoms.

These determinations often relate to situations of political violence or authoritarian regimes. For instance, the Inter-American Commission provided a long list of so-called serious violations when examining (among others) political violence in Honduras. It condemned, as serious, violations of political rights, such as the right to participate in political life and the right to serve in public office. Ministers, governors, members of congress, and mayors were

[37] Among others, IACtHR, *Herrera-Ulloa v Costa Rica ('La Nación' Newspaper Case)*, Provisional Measures Order, 7 September 2001; IACtHR, *Marta Colomina and Liliana Velásquez v Venezuela*, Provisional Measures Order, 2 December 2003.

[38] Among others, Situation of human rights in the DPRK, UNGA Res 75/190 (16 December 2020) para 2 (hereinafter UNGA Res 75/190 (2020)); Situation of human rights in Myanmar, UNGA Res 63/245 (24 December 2008) para 2(b). See further Linos-Alexander Sicilianos, 'L'influence des droits de l'homme sur la structure du droit international, Première partie: La hiérarchisation de l'ordre juridique international' (2012) 117 RGDIP 5, 23 (hereinafter Sicilianos, 'L'influence des droits'). Similar practice from other UN bodies: Technical assistance and capacity-building for Yemen in the field of human rights, UNHRC Res 45/26 (6 October 2020) para 7 (hereinafter UNHRC Res 45/26 (2020)); Guinea-Bissau, UNSC Res 2103 (22 May 2013) Preamble, para 9 (hereinafter UNSC Res 2103 (2013)); UNHRC, 'First Report of the independent international commission of inquiry on the Syrian Arab Republic' (23 November 2011) A/HRC/S-17/2/Add1, paras 84–96.

targets of reprisals, threats, acts of violence, budgetary cuts, and military occupation of their offices.[39]

There are also individual instances where the violation of (potentially almost every) other human rights may qualify as serious because it affected or put at risk one of the rights listed above—directly attacking the values they protect. In 1988, Quiroga came to the conclusion that for a violation to qualify as gross, 'the rights to life, to personal security or to personal freedom must be *either continuously and massively affected* by the violations, *or sporadically affected but continuously threatened*, while other human rights are being massively violated'.[40] For instance, the Committee on Economic, Social and Cultural Rights has condemned as gross violations measures restricting the movement of civilians and, as a consequence, severing their access to food, water, healthcare, education, and work.[41] Also, the violation of the right to a fair trial, despite its centrality within the human rights protection system,[42] is defined as serious only in cases where the right to life is at risk of being violated, particularly in systems where the death penalty is still carried out.[43]

Lastly, the presence of other factors may have contributed to the gravity of a human rights violation, such as the effect of the violations on the overall life of the victims, their systematic character, or their scale.[44] Partially rejecting the 'specific rights' criterion, Bassiouni underlined that the term 'gross' in Basic Principles and Guidelines describes the severity of a violation rather than a violation of a particular category of rights.[45] The illegal expropriation of

[39] See IAComHR, Report on 'Honduras: Human Rights and the Coup d'état' (30 December 2009) OEA/Ser.L/V/II. Doc 55, paras 551, 555, 441. Repeated in IAComHR, Preliminary Observations of the Inter-American Commission on Human Rights on its visit to Honduras (15–18 May 2010, Report on 3 June 2010) OEA/Ser.L/V/II. Doc 68, para 9. Similarly, the ACtHPR, *African Commission on Human and Peoples' Rights v The Republic of Kenya*, Order of Provisional Measures, App No 006/2012, 15 March 2013 (hereinafter *African Commission v Kenya* (Provisional measures)). See also CERD Committee, Decision 1(63) on the Lao People's Democratic Republic (21 August 2003) CERD/C/63/Dec1, para 2 (hereinafter CERD Committee, Decision 1(63) on the Lao People's Democratic Republic).

[40] Quiroga, *The Battle of Human Rights* (n 3) 15 (emphasis added).

[41] Notably, ESCR Committee, Concluding observations on Israel (31 August 2001) E/C12/1/Add69, para 704.

[42] Without access to the judicial system and, even more, a 'fair' judicial system, none of the other human rights can be effectively protected. CCPR Committee, 'General comment 32: Article 14, Right to equality before courts and tribunals and to fair trial' (23 August 2007) CCPR/C/GC/32. This applies to the principle of legality as well. Indirect references could be inferred when condemning as serious practices that are directly attached to their respect, such as 'summary executions'. For instance, CCPR Committee, Concluding Observations on Cameroon (4 August 2010) CCPR/C/CMR/CO/4, para 18.

[43] Among others, IAComHR, *Abu-Ali Abdur' Rahman v US* (Merits), Case 21422, Report No 13/14, 2 April 2014, paras 94–95; IAComHR, *Jeffrey Timothy Landrigan v US* (Merits), Case 12776, Report No 81/11, 21 July 2011, para 64.

[44] See Sections 1.1.2 et seq.

[45] 'Report of the independent expert on the right to restitution, compensation and rehabilitation for victims of grave violations of human rights and fundamental freedoms, Mr M. Cherif Bassiouni', submitted pursuant to ComHR resolution 1998/43 (8 February 1999) E/CN4/1999/65, para 85.

indigenous peoples' lands and other cases of property destruction constitute typical examples. For instance, the seizure of indigenous peoples' land wipes out their means and purpose of living, to the extent that their rights to life and integrity are at stake. In the *Operation Genesis* case, the Inter-American Court stated

> that the destruction of the homes of the inhabitants of the communities of the Cacarica River basin, in addition to constituting a major financial loss, resulted in the inhabitants losing their *basic means of subsistence*, which means that *the violation of the right to property in this case was particularly serious.* Thus, the Colombian Constitutional Court has established that 'property should be considered a fundamental right, provided that it is related to the maintenance of material conditions of existence, and that disregarding it affects equality and the possibility of leading a decent life.'[46]

Likewise, the land redistribution scheme in Zimbabwe that deprived 700,000 Zimbabweans of their homes, their source of livelihood, or both, has been estimated to amount to a serious violation of human rights to the extent of justifying third-party countermeasures.[47]

1.1.1.3 On the lack of hierarchy within human rights

Accepting that the violation of certain rights will more likely qualify as serious compared to others does not automatically imply that these rights are hierarchically superior to others.[48] The debate regarding the hierarchy of human rights is an old debate and is closely linked to the determination of the rights as fundamental, core, or basic. Some authors support the division between hierarchically superior rights and other rights.[49] The present author does not

[46] IACtHR, *Displaced Communities of African Descent of the Basin of the River Cacarica (Operation Genesis) v Colombia* (Preliminary objections, merits, reparations and costs) 20 November 2013, para 352 (emphasis added) (hereinafter *Displaced Communities of African Descent of the Basin of the River Cacarica (Operation Genesis) v Colombia).*

[47] UN Secretary General, 'Report of the Fact-Finding Mission to Zimbabwe to assess the Scope and Impact of Operation Murambatsvina by the UN Special Envoy on Human Settlements Issues in Zimbabwe Mrs Anna Kajumulo Tibaijuka' (18 July 2005). The EU imposed third-party countermeasures against Zimbabwe: Council Decision 2011/101/CFSP concerning restrictive measures against Zimbabwe (15 February 2011) OJ L 121/11, 11. Earlier, Prohibition of forced evictions, ComHR Res 2004/28 (16 April 2004) Preamble, para 4, Operative para 1.

[48] For a different view, see Fatsah Ouguergouz, *The African Charter on Human and Peoples' Rights, A Comprehensive Agenda for Human Dignity and Sustainable Democracy in Africa* (Martinus Nijhoff Publishers 2003) 622–23.

[49] Antonio Cassese, 'A Plea for a Global Community Grounded in a Core of Human Rights' in Antonio Cassese (ed), *Realizing Utopia: The Future of International Law* (OUP 2012) 140; Theodor Meron, 'On a Hierarchy of International Human Rights' (1986) 80 AJIL 1.

entirely dismiss this debate but argues that it is not relevant for determining what amounts to a serious violation of human rights. The distinction between 'basic' or 'fundamental' and other rights is not always easy to define.[50] This difficulty almost ceases when focusing on serious and non-serious violations of human rights.

Any attempt to differentiate between human rights or the severity of their violation has immediately been rejected as introducing a hierarchy among human rights. Human rights have always been described as equal, indivisible, and interrelated.[51] Nevertheless, gravity qualifiers do allow for a more unified approach to human rights, whether they are categorised as civil and political, or economic, social, and cultural rights. Interestingly, van Boven does not question the axiomatic value of the principle of interdependence and indivisibility of all human rights when affirming that 'certain human rights represent or embody core attributes to human life and human dignity'.[52] The fact that certain human rights have acquired other additional characteristics (such as *jus cogens* status) neither makes each violation serious nor automatically places them in a hierarchically superior position.[53]

The determination of gravity should not be understood as dividing human rights into two categories: those the violation of which is serious and those the violation of which is not. First, the violation of any right may qualify as serious in certain aggravating circumstances. Second, even with regard to those rights violation of which more regularly qualifies as serious, such as the right to life, not all violations qualify as serious. Third, the current practice has never justified the classification of certain violations as serious based on their hierarchical superiority. It rather underlines the serious nature of certain violations that justifies the intervention of the international community; it is not a question of the clashing of norms.

1.1.2 The 'irreparable impact' element

There is another element that arguably could more persuasively justify the suggestion that the violation of any human right in specific circumstances can potentially amount to a serious violation of human rights. Indeed, despite its

[50] Maurizio Ragazzi, *The Concept of International Obligations Erga Omnes* (OUP 2000) 139.

[51] 'All human rights are universal, indivisible and interdependent and interrelated.' Vienna Declaration and Programme of Action, adopted by the World Conference on Human Rights in Vienna (25 June 1993) para 5.

[52] van Boven, 'Categories of Rights' (n 35) 142. See also Pierre Sob, 'Article 58' in Maurice Kampto (ed), *La Charte africaine des droits de l'homme et des peuples et le protocole y relatif portant création de la Cour africaine des droits de l'homme: Commentaire article par article* (Bruylant 2011) 1073.

[53] Martin Scheinin, 'Core Rights and Obligations' in Dinah Shelton (ed), *The Oxford Handbook of International Human Rights Law* (OUP 2014) 532.

close connection to the 'protected value' element, the irreparability of the harm a human rights violation may cause to the victims should be understood as an autonomous (if not primary) element influencing the gravity equation by itself.[54] The 'irreparable impact' element has two components: first, human rights violations may cause such harm that a return to the previous position is impossible (one can never bring back the dead); second, certain violations can never be suitably repaired due to the nature of the harm they have caused.[55]

Undeniably, there is a kind of irreversibility in the violation of any human right. However, the hope is that most rights that have been violated could eventually either be reinstated or be fairly compensated in law, by the punishment of those responsible and/or monetary compensation for the damage caused by the violation. But this is not always possible. As the Inter-American Court has stressed:

> [S]exual rape is an extremely traumatic experience that may have *serious consequences* and it causes great physical and psychological damage that leaves the victim 'physically and emotionally humiliated', [a] *situation difficult to overcome with time, contrary to what happens with other traumatic experiences*.[56]

The CERD Committee, in the 2007 'Early-Warning and Urgent Action Procedure' Guidelines—a procedure that is triggered in cases of serious violations of the International Convention on the Elimination of All Forms of Racial Discrimination (CERD)—explicitly underlined that, depending on the circumstances, 'the irreparable harm that may be caused to victims' should be taken into account to identify a serious violation.[57]

The irreparable harm can be assessed either before the violation occurs (*ex-ante*), or after the violation has taken place (*post facto*). For instance, international human rights courts always take into account the consequences of a violation for the victims in order to be able to calculate the compensation they will be awarded.[58] Arguably, the classification of a human rights violation as

[54] See ECtHR, *Nagmetov v Russia* (GC), App no 35589/08, 30 March 2017, para 81; ECtHR, *Varnava and others v Turkey* (GC), App nos 16064/90, 16065/90, 16066/90, 16068/90, 16069/90, 16070/90, 16071/90, 16072/90, and 16073/90, 18 September 2009, para 224.

[55] Eva Rieter, *Preventing Irreparable Harm, Provisional Measures in International Human Rights Adjudication* (Intersentia 2010) 209 (hereinafter Rieter, 'Preventing Irreparable Harm').

[56] IACtHR, *Miguel Castro-Castro Prison v Peru* (Merits, reparations and costs) 25 November 2006, para 311 (emphasis added) (hereinafter *Miguel Castro-Castro Prison v Peru*).

[57] CERD Committee, Guidelines for the Early Warning and Urgent Action Procedure (2007) A/62/18, 117, para 12 (hereinafter CERD Committee, Guidelines for EWA (2007)).

[58] Among others, ECtHR, *Aksoy v Turkey* (n 24) para 113; ECtHR, *Aydin v Turkey*, App no 57/1996/676/866, 25 September 1997, para 131 (hereinafter *Aydin v Turkey*); but also IACtHR, *The Ituango*

serious should primarily be based on the assessment of the potential irreparable impact on the victims before the violation occurs.[59] In several instances, it is essential to make an *ex-ante* determination of a human rights violation as serious. For example, in arms control practice, the 'consequences of the actual violation' were enumerated as a crucial factor in determining whether a violation is serious.[60] However, the ATT requires that the exporting state should evaluate whether there is a potential risk that the exported arms will be used to commit or facilitate 'serious violations of international human rights law' in the future—that is, before the violations occurred.[61] Such assessments can only be made *ex-ante*.

In the opinion of the present author, the 'irreparable impact' element captures the interdependent and intersecting nature of human rights in a manner that the 'protected value' element is unable to describe.[62] The irreparability of harm illustrates more plainly how the violation of a potentially wide array of human rights may amount to a serious violation for the international community. This permits for a determination of gravity in the broader situation within which the violations have occurred. Rieter underlined that determinations should be contextual: 'in a climate of harassment against journalists or the judiciary, it is no longer possible to speak of reversible harm to the claim.'[63] In recognition of this premise, regional human rights courts have gradually broadened (to a greater or lesser degree) the material scope of interim measures that are adopted when an alleged violation risks causing irreparable damage to the victims in the most obvious, serious, and urgent situations, including the right to respect for private and family life, especially when the well-being of a child is at issue, the right to a fair trial,[64] and the protection of an indigenous community's property rights.[65]

Massacres v Colombia (Preliminary Objections, merits, reparations, and costs) 1 July 2006, para 366 (hereinafter *The Ituango Massacres v Colombia*).

[59] George Abi-Saab, 'The Uses of Article 19' (1999) 10 EJIL 339, 341.

[60] Council of the European Union, User's Guide to Council Common Position 2008/944/CFSP defining common rules governing the control of exports of military technology and equipment (updated) (16 September 2019) 12189/19, 47 (hereinafter Council of the EU, User's Guide 2019).

[61] Article 7, ATT (adopted on 2 April 2013) UNGA Res 67/234 (hereinafter ATT). See Clapham and others (eds), *The Arms Trade Treaty* (n 6) 260–71.

[62] On this debate, see Ioana Cismas, 'The Intersection of Economic, Social, and Cultural Rights and Civil and Political Rights' in Eibe Riedel, Gilles Giacca, and Christophe Golay (eds), *Economic, Social, and Cultural Rights in International Law: Contemporary Issues and Challenges* (OUP 2014).

[63] Rieter, 'Preventing Irreparable Harm' (n 55) 718.

[64] ECtHR, Factsheet—Interim Measures, Press Unit (April 2021) 2.

[65] Yves Haeck and Clara Burbano Herrera, 'Interim Measures in the Case Law of the European Court of Human Rights' (2003) 21 NQHR 625, 672. Rieter concluded that there is a high probability that the irreparable impact criterion will be used to further expand the scope of provisional measures. Rieter, 'Preventing Irreparable Harm' (n 55) 715.

As a result, violations of the right to property, as well as forcible transfers, have been understood as serious violations of human rights. The UN Human Rights Council has condemned the forcible transfer of Palestinians and the acquisition of Palestinian land.[66] The CERD Committee has affirmed, while operating under an urgent procedure reserved for serious violations of the Convention, that the expropriation of indigenous peoples' and ethnic groups' lands, or destruction of their houses, has devastating consequences for their lives, health, culture, and environment.[67] Similarly, another set of letters and decisions refers to evictions of Roma people in Great Britain, the Czech Republic, and Slovakia, and underlines the impact of such evictions on multiple levels of Roma people's lives.[68] Likewise, the European Court concluded that the intentional burning of houses by the police as part of an official governmental policy, leaving the victims defenceless and exposed without any assistance, constituted a serious violation of both the right to privacy and the right to property.[69]

Various UN human rights treaty bodies have consistently defined violations 'as "grave" if they are likely to produce substantial harm to victims'.[70] It is not suggested that any violation will potentially amount to a serious violation of human rights. Not every human rights violation has an irreparable impact on its victims. In due course, the notion of 'irreparable impact' could allow the inclusion, apart from the traditional and most obvious cases of irreparability, of

[66] Right of the Palestinian people to self-determination, UNHRC Res 40/22 (22 March 2019) Preamble, para 10.

[67] Among others, CERD Committee, Decision 1(77) on Kyrgyzstan (27 August 2010) CERD/C/NGA/DEC/1 (hereinafter CERD Committee, Decision 1(77) on Kyrgyzstan); CERD Committee, Decision 3(62) on Suriname (12 March 2003) CERD/C/62/Dec/3, para 3 (hereinafter CERD Committee, Decision 3(62) on Suriname); CERD Committee, Decision 8(46) on Papua New Guinea (16 March 1995) CERD/C/60/CO/10, 8–9. See also CCPR Committee, Concluding Observations on Chad (11 August 2009) A/64/40, 74, para 10.

[68] See CERD Committee, Decision 2(53) on the Czech Republic (11 August 1998) CERD/C/348; CERD Committee, Letter to Slovakia (27 August 2010) <https://www.ohchr.org/EN/HRBodies/CERD/Pages/EarlyWarningProcedure.aspx> accessed 16 September 2021; CERD Committee, Letter to the United Kingdom (12 March 2010) <https://www.ohchr.org/EN/HRBodies/CERD/Pages/EarlyWarningProcedure.aspx> accessed 16 September 2021.

[69] ECtHR, *Akdivar and others v Turkey (Article 50)* (GC), App no 21893/93, 1 April 1998, para 37 (hereinafter *Akdivar ao v Turkey (Article 50)*). See also ECtHR, *Moldovan and others v Romania (No 2)*, App nos 41138/98 and 64320/01, 12 October 2004, para 109.

[70] Notably Committee of the Convention on the Elimination of Discrimination against Women (hereinafter CEDAW Committee), 'Inquiry Concerning South Africa Conducted under Article 8 of the Optional Protocol to the Convention' (2021) CEDAW/C/ZAF/IR/1, para 113; CRC Committee, 'Inquiry Concerning Chile under Article 13 of the Optional Protocol to the Convention on the Rights of the Child on a Communications Procedure', (6 May 2020) CRC/C/CHL/IR/1, para 111 (hereinafter CRC Committee, 'Inquiry Concerning Chile'); CRPD Committee, 'Inquiry Concerning Hungary under Article 6 of the Optional Protocol to the Convention', (2020) CRPD/C/HUN/IR/1, para 108 (hereinafter CRPD Committee, 'Inquiry Concerning Hungary').

more complex cases (that can also, in certain circumstances, attack the core of the existence of persons).

1.1.3 The vulnerability element

The vulnerable position in which victims of human rights violations find themselves is the last qualitative element that may influence the classification of a violation as serious. Vulnerability is today frequently incorporated in legal analysis adapted to the circumstances of a particular case and victim.[71] In the *Massacres of El Mozote and Nearby Places* case, the Inter-American Court underlined that the violation of the right to life 'was aggravated with regard to the children, and also to the women who were pregnant'.[72] In the *Akdivar* case, the European Court took into account the villagers' vulnerable position due to the overall context in south-east Turkey.[73] The UN General Assembly also repeatedly condemns as serious violations: discrimination against or the targeting of ethnic minorities, discrimination and sexual violence against women, the malnourishment of children and their use as child soldiers, and the detention or execution of opposition parties;[74] and in the case of North Korea, it has also included the protection of persons with disabilities and workers' rights.[75] The UN Human Rights Council has equally condemned as a gross violation the persecution of specific groups, including: protesters, refugees, human rights defenders, and journalists.[76]

Vulnerability should be broadly understood to include the trauma and harsh conditions faced by a group within a population, but also the personal

[71] Lourdes Peroni and Alexandra Timmer, 'Vulnerable Groups: The Promise of an Emerging Concept in European Human Rights Convention Law' (2013) 11 ICON 1056, 1057 (hereinafter Peroni and Timmer, 'Vulnerable Groups').

[72] *Massacres of El Mozote and nearby Places v El Salvador* (n 34) para 156. See also IACtHR, *Santo Domingo Massacre v Colombia* (Preliminary objections, merits and reparations) 30 November 2012, paras 192, 239; *The Ituango Massacres v Colombia* (n 58) paras 212, 244; IACtHR, *Gómez-Paquiyauri Brothers v Peru*, 8 July 2004, para 76.

[73] ECtHR, *Akdivar and others v Turkey* (GC), App no 21893/93, 16 September 1996, para 105 (hereinafter *Akdivar ao v Turkey*). The Court made similar comments with regard to the situation of enforced disappearances in Chechnya. Among others, see *Aslakhanova ao v Russia* (n 24) paras 216–19. On enforced disappearances, see also IACtHR, *Anzualdo Castro v Peru* (Preliminary objection, merits, reparations and costs) 22 September 2009, para 103; IACtHR, *Ticona Estrada et al v Bolivia* (Merits, reparations and costs) 27 November 2008, para 60.

[74] The UN General Assembly had already referred in 1974 to political prisoners in Chile. UNGA Res 3219(XXIX) (n 30) para 3. More recently, Situation of human rights in the Islamic Republic of Iran, UNGA Res 75/191 (16 December 2020) para 25 (hereinafter UNGA Res 75/191 (2020)); Situation of human rights in the Syrian Arab Republic, UNGA Res 74/169 (18 December 2019) para 11 (hereinafter UNGA Res 74/169 (2019)); Situation of Human Rights in Myanmar, UNGA Res 55/112 (4 December 2000). See also Security Council practice, indicatively Haiti, UNSC Res 2180 (14 October 2014) para 20; Côte d'Ivoire, UNSC Res 1975 (30 March 2011) para 5.

[75] Notably, UNGA Res 75/190 (2020) (n 38) para 2.

[76] Among others, UNHRC Res 45/26 (2020) (n 38) para 7; Situation of human rights of Rohingya Muslims and other minorities in Myanmar, UNHRC Res 42/3 (26 September 2019) para 1.

circumstances that may endanger a person. Certain groups of persons may be put in a more vulnerable position due to the fact that their group is targeted. Examples of underprivileged population groups because they have been targeted include members of indigenous communities,[77] as well as the Roma and Travellers.[78] They remain marginalised at the lowest levels of society because they have been persecuted and undermined for hundreds of years, lacking the means to defend themselves.[79] Individuals may also be in a vulnerable position because they are members of 'particularly underprivileged and vulnerable population group in need of special protection', such as asylum seekers.[80] Children or the elderly are specific categories of the population whose vulnerability emanates from their limited capacity to protect themselves.

Additionally, there is circumstantial vulnerability where any person may find themselves in a situation that leaves them exposed to abuse. In the *Vélez Loor* case, the Inter-American Court provided critical analysis of the complex situation and accumulation of factors that put the undocumented immigrants in a vulnerable position.[81] In certain instances, it is the gravity of a violation that puts the victims in a particularly vulnerable position.[82] The European Court has stressed that '*[r]ape of a detainee by an official* of the State must be considered to be *an especially grave and abhorrent form of ill-treatment* given the *ease* with which the offender can *exploit the vulnerability and weakened resistance of his victim*'.[83] Furthermore, the personal situation of the victim may aggravate the situation. Sexual orientation has been recognised as an additional factor increasing the vulnerability of the victim, who already belonged in the vulnerable category of asylum seekers.[84]

[77] *African Commission v Kenya* (Provisional measures) (n 39) para 3. On indigenous people and vulnerability, see also Rieter, 'Preventing Irreparable Harm' (n 55) 708–11.

[78] ECtHR, *DH and others v the Czech Republic* (GC), App no 57325/00, 13 November 2007, para 182. See further ECtHR, Factsheet—Roma and Travellers, Press Unit (April 2021).

[79] Similarly, *Displaced Communities of African Descent of the Basin of the River Cacarica (Operation Genesis) v Colombia* (n 46) para 354. Connecting harm and vulnerability, see CRPD Committee, 'Inquiry Concerning Hungary' (n 70) para 107.

[80] ECtHR, *MSS v Belgium and Greece* (GC), App no 30696/09, 21 January 2011, para 251. Similarly, on human rights defenders, IACtHR, *Valle Jaramillo et al v Colombia* (Merits, reparations, and costs) 27 November 2008, para 96.

[81] IACtHR, *Vélez Loor v Panama* (Preliminary objections, merits, reparations and costs) 23 November 2010, paras 98, 207; *The Ituango Massacres v Colombia* (n 58) para 212. See also ESCR Committee, Concluding observations on the DRC (17 November 2009) 67, para 308. Audrey R Chapman and Benjamin Carbonetti, 'Human Rights Protections for Vulnerable and Disadvantaged Groups: The Contributions of the UN Committee on Economic, Social and Cultural Rights' (2011) 33 HRQ 682, 682–732 (hereinafter Chapman and Carbonetti, 'Human Rights Protections').

[82] Alexander HE Morowa, 'Vulnerability as a Concept of International Human Rights Law' (2003) 6 J Intl Rel Dev 139, 149 (hereinafter Morowa, 'Vulnerability as a Concept').

[83] *Aydin v Turkey* (n 58) para 83 (emphasis added). Similarly, see *Aksoy v Turkey* (n 24) paras 56, 78, 98. See also *Miguel Castro-Castro Prison v Peru* (n 56) para 311.

[84] ECtHR, *OM v Hungary*, App no 9912/15, 5 July 2016, para 53.

Typically, women, children, the young, the elderly, indigenous people, ethnic and other minorities, migrants, asylum seekers, internally displaced people, stateless persons, the homeless, detainees and prisoners, physically and mentally handicapped people, and civilians during armed conflict have been listed or mentioned as vulnerable.[85] However, it is increasingly recognised that vulnerability is not limited to a specific closed number of groups.[86] It is rather evaluated on the basis of various factors and the particular circumstances present. Peroni and Timmer identify, as possible indicators of vulnerability, prejudice and stigmatisation, dependency on the state, and social exclusion and disadvantage.[87] The various human rights bodies do not have a common approach on the matter, not even within their own practice.[88] Nevertheless, the presence of vulnerability does not automatically and unconditionally indicate that a serious violation of human rights was committed. In most cases, it is the combination of qualitative and external elements that renders an ordinary violation of human rights a serious violation of human rights.

2. The external elements

The external elements describe the manner in which the violation has been committed, or otherwise the circumstances in which the violation occurred. Commonly, these include the massive and the systematic or organised character of the violations. Occasionally, the duration and the geographic spread of the violation are also taken into account. Similarly to the qualitative elements, you find parts of the one element leaking into the other, making it difficult to distinguish them on occasion. To prove the systematic character, the number of violations that occurred will often be taken into account. Equally, the intensity of the external circumstances within which the violations occurred can shift, depending on the qualitative elements present in a situation before it is characterised as serious.

[85] Morowa, 'Vulnerability as a Concept . . .' (n 82) 141.
[86] On argument that human rights instruments, by focusing on specific groups' vulnerability, have excluded other forms of vulnerability, see Peroni and Timmer, 'Vulnerable Groups' (n 71) 1061–62.
[87] Ibid, 1070. Fineman proposed to concentrate on societal structures: Martha Albertson Fineman, 'The Vulnerable Subject: Anchoring Equality in the Human Condition' (2008) 20 Yale JL Fem 1, 1.
[88] Chapman and Carbonetti, 'Human Rights Protections' (n 81) 722–29; Ivona Truscan, 'Considerations of Vulnerability: From Principles to Action in the Cases Law of the European Court of Human Rights' (2013) 36 Retfærd Årgang [Nordic Journal of Law and Justice] 64, 65.

2.1 The quantitative element

'Quantity' has long been recognised as an aggravating factor in international practice. The widespread context is a recurring condition in composite criminal acts, such as crimes against humanity or apartheid.[89] However, beyond the strict confines of international criminal law, the large number of victims and/or violations features in multiple instances of human rights violations that have been characterised as serious. For instance, the Inter-American Court of Human Rights, which from its earliest days was confronted with cases presenting massive human rights violations, has repeatedly recognised the quantitative element as an aggravating factor.[90] Also, the Inter-American Commission, soon after its creation, established a country report procedure to look at the general situation in a country when the Commission receives a number of complaints of serious and large-scale violations.[91]

Similarly, the UN Human Rights Council's Complaint Procedure (former 1503 Procedure), which is activated for cases of gross violations of human rights, is conditioned upon the occurrence of large-scale violations.[92] The CERD Committee has also officially included the '*scale* of the situation' as a determining factor of a 'serious violation of the Convention'.[93] Without having adopted official guidelines, the UN treaty bodies have been taking into account the scale of violations to identify gravity.[94] For instance, the large number of victims was a crucial factor for the Committee on the Elimination of Discrimination against Women to classify violations in Mexico as grave

[89] Article 7, Rome Statute of the International Criminal Court (adopted 17 July 1998) 2187 UNTS 3.

[90] Among others, IACtHR, *Río Negro Massacres v Guatemala* (Preliminary objection, merits, reparations and costs) 4 September 2012, para 190; *Vera Vera et al v Ecuador* (n 13) para 117; IACtHR, *Plan de Sánchez Massacre v Guatemala* (Merits) 29 April 2004, para 51 (hereinafter *Plan de Sánchez Massacre v Guatemala*).

[91] Among others, IAComHR, 'Report on the Situation of Human Rights in Venezuela' (29 December 2003) OEA/Ser.L/V/II.118, para 578 (hereinafter IAComHR, 'Report on the Situation of Human Rights in Venezuela'). See Maria Luisa Bartolomei, *Gross and Massive Violations of Human Rights in Argentina 1976–1983: An Analysis of the Procedure under ECOSOC Resolution 1503* (Juristförlaget, 1994) 263.

[92] Institution-building of the United Nations Human Rights Council, UNHRC Res 5/1 (18 June 2007) paras 85 et seq; ECOSOC Res 1503 (1970) (n 1) para 1. See also Maxime E Tardu, 'United Nations Response to Gross Violations of Human Rights: The 1503 Procedure' (1980(20 SantClLR 559, 583–84 (hereinafter Tardu, 'United Nations Response'); Ermacora, 'Procedures to Deal' (n 5) 678–79.

[93] CERD Committee, Guidelines for EWA (2007) (n 57) para 12 (emphasis added). CERD Committee, Decision 1(78) on Côte d'Ivoire (4 March 2011) CERD/C/CIV/DEC/2, para 1 (hereinafter CERD Committee, Decision 1(78) on Côte d'Ivoire); CERD Committee, Decision 2(47) on the situation in Bosnia and Herzegovina (17 August 1995) A/50/18, 11.

[94] Notably, CRC Committee, 'Inquiry Concerning Chile' (n 70) para 111; CRPD Committee, 'Inquiry Concerning Spain Carried out by the Committee under Article 6 of the Optional Protocol to the Convention', (2018) CRPD/C/ESP/IR/1, para 79 (hereinafter CRPD Committee, 'Inquiry Concerning Spain').

violations of the respective Convention.[95] The continuity and repetition of violations, irrespective of whether there is a plan or policy, demonstrates a critical malfunction of the system.[96]

Various qualifiers have been used interchangeably to describe the large scale of human rights violations, including widespread, massive, and gross.[97] The aggravating effect of the number of violations will depend on the presence of other factors, such as the rights affected or the size of the targeted group, as well as the systematic nature of the violations. The dividing line between widespread and systematic is often quite blurred, as a degree of the one is always required in order to prove the existence of the other. For instance, the UN Committee against Torture is using the widespread character of violations as evidence of the existence of a systematic practice.[98]

The number of victims or violations required for violations to qualify as serious is nowhere specified. Indeed, the use of qualifiers instead of a rigid numerical threshold is common practice in international law.[99] The threshold is relative to the context of each case. For instance, the violation of the rights of 15,000 people of the Ogiek Community of the Mau Forest, an indigenous minority ethnic group comprising 20,000 people in total, was characterised as massive;[100] while the European Court qualified as serious more than 220 cases of enforced disappearance in the Chechnya and Ingushetia regions.[101]

The quest for a numerical threshold recalls the 'Paradox of the Heap'; how many grains does it take to make a heap of sand? There is a certain moment when everyone agrees that a group of violations becomes widespread or massive. However, when exactly a series of violations become massive or

[95] CEDAW Committee, 'Report on Mexico produced by the Committee on the Elimination of Discrimination against Women under article 8 of the Optional Protocol to the Convention, and reply from the Government of Mexico' (27 January 2005) CEDAW/C/2005/OP8/MEXICO, para 263 (hereinafter CEDAW Committee, 'Report on Mexico').

[96] ECtHR, *Assenov and others v Bulgaria*, App no 24760/94, 28 October 1998, para 175 (hereinafter *Assenov ao v Bulgaria*); ECtHR, *Labita v Italy* (GC), App no 26772/95, 6 April 2000, para 207. See also CRPD Committee, 'Inquiry Concerning Spain' (n 94).

[97] The CEDAW Committee refers cumulatively to the widespread character of violations and the large number of victims. In such cases, 'widespread' is probably used to describe the geographical scope. CEDAW Committee, 'Report on Mexico' (n 95) para 263. *Gross* is used either to mean massive, or (next to widespread) to indicate the importance of the nature of the rights violated. ARSIWA with commentaries (n 16) 113, para 8.

[98] Among others, CAT Committee, 'Report on Nepal under Article 20 of the Convention adopted by the Committee against Torture under article 20 of the Convention' (5 October 2012) A/67/44, 299, para 97 (hereinafter CAT Committee, 'Summary account on Nepal').

[99] Jean Salmon, 'Les obligations quantitatives et l'illicéité' in Laurence Boisson de Chazournes and Vera Gowlland-Debbas (eds), *L'ordre juridique international, un système en quête d'équité et d'universalité/The International Legal System in Quest of Equity and Universality, Liber Amicorum Georges Abi-Saab* (Martinus Nijhoff Publishers 2001) 310.

[100] *African Commission v Kenya* (Provisional measures) (n 39) para 3.

[101] *Aslakhanova ao v Russia* (n 24) paras 216–18.

widespread is not clear. Wherever it may be set, the limit will remain arbitrary. It would not be possible to say that 10,000 violations qualify as massive while 9,999 do not.

Yet it follows that not every situation presenting a large scale of human rights violations is viewed as a serious violation. For example, the considerable delay in progressing trials in Italy and other countries is affecting a large number of victims, primarily violating their right to a fair trial. However, these violations do not automatically amount to serious violations of human rights, and they have not been defined as such so far. Consider, for instance, the distinction the European Court made, in the course of a pilot-judgment procedure, between cases concerning violations of Article 6 of the ECHR (right to a fair trial) and violations of Article 3 of the ECHR (prohibition of torture). In the latter instance, the European Court has decided to examine each case separately due to the severity of the violations.[102]

Despite the wide recognition of the influence of the quantitative element, it is not a *sine qua non* for a human rights violation to amount to a serious violation. Therefore, a single human rights violation against a single victim may qualify as serious, albeit depending on other factors. It is no coincidence that the recent ATT refers to 'a serious violation of international human rights law'.[103] Indeed, similarly, going back to the European Court, it has underlined the serious nature of individual cases of torture.[104] The impact on a victim—that person's vulnerable position which is susceptible to abuse—would influence such a determination.

Inevitably, the mandate of the organ that makes the gravity classification is also crucial for the determination of a single instance as a serious violation. For example, the situations the UN Security Council qualifies as serious violations of human rights inevitably are of a widespread character—such as the situations in the Democratic Republic of the Congo and Libya.[105] Its primary responsibility is the maintenance of international peace and security.[106] Nonetheless, even the UN political organs have on rare occasions adopted resolutions on

[102] *Ananyev ao v Russia* (n 24) para 236.

[103] Article 7(1)(b)(ii), ATT (n 61). For instance, in arms control practice, the widespread character of violations is used as one of the indicators of serious violations of human rights, but the absence of widespread practices does not exclude the determination of a violation as serious. European Council, User's Guide, 2009 (n 60) 41.

[104] *Assenov ao v Bulgaria* (n 96) para 175; *Aksoy v Turkey* (n 24) para 113.

[105] See respectively, The situation concerning the Democratic Republic of the Congo, UNSC Res 2409, 27 March 2018; Libya, UNSC Res 1970 (26 February 2011) Preamble, paras 2, 6 (hereinafter UNSC Res 1970 (2011)). But also UNSC Res 2428 (2018) (n 29); UNSC Res 2134 (2014) (n 32), Preamble para 5.

[106] Article 24(1), Charter of the United Nations, San Fransisco (adopted 26 June 1945) 1 UNTS XVI.

named individuals. For example, the UN General Assembly condemned the failure to respect fair trial guarantees and the use of torture to extract confessions in the case of Navid Afkari in Iran.[107] Earlier, it had condemned the arrest and called for the release of the then General Secretary of the National League for Democracy, Aung San Suu Kyi, and other political prisoners.[108]

On the one hand, it could be argued that such resolutions demonstrate the politicised nature of such decisions, which in any case is not denied here. On the other hand, attacks against persons with high visibility bear an additional gravity that one cannot deny. The assassination of a politician may cause social alarm, while the fact that such high-profile figures are attacked constitutes an indicator of the higher risk for the wider 'unknown masses'.[109] They may have a further, chilling effect on or a destabilising impact in the broader region, leading to further human rights violations.

2.2 The 'systematic character' element

It is also widely agreed today that violations committed in a systematic manner entail an additional aggravating element. As the Inter-American Court underlined, 'the systematic practice of forced disappearance entails a disregard of the obligation to organize the State apparatus so as to ensure the rights recognized in the Convention, which reproduces the conditions of impunity so that this type of event is repeated'.[110] The systematic character of human rights violations appears as a separate 'aggravating' classification, alongside the broader 'serious, grave, or gross' qualifiers in various human rights treaties. The exceptional inquiry procedure under the Optional Protocol to the Convention on the Elimination of all Forms of Discrimination Against Women may be seized for situations of 'grave or systematic' violations of the Convention.[111] Apart

[107] UNGA Res 75/191 (2020) (n 74) para 25.

[108] Situation of human rights in the Syrian Arab Republic, UNGA Res 68/182 (18 December 2013) para 2 (hereinafter UNGA Res 68/182 (2013)); Situation of human rights in Myanmar, UNGA Res 61/232 (22 December 2006) paras 2(b)–(c), 3. See also Menno T Kamminga, *Inter-State Accountability for Violations of Human Rights* (University of Pennsylvania Press 1992) 104–05.

[109] On social alarm as a non-quantitative gravity factor, see ICC, *Prosecutor v Lubanga, Decision on the Prosecutor's Application for a Warrant of Arrest, Article 58*, ICC-01/04-01/06, 10 February 2006, para 46. See further on social alarm Kevin Jon Heller, 'Situational Gravity Under the Rome Statute' in Carsten Stahn and Larissa van den Herik (eds), *Future Perspectives on International Criminal Justice* (Asser 2010) 235–40 (hereinafter Heller, 'Situational Gravity').

[110] IACtHR, *García and Family v Guatemala* (Merits, reparations and costs) 29 November 2012, para 130.

[111] Article 8, Optional Protocol to the Convention on the Elimination of All Forms of Discrimination against Women (adopted 6 October 1999) 2131 UNTS 83. Also repeated in Article 13, Optional Protocol to the Convention on the Rights of the Child on a communications procedure, UNGA Res

from the UN treaty bodies, where the systematic character of violations is part of their mandate, other bodies, including the regional human rights courts and the UN political bodies, also continue to identify the systematic character of violations as a distinctive aggravating factor.

Despite the wide recognition of the significance of the systematic practice of human rights violations, there is no unified approach regarding the criteria that determine that violations are committed systematically. Even in international criminal law, where the question has been addressed more consistently, there is still a debate on the details.[112] The ILC described 'systematic violation' as a violation that 'would have to be carried out in an organized and deliberate way'.[113]

According to the European Court, '[a]n administrative practice involves two distinct elements: a repetition of acts and official tolerance'.[114] The 'repetition of acts' describes 'an accumulation of identical or analogous breaches which are sufficiently numerous and inter-connected not to amount to merely isolated incidents or exceptions but to a pattern or system'.[115] The responsible officials tolerate these illegal acts by not punishing them or trying to prevent them.[116] While the Court does not require the existence of an official policy, the situation must be such that it was inconceivable that the authorities of a state were unaware of such a practice.[117] The inability to access local remedies is also an indicator of the existence of an administrative practice. In *Kaverzin v Ukraine*, the Court underlined that the previous judgments proved

66/138 (19 December 2011); Article 6, Optional Protocol to the Convention on the Rights of Persons with Disabilities (adopted 13 December 2006) 2518 UNTS 283; Article 11, Optional Protocol to the International Covenant on Economic, Social and Cultural Rights, UNGA Res 63/117 (10 December 2008). Article 20 of the Convention against Torture and Other Cruel, Inhuman or Degrading Treatment or Punishment ((adopted 10 December 1984) 1465 UNTS 85) refers to situations where 'torture is being systematically practised'.

[112] Compare ICC, *Decision Pursuant to Article 15 of the Rome Statute on the Authorization of an Investigation into the Situation in the Republic of Kenya*, Pre-Trial Chamber II, 31 March 2010, ICC-01/09, para 96; ICTR, *Prosecutor v Akayesu*, Judgment, Trial Chamber I, ICTR-96-4, 2 September 1998, para 580; *Prosecutor v Tadić* (n 17) para 648.

[113] ARSIWA with commentaries (n 16) 113, para 8.

[114] ECtHR, *Georgia v Russia (I)* (Merits, GC), App no 13255/07, 14 July 2014, para 122 (hereinafter *Georgia v Russia (I)*); ECtHR, *Cyprus v Turkey* (GC), App no 25781/94, 10 May 2001, para 99 (hereinafter *Cyprus v Turkey* (GC)); European Commission of Human Rights (EComHR), *Denmark, Norway, Sweden & Netherlands v Greece* (The Greek Case), App nos 3321–3323, 3344/67, Decision, Yearbook of the European Convention on Human Rights, Vol 12-I (1969), 5 November 1969, para 195.

[115] *Aslakhanova ao v Russia* (n 24) para 212; *Georgia v Russia (I)* (n 114) para 123; *Cyprus v Turkey* (GC) (n 114) para 115; ECtHR, *Ireland v UK*, App no 5310/71, 18 January 1978, para 159 (hereinafter *Ireland v UK*).

[116] *Georgia v Russia (I)* (n 114) paras 124, 126; Concurring Opinion of Judge Pinto de Albuquerque, Joined by Judge Vučinić, *Cyprus v Turkey* (GC) (n 114) para 87.

[117] *Ireland v UK* (n 115) para 159; *Georgia v Russia (I)* (n 114) para 124. For a critical view, see Aisling Reidy, Françoise Hampson, and Kevin Boyle, 'Gross Violations of Human Rights: Invoking the European Convention on Human Rights in the Case of Turkey' (1997) 15 NQHR 161, 165.

the recurring nature of the problem, as they revealed similar facts as to when and how torture occurred and the reluctance of the prosecution to investigate those cases.[118]

On the other side of the Atlantic, the existence of a governmental policy amounting to a systematic disregard for human rights has been central to the Inter-American Commission's decision to trigger the general procedure dealing with situations of gross and systematic human rights violations.[119] Without providing a definition similar to that of the European Court, the Inter-American Court took into account certain factors where it concluded that there was a systematic practice. For instance, in *Velásquez-Rodriguez* case, it took into account that almost all the victims were identified as dangerous by the authorities, that state officials usually used the arms employed, that blindfolded victims submitted similar allegations, and that the authorities denied family requests to investigate, in order to conclude that enforced disappearances were practised systematically.[120]

In parallel, though, the Committee against Torture has adopted a restrictive definition of 'systematic practice', which includes the number of complaints from various sources, the similarity of circumstances, the purpose of the torture, the similarity of methods employed, and the fact that such methods were widespread—all taken into account in order to reach the conclusion that torture was practised systematically. Systematic practice is seen as 'habitual, widespread and deliberate'.[121] Here as well, the existence of a policy is used as evidence of the existence of a systematic practice, without being a constitutive factor.[122] Less restrictively, other UN treaty bodies have understood 'systematic' as pertaining 'to the organized nature of the acts leading to the violations

[118] ECtHR, *Kaverzin v Ukraine*, App no 23893/03, 15 May 2012, paras 172–80.

[119] IAComHR, 'Report on Gross Human Rights Violations in the Context of Social Protests in Nicaragua' (21 June 2018) OEA/SerL/V/IIDoc86, paras 54 et seq. See also IAComHR, 'Third Report on the Human Rights Situation in Colombia' (29 February 1999) OEA/Ser.L/V/II.102, para 22 (Chapter IV). See also Cecilia Medina Quiroga, 'The Inter-American System for the Protection of Human Rights' in Catarina Krause and Martin Scheinin (eds), *International Protection of Human Rights: A Textbook* (2nd edn, Åbo Akademi University, Institute for Human Rights 2012) 521.

[120] IACtHR, *Velásquez-Rodriguez v Honduras* (Merits) 29 July 1988, paras 132, 147(d). See also, more recently, IACtHR, *Gelman v Uruguay* (Merits and reparations) 24 February 2011, para 99; IACtHR, *Gomes Lund et al ('Guerrilha Do Araguaia') v Brazil* (Preliminary objections, merits, reparations, and costs) 24 November 2010, para 103; IACtHR, *González et al ('Cotton Field') v Mexico* (Preliminary objection, merits, reparations and costs) 16 November 2009, para 117; IACtHR, *Myrna Mack Chang v Guatemala* (Merits, reparations and costs) 25 November 2003, para 139.

[121] CAT Committee, 'Summary account of the results of the proceedings concerning the inquiry on Turkey' (1 January 1994) A/49/44, 9, para 390. The definition has been reproduced in every report ever since. For instance, CAT Committee, 'Summary account on Nepal' (n 98) 299, para 97.

[122] CAT Committee, 'Summary account on Nepal' (n 98) para 104; CAT Committee, 'Report on Brazil produced by the Committee under Article 20 of the Convention, and reply from the Government of Brazil' (3 March 2009) CAT/C/39/2, paras 178 et seq.

and the improbability of their random occurrence'.[123] The CERD Committee defines 'persistent pattern' as the regular way in which something is happening or is done; that it is the norm, the standard. It hence emphasises the element of repetition.[124]

Like the UN treaty bodies, the various *ad hoc* commissions of inquiry have been identifying systematic practices, taking into account several factors on a case-by-case basis rather than based on a specific definition. For instance, the Commission of Inquiry on Eritrea included

> the high frequency of occurrence of the human rights violations documented and corroborated during the investigation, the number of victims and the replication of the violation during a certain period of time; the type of rights violated; and the systemic nature of these violations, meaning that they cannot be the result of random or isolated acts of the authorities.[125]

Even when reviewing the old UN Complaint Procedure, each author would put emphasis on a different characteristic that could indicate the existence of a systematic violation, be it the number of victims,[126] the violation's duration,[127] or the existence of a governmental policy.[128]

None of the UN political bodies has defined 'systematic', but they all continue to condemn systematic practices of human rights violations as serious violations of human rights. The Security Council condemned as systematic human rights violations and abuses that occurred in East Timor, Somalia, the Democratic Republic of the Congo, and Libya. All these situations involved long-term, persisting situations of violence, where violations occurred in an organised manner and affected a large number of victims. No governmental policy was necessarily present; in some of these cases, there was, in fact, no

[123] CRPD Committee, 'Inquiry Concerning Hungary' (n 70) para 108; CRC Committee, 'Inquiry Concerning Chile' (n 70) para 112; CEDAW Committee, 'Inquiry Concerning the United Kingdom of Great Britain and Northern Ireland under Article 8 of the Optional Protocol to the Convention on the Elimination of All Forms of Discrimination against Women' (2018) CEDAW/C/OP.8/GBR/1, para 80.

[124] CERD Committee, Guidelines for EWA (2007) (n 57) para 12(a). Among others, CERD Committee, Decision 1(78) on Côte d'Ivoire (n 93); CERD Committee, Decision 1(77) on Kyrgyzstan (n 67); CERD Committee, Decision 1(63) on the Lao People's Democratic Republic (n 39); CERD Committee, Decision 3(62) on Suriname (n 67).

[125] UNHRC, 'First report of the commission of inquiry on human rights in Eritrea' (4 June 2015) A/HRC/29/42, para 23.

[126] Tardu stressed that it was hard to conceive of a situation where there was only a single victim or only a single violation occurred. Tardu, 'United Nations Response' (n 92) 583–84.

[127] Ermacora argued that it cannot be a temporary violation. Ermacora, 'Procedures to Deal' (n 5) 678–79.

[128] Tolley, 'The Concealed Crack' (n 5) 448. See also Quiroga, *The Battle of Human Rights* (n 3) 15–16.

effective government at all.[129] Similarly, the General Assembly qualifies as systematic cases that include a large number of victims and a high level of organisation in the commission of violations, often accompanied by a repressive governmental policy.[130]

To recap, in order to examine human rights practice in a unified manner, it is only possible to identify indicators that systematic practices are in place, including: a high degree of organisation, the recurrent violation of certain rights, the method used to commit the violations, a certain number of victims, situations of impunity, and occasionally the existence of a policy. These are not cumulative requirements; not all the above would be present in every case. They also do not need to be present in the same intensity in every case. For example, in Somalia, the persistence over time and the impact on large numbers of specific groups were crucial, even though there was no clear governmental policy.[131] On the other hand, in Libya, the intensity of the violence by the Government, targeting specific parts of the population, shifted the threshold very quickly.[132] As such, systematic violations may not always involve large numbers of victims.[133]

Similar to the widespread element, the systematic character of a violation does not always make it a serious violation. In the pilot-judgment process, the European Court deals with widespread violations that have resulted from a malfunctioning of the national system in the country concerned. The process is triggered when there is a structural and systemic problem that has affected (and will potentially continue to affect) a large number of persons.[134] Pilot-judgment cases are not treated in a similar manner by the Court. While it will usually adjourn all similar cases after pronouncing on the pilot case, the Court does not adjourn the pending cases when they concern serious violations.[135]

[129] Among others, Somalia, UNSC Res 2067 (18 September 2012) para 18 (hereinafter UNSC Res 2067(2012)); UNSC Res 1493 (2003) (n 29) para 8; East Timor, UNSC Res 1272 (25 October 1999) Preamble, para 14.

[130] Among others, UNGA Res 75/190 (2020) (n 38) para 1; UNGA Res 74/169 (2019) (n 74) para 1; Situation of human rights in Myanmar, UNGA Res 72/248 (24 December 2017); GA Res 68/182 (2013) (n 110) para 2; Situation of human rights in Iraq, UNGA Res 57/232 (18 December 2002) para 4(a). Similar practice, Situation of human rights in the Syrian Arab Republic, UNHRC Res 43/28 (22 June 2020) para 1 (hereinafter UNHRC Res 43/28 (2020)); UNHRC Res 40/20 (2019) (n 32) para 1; UNHRC Res 20/13 (2012) (n 31) para 1.

[131] UNSC Res 2067 (2012) (n 129) para 18.

[132] UNSC Res 1970 (2011) (n 105) Preamble, paras 2, 6.

[133] See Daniel Byman, 'Do Targeted Killings Work?' (2006) 85 Foreign Affairs <https://www.foreignaffairs.com/articles/israel/2006-03-01/do-targeted-killings-work> accessed 9 October 2021.

[134] ECtHR, *Burdov v Russia*, App no 33509/04, 15 January 2009, para 122; ECtHR, *Hutten-Czapska v Poland* (GC), App no 35014/97, 19 June 2006, paras 235–37.

[135] Among others, see *Ananyev ao v Russia* (n 24) paras 238–39. See also Antoine Buyse, 'The Pilot Judgment Procedure at the European Court of Human Rights: Possibilities and Challenges' [2009] 'European Court of Human Rights, 50 Years', Special issue, Nomiko Vima [Greek Law Journal] 78, 84.

First, the degree of influence on the seriousness threshold of the systematic character of a violation will depend on its level of organisation and the intention of the perpetrators. Second, the classification of a systematic violation as a serious violation will be a cumulative result together with other factors, including the rights affected and the impact on the victims. For instance, systematic summary executions undoubtedly constitute serious violations of human rights, but the systematic violation of the right to privacy will qualify as serious, albeit not as quickly.[136] Also, in the case of indigenous peoples' land, the violation of their right to property or their right to cultural development becomes serious due to the systematic character of these violations, but also because of the irreparable impact these violations have on the communities as a whole, as their land is essential for the survival of the entire group.[137]

2.3 Other external elements

Two other external elements, associated with the systematic character of violations,[138] may also occasionally be understood to contribute independently to the categorisation of a violation as 'serious': time and space.

2.3.1 The temporal aspect

Continuous, ongoing, persisting, recurring violations all underline either the long duration of one violation against one victim, or the recurrence of multiple violations against different victims over an extended period. Duration may take many forms. For instance, the enforced disappearance of one person is ongoing for as long as the whereabouts of the disappeared remain unknown.[139] Duration as such can contribute to an aggravated form of violation. For instance, the continuation (or repetition for a long period) of inhuman or degrading treatment can lead to the characterisation of the acts as torture.[140] However, duration may also refer to separate instances of enforced disappearance practices affecting different victims over an extended period.

136 See Section 1.1.2.

137 See Section 1.1.3.

138 Quiroga, *The Battle of Human Rights* (n 3) 12.

139 IACtHR, *Torres Millacura et al v Argentina* (Merits, reparations, and costs) 26 August 2011, para 94.

140 *Aslakhanova ao v Russia* (n 24) para 239; ECtHR, *Ivanţoc and others v Moldova and Russia*, App no 23687/05, 15 November 2011, para 122 (hereinafter *Ivanţoc ao v Moldova and Russia*).

The persistence of violations over time has been a critical factor for the involvement of political bodies, such as the UN Security Council[141] and the UN General Assembly.[142] Nonetheless, it is not feasible to determine the exact period of time that needs to elapse for a violation or a series of violations to become serious. It will always depend on the specific circumstances of a particular case. For example, various factors, including the convergence of political considerations, led to the rapid determination of the violations in Libya in 2011 as serious.[143] Similarly, the UN Human Rights Council has repeatedly highlighted the long-standing and ongoing character of situations of gross violations of human rights.[144] Ermacora, when examining the elements of a 'consistent pattern of gross violations' for the Complaint Procedure, identified the time element as a distinct factor, as 'consistent' implies a 'certain continuity whose end cannot be foreseen'.[145] The UN treaty bodies occasionally underline the duration of violations as a separate aggravating factor. For instance, the Committee on the Elimination of Discrimination against Women referred to the continuation of the violations and the duration of the violations.[146] Equally, the persistence of violations is a factor underlined by the CERD Committee, but in connection with the pattern of violations.[147]

2.3.2 The geographic spread aspect

The geographical spread of violations is rarely seen as an autonomous aggravating factor. The qualifier 'widespread' is mostly used to underline the large number of victims or violations, and only occasionally to describe violations that have occurred over a large area. Similarly to the other elements, the area in which violations occur is mostly significant by association with other aggravating factors. For instance, the Committee on the Elimination of

[141] Among others, The situation in Somalia, UNSC Res 2431 (30 July 2018); UNSC Res 2103 (2013) (n 38) Preamble, para 9.

[142] Among others, UNGA Res 74/169 (2019) (n 74) para 11; UNGA Res 68/184 (2013) (n 30) para 5; Situation of Human Rights in Myanmar, UNGA Res 58/247 (23 December 2003) para 3(a); Situation of human rights in Turkmenistan, UNGA Res 56/206 (20 December 2002) para 2.

[143] The UN Security Council adopted its well-known Resolution 1970 on 26 February 2011, not even 10 days after the Libyan Civil War erupted (also referred to as the 17 February Revolution against Gaddafi's regime). UNSC Res 1970 (2011) (n 105).

[144] Among others, Situation of human rights in Myanmar, UNHRC Res 43/3 (22 June 2020) para 1; Situation of human rights in Belarus, UNHRC Res 25/25 (27 June 2014) para 2; The continuing grave deterioration of the human rights and humanitarian situation in the Syrian Arab Republic, UNHRC Res 25/23 (28 March 2014) para 5.

[145] Ermacora, 'Procedures to Deal' (n 5) 678–79. Tardu connected the time requirement to the quantitative element. Tardu, 'United Nations Response . . .' (n 92) 583–84.

[146] CEDAW Committee, 'Report on Mexico' (n 95) paras 260–63.

[147] CERD Committee, Guidelines for EWA (2007) (n 57) para 12(a). Similarly, see IAComHR, 'Report on the Situation of Human Rights in Venezuela' (n 91) para 578.

Discrimination against Women took into account the fact that violations presenting the same characteristics occurred in the same regions, to conclude that they were systematically perpetrated.[148] Also, the Committee against Torture refers to violations that are widespread 'in at least a *considerable part of the territory of the country* in question', in the definition of systematic practices of torture.[149]

The geographical spread of a violation has an impact on the involvement of political bodies. However, in such cases, large numbers of victims and systematic practices are often also present. Most of the situations addressed by the UN Security Council or the UN General Assembly concern, for instance, violent events that have spread all over the country or in a large part of the territory, affecting a large number of civilians, such as Syria or the Democratic Republic of the Congo.[150]

3. The involvement of the state

Besides the qualitative and external elements discussed above, the degree of involvement of the state (directly or indirectly) in the commission of the violations is an aggravating factor in its own right. However, the degree of involvement of the state varies, and as a result, its aggravating impact varies.

3.1 The direct involvement of the state

The direct involvement of the state in the commission of human rights violations may entail different degrees of governmental interference. First, state officials may commit the violations independently. As such it can be an aggravating element on its own. Second, the existence of a governmental policy constitutes the most extreme form of a state's direct involvement, because the state has formulated a plan to commit violations of human rights.[151] Lastly, it may describe situations where private actors act with the approval, acquiescence, or tolerance of the authorities.[152] The identification of the perpetrator of

[148] CEDAW Committee, 'Report on Mexico' (n 95) paras 36–37.

[149] CAT Committee, 'Summary account on Nepal' (n 98) para 97; CAT Committee, 'Summary account on Turkey' (n 121) para 39.

[150] Syria, UNSC Res 2042 (14 April 2012) Preamble, para 4; DRC, UNSC Res 1991 (28 June 2011) Preamble, para 9.

[151] Arguing a policy was imperative for gross violation to occur, see Ermacora, 'Procedures to Deal' (n 5) 679.

[152] Quiroga, *The Battle of Human Rights* (n 3) 16.

a human rights violation or the fault of the state may not matter for engaging the state's responsibility for those violations, but it remains highly relevant with regard to their qualification as serious violations.

Any abuse of human rights may translate into a state's obligations, whether an obligation to respect or to protect. If the state does not fulfil those obligations, it violates the human rights rule irrespective of whether there was any intent (objective responsibility of state).[153] However, even if one accepts the objective responsibility of the state for human rights violations, this should not exclude intent (subjective responsibility) as an aggravating factor.[154] Identifying the intention of those responsible is an exercise that is inextricably related to individual criminal responsibility. In the words of Cançado Trindade, '[t]here are cases ... in which the intention of the State to cause the damage or its negligence in avoiding it can be demonstrated; the fault or guilt becomes, here, the indispensable basis of the responsibility of the State, *aggravated* by this circumstance'.[155]

Any direct violation of human rights by a state official has a double bearing on the matter, as it constitutes an abuse of power and it nullifies the role of the state as the protector of human rights:[156]

> Human rights violations committed by the state are qualitatively different from private injury because of the motives and nature of the conduct as well as the identity of the wrongdoer. Individuals expect protection from the state; indeed, one of its fundamental purposes is to provide the institutional and other means to ensure the safety and well-being of those within its power.[157]

The direct involvement of the state has been explicitly identified as an aggravating factor by both the European and the Inter-American human rights

[153] ARSIWA with commentaries (n 16) 34, para 3.

[154] Alain Pellet, 'Can a State Commit a Crime? Definitely, Yes!' (1999) 10 EJIL 425, 434 (hereinafter Pellet, 'Can a State Commit a Crime? Definitely, Yes!'); Giuseppe Palmisano, 'Les causes d'aggravation de la responsabilité des états et la distinction entre "crimes" et "delits" internationaux' (1994) 98 RGDIP 629, 666 (hereinafter Palmisano, 'Les causes d'aggravation').

[155] Antônio Augusto Cançado Trindade, 'Complementarity between State Responsibility and Individual Responsibility for Grave Violations of Human Rights: The Crime of State Revisited' in Maurizio Ragazzi (ed), *International Responsibility Today, Essays in Memory of Oscar Schachter* (Martinus Nijhoff Publishers 2005) 258 (hereinafter Cançado Trindade, 'Complementarity'). See also Pellet, 'Can a State Commit a Crime? Definitely, Yes!' (n 154) 434; Palmisano, 'Les Causes d'Aggravation (n 154) 666.

[156] See further on the element of 'social alarm' that should arguably also include cases where the perpetrators are those meant to be safeguarding the victims, Heller, 'Situational Gravity' (n 109) 235–40.

[157] Dinah Shelton, *Remedies in International Human Rights Law* (3rd edn, OUP 2015) 61.

courts.[158] In the *Castro-Castro Prison* case, for instance, the Inter-American Court concluded 'that the sexual rape of a detainee *by a state agent* is an *especially gross and reprehensible act*, taking into account ... the *abuse of power* displayed by the agent'.[159] Similarly, the Committee on the Rights of Persons with Disabilities has highlighted the state's intent to commit grave and systematic violations of the Convention.[160]

3.2 On the lack of remedies and impunity

The state's failure to remedy human rights violations should arguably not factored into the equation on its own right when making assessments of gravity. Ensuring respect for the human rights of individuals under their jurisdiction encompasses states' obligations to take measures to cease current or future violations, to punish those responsible, and/or to ensure that an appropriate remedy is provided to the victims.[161] The international institutions often underline the existence of a situation of impunity and the lack of remedies, urging the governments concerned to assume responsibility once they have already been involved.[162] Quiroga had emphasised the inability of the victims to defend themselves at the national level.[163] Yet the links to gravity seem weak. It seems more convincing that the lack of remedies is evidence of the existence of other elements, such as the systematic character of the violation, than an aggravating factor in its own right.[164]

[158] For example, ECtHR, *Tangiyev v Russia*, App no 27610/05, 11 December 2012, para 87; *Akdivar ao v Turkey* (n 73) para 37. Also, *Plan de Sánchez Massacre v Guatemala* (Merits) (n 90) para 2004; *Myrna Mack Chang v Guatemala* (n 120) paras 139, 154.

[159] *Miguel Castro-Castro Prison v Peru* (n 56) para 311 (emphasis added).

[160] CRPD Committee, 'Inquiry Concerning Spain' (n 94) para 79.

[161] On states' positive obligations, see Sandra Krähenmann, 'Positive Obligations in Human Rights Treaties' (Graduate Institute of International and Development Studies 2012) (hereinafter Krähenmann, 'Positive Obligations').

[162] For instance, the Security Council repeatedly asks state authorities to bring the perpetrators of serious violations of human rights to justice, and authorises peacekeeping mandates to assist them in the process. Among others, The situation in Mali, UNSC Res 2531 (29 June 2020) para 28(3)(i); Côte d'Ivoire, UNSC Res 2062 (26 July 2012) paras 12–13; Sudan, UNSC Res 2046 (2 May 2012) para 7.

[163] Quiroga, *The Battle of Human Rights* (n 3) 16–18. Cançado Trindade argues that the lack of structure in public power, leading to impunity, is an aggravating factor. However, he connects it also to the abuse of the deficiencies of the system to commit grave violations. Cançado Trindade, 'Complementarity' (n 155) 264.

[164] CAT Committee, Summary account of the results of the proceedings concerning the inquiry on Serbia and Montenegro (1 October 2004) CAT/C/XXXII/Misc.2, paras 211–12; CAT Committee, 'Activities of the Committee under Article 20 of the Convention for Sri Lanka' (17 October 2002) A/57/44(SUPP) 69, paras 178, 183 (hereinafter CAT Committee, Article 20 Activities for Sri Lanka). See also CEDAW Committee, 'Report on Mexico' (n 95) paras 8 et seq, 261.

The international community has only a subsidiary role and reacts only when the state primarily responsible is unwilling or unable to ensure respect for human rights. Already, there is a procedural condition for individual complaints of violations of human rights to reach the international monitoring bodies only after local remedies have been exhausted.[165] By default, all instances of human rights violations that are discussed at international level will not have been remedied (at least not appropriately). Otherwise, there would be no need for international society to react in the first place. As a result, any assessment of the aggravating influence of the lack of remedies and the situation of impunity seems unwarranted. It seems more convincing that the gravity of the violation heightens the obligation to punish the perpetrators and to provide remedies, rather than a distinct element of gravity qualifications. For instance, regional human rights courts request a more thorough investigation or award higher compensation when serious violations have been committed.[166]

3.3 Disregard of international procedures

The refusal of the government to collaborate with the judicial and other international procedures that monitor instances of human rights violations, and the deliberate obstruction of the process before the regional human rights courts, is always subsequent to the violation at issue. The influence on any gravity qualification of the behaviour of state officials in the course of the judicial or other international proceedings also seems weak. Yet, for instance, the European Court underlined the aggravated responsibility of the state in those cases where it receives evidence that a state actively attempted to sabotage individual applications reaching the European Court, or otherwise interfered to alter the outcome of the proceedings.[167] Furthermore, it has declared:

> The violation of Article 3 [ECHR] is *further aggravated* by the fact that Mr Ivanţoc and Mr Popa's conditions of detention occurred after the Court's judgment of 8 July 2004 ordering the respondent States to put an end to their arbitrary detention and to secure their immediate release.[168]

[165] See, though, on the tendency to involve the international mechanisms directly, Sicilianos, 'L'influence des droits' (n 38) 14.
[166] *Myrna Mack Chang v Guatemala* (n 123) para 139.
[167] See also *Assenov ao v Bulgaria* (n 96) para 175; ECtHR, *Boicenco v Moldova*, App no 41088/05, 11 July 2006, para 159; *Akdivar ao v Turkey (Article 50)* (n 69) para 175.
[168] *Ivanţoc ao v Moldova and Russia* (n 140) paras 126, 134, 144 (emphasis added).

Tigroudja has criticised these references to 'aggravated responsibility' by the European Court, because they misrepresent both the notion and its importance. She maintains that such references aim at stigmatising states that do not comply with the Court's decisions or impede access to judicial mechanisms, but the violations themselves do not necessarily amount to 'international crimes of states'.[169]

Such forms of public and direct disregard of the international judicial mechanisms signal a degree of disrespect for the broader international legal order and its values, and as such cannot be ignored. The lack of willingness of state officials to collaborate with international organs, as well as any attempts to prevent victims from reaching international procedures, may be an indicator of the state's potential direct involvement in the commission of human rights violations. Nevertheless, the aggravating effect of a state's behaviour before international procedures should not be seen as a distinct element, as it can only be assessed after the violations have already occurred. In any event, the presence of other factors will arguably be sufficient for any classification of gravity.

That said, the behaviour of official authorities and their degree of collaboration with international procedures seem to influence the determination of violations as serious in a strategic manner. The state's behaviour impacts both the classification of a violation as serious and the activation of exceptional procedures relating to serious violations of human rights. For instance, the African Commission seems to have developed a practice where it condemns violations as serious mainly when the state concerned does not collaborate with the Commission and does not respond to the application. The condemnation of violations as 'serious or massive' in the African system carries strong political weight, since the determination can potentially trigger an Article 58 procedure, which authorises the Commission to refer cases of 'serious or massive' violations to the Assembly of the African Union.[170] However, this practice can have unfortunate effects. For instance, a case against Kenya seemed to bring together all the elements required in a situation of serious and massive violations. Nevertheless, the Commission refrained from qualifying the situation as serious, since the Kenyan Government eventually collaborated.[171] The absence of gravity classification functions as a form of reward for any state that collaborates with the international bodies to bring serious violations to an end.

[169] Tigroudja, 'Violation de droits de l'homme' (n 4) 760–61.

[170] Article 58, African Charter on Human and Peoples' Rights ('Banjul Charter') OAU (adopted 27 June 1981).

[171] AComHPR, *Centre for Minority Rights Development (Kenya) and Minority Rights Group (on behalf of Endorois Welfare Council) v Kenya*, Comm 276/2003 (4 February 2010).

On the one hand, this confirms that any gravity classification at international level, particularly outside judicial proceedings, is decided with political considerations and balances in mind. The international system lacks a central authority, and its functioning still heavily depends on each independent state's willingness to collaborate with international organs. To the extent that a state appears to collaborate, international bodies will refrain from publicly accusing the state of committing serious violations of human rights. On the other hand, such considerations demonstrate that determinations of gravity matter to states, and the international organs use this as leverage. This was the case with the situation of serious violations of human rights in Eritrea, where the UN Human Rights Council decided to shift the discussions from the confidential Complaint Procedure to the public sphere, due to the lack of collaboration exhibited by Eritrean officials.[172]

3.4 Non-state actors' acts and serious violations of human rights

The recognition of the involvement of the state as an aggravating factor does not exclude instances where violations committed by non-state actors (including armed groups or individuals) qualify as serious or grave. Certain violations or abuses will be considered as serious because of the state's direct involvement, while others will be serious independently of who the perpetrators are. There are two different entry points with regard to the aggravated nature of private acts.

Primarily, violations of international human rights law may qualify as serious where the state has failed to fulfil its procedural obligations, such as the obligation to investigate. It is possible to imagine a scenario where the state did not commit the actual murder or cause the disappearance (or at least there is no evidence confirming its direct involvement), but it nevertheless did not fulfil its obligations to protect individuals against such abuses, proactively or after the events took place. As mentioned above, the failure to investigate (even

[172] The situation in Eritrea was initially discussed under the confidential Complaint Procedure following reports that serious violations of human rights had been committed. The UN Human Rights Council decided to discontinue the confidential procedures in order to enable public consideration of the same matter, and appointed for that purpose a Special Rapporteur to inquire further into the situation. Among the reasons for this decision was the lack of collaboration of the Government. Situation of human rights in the Syrian Arab Republic, UNHRC Res 21/26 (28 September 2012); Situation of human rights in Eritrea, UNHRC Res 20/20 (6 July 2012). See 'History of Situations Considered since the Establishment of the Complaint Procedure, UNHRC' <http://www.ohchr.org/EN/HRBodies/HRC/ComplaintProcedure/Pages/HRCComplaintProcedureIndex.aspx> accessed 16 September 2021.

cases concerning the right to life) may amount to a serious violation, although not always.[173] Only in specific cases have the regional courts concluded that the violation of the obligation to investigate amounts to a serious violation.

Remarkably, the Inter-American Court underlined that preventing the survivors and the victims' next-of-kin from being heard by a judge and receiving judicial protection revealed a serious violation of the state's international obligation to investigate and punish the grave human rights violations relating to the massacres of El Mozote and nearby places.[174] Similarly, in the *'Beslan School Siege'* case, Russian security forces stormed a school gymnasium where 800 children and 300 adults had been held hostage for three days. The European Court found four separate violations of the right to life, including a serious breach of the obligation to investigate, where the Court concluded that '[t]he failure to ensure that relevant material evidence was adequately secured, collected and recorded constituted a serious breach of the requirements of an effective investigation in the present case'.[175] On the other hand, in the *Vera-Vera* case, the victim was found shot while in police custody and died because he was not provided with appropriate medical care in time. From the facts of the case, the Inter-American Court was not able to conclude with absolute certainty that the state was responsible for the wounding of the victim, but held the state responsible for a failure to investigate. Therefore, it concluded that the violations were not of a serious nature.[176]

The above reflections are in line with the traditional understanding of international human rights law, which has mainly revolved around the obligations of states towards individuals.[177] Yet while the direct involvement of the state can be an aggravating factor, it should not be understood as a prerequisite for the qualification of a human rights violation as serious. There is a movement

[173] The legal basis for an obligation to investigate varies. It has been understood as a procedural obligation deriving directly from the right to life or the right not to be forcibly disappeared, but it is also an inextricable part of the right to a remedy. Articles 2 and 13, European Convention for the Protection of Human Rights and Fundamental Freedoms (as ammended by subsequent protocols) (adopted 4 November 1950) (CETS No 5, Rome, Council of Europe; Article 1, CED (n 19). For an in-depth analysis of the obligation to investigate and other positive obligations, see Krähenmann, 'Positive Obligations' (n 161).

[174] *Massacres of El Mozote and nearby Places v El Salvador* (n 34) 295.

[175] *Tagayeva ao v Russia* (n 34) para 516.

[176] *Vera Vera et al v Ecuador* (n 13) paras 117–18. See also IACtHR, *Vélez Restrepo and family v Colombia* (Preliminary objection, merits, reparations and costs) 3 September 2012, paras 280–84.

[177] On this debate, see Andrew Clapham, 'Non-State Actors' in Daniel Moeckli and others (eds), *International Human Rights Law* (3rd edn, OUP 2018); Nehal Bhuta, 'The Role International Actors Other Than States Can Play in the New World Order' in Antonio Cassese (ed), *Realizing Utopia: The Future of International Law* (OUP 2012); W Michael Reisman, 'The Quest for World Order and Human Dignity in the Twenty-First Century: Constitutive Process and Individual Commitment' (2012) 351 RCADI 9.

towards recognising that (at least) armed groups have human rights obligations too, even if the legal basis for these obligations is unsettled.[178] As the analysis here focuses primarily on sources from international practice, there are inevitably fewer examples of serious violations of human rights where the state has no involvement, but this does not exclude the commission of serious violations of human rights by non-state actors.

Pointing in this direction, when necessary and within the scope of their competences, different international bodies and institutions have condemned as serious violations (or abuses)[179] of human rights acts committed by non-state actors. This practice can be primarily observed before political bodies. The mandate of various human rights bodies (including regional human rights courts and UN treaty bodies) is still limited when examining violations committed by states. They have jurisdiction to deal with acts committed by private parties (violations at least under national law) only to the extent that the state fails to protect the individuals' rights from private actors. However, this does not exclude the responsibility of non-state actors outside the scope of the treaties.

Notably, the UN Security Council recurrently condemns as serious the acts of all the parties taking part in incidents of violence.[180] The determination of the perpetrators has a secondary role for the UN General Assembly as well. However, particularly in the case of armed conflicts, it refers to all parties to the conflict when condemning serious violations or abuses of human rights.[181] Resolutions of the UN Human Rights Council have increasingly addressed the behaviour of non-state actors and repeatedly condemned serious violations of

[178] See Katharine Fortin, *The Accountability of Armed Groups under Human Rights Law* (OUP 2017); Andrew Clapham, 'Human Rights Obligations of Non-State Actors in Conflict Situations' (2006) 88 IRRC 491.

[179] There is a tendency within UN political bodies' practice to refer to 'abuses' instead of 'violations' when referring to acts committed by non-state actors. For instance, the Human Rights Council condemned 'the gross *abuses* of international human rights law ... perpetrated by the terrorist group Boko Haram' (Atrocities committed by the terrorist group Boko Haram and its effects on human rights in the affected States, UNHRC Res S-23/1 (1 April 2015) para 1 (emphasis added) (hereinafter UNHRC Res S-23/1 (2015)). However, the UN bodies' practice is not systematic. They use both terms interchangeably. In any case, the term 'abuse' does not have any legal content and therefore is misleading. On an analysis of Human Rights Council practice, see Annyssa Bellal, 'Human Rights Obligations of Armed Non-State Actors: An Exploration of the Practice of the UN Human Rights Council', Geneva Academy of International Humanitarian Law and Human Rights (2016) <https://www.geneva-academy.ch/joomlatools-files/docman-files/InBrief7_web.pdf> accessed 16 September 2021.

[180] Notably, CAR, UNSC Res 2149 (10 April 2014) para 9; Middle East (Syria), UNSC Res 2043 (21 April 2012) Preamble, para 4; Reports of the Secretary-General on the Sudan, UNSC Res 1935 (30 July 2010) Preamble, para 12; The Great Lakes region, UNSC Res 1653 (27 January 2006) para 8; DRC, UNSC Res 1468 (20 March 2003) para 6.

[181] Notably, UNGA Res 74/169 (2019) (n 74) paras 11, 14; UNGA Res 68/182 (2013) (n 108) para 2; Situation of human rights in the DRC, UNGA Res 60/170 (16 December 2005) para 5; Question of human rights in Afghanistan, UNGA Res 56/176 (19 December 2001) para 12.

human rights committed by armed opposition groups. It has, among others, condemned violations committed by the Islamic State, Al Shaabab, and Boko Haram.[182] A similar understanding that non-state armed groups may commit human rights violations is also reflected in the practice of commissions of inquiry.[183]

4. The contextual aspect

All the above-analysed elements contribute to the determination of a violation of human rights as serious. Nonetheless, such classification of human rights violations seems to further depend on the context within which the particular violation occurred. 'Context' can be understood in its wider sense as the overall situation, the glue that brings together all other elements, but also more concretely it describes situations, such as an armed conflict or a totalitarian regime, or even a peaceful democratic nation within which serious violations of human rights occurred. The context should not be seen as an aggravating element per se. The context rather highlights the relative nature of the notion of serious violations, without significantly altering the threshold of gravity for the international community. The contextual element is not explicit; however, it contributes to the logical resolution of the gravity equation.

It suffices to think of situations of widespread violence and instability, such as armed conflicts,[184] where violations of the human rights frequently associated with serious violations (such as the right to life, freedom from torture, and right to liberty) are routinely committed. In such contexts, the overall chaos ultimately absorbs those violations of human rights that in a peacetime context would immediately be identified as serious, even if they have had devastating effects on the victims. It is practically impossible to deal with all the violations that have occurred in such situations. For example, blatant systematic

[182] Among others, UNHRC Res 43/28 (2020) (n 130) para 57; UNHRC Res S-23/1 (2015) (n 179) para 1; Assistance to Somalia in the field of human rights, UNHRC 17/25 (17 June 2011) para 2.

[183] Notably, UNHRC, 'Report of the International Commission of Inquiry to investigate all alleged violations of international human rights law in the Libyan Arab Jamahiriya' (12 January 2012) A/HRC/17/44, para 62. For further practice, see Theo Boutruche, 'Selecting and Applying Legal Lenses in Monitoring, Reporting, and Fact-Finding Missions' (SSRN 2013) SSRN ID 2337437, 31–32 <http://papers.ssrn.com/abstract=2337437> accessed 9 October 2021.

[184] On the applicability of international human rights law in armed conflicts, see: Ilia Maria Siatitsa and Maia Titberidze, 'Human Rights in Armed Conflict: Ten Years of Affirmative State Practice within United Nations Resolutions' (2012) 3 JIHLS 233, 233–62; Louise Doswald-Beck, *Human Rights in Times of Conflict and Terrorism* (OUP 2011) 5–9; Cordula Droege, 'Elective Affinities? Human Rights and Humanitarian Law' (2008) 90 IRRC 501, 501–48.

violations of the freedom of assembly will not necessarily be considered as serious in a situation of widespread violence.

On the other hand, in peaceful democratic states, the inability or unwillingness of the authorities to react to certain violations is more shocking. The same violations, such as violations of freedom of assembly, are more likely to be considered as serious during peacetime—albeit not always.[185] In one case, the Committee reached the conclusion that torture was not practised systematically because it was a result of an armed conflict.[186] In parallel, the list of rights the violation of which is identified as serious seems to grow when addressing long-standing oppressive regimes. For example, the UN General Assembly's resolutions on North Korea or Myanmar condemn as serious a wide range of human rights violations. The list of serious violations committed by North Korea has been growing since 2005 to include, beyond torture and other cruel, inhuman, or degrading treatment or punishment, also limitations imposed on every person who wishes to move freely; the situation of refugees and asylum-seekers; restrictions on the freedoms of thought, conscience, religion, opinion and expression, peaceful assembly and association; the rights to privacy and equal access to information; violations of economic, social, and cultural rights; particular violations of the rights of women, children, persons with disabilities, and workers; and others.[187] The level of control and organisation of the state authorities, the intentional repression of human rights, and the duration of the totalitarian regimes contribute to the determination of violations as serious.[188]

5. The 'iceberg' of serious violations of human rights

To sum up, the classification of a violation of human rights as serious in international practice is a result of the combination of various aggravating elements. The irreparable impact on victims, together with the value protected by the human rights rule and the degree of vulnerability a situation presents for the victims, has considerable weight in the gravity equation. The external elements relate more to the manner in which the violations have been committed,

[185] For example, Amnesty International, 'Turkey accused of gross human rights violations in Gezi Park protests', 2 October 2013 <https://www.amnesty.org/en/latest/news/2013/10/turkey-accused-gross-human-rights-violations-gezi-park-protests/> accessed 16 September 2021.

[186] CAT Committee, Article 20 Activities for Sri Lanka (n 164) para 181.

[187] UNGA Res 75/190 (2020) (n 38) para 2; Situation of human rights in the DPRK, UNGA Res 60/173 (15 December 2005) para 1(b).

[188] For arms transfers, the User's Guide distinguishes between situations of internal repression and other situations of serious violations of human rights to restrict the arms exports to the first of these. Council of the EU, User's Guide 2019 (n 60) 39.

including their scale, their systematic character, their duration, and the involvement of the state. These recurring elements in instances of gravity determinations signify a certain convergence in the international community's understanding of serious violations of human rights.

A serious violation of human rights could be described as any human rights violation that is likely to have an irreparable impact on the victim, who at that moment is deprived of state protection in a specific context. However, this definition neither incorporates all the identified elements nor demonstrates the delicate balance between the different elements. Any attempt to encapsulate serious violations of human rights in a rigid abstract definition would result in excessive formalism. As Schachter concluded while attempting to define the notion of 'the dignity of the human person', its 'intrinsic meaning has been left to intuitive understanding, ... "I know when I see it even if I cannot tell you what it is."'[189]

Serious violations of human rights could be pictured as an iceberg floating in a sea of human rights violations—or several icebergs for that matter. The water's surface could be understood as the threshold above which the international community may react; 90 per cent of the serious violations of human rights lie below the waterline.[190] What the international community eventually touches is only the tip of the iceberg. International organs deal with violations around the globe; they will never have the resources to address more than a fraction of those situations that fall within the category 'serious violations of human rights'. Therefore, they have to make intelligent decisions and prioritise certain situations over others.

Lastly, the contours of the iceberg's surface are not straight, and the dividing line between the berg and the waters within which it floats can become blurred; after all, they are made of the same substance—human rights violations. As was stated at the very beginning of this chapter, 'any human rights violation involves a level of severity by its own nature, because it implies a breach of certain State obligations to respect and guarantee the rights and freedoms for people'.[191] Gravity signifies the seriousness of an act in comparison to another less serious act; there is already an unlawful act (a violation of international human rights law), which in addition is identified as serious.

[189] Oscar Schachter, 'Human Dignity as a Normative Concept' (1983) 77 AJIL 848, 848.

[190] The density of ice is 0.92g/ml and the density of water is 1.0g/ml (1.03g/ml for salt water). This means that the ice has nine-tenths, or 90 per cent, of water's density, and so 90 per cent of the iceberg is below the surface of the water.

[191] *Vera Vera et al v Ecuador* (n 13) para 118.

Undoubtedly, since the notion of serious violations of human rights has developed through practice, certain discrepancies and irregularities are inevitable. Gravity is not an absolute value. Yet, in spite of all the discrepancies, there is a considerable (not absolute) degree of convergence. The fact that specific violations have not qualified as serious does not negate this conclusion. Conflicting interests in international relations do influence the determination of a situation as serious, particularly by political organs.[192] For instance, the UN Security Council immediately reacted to the situation in Libya, but shortly after failed to respond to the situation in Syria. Also, situations such as the one in North Korea can be ignored for decades before they eventually attract the attention of the international organised society: it took fifty years for the UN Human Rights Council to establish a Commission of Inquiry. To conclude, 'a serious violation of human rights' is a notion that is and will be relative in time. It is a dynamic concept, the content of which evolves in accordance with the changing requirements of the international community.

Referring to 'fundamental norms', Gowlland-Debbas adds, 'as to the process of their formation it appears to be not a specific source from which they emanate, for there is none, but the recognition by the international community of the overriding qualities of their content'.[193] They will to an extent adapt and reflect the particularities of the period during which they are used. They will continue evolving depending on future experiences and circumstances.[194] The violations of human rights that are perceived as serious could probably expand. The more people are exposed to human rights values, the more the universally accepted values and principles of the international community should grow. Nonetheless, there is also the risk that increased exposure of the world to human rights violations might narrow the violations of human rights that are perceived to be serious, as we become 'accustomed' to hearing about atrocities.

The notion of 'serious violations of human rights' remains flexible, relative, and politically charged. Its characteristics would have been problematic in international criminal law, where the strict delimitation of notions becomes imperative.[195]

[192] Bertrand Ramcharan, *The Security Council and the Protection of Human Rights* (Martinus Nijhoff Publishers 2002).

[193] Vera Gowlland-Debbas, 'Security Council Enforcement Action and Issues of State Responsibility' (1994) 43 ICLQ 55, 70.

[194] Paul Tavernier, 'L'identification des règles fondamentales, un problème résolu?' in Christian Tomuschat and Jean-Marc Thouvenin (eds), *The Fundamental Rules of the International Legal Order: 'Jus Cogens' and Obligations 'Erga Omnes'* (Martinus Nijhoff Publishers 2006) 15.

[195] Antonio Cassese and Paola Gaeta, *Cassese's International Criminal Law* (3rd edn, OUP 2013) 27ff.

However, for a special regime in international human rights law this is an asset. These characteristics have facilitated the formation gradually and discretely of a special regime around those serious violations of human rights that involve treaty provisions, UN resolutions, human rights courts judgments, and other instruments.

2

The monitoring component

The first operational component of the special regime around serious violations of human rights is a diverse network of special monitoring processes. Their material scope is formally or informally limited to serious violations of human rights. Beyond their material scope, their formal institutional character and their means of operation, constituting primarily promotional and declaratory processes, bring them together. They operate on the basis of dialogue and co-operation with all interested parties by monitoring, inquiring, documenting, and reporting serious violations of human rights. However, they lack the power to force the abusers into compliance.

At the very beginning, the gravity of human rights violations was invoked to expand the mandates of the various newly established human rights bodies. In the aftermath of the Second World War, even when international organisations such as the United Nations (UN) were founded and the first human rights treaties were adopted,[1] human rights were understood as part of the exclusive jurisdiction of states.[2] The 1948 Universal Declaration of Human Rights, for instance, whilst it had an immense influence on the development of international instruments, at the moment of its adoption was supposed to be just an aspirational document.[3] It took several steps for human rights obligations to be fully integrated into the international legal framework and to be excepted from the exclusive domestic jurisdiction of states.[4] The gravity of violations had a role in this evolution.

Any response to human rights situations was seen as a *sui generis* exceptional response to situations of extreme gravity that, as a result, justified exceptional

[1] For a brief overview of the evolution of the human rights framework, see Andrew Clapham, *Brierly's Law of Nations: An Introduction to the Role of International Law in International Relations* (7th edn, OUP 2012), 235–40 (hereinafter Clapham, *Brierly's Law of Nations*).

[2] Article 2(7), Charter of the United Nations, San Francisco (adopted 26 June 1945) 1 UNTS XVI. On the UN organs' practices that contributed to the reinterpretation of the principle of non-intervention, see Rosalyn Higgins, *The Development of International Law Through the Political Organs of the United Nations* (OUP 1963) (hereinafter Higgins, *The Development of International Law*).

[3] Georg Nolte, 'Article 2(7)' in Bruno Simma and others (eds), *The Charter of the United Nations: A Commentary* (3rd edn, OUP 2012) 296–97 (particularly para 40).

[4] On the evolution of the interpretation of Article 2(7), UN Charter, see Benedetto Conforti and Carlo Focarelli, *The Law and Practice of the United Nations* (5th edn, Brill/Nijhoff 2016) 167–89 (hereinafter Conforti and Focarelli, *The Law and Practice of the UN*).

Serious Violations of Human Rights. Ilia Siatitsa, Oxford University Press. © Ilia Siatitsa 2022.
DOI: 10.1093/oso/9780192863041.003.0003

measures.[5] Notably, the first UN General Assembly resolutions regarding the apartheid regime condemned the Union of South Africa for discriminating against citizens of Indian origin in contravention of their bilateral agreements, and were adopted upon request by the Indian Government.[6] It eventually was the commission of 'gross violations of human rights' in the apartheid regime in South Africa[7] that allowed the UN human rights bodies to 'intervene' in country-specific human rights situations.[8] The human rights system eventually expanded to reach its current form.[9] Today, the various international bodies and decision-making procedures address all human rights matters, and their mandates range from standard-setting mechanisms to action taken in specific human rights situations.[10] There is no barrier regarding the human rights issues upon which they might act—from extrajudicial killings to the human rights of older persons.[11] As it was conclusively stated in the 1993 Vienna Declaration, 'the promotion and protection of all human rights is a legitimate concern of the international community'.[12]

This development has created the impression that the distinction between serious and other human rights violations was no longer of relevance. However, in fact, it did not entirely eliminate this distinction. On the contrary, within the continually growing human rights framework, there is still also a continually expanding set of procedures, particularly within the UN,[13] that

[5] See Great Britain's statement quoted in Newell Stultz, 'The Apartheid Issue at the General Assembly: Stalemate or Gathering Storm?' (1987) 86 African Affairs 25, 31. See also Jeroen Gutter, 'Special Procedures and the Human Rights Council: Achievements and Challenges Ahead' (2007) 7 HRL Rev 93, 97 (hereinafter Gutter, 'Special Procedures').

[6] Notably, Treatment of Indians in the Union of South Africa, UNGA Res 44(I) (8 December 1946) (hereinafter UNGA Res 44(I) (1946)).

[7] The apartheid regime in South Africa presented the necessary political elements to modify the existing paradigm: (i) it was a grave situation; (ii) in which neither the Western nor the Eastern blocs had important interests; (iii) in which the new African states, fighting against racism and colonialism, were very keen on interfering; and (iv) the public had for a long period been pushing for some kind of response from the UN human rights body. For a thorough analysis of politics at that time, see Theresa D Gonzales, 'The Political Sources of Procedural Debates in the United Nations: Structural Impediments to Implementation of Human Rights' (1980) 13 NYUJILP 427, 427–72 (hereinafter Gonzales, 'The Political Sources').

[8] See Conforti and Focarelli, *The Law and Practice of the UN* (n 4) 180–81.

[9] See Clapham, *Brierly's Law of Nations* (n 1) 235–40.

[10] On the UN and human rights, see Philip Alston and Frédéric Mégret (eds), *The United Nations and Human Rights: A Critical Appraisal* (2nd edn, OUP 2020). See also Catarina Krause and Martin Scheinin, *International Protection of Human Rights: A Textbook* (2nd edn, Åbo Akademi University 2012).

[11] It suffices to look at the titles of the UN Human Rights Council's sessions. 'UNHRC: Sessions' <http://www.ohchr.org/EN/HRBodies/HRC/Pages/Sessions.aspx> accessed 9 August 2021 (hereinafter 'UNHRC: Sessions').

[12] Vienna Declaration and Programme of Action, adopted by the World Conference on Human Rights in Vienna (25 June 1993) para 4.

[13] The primary focus hereinafter is on the UN system, where numerous procedures and mechanisms predominantly developed, with complementary references to other systems at regional and national levels when this is useful. On the central role of the UN, see Alan Boyle and Christine Chinkin,

focus specifically (and often exclusively) on serious violations of human rights, as opposed to all human rights violations. Serious violations of human rights as such remain a matter of international concern.

1. Country-specific inter-governmental procedures

The adoption of the so-called country-specific resolutions and the formation of special procedures to discuss and condemn instances of serious violations of human rights as opposed to any violation of human rights, by inter-governmental organs, such as the UN General Assembly, prominently validate the international attention to serious violations of human rights. While various political bodies may have developed similar practices, it suffices to look into the two main political organs of the United Nations that have a direct mandate to, and consistently and recurrently do, deal with human rights issues, that is, the UN Human Rights Council and the UN General Assembly.[14]

1.1 The UN Human Rights Council and serious violations of human rights

The UN Human Rights Council is the UN political body entrusted with a broad set of governance functions, potentially covering any human rights issue its members decide to take up.[15] As set out in 2006, it is the main inter-governmental organ of the United Nations responsible for 'promoting universal respect for the protection of all human rights and fundamental freedoms for all', and particularly for addressing 'situations of violations of human rights, including *gross and systematic* violations'.[16]

The Council's predecessor, the Commission on Human Rights,[17] was initially conceived as merely a standard-setting body.[18] Yet, under the pressure

The Making of International Law (OUP 2007) 109 (hereinafter Boyle and Chinkin, *The Making of International Law*).

[14] On the UN Security Council practice, see Chapter 3.

[15] Human Rights Council, UNGA Res 60/251 (15 March 2006) paras 8, 10 (hereinafter UNGA Res 60/251(2006)). For a detailed overview, see Bertrand G Ramcharan, *The UN Human Rights Council* (Routledge 2011) 15–105.

[16] UNGA Res 60/251(2006) (n 15) paras 2–3 (emphasis added).

[17] The Council replaced the Commission in 2006. UNGA Res 60/251(2006) (n 15) para 1.

[18] One of the first acts of the Commission on Human Rights in 1946 was to unanimously agree that the Commission had no power to take action as regards any human rights complaints (Communications concerning human rights, ECOSOC Res 75(V) (5 August 1947)). On the first 20 years, see James

of numerous human rights complaints, the Economic and Social Council (ECOSOC) eventually authorised the Commission 'to examine information relevant to *gross violations of human rights* and fundamental freedoms'.[19] Ultimately, it was this authorisation that inspired the development of similar types of procedures before other UN processes and beyond.[20] Soon after, Resolution 1503 established a confidential procedure that allowed the Commission of Human Rights to examine individual complaints for such violations.[21]

Today, the UN Human Rights Council may consider any human rights matter, irrespective of its gravity.[22] Through thematic resolutions and special procedures, the Council offers the forum where international standards are developed and solutions to issues of global concern are devised.[23] Notably, through the unique Universal Periodic Review (UPR), states' representatives gather to assess and review the human rights situation in each and every country around the globe that is a member of the UN.[24] Nonetheless, these developments did not entirely eliminate the original procedures that were put in place after the adoption of Resolution 1235 to address specifically situations of serious violations of human rights. The Human Rights Council retains today an elaborate system of special procedures where only situations of serious violations of human rights are discussed. Without considerably departing from previous practices, there are at least three avenues through which situations of serious violations of human rights are examined at an inter-governmental level before the Council.

Frederick Green, 'Changing Approaches to Human Rights: The United Nations, 1954 and 1974' (1977) 12 TILJ 223.

[19] Question of the violation of human rights and fundamental freedoms, including policies of racial discrimination and segregation and of apartheid, in all countries, with particular reference to colonial and other dependent countries and territories, ECOSOC Res 1235 (6 June 1967) paras 2–3 (emphasis added) (hereinafter ECOSOC Res 1235 (1967)).

[20] On regional organisations, see Fatsah Ouguergouz, *The African Charter on Human and Peoples' Rights, A Comprehensive Agenda for Human Dignity and Sustainable Democracy in Africa* (Martinus Nijhoff Publishers 2003); Cecilia Medina Quiroga, *The Battle of Human Rights: Gross, Systematic Violations and the Inter-American System* (Kluwer 1988).

[21] Procedure for dealing with communications relating to violations of human rights and fundamental freedoms, ECOSOC Res 1503(XLVIII) (27 May 1970) (hereinafter ECOSOC Res 1503(XLVIII)).

[22] Andrew Clapham and Jo Bourke, *The Promotion and Protection of All Human Rights is a Legitimate Concern of the International Community* (The Graduate Institute of International Studies 1999) 36.

[23] Institution-building of the United Nations Human Rights Council, UNHRC Res 5/1 (18 June 2007) (hereinafter UNHRC Res 5/1 (2007)).

[24] ibid paras 1–38. On UPR, see Constance De La Vega and Tamara N Lewis, 'Peer Review in the Mix: How the UPR Transforms Human Rights Discourse' in M Cherif Bassiouni and William A Schabas (eds), *New Challenges for the UN Human Rights Machinery: What Future for the UN Treaty Body System and the Human Rights Council Procedures?* (Intersentia 2011).

As a first step (albeit not always), the Council will examine situations revealing a consistent pattern of gross violations of human rights through the neglected and today confidential Complaint Procedure.[25] Following individual or collective complaints, if there is sufficient reliable information to suggest that such violations occurred, a confidential inquiry is conducted.[26] This entirely confidential procedure is supposed to pre-empt public debate and allow the state concerned to react promptly before being exposed to public criticism. The only exception to the confidentiality rule is an occasional periodic publication of the list of situations that have been referred to the Human Rights Council.[27]

The ultimate threat to the government concerned is that the Council may eventually decide to bring the situation forward for public discussion. Due to the lack of collaboration of the Government of Eritrea following several complaints under the confidential Complaint Procedure, the situation was brought forward for public debate, which led to the adoption of several country-specific resolutions condemning the Government of Eritrea and, ultimately, to the appointment of a Special Rapporteur and then a Commission of Inquiry.[28]

The public debate around a country-specific situation is the second and more invasive avenue through which serious violations of human rights are examined before the Human Rights Council.[29] Often today, situations are brought directly to public debate. Despite the Council's general mandate to monitor respect for human rights, the country-specific resolutions focusing on serious violations of human rights still occupy a significant part of its annual workload. For instance, during its three sessions in 2020, sixteen resolutions focused on the human rights situations in specific countries (including Belarus, Burundi, Democratic People's Republic of Korea (DPRK or North Korea), Eritrea, Iran, Myanmar, occupied Syrian Golan, the Occupied Palestinian Territory, South

[25] UNHRC Res 5/1 (2007) (n 23) paras 85–109. Initially regulated by ECOSOC Res 1503(XLVIII) (n 21).

[26] UNHRC Res 5/1 (2007) (n 23) paras 87, 100.

[27] 'List of Situations Referred to the Human Rights Council under the Complaint Procedure since 2006' (last updated in October 2014) <http://www.ohchr.org/Documents/HRBodies/ComplaintProcedure/SituationsConsideredUnderComplaintProcedures.pdf> accessed 9 August 2021. On the ECOSOC Res 1503 procedure, see Howard Tolley, 'The Concealed Crack in the Citadel: The United Nations Commission on Human Rights' Response to Confidential Communications' (1984) 6 HRQ 420, 447–49.

[28] Situation of human rights in Eritrea, UNHRC Res 26/24 (27 June 2014) para 7 (Commission of Inquiry) (hereinafter UNHRC Res 26/24 (2014)); Situation of human rights in Eritrea, UNHRC Res 21/1 (26 September 2012) para 1 (discontinued confidential procedure); Situation of human rights in Eritrea, UNHRC Res 20/20 (6 July 2012) para 4 (Special Rapporteur) (hereinafter UNHRC Res 20/20 (2012)).

[29] Originates from the ECOSOC Res 1235 (1967) (n 19).

Sudan, Syria, Venezuela, and Yemen).[30] Similar resolutions are adopted every year, covering the human rights situation in these or other countries.[31]

Such resolutions point the finger at specific countries and are adopted following a careful calculation of political costs.[32] To an extent, the political costs are relative to the gravity of the violations. The more serious the violations, the more probable it is that member states will be ready to adopt a resolution. The gravity of violations increases public pressure and the risks of spill-over effects and other harm to global affairs, thus justifying the political costs of responding to such violations. As a result, country-specific scrutiny is limited to serious violations of human rights mostly of a systematic character and potentially on a large scale.[33]

The third avenue through which the Human Rights Council discusses situations of serious violations of human rights is through summoning emergency Special Sessions.[34] Between 2006 and October 2021 the Council called thirty such sessions.[35] They are called to discuss urgent situations of human rights violations that require immediate attention.[36] As with any political procedure, there are no clear guidelines on the situations that trigger a Special Session. The rules of procedure do not even require a gravity threshold.[37] Nevertheless, the urgent nature of a situation is inevitably calculated on the basis of the gravity of the human rights violations, entailing an irreversible impact on the victims.[38] Such sessions have so far been summoned only as a response to situations of serious violations of human rights. The Council has held Special Sessions to discuss the human rights situation in Burundi, CAR, Côte d'Ivoire, Iraq (ISIS), Libya, Myanmar, South Sudan, Sri Lanka, Sudan (Darfur), and Syria (with regard to government and ISIS abuses).[39] It has also convened to discuss major

[30] Available at 'UNHRC Documents and Resolutions' http://www.ohchr.org/EN/HRBodies/HRC/Pages/Documents.aspx accessed 9 August 2021.

[31] ibid.

[32] See Olivier de Frouville, 'Building a Universal System for the Protection of Human Rights: The Way Forward' in M Cherif Bassiouni and William A Schabas (eds), *New Challenges for the UN Human Rights Machinery: What Future for the UN Treaty Body System and the Human Rights Council Procedures?* (Intersentia 2011) 241–66 (hereinafter de Frouville, 'Building a Universal System').

[33] Philip Alston, 'The Commission on Human Rights' in Philip Alston (ed), *The United Nations and Human Rights: A Critical Appraisal* (OUP 1992) 161–64 (hereinafter Alston, 'The Commission on Human Rights').

[34] UNHRC Res 5/1 (n 23) paras 119–28. The Special Session already existed before the Commission on Human Rights, albeit rarely used. Alston, 'The Commission on Human Rights' (n 33).

[35] 'UNHRC: Special Sessions' <https://www.ohchr.org/EN/HRBodies/HRC/SpecialSessions/Pages/SpecialSessions.aspx> accessed 9 August 2021 (hereinafter 'UNHRC: Special Sessions').

[36] 'UNHRC: Sessions' (n 11).

[37] A Special Session can be convened at the request of a member of the Council with the support of one-third of the membership of the Council. UNGA Res 60/251 (2006) (n 15) para 10; Rule 6, Rules of Procedure, UNHRC Res 5/1 (n 23).

[38] See Chapter 1.

[39] 'UNHRC: Special Sessions' (n 35).

incidents in the Occupied Palestinian Territory since 2006, and the activities of Boko Haram.[40] Special Sessions result in the adoption of resolutions condemning serious violations of human rights and recommending urgent measures.[41]

1.2 The UN General Assembly country-specific resolutions

Other UN inter-governmental organs also single out serious violations of human rights. Notably, the UN General Assembly annually adopts country-specific resolutions to address situations of serious violations of human rights. It has an express mandate to discuss *any* human rights issues,[42] and it thematically addresses various human rights issues of global significance.[43] Yet it has so far adopted country-specific resolutions primarily in instances of serious violations of human rights.[44]

During the first years, the General Assembly dealt only with the decolonisation process and inter-state matters. The first step was taken in the 1950s, when the Assembly condemned South African racial practices regarding the treatment of citizens of Indian origin, at the Indian Government's request.[45] It was in 1974 that the General Assembly finally adopted a country-specific resolution, entitled 'Protection of human rights in Chile'. It condemned the gross and flagrant violations of human rights by the Pinochet regime against the Chilean population—against its *own* population.[46] Following this instance, the General

[40] The 30th, 28th, 21st, 12th, 9th, 6th, 3rd, and 1st Special Sessions focused on the Occupied Palestinian Territory; the 23rd Special Session focused on Boko Haram. ibid.

[41] Notably, The human rights situation in the Syrian Arab Republic, UNHRC Res 34/26 (24 March 2017) paras 6–9; The human rights situation in the Syrian Arab Republic, UNHRC Res 31/17 (23 March 2016) paras 6–10; Preventing the deterioration of the human rights situation in Burundi, UNHRC Res S-24/1 (22 December 2015) Preamble, paras 11, 4.

[42] Articles 10 and 13(c), Charter of the United Nations, San Fransisco (adopted 26 June 1945) 1 UNTS XVI.

[43] In its 74th session (2019–20), the General Assembly adopted resolutions on The human rights to safe drinking water and sanitation, UNGA Res 74/141, (18 December 2019); Protection of and assistance to internally displaced persons, UNGA Res 74/160 (18 December 2019) (hereinafter UNGA Res 74/160 (2019)); The safety of journalists and the issue of impunity, UNGA Res 74/157 (18 December 2019).

[44] At least since its 61st session, the General Assembly adopts on average four country-specific resolutions per session. For example, 'UNGA: 74th Session (2019–2020)' <https://research.un.org/en/docs/ga/quick/regular/74> accessed 9 August 2021.

[45] UNGA Res 44(I) (1946) (n 6). The Greek civil war was discussed only to call on Albania, Bulgaria, and Yugoslavia to stop providing any form of assistance to the 'guerrillas'. Threats to the political independence and territorial integrity of Greece, UNGA Res 109 (II) (21 October 1947). For a historical overview, see Antonio Cassese, 'The General Assembly: Historical Perspective 1945–1989' in Philip Alston (ed), *The United Nations and Human Rights: A Critical Appraisal* (CUP 1992). Conforti and Focarelli, *The Law and Practice of the UN* (n 4) 180–81.

[46] UNGA Res 3219(XXIX) (6 November 1974).

Assembly's practice gradually expanded to include situations in other countries, such as Guatemala and El Salvador in 1980.[47] Over the past ten years, the General Assembly has adopted resolutions regarding the human rights situations in Syria,[48] Myanmar,[49] Iran,[50] North Korea,[51] Belarus,[52] the Occupied Territories,[53] and, more recently, Crimea and Sevastopol (Ukraine).[54]

There may be no formal criteria for determining which situations will be assessed before the General Assembly. Nevertheless, the restriction of country-specific resolutions to serious violations of human rights is confirmed both factually, by examining the situations under consideration before the Assembly, and verbally, by looking at the language used in its resolutions. First, all the human rights situations discussed before the Assembly over the past ten years exhibit the characteristics of serious violations of human rights.[55] The General Assembly has so far looked only at large-scale situations, which involve widespread and systematic abuses. Variously, the situations under examination concern violations of the right to life, ill-treatment, and arbitrary detention, as well as violations of the right to privacy and the freedoms of movement, religion, and expression.[56]

Second, almost all of these resolutions explicitly condemn the commission of serious violations of human rights.[57] The language, being descriptive rather than normative, varies from one resolution to the next; all the qualifiers—gross,

[47] See Menno T Kamminga, *Inter-State Accountability for Violations of Human Rights* (University of Pennsylvania Press 1992) 88 (hereinafter Kamminga, *Inter-State Accountability*).

[48] Among others, UNGA Res 74/160 (2019) (n 43); Situation of human rights in the Syrian Arab Republic, UNGA Res 70/234 (23 December 2015).

[49] The General Assembly has been adopting resolutions on Myanmar every year since 1991 (46th session) until its 70th session, and again since its 72th session. Notably, Situation of human rights of Rohingya Muslims and other minorities in Myanmar, UNGA Res 74/246 (27 December 2019); Situation of human rights in Myanmar, UNGA Res 70/233 (23 December 2015); Situation in Myanmar, UNGA Res 46/132, (17 December 1991).

[50] The General Assembly has been adopting resolutions on Iran annually since 1985 (40th session), except for four sessions (46th, 47th, 51st, 57th). Situation of human rights in the Islamic Republic of Iran, UNGA Res 74/167 (18 December 2019); Situation of human rights in the Islamic Republic of Iran, UNGA Res 70/173 (17 December 2015); Situation of human rights in the Islamic Republic of Iran, UNGA Res 40/141 (13 December 1985).

[51] First resolution adopted on 60th session: Situation of human rights in the DPRK, UNGA Res 73/180 (17 December 2018); Situation of human rights in the DPRK, UNGA Res 60/173 (15 December 2005) (hereinafter UNGA Res 60/173 (2005)).

[52] Belarus was on the agenda for two years: Situation of human rights in Belarus, UNGA Res 62/169 (18 December 2007); Situation of human rights in Belarus, UNGA Res 61/175 (19 December 2006).

[53] With its own separate Item in the agenda, there are multiple resolutions every year. One of the earliest resolutions: Respect for and implementation of human rights in occupied territories, UNGA Res 2443 (XXIII) (19 December 1968).

[54] Situation of human rights in the Autonomous Republic of Crimea and the city of Sevastopol, Ukraine, UNGA Res 74/168 (18 December 2019); Situation of human rights in the Autonomous Republic of Crimea and the city of Sevastopol (Ukraine), UNGA Res 71/205 (19 December 2016).

[55] But even before, see Kamminga, *Inter-State Accountability* (n 47) 85–86.

[56] See Chapter 1.

[57] See notably resolutions listed nn 49–54.

grave, and serious—are used interchangeably.[58] Finally, there is a pragmatic argument as to why there is a threshold above which the Assembly adopts country-specific resolutions. The 'parliamentary' body of the United Nations comprises all 193 member states, whose country-specific resolutions correspond to a very limited part of its annual workload, and can only deal with the most serious situations of human rights violations.

Decisions on the countries examined under the country-specific resolutions remain highly political.[59] External considerations, such as the government's willingness to collaborate, still remain an important factor, as the entity primarily responsible is the state under whose jurisdiction these violations occurred.[60] By way of illustration, the situation in Myanmar, which had been under consideration for 24 consecutive sessions, was removed in 2016, despite the serious allegations of ethnic cleansing of the Rohingya minority persisting in the country. The steps taken towards democratic rule and the rise to power of a party that was ready to engage at an international level determined this decision.[61] Eventually, Myanmar was reintroduced to the agenda two years later.[62] Nonetheless, political selectivity does not altogether eliminate the significance of the process that is in fact limited to states where serious violations are committed. Many situations that meet the threshold of serious violations of human rights have not been discussed before the General Assembly, but also country-specific resolutions have not been adopted for any situation below that threshold.[63]

These resolutions contribute to the consolidation of the principles encompassed in serious violations of human rights that constitute as such matters of international concern.[64] These are authoritative procedures that often set the foundations for further action at every level: (i) the state concerned; (ii) other decision-making processes; as well as (iii) further measures within the same organ. First, resolutions adopted by inter-governmental organisations are

[58] ibid.

[59] The states under scrutiny never fail to highlight the political nature of the process in order to undermine its credibility. For instance, the representatives of Syria, Iran, and North Korea underlined the politicised, selective, double-standard nature of this process during the 69th session. UNGA, 69th session, Verbatim record of the 73rd plenary meeting (18 December 2014) A/69/PV73. See also Andrew Clapham, 'The General Assembly' in Philip Alston and Frédéric Mégret (eds), *The United Nations and Human Rights: A Critical Appraisal* (2nd edn, OUP 2020).

[60] See ECtHR, *Ilaşcu and Others v Moldova and Russia*, App no 48787/99, 8 July 2004.

[61] The National League for Democracy Party—the party of Aung San Suu Kyi—won the general elections on 8 November 2015.

[62] Situation of human rights in Myanmar, UNGA Res 72/248 (24 December 2017). See also n 49.

[63] The fact that resolutions addressing the treatment of single individuals have been adopted does not negate the gravity aspect. See Section 2.1, Chapter 1.

[64] On the legal effect of international organs' decisions, see Boyle and Chinkin, *The Making of International Law* (n 13) 211ff; Higgins, *The Development of International Law* (n 2).

often a key element in pushing states towards compliance with international standards. Second, their determinations are still used as an indicator for other decisions. For example, in arms control, the European Union refers to these decisions when assessing whether serious violations have occurred and, as a result, whether they should ban an arms export.[65] Lastly, the political organs regularly adopt further measures through these processes—within the framework of their mandates—aimed at addressing situations of serious violations of human rights. Among other things, they may subject a state to further international scrutiny, though inquiries and monitoring processes.

2. Extra-conventional international inquiry and fact-finding mechanisms

Beyond the inter-governmental procedures, there is today a complex and continually expanding network of extra-conventional special procedures and mechanisms dedicated exclusively to the monitoring and recording of situations of serious violations of human rights. These mechanisms are often the result of the country-specific resolutions adopted by the UN Human Rights Council or the UN General Assembly, but also by the UN Security Council (albeit less frequently). Operating outside the framework of human rights treaties, they constitute the backbone of the UN's investigative, supervisory, and promotional activities.[66] Increasingly, other regional international organisations have been establishing similar regional inquiry processes.[67]

The establishment of all these inquiry and monitoring procedures demonstrates as such the eminence of serious violations of human rights as a distinct category of human rights violations, but also speak to the formation of a special regime. *Ad hoc* investigatory bodies may be regularly established in international law for resolving a wide array of matters of international concern and political significance. However, the constant and recurrent recourse to such mechanisms for serious violations of human rights sets them apart. In fact, the recurring and frequent recourse to these inquiry and monitoring procedures elevates them to an important component of the special regime

[65] Article 2(b), EU Council Common Position 2008/944/CFSP (8 December 2008) OJEU, L 335/99.

[66] For a comparison between individual complaints and inquiry bodies, see Nigel Rodley, 'The United Nations Human Rights Council, Its Special Procedures, and Its Relationship with the Treaty Bodies: Complementarity or Competition?' in Kevin Boyle (ed), *New Institutions for Human Rights Protection* (OUP 2010) 56–7, 63.

[67] See Section 2.2.2.

around serious violations of human rights. At the moment of writing, there are ongoing special inquiries and monitoring procedures reporting on situations around the globe—Belarus, Burundi, Libya, Sri Lanka, Syria, and elsewhere.[68] Undoubtedly there are still 'culprits' that manage to evade scrutiny. For instance, the Yemeni conflict is one of the darker, largely ignored instances in contemporary history.[69] Nevertheless, the number of situations with some sort of scrutiny is steadily increasing.

2.1 Their common features

These inquiries and monitoring procedures appear under various labels, forms, and structures. The conditions for the establishment and functions of extra-conventional mechanisms are nowhere outlined.[70] They are labelled special rapporteurs, commissions of inquiry, truth commissions, high-level panels, and so on. Any attempt to categorise them perfectly and in full would be overly simplistic. Each of these bodies can be seen as unique, even within the same category; each is tailored to the circumstances of the particular situation for which it has been established.[71]

Their functions also vary. They may have a purely fact-finding and documentary function (to establish the facts), a quasi-prosecutorial function (to identify those responsible), a conciliation function (to seek solutions), or a combination of these.[72] For example, the mandate of a UN special rapporteur may (or may not) include: inquiries into and receipt of information with respect to a specific situation, engagement in dialogue with the state concerned, on-site visits, consultations with civil society, follow-ups on a situation, as well as recommendations regarding the necessary steps to be taken. Similarly, a UN commission of inquiry is established, among other things, to make an account of past and complicated events, identify the responsible

[68] See practice Section 2.2.

[69] It was only on 29 September 2017 that the UN Human Rights Council managed to agree on the establishment of a 'Group of Eminent Experts on the situation of human rights in Yemen'. Human rights, technical assistance and capacity-building in Yemen, UNHRC Res 36/31 (29 September 2017) para 16.

[70] On their unco-ordinated proliferation, see Tania Baldwin-Pask and Patrizia Scannella, 'The Unfinished Business of a Special Procedures System' in M Cherif Bassiouni and William A Schabas (eds), *New Challenges for the UN Human Rights Machinery: What Future for the UN Treaty Body System and the Human Rights Council Procedures?* (Intersentia 2011) 419.

[71] It is difficult to find a one-size-fits-all definition, even for each separate category. Gutter, 'Special Procedures' (n 5) 99.

[72] Alston, 'The Commission on Human Rights' (n 33) 167–68.

entities, and increasingly collect evidence that could potentially serve future prosecutions.[73]

Despite their differences, these procedures still share certain distinctive features. First and foremost, they share a common purpose and a common function. These country-specific inquiry and monitoring procedures are triggered or established only when there is reliable information that serious violations of human have occurred, and not for each and every human rights violation. No matter what their supplementary functions are, their principal function is the quest for the truth regarding past serious violations of human rights that occurred in a specific situation. As such, they constitute *ad hoc* responses to extraordinary situations that cannot be dealt through the ordinary mechanisms. Second, these procedures are all officially authorised and/or established by inter-governmental organs. Third, they are all composed of independent experts authorised to inquire into, record, or monitor situations where such violations have occurred.[74] Fourth, they are a form of temporary response—set up for a specific period of time, which might be extended for longer or shorter periods[75]—aiming at addressing an extraordinary situation. Fifth, the scope of their mandate is limited to one particular country, region, or incident. For instance, inquiry bodies have been established only for Darfur in Sudan (and not for the entire country),[76] or to inquire into the violations that occurred during the Flotilla incident.[77]

Lastly, there is no legal obligation to establish or trigger any of these processes, nor are their findings and conclusions legally binding. While there have been attempts to establish a more objective process for their establishment,[78] there are also convincing arguments against making the option to create such

[73] Larissa van den Herik, 'An Inquiry into the Role of Commissions of Inquiry in International Law: Navigating the Tensions between Fact-Finding and Application of International Law' (2014) 13 CJIL 507, 511–12 (hereinafter van den Herik, 'An Inquiry').

[74] UNHRC Res 5/1 (n 23) paras 89–99. For a historical overview, see van den Herik, 'An Inquiry' (n 73) 507–37.

[75] Some mandates have lasted for over twenty years, including those for Palestine, Cambodia, and Myanmar. For an overview, see Philip Alston and Sarah Knuckey (eds), *The Transformation of Human Rights Fact-Finding* (OUP 2015)(hereinafter Alston and Knuckey, *The Transformation of Human Rights Fact-Finding*).

[76] Among others, International Commission of Inquiry on Darfur, UNSC Res 1564 (18 September 2004) (hereinafter UNSC Res 1564 (2004)).

[77] International Fact-finding Mission to Investigate Violations of International Law, Including International Humanitarian and Human Rights Law, Resulting from the Israeli Attacks on the Flotilla of Ships Carrying Humanitarian Assistance, UNHRC Res 14/1 (23 June 2010) (hereinafter UNHRC Res 14/1 (2010)).

[78] On the proposal to introduce objective criteria, see Olivier de Frouville, 'Les organes subsidiaires de la commission des droits de l'homme des Nations Unies, Rapport Général' in Emmanuel Decaux (ed), *Les Nations Unies et les droits de l'homme: enjeux et défis d'une réforme* (Pedone 2006) 198 (hereinafter de Frouville, 'Les organes subsidiaires').

inquiries a standard obligation.[79] By becoming members of the UN, states have in a way already accepted that they might be subjected to such supervision. However, the states concerned do not even have a straightforward obligation to collaborate. Only '[a] good faith intent to provide as much information as possible, to preserve and make publicly available any existing state archives, can be expected'.[80] Indeed, the UN Human Rights Council has been establishing commissions of inquiry without the agreement—even in the absence of approval—of the state concerned, as it has done, for instance, with regard to Syria, North Korea, and Eritrea. In any event, the inquiry bodies do not access the territory of the state concerned without its approval.

These mechanisms, adopted mostly with the consent of the state concerned, amount to a form of 'soft' intervention, with primarily a promotional character.[81] The political bodies that create them, most often than not, do not have the competence to bind the states. For instance, the UN Human Rights Council, an inter-governmental body without any legally binding authority, cannot bestow binding powers on an inquiry mechanism. Due to these specific features, they can be seen as either quasi-political or quasi-judicial mechanisms, depending on the point of departure. Darcy, for instance, argues that commissions of inquiry have a quasi-judicial character because they eventually engage in legal analysis of the situation for which they are assembled.[82]

2.2 An overview of inquiry and fact-finding mechanisms

2.2.1 The UN network of monitoring mechanisms

Ad hoc inquiry and monitoring mechanisms are regularly established under the auspices of the UN, to assess the validity of serious violations of human rights allegations committed at a specific time or in a specific place and further monitor the situation.[83] Despite their temporary and non-binding character,

[79] Hayner reflects on the option to consider the creation of truth commissions as a standard obligation and advocates against the idea. Priscilla B Hayner, *Unspeakable Truths: Transitional Justice and the Challenge of Truth Commissions* (Routledge 2011)18 (hereinafter Hayner, *Unspeakable Truths*).

[80] ibid 24. For an opposite view, see Menno T Kamminga, 'The Thematic Procedures of the UN Commission on Human Rights' (1987) 34 NILR 299, 322. See also Miko Lempinen, *Challenges Facing the System of Special Procedures of the United Nations Commission on Human Rights* (Institute for Human Rights–Åbo Akademi University 2001) 214–15 (hereinafter Lempinen, *Challenges Facing the System of Special Procedures*).

[81] Malcolm N Shaw, *International Law* (8th edn, CUP 2017) 84–8.

[82] Shane Darcy, 'Laying the Foundations: Commissions of Inquiry and the Development of International Law' in Christian Henderson (ed), *Commissions of Inquiry: Problems and Prospects* (Hart Publishing 2017) (hereinafter Darcy, 'Laying the Foundations').

[83] Christian Henderson (ed), *Commissions of Inquiry: Problems and Prospects* (Hart Publishing 2017); Alston and Knuckey, *The Transformation of Human Rights Fact-Finding* (n 75).

they are considered today to form part of the regular arsenal to address instances of serious violations of human rights.[84]

The UN Human Rights Council has a constantly evolving system of

> mandated commissions of inquiry, fact-finding missions and investigations [that] are increasingly being used to respond to situations of *serious violations of international humanitarian law and international human rights law*, whether protracted or resulting from sudden events, and to promote accountability for such violations and counter impunity.[85]

At the time of writing, there were about ten UN Human Rights Council country-specific mandated investigations in Burundi, Libya, South Sudan, Syria, Venezuela, Yemen, and others.[86] Also, there were at least ten special country-specific procedures mandates, working on the human rights situations in, among others, CAR, Iran, the Occupied Palestinian Territory, and Somalia.[87] The thematic special rapporteur is a type of procedure that lends itself both to the general human rights regime and the special regime.[88]

Similarly, albeit less frequently, both the UN General Assembly and the UN Security Council have set up commissions of inquiry, high-level panels, and other investigatory schemes to report on allegations of commission of serious violations of human rights. The first General Assembly fact-finding mission concerned the plight of Buddhists in South Vietnam in the early 1960s.[89] Later, experts were sent to Cambodia.[90] The UN Security Council directly mandated

[84] UNHRC, Code of Conduct for Special Procedures Mandate-holders of the Human Rights Council (18 June 2007) A/HRC/RES/5/2 (hereinafter UNHRC, Code of Conduct for Special Procedures); OHCHR, Commissions of Inquiry and Fact-finding Missions on International Human Rights and Humanitarian Law: Guidance and Practice (2015) (hereinafter OHCHR, Guidance and Practice).

[85] 'UNHRC: International Commissions of Inquiry, Commissions on Human Rights, Fact-Finding Missions and Other Investigations' <http://www.ohchr.org/EN/HRBodies/HRC/Pages/COIs.aspx> accessed 9 August 2021 (emphasis added).

[86] 'UNHRC: List of HRC-Mandated Commissions of Inquiries/Fact-Finding Missions & Other Bodies (as of October 2019)' <http://www.ohchr.org/EN/HRBodies/HRC/Pages/ListHRCMandat.aspx> accessed 9 August 2021.

[87] 'UNHRC: Country Mandates' <https://spinternet.ohchr.org/ViewAllCountryMandates.aspx?lang=en> accessed 9 August 2021.

[88] Historically, the first thematic special procedures were established to respond to serious violations of human rights, including enforced disappearances, extrajudicial, summary or arbitrary executions, torture and the sale of children. Gonzales, 'The Political Sources' (n 7) 431.

[89] UNGA, 18th session, Verbatim record of the 1239th Plenary Meeting (11 October 1963) A/PV1239, paras 170–74.

[90] Human rights situation in Cambodia, UNGA Res 52/135 (12 December 1997).

investigations in Rwanda and Darfur.[91] It is not uncommon today to have more than one mechanism established for the same situation.[92]

In addition, the UN Office of the High Commissioner for Human Rights (OHCHR) has increasingly been initiating inquiries either upon request by the inter-governmental bodies,[93] or directly from its mandate[94] on its own motion.[95] Its Rapid Response Unit has conducted or facilitated missions in the Occupied Palestinian Territories, North Korea, Syria, Sri Lanka, and CAR, and has established monitoring teams in Lebanon, Mali, the CAR, and Ukraine.[96] It also occasionally conducts 'mapping' exercises[97] and regularly takes part in UN Peacekeeping Operations to, among other things, monitor, investigate, and report human rights violations.[98] These procedures, established as a response to serious violations of human rights, inevitably also focus on serious violations of human rights even when this is not explicitly stated in their respective mandates.[99]

[91] UNSC Res 1564 (2004) (n 76); Commission of Experts to examine violations of international humanitarian law committed in Rwanda, UNSC Res 935 (1 July 1994); Former Yugoslavia, UNSC Res 780 (6 October 1992).

[92] For example, UNSC Res 1564 (2004) (n 76) para 12; Follow-up to decision S-4/101 of 13 December 2006 adopted by the Human Rights Council at its fourth special session titled: Situation of human rights in Darfur, UNHRC Res 4/8 (30 March 2007) para 6. Similarly, Flotilla incident: Report of the Secretary-General's Panel of Inquiry on the 31 May 2010 Flotilla Incident (September 2011); UNHRC Res 14/1 (2010) (n 77).

[93] Recent examples include: Technical assistance and capacity-building to improve human rights in Libya, UNHRC Res 28/30 (27 March 2015); International Commission of Inquiry on the Central African Republic in CAR, UNSC Res 2127 (5 December 2013); Secretary-General's Panel of Experts on Accountability in Sri Lanka (22 June 2010) SG/SM/12967.

[94] High Commissioner for the promotion and protection of all human rights, UNGA Res 48/141 (20 December 1993).

[95] Among others, the OHCHR Mission in Mali (2013); the OHCHR mission on the situation of human rights in Honduras since the coup d'état of 28 June 2009 (2009). See Felice D Gaer and Christen L Broecker (eds), *The United Nations High Commissioner for Human Rights: Conscience for the World* (Martinus Nijhoff Publishers 2014).

[96] 'OHCHR in the World: making human rights a reality on the ground' <http://www.ohchr.org/EN/Countries/Pages/WorkInField.aspx> accessed 9 August 2021.

[97] OHCHR, 'Report of the Mapping Exercise Documenting the Most Serious Violations of Human Rights and International Humanitarian Law Committed within the Territory of the Democratic Republic of the Congo between March 1993 and June 2003' (2010) <http://www.ohchr.org/Documents/Countries/CD/DRC_MAPPING_REPORT_FINAL_EN.pdf> accessed 9 August 2021 (hereinafter OHCHR 'Report of the Mapping Exercise Documenting … Democratic Republic of the Congo'); OHCHR, 'The Nepal Conflict Report' (2012) <http://www.ohchr.org/EN/Countries/AsiaRegion/Pages/NepalConflictReport.aspx> accessed 9 August 2021.

[98] For a detailed account of the human rights functions of UN Peacekeeping Operations, see Mari Katayanagi, *Human Rights Functions of United Nations Peacekeeping Operations* (Martinus Nijhoff Publishers 2002).

[99] Annyssa Bellal, 'Building Respect for the Rule of Law in Violent Contexts: The Office of the High Commissioner for Human Rights' Experience and Approach' (2014) 96 IRRC 881, 897–98.

2.2.2 The regional international inquiries

Next to the UN, regional organisations have been establishing their own *ad hoc* inquiries and monitoring mechanisms in cases of serious violations of human rights, albeit less frequently. Their choice of form and structures often mirror the UN procedures, but they also reflect the peculiarities of the regional mechanisms. The Inter-American Commission was the first regional monitoring body to develop a practice of reporting situations of serious violations of human rights.[100] It interpreted its mandate to allow it to look into the general human rights situation in countries where gross and systematic violations were allegedly taking place.[101] It has used these reports to inform the political organs of the Organization of American States and to push for their intervention. One of the first and most successful examples was its interference during the Pinochet dictatorship in Chile.[102]

On the other side of the Atlantic, regional African organs are increasingly also setting up similar *ad hoc* mandates. The African Union established a Commission of Inquiry on South Sudan.[103] The African Commission on Human and People's Rights has also organised various missions.[104] In Europe, the Commissioner for Human Rights of the Council of Europe has organised investigations in cases of serious violations of human rights when deemed necessary.[105] The Commissioner actively participates in inquiries and travels to the regions under investigation, including Chechnya,[106] as well as Georgia and Russia over South Ossetia,[107] and Armenia and Moldova over election

[100] Article 41(d), American Convention on Human Rights ('Pact of San José'), San José, Costa Rica (adopted 22 November 1969).

[101] On past practice, see O Hilaire Sobers, 'The Inter-American System of Human Rights' in Gentian Zyberi and Kevin Mason (eds), *An Institutional Approach to the Responsibility to Protect* (CUP 2013) 468.

[102] For a detailed account, see Cecilia Medina Quiroga, 'The Inter-American System for the Protection of Human Rights' in Catarina Krause and Martin Scheinin (eds), *International Protection of Human Rights: A Textbook* (2nd edn, Åbo Akademi University, Institute for Human Rights 2012) 520–21.

[103] AU, 'Final Report of the African Union Commission of Inquiry on South Sudan' (15 October 2014) 8. See Rob Grace, 'Lessons from Two Regional Missions: Fact-Finding in Georgia and South Sudan' in Christian Henderson (ed), *Commissions of Inquiry: Problems and Prospects* (Hart Publishing 2017) 65.

[104] Rachel Murray and Debra Long, *The Implementation of the Findings of the African Commission on Human and Peoples' Rights* (CUP 2015).

[105] On OSCE, see Martina Huber and others, *The Effectiveness of OSCE Missions: The Cases of Uzbekistan, Ukraine and Bosnia and Herzegovina* (Conflict Research Unit, Netherlands Institute of International Relations 'Clingendael' 2003).

[106] Commissioner for Human Rights (CoE), 'Report by Thomas Hammarberg Commissioner for Human Rights of the Council of Europe Following his Visit to the Russian Federation' (Chechen Republic and the Republic of Ingushetia) on 2–11 September 2009 (2009) CommDH(2009)36.

[107] Commissioner for Human Rights (CoE), 'Report on Human Rights Issues Following the August 2008 Armed Conflict in Georgia by Thomas Hammarberg Commissioner for Human Rights of the Council of Europe' (2010) CommDH(2010)40; Commissioner for Human Rights (CoE), 'Human Rights in Areas Affected by the South Ossetia Conflict, Special Mission to Georgia and Russian

violence.[108] Furthermore, Article 52 of the ECHR authorises the Secretary-General of the Council of Europe to request any High Contracting Party to provide an explanation in relation to the effective implementation of any of the provisions of the Convention.[109] This option has been used only in cases presenting serious violations of human rights. Among others, the situation in Chechnya during 1999 and 2000,[110] and following allegations in 2005 about the existence of secret Central Intelligence Agency (CIA) detention centres, triggered such requests.[111]

2.3 Monitoring serious violations of human rights

The decision to establish an extra-conventional international human rights mechanism at international level is always the result of careful weighing up of all factors in a specific situation from all sides—inevitably depending on the convergence of the interests of states.[112] As Lempinen points out, '[t]here is always a different reasoning in the choice of voting'.[113] All these monitoring bodies are created by a political entity through a political process, and they report back to the same political entity that established them. Still, serious violations of human rights remain a *sine qua non* in order to establish any new *ad hoc* monitoring mechanism for a specific situation.

Federation by Thomas Hammarberg Council of Europe Commissioner for Human Rights' (2008) CommDH(2008)22.

[108] Respectively: Commissioner for Human Rights (CoE), 'Report by Thomas Hammarberg Commissioner for Human Rights of the Council of Europe Following His Visit to Moldova 25 to 28 April 2009' (2009) CommDH(2009)27; Commissioner for Human Rights (CoE), 'Special Mission to Armenia Summary of Findings by Thomas Hammarberg Commissioner for Human Rights of the Council of Europe, Yerevan 13–15 July 2008', (2008) CommDH(2008)29; Commissioner for Human Rights (CoE), 'Special Mission to Armenia by Thomas Hammarberg Commissioner for Human Rights of the Council of Europe, Yerevan 12–15 March 2008' (2008) CommDH(2008)11REV.

[109] European Convention for the Protection of Human Rights and Fundamental Freedoms ((as ammended by subsequent protocols) (ECHR) (adopted 4 November 1950) CETS No 5, Council of Europe.

[110] Council of Europe, Secretary-General, 'Request for explanations concerning the manner in which the Convention is implemented in Chechnya and the risks of violation which may result therefrom, Report by the Secretary General on the use his powers under Article 52 of the European Convention on Human Rights in respect of the Russian Federation' (10 May 2000) SG/Inf(2000)21.

[111] Council of Europe, Secretary-General, 'Secretary General's supplementary report under Article 52 ECHR on the question of secret detention and transport of detainees suspected of terrorist acts, notably by or at the instigation of foreign agencies' (14 June 2006) SG/Inf(2006)13.

[112] On a past attempt to make the process more objective, see de Frouville, 'Les organes subsidiaires' (n 78) 198.

[113] Lempinen, *Challenges Facing the System of Special Procedures* (n 80) 124.

The mandates of extra-conventional *ad hoc* monitoring mechanisms interchangeably authorise them to inquire into and report on all human rights, or on serious violations of human rights. The Commission of Inquiry on Eritrea was initially mandated to 'investigate violations of international human rights law', but after its first report it was asked to 'investigate systematic, widespread and gross violations of human rights . . ., including where these violations may amount to crimes against humanity'.[114] Similarly, the initial mandate of the Commission of Inquiry on Syria referred simply to all human rights law violations, but later on the Commission was asked 'to continue to update its mapping exercise of gross violations of human rights in the Syrian Arab Republic since March 2011'.[115] The Fact-Finding mission on Libya has a mandate to investigate all human rights violations.[116] The Commission of Inquiry on the DPRK was from the beginning requested to 'investigate systematic, widespread and grave violations of human rights', including crimes against humanity.[117] Increasingly, country-specific special rapporteurs are authorised to monitor the human rights situation overall.[118]

The decision as to which type of mechanism should be established depends on the political considerations regarding a particular situation at a specific time, and not so much on the threshold of violations.[119] Recently, it may appear that the Human Rights Council distinguishes between the mandates of the UN country-specific special rapporteurs and the commissions of inquiry, as it has been establishing both forms of monitoring for the same situation[120]—the former having a more general monitoring, advisory role, while the latter focuses primarily on inquiring into and reporting serious violations. The

[114] Situation of Human Rights in Eritrea, UNHRC Res 29/18 (2 July 2015) para 10; UNHRC Res 26/24 (2014) (n 28) para 8.

[115] Respectively: Situation of human rights in the Syrian Arab Republic, UNHRC Res 21/26 (28 September 2012) para 18; Independent International Commission of Inquiry on the Syrian Arab Republic, UNHRC Res S-17/1 (18 October 2011) (hereinafter UNHRC Res S-17/1 (2011)).

[116] Technical assistance and capacity-building to improve human rights in Libya, UNHRC Res 43/39 (22 June 2020).

[117] Situation of human rights in the DPRK, UNHRC Res 22/13 (21 March 2013) (hereinafter UNHRC Res 22/13 (2013)) para 5.

[118] Notably, Technical assistance to the Central African Republic in the field of human rights, UNHRC Res 24/34 (27 September 2013); Situation of human rights in Belarus, UNHRC Res 20/13 (5 July 2012); Situation of human rights in the DPRK, ComHR Res 2004/13 (15 April 2004) (hereinafter ComHR Res 2004/13 (2004)); but even older Situation of human rights in the Sudan, ComHR Res 1993/60 (10 March 1993).

[119] OHCHR, Fact Sheet No 27: Seventeen Frequently Asked Questions about United Nations Special Rapporteurs. See also before Alston, 'The Commission on Human Rights' (n 33) 165.

[120] See notably regarding the situations in Syria and Eritrea: UNHRC Res 26/24 (2014) (n 28) para 7 (Commission of Inquiry); UNHRC Res 20/20 (2012) (n 28) para 4 (Special Rapporteur); The human rights situation in the Syrian Arab Republic, UNHRC Res S-18/1 (2 December 2011) (Special Rapporteur) (hereinafter UNHRC Res S-18/1 (2011)); UNHRC Res S-17/1 (2011) (n 115).

systematic recourse to such bodies may gradually sharpen these distinctions, but it is too soon to be certain. In the case of Eritrea, the two bodies operated simultaneously;[121] while in the case of Syria, the mandate of the Special Rapporteur will begin only once the Commission of Inquiry is dissolved.[122]

Enjoying wide discretionary powers as to how they operate, there are enormous differences of style, methodology, content, and focus from one report to another.[123] Yet, even in instances where their mandate authorised them to look into all human rights violations that occur in a situation, these bodies never actually report on all human rights violations.[124] The overall situation, the timeframe and other factors may influence the content of their reports. Yet whether a mechanism is operating for many decades or just examining a specific incident,[125] they will still prioritise and report on serious violations of human rights.[126]

The proliferation of mechanisms in itself reinforces the understanding that a distinction is made in practice between these and other human rights violations. Officially formed by governments, these inquiries are considered authoritative sources, providing an account of instances of serious violations of human rights in a seemingly 'de-politicised' manner.[127] They could be understood as providing a quasi-judicial assessment of the particular situation aimed

[121] UNHRC 'First Report of the Special Rapporteur on the situation of human rights in Eritrea, Sheila B Keetharuth' (28 May 2013) A/HRC/23/53; UNHRC, 'First report of the commission of inquiry on human rights in Eritrea' (4 June 2015) A/HRC/29/42.

[122] UNHRC Res S-18/1 (2011) (n 120) para 10.

[123] Alston concluded already in 1992, 'whether they have been asked to "study", "inquire into", "investigate", "monitor", "examine" most rapporteurs have tended to assume considerable flexibility and to approach each situation as they see fit'. Alston, 'The Commission on Human Rights' (n 33) 167.

[124] See further examples in Chapter 1.

[125] For instance, the Commission of Inquiry on Syria was established in 2011 and at the time of writing is still operating. The Special Rapporteur on the situation of human rights in the Palestinian territories occupied since 1967 was appointed in 1993, and continues to monitor the situation to this day.

[126] Notably, UNHRC, 'Report of the Independent International Commission of Inquiry on the Syrian Arab Republic' (11 March 2021) A/HRC/46/55; UNHRC, 'Report of the independent commission of inquiry established pursuant to Human Rights Council resolution S-21/1' (24 June 2015) A/HRC/29/52; UNHRC, 'Report of the Special Rapporteur on the situation of human rights in Myanmar, Yanghee Lee' (23 March 2015) A/HRC/28/72; UNHRC, 'Eight Report of the independent international commission of inquiry on the Syrian Arab Republic' (13 August 2014) A/HRC/27/60; UNHRC, 'Report of the commission of inquiry on human rights in the DPRK' (7 February 2014) A/HRC/25/63; UNHRC, 'Report of the Special Rapporteur on the situation of human rights in Belarus' (18 April 2013) A/HRC/23/52; OHCHR 'Report of the Mapping Exercise Documenting ... Democratic Republic of the Congo' (n 97).

[127] See de Frouville, 'Building a Universal System' (n 32) 260. UNHRC, Code of Conduct for Special Procedures (n 84); OHCHR: Guidance and Practice (n 84). For a critical assessment of the fragility of this perception, see Miko Lempinen, *The United Nations Commission on Human Rights and the Different Treatment of Governments: An Inseparable Part of Promoting and Encouraging Respect for Human Rights?* (Åbo Akademis Förlag—Åbo Akademi University Press 2005) 19. For an in-depth analysis of personal biases and impartiality, see Frédéric Mégret, 'International Judges and Experts' Impartiality and the Problem of Past Declarations' (2011) 10 The Law and Practice of International Courts and Tribunals 31.

at clarifying past events, or even ongoing situations, through a legal assessment of applicable legal standards.[128] Whether they are created to actively seek evidence or to receive information, they have to decide whether the information is relevant and make legal determinations. They need to assess if evidence proves the occurrence of a violation, what kind of violation, who was responsible, and, in some instances, even who the perpetrator was.[129] Yet *ad hoc* extra-conventional monitoring mechanisms are not the only bodies that perform such functions, there are also multiple permanent treaty-based inquiry procedures that respond to serious violations of human rights by design.

3. The treaty-based inquiry mechanisms

Beyond inter-governmental processes condemning serious violations of human rights and *ad hoc* inquiries recording and shaming the commission of such violations, 'serious violations of human rights' have found their way into various human rights treaties establishing permanent urgent inquiry procedures. The inclusion of serious violations of human rights in treaty provisions constitutes an outright recognition of the normative value of these violations as a separate legal category of human rights violations.

3.1 UN treaty bodies *proprio motu* inquiry powers

Several UN human rights treaties explicitly authorise their respective UN human rights treaty bodies to initiate urgent inquiries when they receive reliable information that serious violations of human rights covered by their respective mandates have been committed. These permanent special procedures essentially allow the monitoring bodies to divert from the regular proceedings (namely, state reports or individual communications)[130] and establish a new

[128] Darcy, 'Laying the Foundations' (n 82) 231–56. For a critical assessment on the matter, see Lyal S Sunga, 'What Should Be the UN Human Rights Council's Role in Investigating Genocide, War Crimes and Crimes against Humanity?' in M Cherif Bassiouni and William A Schabas (eds), *New Challenges for the UN Human Rights Machinery: What Future for the UN Treaty Body System and the Human Rights Council Procedures?* (Intersentia 2011) 344 (hereinafter Sunga, 'What Should Be the UN Human Rights Council's Role').

[129] On tendency to focus on international crimes, see Sunga, 'What Should Be the UN Human Rights Council's Role' (n 128) 326–28. Similarly for truth and reconciliation commissions, see Hayner, *Unspeakable Truths* (n 79) 121–22, 130–31.

[130] For a further information, see Suzanne Egan, *The UN Human Rights Treaty System: Law and Procedure* (Bloomsbury Professional 2011) 131–77, 253–450 (hereinafter Egan, *The UN Human Rights Treaty System*).

line of communication with the respective government, focusing on a situation of serious violations of human rights.

The first body vested with the power to initiate an inquiry if it receives reliable information that 'torture is being *systematically* practised' was the Committee against Torture in 1984.[131] None of the human rights treaties that preceded it included such a distinction.[132] Following the formula set out in the Convention against Torture, the inquiry procedure has been introduced in every UN human rights treaty adopted ever since, with minor variations. Five other UN treaty bodies are authorised to initiate an inquiry of their own motion in cases of '*grave or systematic* violations by a State Party of rights set forth in the Convention'.[133]

The structure of all these procedures is very similar.[134] In all cases, the committees will request the government to submit an urgent report or statement on the situation in question. If possible, and depending on the respective government's approval, they will make an on-site visit. By the end of the process, the supervisory body will adopt some kind of conclusions, whether in the form of a report, summary account, decision, or resolution. These conclusions provide an account of the situation, accompanied by a legal assessment and recommendations. The whole process is confidential.[135] The committees can publish summary accounts of the inquiries' results only after prior consultation with the state concerned. Despite the confidentiality clause, various committees have been increasingly publishing their findings, providing some insights to the process.

[131] Article 20, Convention against Torture and Other Cruel, Inhuman or Degrading Treatment or Punishment (adopted 10 December 1984) 1465 UNTS 85 (hereinafter CAT).

[132] Referring to: International Convention on the Elimination of All Forms of Racial Discrimination (adopted 7 March 1966) 660 UNTS 195 (hereinafter CERD); International Covenant on Civil and Political Rights (adopted 16 December 1966) 999 UNTS 171 (hereinafter ICCPR); International Covenant on Economic, Social and Cultural Rights (adopted 16 December 1966) 993 UNTS 3; Convention on the Elimination of All Forms of Discrimination against Women (adopted 18 December 1979) 1249 UNTS 13 (hereinafter CEDAW).

[133] Articles 13–14, Optional Protocol to the Convention on the Rights of the Child on a communications procedure (adopted 19 December 2011) UNGA Res 66/138 (hereinafter OP-CRC-IC); Article 11, Optional Protocol to the International Covenant on Economic, Social and Cultural Rights (adopted 10 December 2008) UNGA Res 63/117 (hereinafter OP-ICESCR); Articles 6–8, Optional Protocol to the Convention on the Rights of Persons with Disabilities (adopted 13 December 2006) 2518 UNTS 283 (hereinafter OP-CRPD); Articles 8–9, Optional Protocol to the Convention on the Elimination of All Forms of Discrimination against Women (adopted 6 October 1999) 2131 UNTS 83 (hereinafter OP-CEDAW). Article 33, International Convention for the Protection of All Persons from Enforced Disappearance ((adopted 20 December 2006) 2716 UNTS 3) (hereinafter CED) refers to a party's 'seriously violating the provisions of this Convention'.

[134] For a more detailed (albeit still brief) overview of these procedures, see Egan, *The UN Human Rights Treaty System* (n 130) 179–219.

[135] Only the CED (n 133) does not require that the proceedings under Article 33 are confidential.

Under these procedures, the groups of independent experts (that is the monitoring bodies and not political representatives) are authorised to decide on their own initiative to initiate an urgent inquiry at any moment against any member state (that has agreed to be potentially subject to such a process), arguably without any further political interference.[136] The inquiry process allows the monitoring bodies to tackle situations of serious violations that would not be adequately addressed under the regular reporting procedures or following individual complaints. They also have the liberty to examine a broader range of issues, as they are not limited by the content of the submitted state reports or individual complaints.[137]

This kind of power has been a significant development in the international legal order, and it is still perceived as intrusive into the internal affairs of states. Neither the European Court nor the Inter-American Court has *ab initio* investigatory powers outside the cases pending before them.[138] Additionally, the *ad hoc* monitoring procedures discussed in the previous section depend on the inter-governmental bodies' decision. These treaty-based provisions as such have a deterrent effect on states parties to the respective treaties, which are arguably more eager to collaborate with the treaty bodies under the regular procedures in order to avoid being brought under the microscope of emergency inquiries. Yet the treaties are restricting the committees' powers.

First, most conventions contain an opt-out clause, allowing signatory states to declare that they do not recognise this competence.[139] Second, eventually the whole process depends heavily on states' co-operation every step of the way. While a state cannot formally block the procedure, it can delay it by disrupting

[136] Chris Ingelse, *United Nations Committee Against Torture: An Assessment* (Kluwer 2001) 79–80 (hereinafter Ingelse, *United Nations Committee Against Torture*).

[137] The information triggering the process can come from any source, including victims and non-governmental organisations. The CRPD Committee can also proactively initiate a procedure based on information gathered by itself. Article 6, OP-CRPD (n 133).

[138] The European Court of Human Rights (ECtHR) has the power to decide at any stage of a case to conduct an on-site visit or any other investigation it deems necessary. But it cannot initiate an investigation outside a pending case. Article 19(2), ECtHR, Rules of Court, 14 November 2016 (see also Rule A1(3), Annex to the rules (concerning investigations)). Interestingly, a recent empirical study revealed that 90 per cent of the cases where an on-site investigation was undertaken by either of the European Convention bodies, concerned violations of Articles 2 (killings and disappearances) or 3 (ill-treatment). Philip Leach, Costas Paraskeva, and Gordana Uzelac, 'International Human Rights & Fact-Finding; An Analysis of the Fact-Finding Missions Conducted by the European Commission and Court of Human Rights', Report by the Human Rights and Social Justice Research Institute at London Metropolitan University (2009) <http://www.academia.edu/1315823/INTERNATIONAL_HUMAN_RIGHTS_and_FACT-FINDING> (accessed 11 October 2021), 24–30.

[139] Article 28, CAT (n 131); Article 10, OP-CEDAW (n 133); Article 8, OP-CRPD (n 133); Article 13(7), OP-CRC-IC (n 133). See, for an opt-in clause, Article 10, OP-ICESCR (n 133). See Manfred Nowak and Elizabeth McArthur, *The United Nations Convention Against Torture: A Commentary* (OUP 2008) 674–84; Ingelse, *United Nations Committee Against Torture* (n 136) 163.

the investigatory process, by not communicating, denying access, and delaying its responses. The Committee against Torture has repeatedly pointed out the methods authorities have used to delay the process.[140]

Despite these shortcomings, publicly available information indicates that the committees have been increasingly initiating such inquiry procedures. The Committee against Torture had at the time of writing completed ten inquiries, the most recent in Egypt, Lebanon, Nepal, and Brazil.[141] Similarly, the Committee on the Elimination of Discrimination against Women has made public seven inquiry procedures in countries such as Canada, Kyrgyzstan, and Mali.[142] Most recently, both the Committee on the Rights of the Child and the Committee on the Rights of Persons with Disabilities have also made public their findings on grave and systematic violations committed in Chile, Spain, and the United Kingdom.[143]

3.2 The CERD's Emergency and Early-Warning Procedure

In the absence of explicit treaty provisions, other human rights monitoring organs have developed, or at least attempted to develop, procedures in order to deal with situations of serious violations of human rights. Pushed by the tragic events in the former Yugoslavia and Rwanda, a couple of UN treaty bodies attempted in the early 1990s to establish an *Exceptional Report Procedure*, by

[140] For instance, CAT Committee, 'Summary account of the results of the proceedings concerning the inquiry on Egypt', (9 July 1996) A/51/44. See Egan, *The UN Human Rights Treaty System* (n 130) 197.

[141] Respectively, CAT Committee, 'Summary Account of the Results of the Proceedings of the Inquiry on Egypt', (23 June 2017) A/72/44, 12; CAT Committee, 'Summary account of the result of the proceedings concerning the inquiry on Lebanon', (2 October 2014) A/69/44, 265; CAT Committee, 'Report on Nepal under Article 20 of the Convention adopted by the Committee against Torture under article 20 of the Convention' (5 October 2012) A/67/44, 177; CAT Committee, 'Report on Brazil produced by the Committee under Article 20 of the Convention, and reply from the Government of Brazil' (3 March 2009) CAT/C/39/2.

[142] Respectively, CEDAW Committee, 'Report of the inquiry concerning Canada of the Committee on the Elimination of Discrimination against Women under article 8 of the Optional Protocol to the Convention on the Elimination of All Forms of Discrimination against Women' (30 March 2015) CEDAW/C/OP.8/CAN/1; CEDAW Committee, 'Inquiry Concerning Kyrgyzstan under Article 8 of the Optional Protocol to the Convention on the Elimination of All Forms of Discrimination against Women' (21 September 2018) CEDAW/C/OP.8/KGZ/1; CEDAW Committee, 'Inquiry Concerning Mali under Article 8 of the Optional Protocol to the Convention on the Elimination of All Forms of Discrimination against Women' (24 December 2019) CEDAW/C/IR/MLI/1.

[143] Respectively, CRC Committee, 'Inquiry Concerning Chile under Article 13 of the Optional Protocol to the Convention on the Rights of the Child on a Communications Procedure' (6 May 2020) CRC/C/CHL/IR/1; CRPD Committee, 'Inquiry Concerning Spain Carried out by the Committee under Article 6 of the Optional Protocol to the Convention' (4 June 2018) CRPD/C/ESP/IR/1; CRPD Committee, 'Inquiry Concerning the United Kingdom of Great Britain and Northern Ireland Carried out by the Committee under Article 6 of the Optional Protocol to the Convention' (24 October 2017) CRPD/C/15/4.

inferring this power from their founding treaties.[144] Due to the limited response by the states concerned, this was scarcely used and was quickly abandoned. The Human Rights Committee used this process between 1991 and 1996 to receive reports from former Yugoslav States, but not since.[145] Similarly, CEDAW Committee had only four reports, including on the Federal Republic of Yugoslavia, Croatia, Rwanda, and the DRC (former Zaire).[146]

During the same period, in 1993, the Committee on Elimination of All Forms of Discrimination (CERD) also introduced the Emergency and Early-Warning Procedure that is still in operation.[147] The procedure was founded on the implied powers of the Committee.[148] It has no explicit basis in the treaty text.[149] None of the state parties has contested the legal validity of this process. Notably, it has proved to be prolific and active 'treaty-based' special procedure responding to serious violations of human rights. The CERD Committee has adopted multiple decisions and initiated even more discussions under this procedure.[150]

Under the Emergency and Early-Warning Procedure, the Committee will examine serious violations of the Convention at any time, irrespective of any reporting cycle. Any member state may be covered; there is no opt-out clause for state parties, as there is no treaty provision. For the rest, the procedure does not substantially differ from the above-mentioned inquiry procedures. Under this process, if the Committee decides to examine a situation outside the regular reporting cycle, it will send a letter to the government concerned

[144] Respectively, Article 40(1)(b), ICCPR (n 132); Article 18(1)(b), CEDAW (n 132). See Wouter Vandenhole, *The Procedures Before the UN Human Rights Treaty Bodies: Divergence or Convergence?* (Intersentia 2004) 170.

[145] CCPR Committee, 'Early-warning measures and urgent procedures, Working Methods' <http://www.ohchr.org/EN/HRBodies/CCPR/Pages/WorkingMethods.aspx> accessed 11 August 2021; CCPR Committee, 'The Committee's procedures in dealing with emergency situations' (1994) A/49/40 (Vol I)) 9, para 47.

[146] See Carmel Shalev, 'State Reporting and the Convention on the Elimination of All Forms of Discrimination Against Women' in Anne F Bayefsky (ed), *The UN Human Rights Treaty System in the 21st Century* (Kluwer 2000) 27, fnn 12–13.

[147] CERD Committee, 'Prevention of racial discrimination, including early warning and urgent procedures: working paper adopted by the Committee on the Elimination of Racial Discrimination' (1993) A/48/18, 125.

[148] Régis de Gouttes, 'Le rôle du comité des nations unies pour l'élimination de la discrimination raciale' (2001) 46 RTDH 567, 582–83; Régis de Gouttes, 'La Convention internationale et le Comité des nations unies sur l'élimination de la discrimination raciale' (1996) 28 RTDH 515, 526–28 (hereinafter de Gouttes, 'La Convention internationale').

[149] Theo van Boven, 'Prevention, Early-Warning and Urgent Procedures; a New Approach by the Committee on the Elimination of Racial Discrimination' in PJIM de Waart, Erik Denters, and Nico Schrijver (eds), *Reflections on International Law from the Low Countries in Honour of Paul de Waart* (Martinus Nijhoff Publishers 1998) 165.

[150] CERD decisions since 2003: CERD Committee, 'Early-Warning Measures and Urgent Procedures' <http://www.ohchr.org/EN/HRBodies/CERD/Pages/EarlyWarningProcedure.aspx> accessed 11 August 2021 (hereinafter CERD Committee, 'EWA').

asking for the submission of a special report on the matter under consideration. At the end of the process, the CERD Committee may adopt a decision, providing an account of its findings and recommendations.[151]

Still, the CERD Committee regularly optimises its mode of operation.[152] Notably, it has readjusted the types of situation subject to examination. The Emergency and Early-Warning Procedure was first established in 1993 as a response to criticisms that the Committee had remained silent in the face of the escalating situation in the Balkans.[153] The CERD Committee's rather ambitious intention was to offer its assistance in situations of ongoing conflict and uprising. Initially, the CERD Committee focused on situations in the former Yugoslavia, Rwanda, Burundi, Papua New Guinea, Chechnya, and Palestine.[154] Only occasionally did its decisions concern cases relating to indigenous peoples' matters, such as the 1998 reform of the Native Title Act in Australia.[155]

In the course of its operation, the Committee realised that it would be more effective and efficient to focus on more stable contexts and situations that had received less attention at international level as they had not yet escalated into armed conflicts. For instance, it issued an emergency statement regarding the impact of the spread of the coronavirus (COVID-19) pandemic to indigenous people in Peru.[156] Earlier, it had adopted a decision following the horrific events in Charlottesville, Virginia, of 11–12 August 2017.[157] Its approach regarding those violations that constitute serious violations of the Convention has matured alongside the international community's approach, that is, the realisation that various violations of human rights may have an irreparable impact on the victims even though it might not be evident at first glance.[158] Its members may still feel compelled to make statements or adopt decisions condemning major contemporary instances of violence, such as the situations in Libya, Syria, and Iraq (with respect to IS), but these situations do not constitute their main focus.

[151] CERD Committee, Guidelines for the Early Warning and Urgent Action Procedure (2007), 119, para 21 (hereinafter CERD Committee, 'Guidelines for EWA'). See also, Michael O'Flaherty, *Human Rights and the UN: Practice Before the Treaty Bodies* (Kluwer 2002) 89.

[152] CERD Committee, 'Guidelines for EWA' (n 151).

[153] de Gouttes, 'La Convention Internationale' (n 148) 526.

[154] CERD Committee, 'EWA' (n 150).

[155] CERD Committee, Decision 2(54) on Australia (18 March 1999) A/54/18, 6.

[156] CERD Committee, Statement 2 (2020): Peru (7 August 2020). See also general statement, CERD Committee, Statement 3 (2020) on the coronavirus (COVID-19) pandemic and its implications under the International Convention on the Elimination of All Forms of Racial Discrimination (7 August 2020).

[157] This incident involved hundreds of white nationalists, neo-Nazis, and Ku Klux Klan members clashing with counter-protesters in the streets, and a car ploughing into the crowds. CERD Committee, Decision 1(93) on United States of America (18 August 2017).

[158] On the gravity threshold, see Chapter 1.

3.3 The restrictive approach of the African Charter

From the regional mechanisms, only the African system provides for a procedure closely resembling the CERD Emergency and Early-Warning Procedure. Article 58 of the African Charter on Human and Peoples' Rights requires the African Commission on Human and Peoples' Rights to inform the Assembly of Heads of States of the African Union (and the relevant government) when it has received communications that reveal the existence of a series of serious or massive violations of human rights, and subsequently to conduct an inquiry.[159] Its wording has been inspired by the (former 1503) Complaint Procedure and the UN human rights treaties.[160] Nevertheless, the procedure is much more restrictive than that provided for the UN treaty bodies. The Commission cannot start an inquiry on its own motion; it depends upon authorisation by the Assembly of Heads of States. Also, it cannot use every source of information; its inquiries should be based on already submitted communications. Lastly, the entire process is confidential.[161]

This provision establishes a direct and official line of communication between the independent human rights monitoring body and the political organ of the regional organisation. It essentially requires the independent body to warn the political body when it concludes that political interference is necessary to resolve a situation. The Commission initially attempted to refer situations to the Assembly, particularly the situations in Burundi, the DRC (former Zaire), Malawi, Rwanda, and Sudan.[162] However, the Assembly did not respond.[163] As a result, while the Commission continues to condemn states for serious and massive violations, it does not appear to transmit the cases to the Assembly—at least formally.[164] In that sense, Article 58 seems so far to remain a dead letter.

[159] African Charter on Human and Peoples' Rights ('Banjul Charter') OAU (adopted 27 June 1981) (hereinafter ACHPR).

[160] Pierre Sob, 'Article 58' in Maurice Kampto (ed), *La Charte africaine des droits de l'homme et des peuples et le protocole y relatif portant création de la Cour africaine des droits de l'homme: Commentaire article par article* (Bruylant 2011) 1073.

[161] Articles 58(2) and 59(1), ACHPR (n 159).

[162] Frans Viljoen, 'The African System of Human Rights' in Gentian Zyberi and Kevin Mason (eds), *An institutional approach to the responsibility to protect* (CUP 2013) 497 (hereinafter Viljoen, 'The African System'); Oji Umozurike, *The African Charter on Human and Peoples' Rights* (Martinus Nijhoff Publishers 1997) 77 (hereinafter Umozurike, *The African Charter*) .

[163] Notably, African Commission on Human and Peoples' Rights (AComHPR), *Lawyers Committee for Human Rights v Zaire*, Comm 47/90, 7th ACHPR AAR Annex IX (1993–1994). See further, Viljoen, 'The African System' (n 162) 497; Umozurike, *The African Charter* (n 162) 77.

[164] See AComHPR, *Krishna Achuthan (on behalf of Aleke Banda), Amnesty International (on behalf of Orton and Vera Chirwa) v Malawi*, Comm Nos 64/92, 68/92, and 78/92, Decision on Merits (22 March 1995); AComHPR, *Organisation Mondiale Contre la Torture and Association Internationale des Juristes Democrates) Commission Internationale des Juristes (CIJ), Union Interafricaine des Droits de*

Nonetheless, more recently, Article 58 was silently amended by Article 5(1)(a) of the Protocol to the Banjul Charter, which allows the Commission to submit cases that reveal the existence of a series of serious or massive violations of human rights to the African Court, while retaining the option to refer a situation to a political body.[165] With this amendment, judicial consideration replaced political decision-making.[166] Subsequently, the Commission submitted an application against Libya in 2011. The Court immediately responded and decided to adopt provisional measures.[167] Unfortunately, there is no indication that 'any Libyan government' tried to adopt those measures.[168]

The inclusion of serious violations of human rights in treaty provisions constitutes an official form of recognition by member states. States, by designing and signing these provisions, have delegated the decision to initiate urgent inquiries regarding serious violations of human rights to permanent monitoring bodies composed of independent experts. Yet serious violations of human rights have been having an impact at the national level, too, where states are increasingly, with pressure from and the assistance of the international community, creating hybrid monitoring mechanisms.

4. The national monitoring mechanisms

In parallel with international inquiry and monitoring bodies, the last few years have also seen the development of special *ad hoc* monitoring mechanisms at the domestic level, as a result of and in response to serious violations of human rights—namely, truth and reconciliation commissions and national commissions of inquiry. Parallels can be drawn between the functions of various international bodies and those of national monitoring mechanisms, therefore

l'homme v Rwanda, Comm 27/89, 46/91, 49/91, 99/93, Decision on Merits, October 2006, 10th ACHPR AAR Annex X (1996–1997). In the case of Sudan, the Commission concluded that there was no need for a referral as the Assembly was already involved in the matter: AComHPR, *Sudan Human Rights Organisation & Centre on Housing Rights and Evictions (COHRE) v Sudan*, Comm 279/03-296/05, Decision on Merits, 27 May 2009.

[165] Protocol to the African Charter on Human and Peoples' Rights on the Establishment of the African Court on Human and Peoples' Rights (adopted 10 June 1998); Articles 84(2) and 118, Rules of Procedure of the African Commission on Human and Peoples' Rights (2010).

[166] Viljoen, 'The African System' (n 162) 504, 506.

[167] ACtHPR, *African Commission on Human and Peoples' Rights v Great Socialist People's Libyan Arab Jamahiriya*, App No 04/2011, Order for Provisional Measures, 15 March 2011.

[168] ACtHPR, *African Commission on Human and Peoples' Rights v Great Socialist People's Libyan Arab Jamahiriya*, App No 04/2011, Order, 15 March 2013. The African Court also issued a judgment on a subsequent application: ACtHPR, *African Commission on Human and Peoples' Rights v Libya*, App No 02/2013, 3 June 2013.

giving them a place in the special regime described therein.[169] They are all primarily established as a response to events where serious violations of human rights occurred, but they also increasingly present international characteristics, in an attempt to uphold international standards.[170] Ultimately, their establishment is becoming a matter of international concern, and is even used as a piece of the puzzle in peace negotiations. For example, the Commissions in Sierra Leone and Liberia were a result of agreements reached during peace negotiations.[171] In East Timor, it was the United Nations that established the Truth and Reconciliation Commission.[172]

The term 'truth and reconciliation commissions' is used here to describe all those bodies comprised of independent experts, established temporarily, primarily by governments, with or without the involvement of international actors.[173] They are established as a response to a violent past, always including serious violations of human rights, such as massacres, extrajudicial killings, enforced disappearances, torture practices, or most often a combination of all of these. The South African Commission resulted from the apartheid regime; the Chilean Commissions were established following the fall of the brutal Pinochet dictatorship; the Burundian Commission came into being to face acts of violence committed during the cyclical conflict that devastated the country from the date of independence on 1 July 1962; and so on.[174]

Most of the truth and reconciliation commissions have been explicitly authorised to investigate and record instances or patterns of gross violations of human rights.[175] The National Commission for Truth and Reconciliation in Chile was mandated 'to clarify in a comprehensive manner the truth about the most serious human rights violations committed in recent years' in Chile,[176]

169 'Report of the Special Rapporteur on the promotion of truth, justice, reparation and guarantees of non-recurrence, Pablo de Greiff' (28 August 2013) A/HRC/24/42, para 37 (hereinafter 'Report on the promotion of truth ...' (2013)).

170 Cheryl Lawther, 'Transitional Justice and Truth Commissions' in Cheryl Lawther, Luke Moffett, and Dov Jacobs (eds), *Research Handbook on Transitional Justice* (Edward Elgar 2017) (hereinafter Lawther, 'Transitional Justice').

171 Eric Brahm, 'Judging Truth: The Contributions of Truth Commissions in Post-Conflict Environments' in Noha Shawki and Michaelene Cox (eds), *Negotiating Sovereignty and Human Rights; Actors and Issues in Contemporary Human Rights Politics* (Ashgate 2009) 131.

172 UN Transitional Administration in East Timor (UNTAET), Regulation 2001/10 on the Establishment of a Commission for Reception Truth and Reconciliation in East Timor, (13 July 2001) UNTAET/REG/2001/10.

173 There is no agreed definition of truth and reconciliation commissions. Most authors focus on common features that the various bodies share. See Valentina Cadelo, 'Truth and Reconciliation Commissions' in Niccolò Pons and Drazan Djukic (eds), *Companion of International Humanitarian Law: Lexicon* (Brill 2018) 701; Hayner, *Unspeakable Truths* (n 79) 10–13.

174 See Hayner, *Unspeakable Truths* (n 79) 45–74.

175 'Report on the promotion of truth ...' (2013) (n 169) para 35.

176 Article 1, Supreme Decree No 355, Diario Oficial (25 April 1990).

while the Truth and Reconciliation Commission in South Africa was asked to build an 'as complete a picture as possible of the nature, causes and extent of gross violations of human rights'.[177] The South African law's phrasing recurred in the mandates of many subsequent commissions. Among the more recent examples is the Truth and Reconciliation Commission in Nepal, which was mandated to investigate 'gross violations of human rights'.[178]

Less frequently, truth commissions have been tasked with clarifying the facts regarding specific serious violations, such as disappeared persons.[179] The few commissions that appear to have even broader mandates—tasked with reporting on any human right violation and abuse committed during a specific period—*de facto* have eventually focused on certain categories of the most serious violations. For instance, the Truth Commission in El Salvador received a general mandate, which was subsequently interpreted as being to consider a limited number of exemplary cases of disappearance, extrajudicial killing, and massacre.[180]

The primary purpose of truth and reconciliation commissions is to seek the truth in the broader sense, and in some cases to reconcile societies emerging from a violent past.[181] They have not been created just to document past events, but also to identify the root causes, the specific circumstances, and to give a voice to the victims. With minor variations, truth and reconciliation commissions have been established in Argentina, El Salvador, South Africa, East Timor, Liberia, Kenya, Sierra Leone, and elsewhere, to investigate and record serious violations of human rights.[182] Two of the most recent examples are to be found in Nepal[183] and Tunisia.[184] Very few commissions have actually been given additional tasks, such as providing amnesties or distributing reparations.[185] Increasingly, though, such commissions are also asked to facilitate the

[177] Article 3(1)(a), South African Promotion of National Unity and Reconciliation Act 1995, Act 34 (26 July 1995) <https://www.justice.gov.za/legislation/acts/1995-034.pdf> accessed 11 August 2021.

[178] Enforced Disappearances Enquiry, Truth and Reconciliation Commission Act 2071, Nepal (11 May 2014) (hereinafter Nepal Act 2014)

[179] National Commission on the Disappeared (Comisión Nacional sobre la Desaparición de Personas, CONADEP) in Argentina, Decree/Decreto 187/83 (15 December 1983).

[180] 'Report on the promotion of truth . . .' (2013) (n 169) para 35. Similarly, Articles 5(a), 5(c), and 6(a), part II, Truth, Justice and Reconciliation Commission Act No 6 of 2008 of Kenya (28 November 2008).

[181] Lawther, 'Transitional Justice' (n 170).

[182] For a schematic overview of truth commissions, see Priscilla B Hayner, 'Truth Commissions: A Schematic Overview' (2006) 88 IRRC 295, 295–310.

[183] 'Truth and Reconciliation Commission, Nepal' <http://www.trc.gov.np/> accessed 21 August 2021.

[184] 'Truth and Dignity Commission of Tunisia' <http://www.ivd.tn/fr/> accessed 13 April 2017.

[185] 'Report on the promotion of truth . . .' (2013) (n 169) paras 37–38. See also Hayner, *Unspeakable Truths* (n 79) 265–67.

prosecution of international crimes.[186] Notably, in Tunisia, the Commission has been collecting evidence and forwarding cases to the Specialised Criminal Chambers.[187]

In parallel, states have also gradually introduced other *ad hoc* inquiry procedures at the domestic level (upholding international standards) as a response to serious violations of human rights. Notably, the Governments of Kyrgyzstan[188] and Bahrain[189], following persistent civil society demands, established national commissions of inquiry to report on the alleged serious violations of human rights that were committed during extremely violent events at a specific moment. Nepal, following the brutal events that occurred during the Civil War that began in 1996, established both a Truth and Reconciliation Commission and a Commission of Inquiry into Disappearances.[190]

There are also additional initiatives that advocate inquiry mechanisms to examine situations that occurred further in the past, often referred to as historical injustices or past mass crimes. New commissions have been established in Australia, Canada, Germany, New Zealand, and the United States to address past injustices. In 2006, for instance, a truth and reconciliation commission was established in Canada to investigate discriminatory policies separating Native American children from their families.[191] Australia has also held a National Inquiry into the Separation of Aboriginal and Torres Strait Islander Children from Their Families.[192] The Inter-American Court even ordered the establishment of a national commission to track the young people who

[186] See Aaron Fichtelberg, 'Transitional Justice and the End of Impunity: Hybrid Tribunals' in Cheryl Lawther, Luke Moffett, and Dov Jacobs (eds), *Research Handbook on Transitional Justice* (Edward Elgar 2017).

[187] Truth and Dignity Commission of Tunisia, 'The Final Comprehensive Report, Executive Summary' (May 2019) <http://www.ivd.tn/rapport/doc/TDC_executive_summary_report.pdf> accessed 11 October 2021.

[188] The Kyrgyzstan Inquiry Commission was mandated to investigate the facts and circumstances relevant to incidents that took place in southern Kyrgyzstan in June 2010, to qualify the violations and crimes under international law, and to determine responsibilities and make recommendations, particularly on accountability measures. 'Report of the Independent International Commission of Inquiry into the Events in Southern Kyrgyzstan in June 2010, Kyrgyzstant Inquiry Commission (KIC)' (2011) <https://reliefweb.int/sites/reliefweb.int/files/resources/Full_Report_490.pdf> accessed 11 August 2021.

[189] The Bahrain Independent Commission of Inquiry was established on 29 June 2011 pursuant to Royal Order No 28 by His Majesty, Hamad bin Isa Al Khalifa. The Commission was tasked with looking into the incidents that occurred during the period of unrest in Bahrain in February and March 2011, and the consequences of these events. 'Report of the Bahrain Independent Commission of Inquiry' (2011) <http://www.bici.org.bh/BICIreportEN.pdf> accessed 11 August 2021.

[190] See Nepal Act 2014 (n 178); 'Truth and Reconciliation Commission, Nepal' (n 183); 'Commission of Investigation on Enforced Disappeared Persons, Nepal' <https://ciedp.gov.np/en/home/> accessed 11 August 2021.

[191] See 'Report on the promotion of truth ...' (2013) (n 169) 12, fn 44.

[192] ibid.

disappeared when they were children during the armed conflict in El Salvador, as a remedial reward.[193]

One of the key features of these inquiry commissions was arguably the desire of the governments concerned to demonstrate compliance with international standards and obligations. They were equipped with internationally renowned human rights experts, with long experience in human rights fact-finding, as an assurance of their independence and impartiality.[194] Their terms of reference, as well as their final reports, were made public. To be sure, the whole process raises questions regarding the level of control of these bodies by national governments and the lack of any assurances that any action will be taken after a report is released. The fact, though, that these bodies were established to inquire into serious violations of human rights that occurred during a specific incident, and that governments felt compelled to establish such bodies to avoid international scrutiny, is an important indication that, today, inquiries into serious violations of human rights have become an almost standard process.

5. A multilateral network of monitoring responses

All these mechanisms and procedures—permanent or temporary, treaty-based or *ad hoc*, political or independent—create a network, at the centre of which is the occurrence of serious violations of human rights. One might imagine spiders' webs, which are complex nets of strong dragline threads (frame, spokes) radiating out from the centre, and elastic, sticky catching threads spiralling into the centre. This web is less symmetrical, but it continually develops, introducing new mechanisms and procedures. They all constitute monitoring responses to serious violations of human rights, and as such they form part of and contribute to the furtherance of the progressively developing special regime around such violations.

The international community lacks general organisation and, as a result, some forms of organisation are designed to protect certain interests without the power to make binding decisions.[195] Each mechanism and procedure is evidence of the position of serious violations of human rights in the international

[193] IACtHR, *Serrano-Cruz Sisters v El Salvador* (Preliminary objections), 23 November 2004, para 183.

[194] The Bahrain Commission of Inquiry was composed of international law experts, including Mahmoud Cherif Bassiouni and Nigel Rodley. The President of the Kyrgyzstan Inquiry Commission was Kimmo Kiljunen, Special Representative for Central Asia, OSCE Parliamentary Assembly.

[195] Giorgio Gaja, 'The Protection of General Interests in the International Community: General Course on Public International Law' (2013) 364 RCADI 9, 32–33.

legal order. Inter-governmental processes and decision-making procedures, such as the UN General Assembly and the UN Human Rights Council, demonstrate the international attention to such situations and constitute a direct recognition of their position in the international community. Ultimately it is states that decided to introduce serious violations of human rights as a separate category of human rights violations in several legally-binding human rights treaties. Equally, the proliferation of *ad hoc* monitoring and inquiry mechanisms at both the international and the national levels, in itself reinforces their position in the international legal order as a category of human rights violations that mobilises certain special procedures.

First, these monitoring procedures and mechanisms are often the first step of the formal mobilisation of the international community in response to serious violations of human rights. The resolutions or independent reports highlighting and condemning specific instances of serious violations of human rights are instrumental in raising awareness regarding such violations. As a matter of fact, they constitute a public acknowledgment of certain events, which contributes to the establishment of a public record of past occurrences. Officially formed by inter-governmental organs or governments directly, *ad hoc* monitoring and inquiry mechanisms are then considered authoritative sources, providing an account of instances of serious violations of human rights.

Second, ultimately, today, these procedures and mechanisms together build the most detailed map of past *serious* violations of human rights that ever existed in international legal history—an official public record of serious violations of human rights. Despite their differences in nature, formality, and legal standing, all these proclamations carry a degree of legitimacy and authority, each in their own right—even if they do not constitute conclusive determinations of a factual situation or a judicial legal assessment. They are not detailed records of each serious violation of human rights that occurred in a given situation, neither are they always accurate. They are, rather, rough sketches of serious violations of human rights that occurred in a particular country or region during a particular (long or short) period of time. Yet they are still so far the most complete record, being formally adopted directly by authoritative organs, that is widely visible and accessible.

Third, the resolutions adopted by inter-governmental organisations to an extent push states towards compliance with international standards, even if they have only a recommendatory power and lack enforcement powers. The country-specific resolutions often call on the states concerned to comply with their obligations and to take steps to remedy the situation. They may also subject a state to further international scrutiny, through *ad hoc* inquiries and monitoring processes. These processes, as well as the initiation of an urgent procedure by a human rights treaty body, constitute a form of public shaming of governments. The monitoring bodies are able to use the treaty-based mechanisms as leverage to ensure that governments will collaborate with them through the regular monitoring procedures.

Fourth, this multilateral network of monitoring responses may have emerged in an unco-ordinated and empirical manner. There is no 'grand design' to create a regime around serious violations of human rights.[196] Yet they occasionally function in a loosely co-ordinated manner. This progressive development has been evident, for instance, with regard to the situation in North Korea—a situation that was ignored for decades due to political considerations.[197] The Commission on Human Rights adopted the first resolution in 2003, and a year later it decided to appoint a Special Rapporteur to monitor and report on the situation.[198] Shortly after, in 2005, the UN General Assembly began to adopt annual resolutions, expressing its concern regarding the commission of serious violations of human rights.[199] In 2013, the UN Human Rights Council established a Commission of Inquiry to investigate such violations.[200] By 2015, for the first time, North Korea was included on the human rights agenda of the UN Security Council. North Korea has been on its agenda for many years for nuclear weapons possession and disarmament, but not for the human rights situation.[201]

Fifth, and in consequence of whether they are created to actively seek evidence or to receive information, the monitoring mechanisms and procedures have to decide whether the information is relevant and make legal determinations. Their assessment of a specific situation may subsequently influence judicial findings, political decision-making processes, and public opinion.[202] Even the determinations of political bodies are used as an indicator for other decisions. For example, in arms control, the European Union refers to these

196 Phrase borrowed from Gutter's article on UN Human Rights Council Special Procedures. Gutter, 'Special Procedures' (n 5) 98.

197 The author is mindful of the primarily political complications that surround any response to the human rights violations committed by North Korea.

198 ComHR Res 2004/13 (2004) (n 118), para 5; Situation of human rights in the DPRK, ComHR Res 2003/10 (16 April 2003).

199 UNGA Res 60/173 (2005) (n 51).

200 UNHRC Res 22/13 (2013) (n 117) para 4.

201 UNSC, 7575th meeting (10 December 2015) S/PV.7575.

202 Dapo Akande and Hannah Tonkin, 'International Commissions of Inquiry: A New Form of Adjudication?' <https://www.ejiltalk.org/international-commissions-of-inquiry-a-new-form-of-adjudication/> accessed 12 August 2021.

decisions when assessing whether serious violations have occurred and, as a result, whether they should ban an arms export.

Lastly, while none of these resolutions, reports, or recommendations are formally binding in the strict sense, they are not devoid of any legal effect. They still have a strong normative impact and a cumulative normative effect.[203] *Ad hoc* monitoring and inquiry mechanisms, despite their temporary character, are considered today to form part of the regular arsenal to address instances of serious violations of human rights.[204] Similarly, truth and reconciliation commissions have today become 'an habitual response to ... the legacies of atrocities'.[205] The practice of special procedures constantly enriches the international community's understanding of this category of violations and creates a constantly multiplying 'jurisprudence' around them.[206] The continued recourse to expressions of gravity enhances the systematisation and progressive solidification of serious violations of human rights as a separate category of human rights violations and of their legal consequences.[207] The various declaratory processes build, through repetition and recurrent recourse, a very persuasive precedent that may eventually lead to the formation of customary law.[208] Notably, a substantive 'side-effect' has been that the continuous recourse to inquiry and fact-finding mechanisms advances and reinforces the right of victims to the truth in cases of serious violations of human rights and the procedural obligations that derive from them.[209]

In any event, these procedures and mechanisms do not stand alone in the international legal system. Serious violations of human rights have further been included within procedures that are found at the heart of the international legal order—that is, the enforcement mechanisms and the secondary obligations of

[203] On the legal effect of international organs' decisions, see Boyle and Chinkin, *The Making of International Law* (n 13) 211ff; Higgins, *The Development of International Law* (n 2).

[204] UNHRC, Code of Conduct for Special Procedures (n 84); OHCHR, Guidance and Practice (n 84).

[205] 'Report on the promotion of truth ...' (2013) (n 169) para 27.

[206] Boyle and Chinkin, *The Making of International Law* (n 13) 156; de Frouville, 'Building a Universal System' (n 32) 266.

[207] Even the consistent use of gravity qualifiers—gross, serious, grave, and others—reinforces its regularisation and enhances its descriptive value. On the power of language in law making, see Stephane Beaulac, *The Power of Language in the Making of International Law: The Word Sovereignty in Bodin and Vattel and the Myth of Westphalia* (Brill/Nijhoff, 2004); W Michael Reisman, 'International Lawmaking: A Process of Communication' (1981) 75 ASILP 101.

[208] On the normative value of UN resolutions, see ICJ, *Legal Consequences of the Construction of a Wall in the Occupied Palestinian Territory*, Advisory Opinion, 9 July 2004, para 86; ICJ, *Legality of the Threat or Use of Nuclear Weapons*, Advisory Opinion, 8 July 1996, para 70.

[209] See Right to the truth, UNHRC Res 9/11 (18 September 2008); Basic Principles and Guidelines on the Right to a Remedy and Reparation for Victims of Gross Violations of International Human Rights Law and Serious Violations of International Humanitarian Law, UNGA Res 60/147 (16 December 2005) Annex, para 22(b). See Chapter 4.

the wrongdoing state. First, the whole enforcement mechanism seems to have advanced to incorporate serious violations of human rights, within and beyond the UN system (Chapter 3). Second, serious violations of human rights have gradually influenced the incidence of the forms of secondary obligations of the wrongdoing state (Chapter 4).

3
The enforcement component

As discussed in Chapter 2, serious violations of human rights have become a matter of international concern, around which a multi-layered, complex network of monitoring and inquiry mechanisms and procedures has been built comprising the monitoring component of the special regime. Yet these procedures and mechanisms do not stand alone. They have been gradually complemented by the second operational component—enforcement. It primarily aims to sanction those responsible for serious violations of human rights and force them to cease committing such violations.

'Enforcement', within the special regime around serious violations of human rights, describes all different forms of measures of constraint taken at the international level as a response to serious violations of human rights, by forcible and other coercive means. On the one hand, the UN Security Council has been authorising and recommending measures to be taken to ensure the cessation of serious violations of human rights in a specific context. On the other hand, 'third' states have been increasingly adopting countermeasures even in the absence of any direct injury or authorisation by the Security Council. The enforcement component of the special regime on serious violations of human rights has grown within both the UN sanctions regime and the inter-state countermeasures framework.

These two types of measures exhibit certain 'irreconcilable' differences that set them apart—not the least that the one is regulated by general public international law and the law of state responsibility, while the UN Charter regulates the other.[1] Nonetheless, under both frameworks, measures are increasingly taken as a response to the same unlawful acts, that is, serious violations of human rights. These unlawful acts are becoming one of the thresholds in the international legal order beyond which the international community, both within and outside the auspices of the UN, has been imposing coercive

[1] Not without a debate, the ILC separated the UN collective security system from the state responsibility regime. See Article 59, ILC, Articles on Responsibility of States for Internationally Wrongful Acts, UNGA Res 56/83 (12 December 2001) (hereinafter ARSIWA). See Maurizio Arcari, 'Responsabilité de l'État pour violations graves du droit international et système de securité collective des Nations Unies' (2005) 21 Anuario de Derecho Internacional 415, 424, 434.

Serious Violations of Human Rights. Ilia Siatitsa, Oxford University Press. © Ilia Siatitsa 2022.
DOI: 10.1093/oso/9780192863041.003.0004

measures to force those responsible to cease such breaches. They have the same objective—to enforce compliance with international law by coercing the wrongdoers to cease these violations. They usually do not intend to punish those responsible or remedy the victims.[2] In such instances, the UN Security Council functions not only as a guarantor of international peace and security but also as an enforcer of international law,[3] while the states that unilaterally adopt third-party countermeasures become (so to speak) representatives of the international community.[4]

1. 'Threat to the peace' and serious violations of human rights

For the first four decades of its existence, the UN Security Council 'did its best to avoid taking up human rights issues'.[5] However, today, it has recognised respect for human rights and fundamental freedoms to form part of the foundations of international peace and security.[6] This transformation occurred slowly and gradually.[7] The first time the Council established a direct link between human rights and the maintenance of the peace was after the Iraqi invasion of Kuwait in 1991,[8] to be repeated shortly afterwards in its response to the conflicts in the former Yugoslavia[9] and Rwanda.[10]

[2] Linos-Alexander Sicilianos, 'Sanctions institutionnelles et contre-mesures: Tendances recentes' in Laura Picchio Forlati and Linos-Alexander Sicilianos (eds), *Economic Sanctions in International Law* (The Centre for Studies and Research in International Law and International Relations, The Hague Academy of International Law, 2004) 13–16 (hereinafter Sicilianos, 'Sanctions institutionnelles'). For an opposing view supporting the penal character of Security Council sanctions, see Robert Jennings and Arthur Watts (eds), *Oppenheim's International Law*, Vol 1: *Peace* (9th edn Longman 1992) 536.

[3] On the Council's police function, see Vera Gowlland-Debbas, 'The Security Council as Enforcer of Human Rights' in Bardo Fassbender (ed), *Securing Human Rights? Achievements and Challenges of the UN Security Council* (OUP 2011) 39–41 (hereinafter 'Gowlland-Debbas, 'The Security Council as Enforcer'); Martti Koskenniemi, 'The Police in the Temple Order, Justice and the UN: A Dialectical View' (1995) 6 EJIL 325 337–39.

[4] Georges Scelle, *Précis de droit des gens, principes et systématique*, Vol I (Dalloz 1932) 43, 54–56, and 217.

[5] Sydney Bailey, *The UN Security Council and Human Rights* (Macmillan 1994) x.

[6] UN Secretary-General, 'In larger freedom: towards development, security and human rights for all', Report (21 March 2005) para 143. See also Bertrand Ramcharan, *The Security Council and the Protection of Human Rights* (Martinus Nijhoff Publishers 2002), 18 (hereinafter Ramcharan, *The Security Council*).

[7] For an overview of this evolution, see Bruno Stagno Ugarte and Jared Genser, 'Evolution of the Security Council's Engagement on Human Rights' in Bruno Stagno Ugarte and Jared Genser (eds), *The United Nations Security Council in the Age of Human Rights* (CUP 2014) 7–14.

[8] Iraq, UNSC Res 688 (5 April 1991) Preamble, para 3, repeated in operative para 1 (hereinafter UNSC Res 688 (1991)).

[9] Notably, Bosnia and Herzegovina, UNSC Res 787 (16 November 1992) Preamble, para 9.

[10] Notably, UN Assistance Mission for Rwanda, UNSC Res 929 (22 June 1994) Preamble, paras 8–10 (hereinafter UNSC Res 929 (1994)).

Human rights issues now regularly appear across the UN Security Council's agenda and activities. For example, the Council orders peacekeepers to refrain from committing any human rights violations, not only serious ones.[11] However, the Council imposes sanctions and other measures under Chapter VII of the UN Charter only for serious violations of human rights—not any human rights violation.[12] Only serious violations of human rights turn the key of 'threat to the peace' that opens the door to the UN collective security system. This premise is confirmed on multiple levels: factually, when examining the situations under consideration; linguistically, from the terminology used in Chapter VII resolutions; and teleologically, with regard to the Council's mandate.

1.1 Factoring gravity in 'threat to the peace' determinations

1.1.1 Situations under Chapter VII of the UN Charter

All the Chapter VII situations where the occurrence of human rights violations has been raised as a matter of concern involve extreme levels of arbitrary loss of life and other serious violations of human rights. The UN Security Council has reacted to horrific events in Burundi, the Central African Republic (CAR), Côte d'Ivoire, the Democratic Republic of the Congo (DRC), Georgia, Iraq, Kosovo, Liberia, Libya, Mali, Rwanda, Somalia, Sudan, Syria, the former Yugoslavia, and Yemen, at various times and on different occasions.[13] It is impossible to overlook the widespread and systematic commission of atrocities in these countries at the particular moments in their history when the Security Council acted upon Chapter VII of the UN Charter.

[11] Yet the responsibility of the peacekeepers for human rights violations was raised as a result of serious violations of human rights committed by them. Among the most recent contributions, see Moritz P Moelle, *The International Responsibility of International Organisations: Cooperation in Peacekeeping Operations* (CUP 2017).

[12] Article 39, Charter of the United Nations, San Francisco (adopted 26 June 1945) 1 UNTS XVI (hereinafter UN Charter).

[13] Among others, Reports of the Secretary-General on the Sudan and South Sudan, UNSC Res 2428 (13 July 2018) para 14(d) (hereinafter UNSC Res 2428 (2018)); The situation concerning the DRC, UNSC Res 2409 (27 March 2018) para 12 (hereinafter UNSC Res 2409 (2018)); Mali, UNSC Res 2295 (29 June 2016); Burundi, UNSC Res 2303 (29 July 2016); Middle East (Syria), UNSC Res 2139 (22 February 2014); Somalia, UNSC Res 2067 (18 September 2012) (hereinafter UNSC Res 2067 (2012)); Middle East (Yemen), UNSC Res 2014 (21 October 2011); Côte d'Ivoire, UNSC Res 1975 (30 March 2011) (hereinafter UNSC Res 1975 (2011)); Libya, UNSC Res 1970 (26 February 2011) (hereinafter UNSC Res 1970 (2011)); Liberia, UNSC Res 1509 (19 September 2003); DRC, UNSC Res 1493 (28 July 2003); Kosovo (FRY), UNSC Res 1199 (23 September 1998) (UNSC Res 1199 (1998)); Georgia, UNSC Res 1036 (12 January 1996); Commission of Experts to examine violations of international humanitarian law committed in Rwanda, UNSC Res 935 (1 July 1994) (hereinafter UNSC Res 935 (1994)); Socialist Federal Republic of Yugoslavia, UNSC Res 713 (25 September 1991) (hereinafter UNSC Res 713 (1991)).

In 2013, the Security Council imposed the sanctions regime in the CAR. By that time, the civil war in the country had already escalated, giving rise to a growing cycle of revenge killings in a war between the government in power, the predominantly Muslim Seleka rebels, and the 'anti-balaka' (a group harbouring hatred towards Muslims).[14] Thousands had been fleeing the areas of conflict, seeking refuge within and outside the country.[15]

Similarly, in South Sudan, the Security Council imposed sanctions in 2015 while condemning past and ongoing human rights violations and abuses, including:

> targeted killings of civilians, ethnically-targeted violence, extrajudicial killings, rape, and other forms of sexual and gender-based violence, recruitment and use of children in armed conflict, abductions, enforced disappearances, arbitrary arrests and detention, violence aimed at spreading terror among the civilian population, and attacks on schools, places of worship and hospitals, as well as United Nations and associated peacekeeping personnel and objects, by all parties ...[16]

In fact, most of the situations examined before the Security Council could be interpreted as having reached the contextual threshold for crimes against humanity—that is 'acts committed as part of a widespread or systematic attack against any civilian population'.[17] Indeed, the Security Council has on several occasions condemned crimes against humanity and other international crimes committed in a specific situation.[18] Also, it regularly calls on governments to bring to justice the perpetrators of international crimes.[19] However, the situations where human rights violations of a certain gravity occurred do not necessarily need to have reached the threshold for crimes against humanity threshold to trigger Chapter VII. To put it differently, crimes against humanity should not be the designated threshold. 'Crimes against humanity' is a much

[14] CAR, UNSC Res 2127 (5 December 2013) (hereinafter UNSC Res 2127 (2013)).

[15] ibid Preamble, paras 4–5. Also CAR, UNSC Res 2134 (28 January 2014) paras 5–6 (hereinafter UNSC Res 2134 (2014)).

[16] Reports of the Secretary-General on the Sudan and South Sudan, UNSC Res 2206 (3 March 2015) Preamble, para 4 (hereinafter UNSC Res 2206 (2015)). Also Reports of the Secretary-General on the Sudan and South Sudan, UNSC Res 2290 (31 May 2016) Preamble, para 7 (hereinafter UNSC Res 2290 (2016)).

[17] Article 7, Rome Statute of the International Criminal Court (adopted 17 July 1998) 2187 UNTS 3 (hereinafter ICC Statute).

[18] Notably, Libya, UNSC Res 1973 (17 March 2011) Preamble, para 7 (hereinafter UNSC Res 1973 (2011)); UNSC Res 2206 (2015) Preamble, para 20.

[19] Among others, The situation in Mali, UNSC Res 2531 (29 June 2020) para 28(e)(i); DRC, UNSC Res 1991 (28 June 2011) para 19.

more restrictive legal term, which most importantly gives rise to individual criminal responsibility. It would be better for the Council to refrain from making legal determinations regarding individual criminal responsibility. If the Council were to rely on legal responsibility in order to take enforcement action, it would be more apt to focus on questions of state responsibility.[20]

1.1.2 The language in Chapter VII resolutions

In many of the Chapter VII resolutions adopted with regard to these situations, the Security Council expressly condemns serious violations of human rights, underlining the aggravated character of the violations by using adjectives such as serious, gross, grave, systematic, and/or widespread.[21]

Since the 1990s, but particularly over the last ten years, the Security Council has explicitly condemned a wide range of acts as serious violations of human rights: mass killings; ethnic cleansing; summary executions; extrajudicial killings; the killing and maiming of children; enforced disappearances; torture; rape and all forms of sexual and gender-based violence; the recruitment, training, and use of child soldiers; other grave violations against children; arbitrary arrests and abductions; arbitrary detention; forcible expulsion; displacement; deportations; forced labour; and others.[22]

It has also occasionally condemned as such the repression of peaceful demonstrations, the impeding of food and medical supplies, the devastation and looting of property, and discrimination against women and girls.[23] Apart from the specific violations, the Security Council also often highlights the vulnerability of certain groups, including broader categories such as children, refugees, and internally displaced people, as well as women and girls, often found in vulnerable positions.[24]

[20] For a critique of Security Council practice for reducing its references to state accountability, see Laurel E Fletcher, 'A Wolf in Sheep's Clothing: Transitional Justice and the Effacement of State Accountability for International Crimes' (2015) 39 FILJ 447, 517.

[21] Notably, UNSC Res 2409 (2018) (n 13) para 9; UNSC Res 2134 (2014) (n 15) para 38; DRC, UNSC Res 2078 (28 November 2012) para 10 (hereinafter UNSC Res 2078 (2012)); Sudan, UNSC Res 2046 (2 May 2012) para 7; Côte d'Ivoire, UNSC Res 2000 (27 July 2011) Preamble, para 13; The Great Lakes Region, UNSC Res 1653 (27 January 2006); DRC, UNSC Res 1468 (20 March 2003); Afghanistan, UNSC Res 1378 (14 November 2001).

[22] The list will differ depending on the situation, notably UNSC Res 2409 (2018) (n 13) para 9; UNSC Res 2078 (2012) (n 21) para 4(e); Haiti, UNSC Res 2070 (12 October 2012) para 18; DRC, UNSC Res 2053 (27 June 2012) Preamble, para 10.

[23] See further Daphna Shraga, 'The Security Council and Human Rights—From Discretion to Promote to Obligation to Protect' in Bardo Fassbender (ed), *Securing Human Rights?: Achievements and Challenges of the UN Security Council* (OUP 2011) 19 (hereinafter Shraga, 'The Security Council and Human Rights').

[24] Among others, Somalia, UNSC Res 2182 (24 October 2014) Preamble, para 14; Haiti, UNSC Res 2180 (14 October 2014) para 20; UNSC Res 2134 (2014) (n 15) Preamble, para 5; Somalia, UNSC Res 2102 (2 May 2013) Preamble, para 9; UNSC Res 2067 (2012) (n 13) para 18; UNSC Res 1975 (2011) (n 13) para 5.

Undoubtedly, the Security Council's practice cannot be taken as definitive. Indeed, the Security Council neither uses one expression systematically, nor chooses the situations to target on the basis of a strict definition of serious violations of human rights.[25] It will equally condemn all human rights violations without using qualifiers as to their gravity—albeit they do factually amount to serious violations of human rights.[26] Any qualification and enumeration of violations can be construed as indicative and descriptive to underline the grave nature of the situation, which then justifies the Council's intervention. However, this does not negate the significance of its practice altogether. The Council's practice reflects a loose factual and highly contextualised approach. The occasional lack of linguistic consistency is remedied by the evidence on the ground, as well as the role of the Security Council in the UN collective security system.[27]

1.1.3 The role of the Security Council

The UN Security Council is the UN's main political organ, whose primary function is to maintain international peace and security.[28] Vested with the power to respond to any situation that appears to destabilise the world order, its agenda is not limited to human rights issues. The primary responsibility to ensure full respect for all human rights and protection from their abuse remains with each state, while the task of promoting and encouraging respect for human rights is reserved to the other UN organs, such as the General Assembly and the Human Rights Council.[29] The Security Council will and should interfere only when violations are gross, extensive, and persistent.[30] Upon deciding to intervene, the Council often underlines 'the unique character of the … situation … and … its deteriorating, complex and extraordinary nature, requiring an immediate and exceptional response'.[31]

[25] Joanna Weschler, 'Acting on Human Rights' in Sebastian von Einsiedel, David M Malone, and Bruno Stagno Ugarte (eds), *The UN Security Council in the 21st Century* (Lynne Rienner Publishers 2015) 274 (hereinafter Weschler, 'Acting on Human Rights').

[26] Among others, Reports of the Secretary-General on the Sudan and South Sudan, UNSC Res 2155 (27 May 2014) Preamble, para 5; CAR, UNSC Res 2149 (10 April 2014) Preamble, para 9 (hereinafter UNSC Res 2149 (2014)); Burundi, UNSC Res 2090 (13 February 2013) Preamble, para 9.

[27] Several authors assume by default the connection to serious or gross violations: Shraga, 'The Security Council and Human Rights' (n 23); Ramcharan, *The Security Council* (n 6); Sydney Bailey, 'The Security Council' in Philip Alston (ed), *The United Nations and Human Rights: A Critical Appraisal* (Clarendon 1992) (hereinafter Bailey, 'The Security Council').

[28] Article 24(1), UN Charter (n 12).

[29] Articles 13(1), 24, 62(a), 68 and 76(c), UN Charter (n 12).

[30] Shraga, 'The Security Council and Human Rights' (n 23) 12; Ramcharan, *The Security Council* (n 6) 3–4; Bailey, 'The Security Council' (n 27) 125.

[31] Somalia, UNSC Res 794 (3 December 1992) Preamble, para 2 (hereinafter UNSC Res 794 (1992)).

Political, financial, and logistical considerations further restrain its ability to act.[32]

1.2 Serious violations of human rights as the 'threat to the peace'?

Undoubtedly, today, serious violations of human rights are an issue of primary concern for the Security Council. Also, the Council does take measures under Chapter VII targeting serious violations of human rights. For instance, the Council has included responsibility for serious violations of human rights as a stand-alone condition for imposing targeted sanctions, such as the freezing of assets and travel bans.[33] However, whether the occurrence of serious violations of human rights can on its own qualify as a threat to the peace is still extensively debated.

On the one side, the 2016 Biersteker study, when analysing the objectives of various sanctions regimes, concluded that '[h]uman rights concerns are routinely invoked, though never as the primary objective'.[34] Similarly, Corten concluded that a threat to international peace has been based on the gravity of the humanitarian situation, but always in combination with other factors, such as the severe loss of authority by the government(s) concerned.[35] Some authors argue that the Security Council's 'practice so far does *not* reflect a sufficiently broad consensus to extend the notion of a threat to the peace to grave violations of human rights as such, *in the absence of the risk of armed conflict*'.[36] To that effect, de Wet justifiably pointed out that accepting that the source of instability (here the gravity of violations) is what triggers the Council's action risks enlarging its discretionary power, which could eventually result in a

[32] See Inger Österdahl, 'The Exception as the Rule: Lawmaking on Force and Human Rights by the UN Security Council' (2005) 10 JC & SL 1, 10 (hereinafter Österdahl, 'The Exception as the Rule').

[33] On the individual sanctions designation criteria, for example: UNSC Res 2428 (2018) (n 13) para 14(d); CAR, UNSC Res 2262 (27 January 2016) para 13(b) (hereinafter UNSC Res 2262 (2016)); UNSC Res 1970 (2011) (n 13) para 22(a). See further Section 1.4, Chapter 2.

[34] Thomas J Biersteker, Sue E Eckert, and Marcos Tourinho, *Targeted Sanctions: The Impacts and Effectiveness of United Nations Action* (CUP 2016) 25 (hereinafter Biersteker, Eckert, and Tourinho, *Targeted Sanctions*).

[35] Olivier Corten, 'Human Rights and Collective Security: Is There an Emerging Right of Humanitarian Intervention?' in Philip Alston and Euan Macdonald (eds), *Human Rights, Intervention, and the Use of Force* (OUP 2008) 95 (hereinafter Corten, 'Human Rights and Collective Security').

[36] Nico Krisch, 'Article 39' in Bruno Simma and others (eds), *The Charter of the United Nations: A Commentary* (3rd edn, OUP 2012) 1287 (hereinafter Krisch, 'Article 39') (emphasis added). Similar view, see also Erika de Wet, *The Chapter VII Powers of the United Nations Security Council* (Hart Publishing 2004) 150–77 (hereinafter de Wet, *The Chapter VII Powers*).

complete erosion of the UN Charter structure, making the concept of threat to the peace 'indefinable'.[37]

Indeed, the Council often underlines the transboundary implications presented by a situation under consideration before it. For instance, in situations such as Iraq, it has emphasised both the massive flows of refugees and the destabilising effects in the region that threaten international peace and security.[38] Similarly, the Security Council declared that it was '[g]ravely alarmed at the rapid deterioration of the situation in Somalia and the heavy loss of human life and widespread material damage resulting from the conflict in the country and *aware of its consequences on stability and peace in the region*'.[39] Even in Libya, the situation invariably invoked as the ultimate expression in practice of the so-called 'responsibility to protect',[40] the Council did not omit to signal its concern 'at the plight of refugees forced to flee the violence in the Libyan Arab Jamahiriya'.[41]

However, serious violations of human rights do not have to occur in the context of an armed conflict to trigger Chapter VII, as has been suggested.[42] Article 39 of the UN Charter—the door to Chapter VII—does not explicitly restrict the Council's authority to situations of armed conflict. On the contrary, the mandate of the UN's predecessor, the League of Nations, *was* restricted to imposing collective sanctions only in the case of war.[43] The 1992 statement of the Security Council, following the first-ever meeting at the level of heads of states, listed human rights issues among the issues that could trigger Chapter VII in the same way as military activities.[44]

More recently, the 2005 World Summit Outcome reinforced the understanding that the Council can use its enforcement powers to protect populations against serious violations of human rights[45] irrespective of the context within which they occur.[46] Additionally, in certain instances, the Security

[37] de Wet, *The Chapter VII Powers* (n 36) 143–44.

[38] UNSC Res 688 (1991) (n 8) Preamble, para 3, Operative para 1.

[39] Somalia, UNSC Res 733 (23 January 1992) Preamble, para 3 (emphasis added). Similar statements in other situations: UNSC Res 1199 (1998) (n 13) Preamble, para 7; UN Assistance Mission for Rwanda, UNSC Res 925 (8 June 1994) Preamble, para 11; UNSC Res 713 (1991) (n 13) Preamble, para 3.

[40] See Section 3, Chapter 2. Alex J Bellamy, 'Libya and the Responsibility to Protect: The Exception and the Norm' (2011) 25 Eth & Int A 263.

[41] UNSC Res 1970 (2011) (n 13) Preamble, para 7.

[42] See n 36.

[43] Article 11, Covenant of the League of Nations including ammendments in force 16 December 1935 (adopted 28 June 1919) 108 LNTS 188.

[44] Note by the President of the Security Council, S/23500 (31 January 1992).

[45] It refers to international crimes—including crimes against humanity, genocide, war crimes, and ethnic cleansing—acts that would also amount to serious violations of human rights. UNGA, 2005 World Summit Outcome (15 September 2005) A/60/L.1, para 139 (hereinafter 2005 Outcome Document).

[46] ibid.

Council refers to serious violations of human rights as a stand-alone ground comprising a threat to the peace. As early as 1992, it concluded that the magnitude of a human tragedy constituted a threat to the peace.[47] Similarly, in 1994, 'ethnic cleansing' was considered to fall within the same category.[48]

Some authors invoke the same practice to build arguments in support of serious violations of human rights as a stand-alone threat to the peace. For instance, Gowlland-Debbas maintained that the fundamental nature of the norms in question as such can trigger the Charter VII enforcement mechanism.[49] Others have defined 'peace' as the absence of human suffering. Some relied on a teleological interpretation of the UN Charter, where in the Preamble the underlying rationale for the maintenance of peace is the prevention of human suffering.[50] An alternative interpretation puts emphasis on the 'international' element, required in Article 39, as including any form of threat to the peace, within or beyond borders, that could be of international concern.[51] It follows that 'serious violations of human rights' breach fundamental common values of the international community, and as such they acquire their international character.

In the end, the Security Council's practice so far can be construed to support either position. A study in 2005 analysed the way the Security Council put emphasis on the protection of human rights when deciding to take measures under Chapter VII. It concluded that the Council considered that human rights concerns in and of themselves can constitute threats to international peace and security.[52] However, using the same resolutions, another study concluded that human rights issues have only been mentioned in relation to other causes of threats to the peace.[53]

The answer is neither black nor white. The UN Security Council addresses complex situations where multiple issues need to be factored in.[54] On the one hand, a 'threat to the peace' is always a multifaceted phenomenon. On the other

[47] UNSC Res 794 (1992) (n 31) Preamble, para 3.

[48] Bosnia and Herzegovina, UNSC Res 941 (23 September 1994) Preamble, para 5.

[49] Gowlland-Debbas, 'The Security Council as Enforcer' (n 3) 48–49.

[50] de Wet lists arguments invoked by Lailach, Martenczuk, and Gading. de Wet, *The Chapter VII Powers* (n 36) 142.

[51] Rosalyn Higgins, 'The Place of International Law in the Settlement of Disputes by the Security Council' (1970) 64 AJIL 1.

[52] Christopher J Le Mon and Rachel S Taylor, 'Security Council Action in the Name of Human Rights: From Rhodesia to the Congo' (2003) 10 UC Dav J Int L & Pol 197, 201, 227.

[53] Mariano J Aznar-Gómez, 'A Decade of Human Rights Protection by the UN Security Council: A Sketch of Deregulation?' (2002) 13 EJIL 223, 225–26 (hereinafter Aznar-Gómez, 'A Decade of Human Rights').

[54] Thomas M Franck, *Recourse to Force: State Action against Threats and Armed Attacks* (CUP 2002) 17 (hereinafter Franck, *Recourse to Force*).

hand, a situation of serious violations of human rights is never the result of a monolithic context.[55] Trying to establish a clear-cut list of situations amounting to a threat to the peace seems an almost otiose and redundant exercise.

To conclude, the occurrence of serious—and not all—violations of human rights is indicative of 'a threat to the peace' in certain situations. It is more difficult, though, to determine whether serious violations of human rights can constitute a threat to the peace in their own right, independently of other factors, such as refugee flows or spill-over effects. Despite the lack of conclusive evidence on the matter, probably such an interpretation of the notion 'threat to the peace' should not be excluded. In fact, a situation of serious violations of human rights can constitute a 'threat to the peace' on its own if the Security Council so decides.[56]

1.3 Limitations in the Security Council's determinations

The conclusion set out above does not suggest that the Security Council will or should respond to every serious violation of human rights. It is not possible to transform serious violations of human rights into an automatic trigger of Chapter VII, nor to invoke a Security Council obligation to trigger Chapter VII in all situations where serious violations of human rights occur. The Council itself is not bound by any previous determination it has made, and has absolutely no obligation to make the same determination in another similar context. It may be expected and pressured to do so, but it is not obliged to.[57] It is rather that a situation of serious violations of human rights opens up this possibility.[58]

The role of the Security Council should be viewed in the context of the system within which it operates. It is part of the UN Charter system, within which it coexists with and complements other organs. It is the executive political organ that intervenes to contain an urgent situation until a permanent solution can be reached.[59] It seldom provides the solution to the long-term

[55] Linos-Alexandre Sicilianos, 'Entre multilatéralisme et unilatéralisme: L'autorisation par le Conseil de sécurité de recourir à la force' (2009) 339 RCADI 9, 51–52 (hereinafter Sicilianos, 'Entre multilatéralisme et unilatéralisme').

[56] Thomas M Franck, *Fairness in International Law and Institutions* (OUP 1998) 224–31.

[57] The possible obligatory precedent is only a political one. Österdahl, 'The Exception as the Rule' (n 32) 14.

[58] See also Theodor Meron, *The Humanization of International Law* (Martinus Nijhoff Publishers 2006) 511.

[59] Nico Krisch, 'Introduction to Chapter VII: The General Framework' in Bruno Simma and others (eds), *The Charter of the United Nations: A Commentary* (3rd edn, OUP 2012) 1247 (hereinafter Krisch, 'Introduction to Chapter VII').

root causes of such violations. Other organs are there for that purpose. Within this system the Council enjoys wide discretion in the choice of situations in which it will intervene and the measures it can take.[60] As Welscher concluded, 'It would be naïve to expect the Council to become a body guided primarily by human rights principles. But is not naïve to expect the Council to appreciate how human rights norms and action can be helpful.'[61]

For instance, the Democratic People's Republic of Korea (DPRK or North Korea) has been on the Security Council's agenda primarily due to its nuclear weapons programme, while the human rights situation in the country has been ignored for decades.[62] Ugarte and Genser pointed out, though, that 'the scale and scope of the killings [are] such that any pretence that they [are] not impacting international peace and security [is] an exercise in sophistry'.[63] Eventually, in 22 December 2014—in response to the findings of the February 2014 Report of the Commission of Inquiry, established by the UN Human Rights Council[64]—the Council added the human rights situation in North Korea to its agenda for a few sessions, as an issue separate from that of non-proliferation.[65] However, no resolution has been adopted on the human rights situation.

Any decision to respond to the dire conditions in North Korea has to be assessed alongside the nuclear threat that country presents, as well as the potential threat to stability in the region. In other words, the Council's lack of action also relates to the geopolitical dynamics and concerns. In that sense, the Council will always be selective, strategically calculating its every choice, and will always prioritise depending on the broader context.[66] Due to its

[60] On an extensive analysis of the Security Council's discretionary powers, see Anne-Laurence Brugere, 'La "menace contre la paix" dans la pratique du Conseil de sécurité des Nations Unies: réflexions sur un concept de droit international' (University of Geneva, 2013) <https://archive-ouverte.unige.ch/unige:34567> accessed 24 September 2021.

[61] Weschler, 'Acting on Human Rights' (n 25) 273–74.

[62] Non-proliferation DPRK, UNSC Res 2321 (30 November 2016); Maintenance of international peace and security: Nuclear non-proliferation and nuclear disarmament, UNSC Res 1887 (24 September 2009); DPRK, UNSC Res 825 (11 May 1993); Complaint of aggression upon the Republic of Korea, UNSC Res 82 (25 June 1950).

[63] Bruno Stagno Ugarte and Jared Genser, 'Evolution of the Security Council's Engagement on Human Rights' in Bruno Stagno Ugarte and Jared Genser (eds), *The United Nations Security Council in the Age of Human Rights* (CUP 2014) 27 (hereinafter 'Evolution of the Security Council's Engagement ...').

[64] UNHRC, 'Report of the commission of inquiry on human rights in the Democratic People's Republic of Korea' (7 February 2014) A/HRC/25/63.

[65] UNSC, Verbatim record of the 8130th meeting (11 December 2017) S/PV8130; UNSC, Verbatim record of the 7830th meeting (9 December 2016) S/PV7830; UNSC, Verbatim record of the 7575th meeting (10 December 2015) S/PV7575.

[66] On competing interests in the Security Council, see the collection of articles in Sebastian von Einsiedel, David M Malone, and Bruno Stagno Ugarte (eds), *The UN Security Council in the 21st Century* (Lynne Rienner Publishers 2015) 57ff.

composition and dependence on the willingness of states to contribute to any measures taken, its discretionary power will always be caught in the middle of political manipulations, subject to abuse from interested states, rather than a careful consideration of facts.[67] However, this observation calls for Security Council reform;[68] it does not cancel out the relevance of serious violations of human rights in determining whether a threat to the peace has occurred.

1.4 The UN Security Council measures

The Security Council enjoys a wide discretionary power as to the measures it can adopt once it identifies a threat to the peace. It is not required to provide any additional justification either for the kind of measures, or for switching from one kind of measure to another. Whether it adopts the measures to directly target the commission of serious violations of human rights or for other reasons, it will not specify. Undoubtedly, when it invokes serious violations to establish the existence of a threat to the peace, the measures it then orders must aim at ceasing those violations as well. Yet, as mentioned above, what qualifies as a threat to the peace is more often than not a complex and multi-layered situation where serious violations of human rights are just one of the principal constituting factors.

Hence, the Council does not distinguish its measures on the basis of the types of threats to the peace they target.[69] Broadly, its coercive measures can be divided into three categories:[70] non-forcible measures (that is sanctions) under Article 41 of the UN Charter;[71] authorisation of the use of force;[72] and peace operations or other exceptional measures.[73] The choice of measures

[67] Ugarte and Genser (eds), 'Evolution of the Security Council's Engagement . . .' (n 63) 26–31.

[68] For a critical view of their effectiveness, see George A Lopez, 'Enforcing Human Rights through Economic Sanctions' in Dinah Shelton (ed), *The Oxford Handbook of International Human Rights Law* (OUP 2014) 788–89.

[69] Aznar-Gómez, 'A Decade of Human Rights' (n 53) 225, 240–41.

[70] This categorisation emerges out of the Security Council's subsequent practice rather than the UN Charter. According to the UN Charter, the UN Security Council can order provisional measures (Article 40), measures not involving the use of force (Article 41), or forcible measures (Article 42). However, the Council has rarely used the provisional measures provisions. Also, the use of force system has never materialised. For an introduction to the UN sanctions, see Simon Chesterman, Ian Johnstone, and David M Malone, *Law and Practice of the United Nations* (2nd edn, OUP 2016) 369–98.

[71] Article 41 of the UN Charter (n 12). See Nico Krisch, 'Article 41' in Bruno Simma and others (eds), *The Charter of the United Nations: A Commentary* (3rd edn, OUP 2012) (hereinafter Krisch, 'Article 41').

[72] The power of the Security Council to authorise use of force is arguably based on a loose interpretation of Articles 42–43 of the UN Charter (n 12) or, more convincingly, on the whole of Chapter VII. See Sicilianos, 'Entre multilatéralisme et unilatéralisme' (n 55) 109–41.

[73] Peacekeeping is not regulated in the UN Charter but has been established utilising implied powers. See Alexander Orakhelashvili, 'The Legal Basis of the United Nations Peace-Keeping Operations' (2002) 43 Va J Intl L 485, 485–524.

depends on the particular situation, the time frame, political will, and available resources. It is always a case-by-case assessment.[74] The measures taken by the Council may be directed at stopping serious violations of human rights alongside other aims, or they may directly focus on ceasing serious violations of human rights.

1.4.1 Measures with multiple objectives

Some of the measures that the UN Security Council orders impact the commission of serious violations of human rights in the relevant context without the Council explicitly making that connection. The Security Council in most cases will condemn serious violations (and abuses) of human rights committed by state and non-state actors in the preambles to its resolutions, but it will not necessarily address the reasons for the measures adopted in the operational part.[75] Yet even if the Council does not expressly state that the measures are also designed to protect human rights, this may be inferred from the resolution as a whole.[76]

Targeted sectoral sanctions, on the basis of Article 41 of the UN Charter, may have this impact. Sectoral sanctions may include arms embargoes, commodity bans, and other more general financial restrictions. They aim at coercing governments and other entities whose conduct and actions are threatening international peace and security to compliance.[77] They usually target the broader ongoing, often escalating, situation, within which serious violations of human rights are also committed. As a result, while sectoral sanctions, such as arms embargoes, are intended to prevent a conflict from escalating and continuing, they simultaneously reduce the risk of human rights abuses occurring and continuing, by preventing coercive means from falling into the wrong hands. Arms embargoes, such as those imposed in the CAR, South Sudan, and Libya,[78] aim at denying human rights abusers the tools of war and repression, while avoiding harming the vulnerable and the innocent. Equally, the establishment of safe zones—such as no-fly zones imposed in Bosnia Herzegovina

[74] For a detailed account of responses to human rights violations between 1946 to 1999, see Katarina Tomaševski, *Responding to Human Rights Violations: 1946–1999* (Martinus Nijhoff Publishers 2000).

[75] See, for instance, UNSC Res 2262 (2016) (n 33); UNSC Res 1970 (2011) (n 13).

[76] In 2021, there were 14 ongoing sanctions regimes. See 'UNSC Sanctions' <https://www.un.org/securitycouncil/sanctions/information> accessed 18 August 2021.

[77] David Cortright, George A Lopez, and Linda Gerber-Stellingwerf, 'Sanctions' in Thomas G Weiss and Sam Daws (eds), *The Oxford Handbook on the United Nations* (OUP 2009).

[78] Respectively, The situation in the Central African Republic, UNSC Res 2588 (29 July 2021) para 1; Reports of the Secretary-General on the Sudan and South Sudan, UNSC Res 2577 (28 May 2021) para 1; The situation in Libya, UNSC Res 2571 (16 April 2021) para 5.

during the Yugoslav war[79]—also aims at protecting individuals against human rights abuses.

Beyond sanctions regimes, other measures taken over the years have also had an impact on serious violations of human rights that occurred in the context under consideration. For instance, the Security Council did establish international criminal tribunals, such as the International Criminal Tribunal for the Former Yugoslavia (ICTY),[80] and referred situations to the ICC—in the cases of Darfur and Libya.[81] These measures address situations where serious violations of human rights have been committed. There is undoubtedly a close relationship between serious violations of human rights and international crimes (particularly crimes against humanity). International criminal justice emerged to protect similar values, and there is a substantive overlap between those acts that amount to international crimes and those that amount to serious violations of human rights.[82]

Also, in two cases—East Timor and Kosovo—where there was a complete collapse of infrastructures and serious violations of human rights had been committed, the Security Council used Chapter VII to allow it to administer those territories.[83] In both cases, in practice the Council (partially or entirely) replaced the governmental apparatus, and in that capacity it took measures to address serious violations of human rights.[84] Amongst the most straightforward examples, in East Timor, the UN Transitional Administration in East Timor (UNTAET) established the Commission for Reception, Truth and Reconciliation in East Timor (CAVR) to investigate serious violations of human rights committed on all sides, between April 1974 and October 1999.[85]

[79] Bosnia and Herzegovina, UNSC Res 781 (9 October 1992) para 1. More recently, Libya UNSC Res 1973 (2011) (n 18) paras 6–12.

[80] Respectively, Establishment of the International Criminal Tribunal for Rwanda (ICTR) and adoption of the Statute of the Tribunal, UNSC Res 955 (8 November 1994) Preamble, para 4; International Criminal Tribunal for the former Yugoslavia (ICTY), UNSC Res 827 (25 May 1993). See also, the International Criminal Tribunal for Rwanda (ICTR) Middle East (Lebanon), UNSC Res 1757 (30 May 2007); Sierra Leone, UNSC Res 1315 (14 August 2000).

[81] Article 13(b), ICC Statute (n 17). Respectively, UNSC Res 1970 (2011) (n 13) para 1; Sudan, UNSC Res 1593 (31 March 2005) para 1. See William Schabas, 'Accountability for International Crimes—Special Tribunals and Referrals to the International Criminal Court' in Stagno Ugarte and Genser (eds), *The United Nations Security Council* (n 63).

[82] See Section 2.3, Introduction.

[83] Respectively: East Timor, UNSC Res 1272 (25 October 1999); Kosovo, UNSC Res 1244 (10 June 1999).

[84] On UN administration of territories, see Carsten Stahn, *The Law and Practice of International Territorial Administration: Versailles to Iraq and Beyond* (CUP 2008) 308–47.

[85] UN Transitional Administration in East Timor (UNTAET), Regulation 2001/10 on the Establishment of a Commission for Reception Truth and Reconciliation in East Timor, (13 July 2001) UNTAET/REG/2001/10 (hereinafter UNTAET, Regulation 2001/10).

The Council does not have to state that these measures will impact human rights, but each of those inevitably should. Beyond the impact that the measures ordered by the Security Council may have on serious violations of human rights due to their being part of the targeted context, the Security Council increasingly has been introducing measures that specifically and expressly target the cessation of serious violations of human rights.

1.4.2 Measures directly targeting serious violations of human rights

The Security Council may not impose an entire sanctions regime exclusively to put an end to serious violations of human rights, but certain measures within the regime are designed with that aim in mind. Such measures eventually operate as responses to these unlawful acts, and they therefore acquire an enforcement function.[86]

1.4.2.1 Individual sanctions against serious violations of human rights

Since 9/11, the Security Council has been increasingly imposing (so-called) individual sanctions, which primarily include the freezing of assets and travel bans.[87] These sanctions are today a regular tool in the sanctions toolbox. Depending on the situation, various designation criteria have been introduced to determine against whom individual sanctions will be imposed. It is not only the commission of terrorist acts. The perpetration of serious violations of human rights is also regularly listed as a stand-alone designation criterion, independent from any other condition.[88] For instance, the wording of Resolution 1970 (2011), which was one of the first resolutions in which the Security Council decided

> that the measures contained in paragraphs 15 and 17 shall apply to the individuals and entities ...; (a) Involved in or complicit in ordering, controlling,

[86] To the extent sanctions aim at putting an end to an illegal situation, they acquire an enforcement role. See Biersteker, Eckert, and Tourinho, *Targeted Sanctions* (n 34) 56–57; Gowlland-Debbas, 'The Security Council as Enforcer' (n 3) 41.

[87] Krisch, 'Article 41' (n 71) 1309. On the so-called smart sanctions, see Laura Picchio Forlati and Linos-Alexander Sicilianos (eds), *Economic Sanctions in International Law* (The Centre for Studies and Research in International Law and International Relations, The Hague Academy of International Law 2004); David Cortright and George A Lopez, *Smart Sanctions: Targeting Economic Statecraft* (Rowman & Littlefield 2002).

[88] Notably, see designation criteria: UNSC Res 2428 (2018) (n 13) para 14(d); CAR, UNSC Res 2339 (27 January 2017) para 17(b); UNSC Res 2290 (2016) (n 16) para 9(c) and (d); UNSC Res 2206 (2015) (n 18) para 7(d); UNSC Res 2134 (2014) (n 15) para 37(b); UNSC Res 2078 (2012) (n 21) para 4(e); Somalia, UNSC Res 2002 (29 July 2011) para 1(e) (hereinafter UNSC Res 2002 (2011)); UNSC Res 1970 (2011) (n 13) para 22(a); DRC, UNSC Res 1807 (31 March 2008) para 13(e); DRC, UNSC Res 1698 (31 July 2006) para 13.

> or otherwise directing the commission of serious human rights abuses against persons in the Libyan Arab Jamahiriya . . .[89]

This process thus involves a double threshold evaluation. First, the decision to impose a sanctions regime is based on the overall situation, within which serious violations may have occurred; and at a second stage, the decision can be made to impose sanctions on an individual, on the basis of their actions that amount to serious violations of human rights. The Council in some resolutions lists both international human rights law violations in general and serious violations of human rights, as two separate criteria for imposing individual sanctions.[90] The repetition seems redundant. While this demonstrates the lack of consistency in the Council's practice, still, individual sanctions cannot but be imposed mostly as a result of the commission of serious violations of human rights.

Even in instances where human rights violations are listed without gravity qualifiers, these sanctions, based on the *chapeau* of the designation criteria, are reserved 'for engaging in or providing support for acts that undermine the peace, stability or security' of the respective country. It is difficult to perceive how just any human rights violation would amount to a threat to an overall situation. It follows that individual sanctions can be imposed against any person responsible for committing serious violations of human rights, irrespective of whether that person's actions also constituted terrorist acts or disrupted international peace and security in any other way.

1.4.2.2 The human rights component in peace operations and monitoring

The inclusion of measures directly targeting serious violations of human rights in a specific context is further illustrated by certain developments in the structure and functions of UN peace operations as their role gradually became more complex, multi-layered, and multifaceted.[91] Human rights issues have been explicitly introduced into the mandate of peace operations.[92] Most of these operations today contain a human rights component (usually headed by a representative of the Office of the High Commissioner for Human Rights

[89] UNSC Res 1970 (2011) (n 13) para 22. See also, UNSC Res 2002 (2011) (n 88) para 1(e).

[90] For instance, UNSC Res 2290 (2016) (n 16) para 9(c)–(d); UNSC Res 2134 (2014) (n 15) para 37(b)). Or it lists only international human rights law as a whole (DRC, UNSC Res 2293 (23 June 2016) para 7(c)).

[91] Peacekeeping has developed over the years, and may include nation-building, peace-enforcement, and even territorial administration. Therefore, the expression 'peace operations' has been preferred, as encompassing all the different functions.

[92] For an in-depth analysis, see Mari Katayanagi, *Human Rights Functions of United Nations Peacekeeping Operations* (Martinus Nijhoff Publishers 2002).

(OHCHR)), with a narrower or broader mandate depending on the particular circumstances on the ground. The human rights component is primarily authorised to focus on observing, investigating, documenting, and reporting on serious violations of human rights.[93]

Similarly, outside the peace operations context, the Council has on several occasions, following the perpetration of serious violations of human rights, established commissions of experts or commissions of inquiry to report on specific situations. These can be understood as part of the monitoring component of the regime.[94] The first post-Cold War commission was established in 1992 to address the situation in the former Yugoslavia,[95] setting the stage for the subsequent commissions on Burundi, Rwanda, Sudan, and Timor-Leste.[96]

1.4.2.3 Authorisation to use force to protect the civilian population

The authorisation to use force runs at the core of the Security Council's role as the gatekeeper of international peace and security. It authorises the use of force, either by permitting the peace forces to use all necessary means or by directly recommending or allowing states to use all necessary means to contain a situation.[97] The aim of forcible measures is often not limited to restoring peace and security, but also extends to protecting the civilian population.

This is becoming evident when it comes to peace operations established by the Council. The latter has been giving peace forces more explicit and stronger civilian protection mandates.[98] Initially, peace forces were authorised to use force only to defend themselves against attacks. However, various factors led to the evolution of their mandate to allow them to 'use all necessary means' to protect the civilian population. The occurrence of serious violations of human rights has been a motivating element in expanding their powers. One of the most tragic moments in peacekeeping history was the events in Srebrenica. The area was designated as a safe haven for Muslim refugees in Bosnia in the

[93] Mari Katayanagi, 'UN Peacekeeping and Human Rights' in Stagno Ugarte and Genser (eds), *The United Nations Security Council* (n 63) 131 (hereinafter Katayanagi, 'UN Peacekeeping and Human Rights').

[94] See Chapter 2.

[95] Former Yugoslavia, UNSC Res 780 (6 October 1992).

[96] Respectively: International Commission of Inquiry in Burundi, UNSC Res 1012 (28 August 1995); UNSC Res 935 (1994) (n 13); Report of the Secretary-General on the Sudan, UNSC Res 1564 (18 September 2004); UNTAET, Regulation 2001/10 (n 85).

[97] See Anne Orford, *Reading Humanitarian Intervention Human Rights and the Use of Force in International Law* (CUP 2003) (hereinafter Orford, *Reading Humanitarian Intervention*); Simon Chesterman, *Just War or Just Peace?: Humanitarian Intervention and International Law* (OUP 2002) 150–51 (hereinafter Chesterman, *Just War or Just Peace?*).

[98] Rosa Brooks, 'Civilians and Armed Conflict' in Stagno Ugarte and Genser (eds), *The United Nations Security Council* (n 63) 64–67; Katayanagi, 'UN Peacekeeping and Human Rights' (n 93) 54–60. See also James Sloan, *The Militarisation of Peacekeeping in the Twenty-First Century* (Hart Publishing 2011).

mid-1990s, to be protected by the Dutch peacekeepers. Faced with an attack, the peacekeepers refused to use weapons to defend the refugees, due to the fact that their mandate allowed them to use force only to defend themselves. The refusal resulted in the massacre of an estimated 8,000 men and boys.[99]

A series of strengthening resolutions cumulated in the adoption of Resolution 1565, in 2004, where the Council gave the United Nations Organisation Mission in the Democratic Republic of the Congo (MONUC, renamed MONUSCO (United Nations Stabilisation Mission in the Congo) in 2010), among many assignments, the power to protect civilians and UN personnel '[using] all necessary means'.[100] Its mandate was strengthened further with Resolution 1906 (2009), in which the Council ordered the Security Council to include training for military and police personnel on the protection of civilians from imminent threats and appropriate responses, including on human rights, sexual violence, and gender issues.[101]

These mandates have been established to ensure stability in war-torn communities, but also to protect the civilian population caught in the middle of conflicts against unlawful attacks. Hence, their aim is also to cease serious violations of human rights. These forces are expected to protect civilians from imminent threats to their physical integrity, violations that in such a context would amount to serious violations of human rights, not against any human rights violation. Missions still in operation in 2021, such as the ones in Mali, CAR, DRC, South Sudan, and Sudan, all included a primary mandate to protect the civilian population from threats of physical violence, within their capabilities and areas of deployment.[102]

Beyond peace operations, where immediate intervention has been deemed necessary, the Council has ordered multilateral forces—dominated by one member state's forces—to use all necessary means to ensure that the humanitarian crisis of an exceptional character

[99] ICJ, *Application of the Convention on the Prevention and Punishment of the Crime of Genocide (Bosnia and Herzegovina v Serbia and Montenegro)*, 26 February 2007.

[100] Democratic Republic of the Congo, UNSC Res 1565 (1 October 2004).

[101] See DRC, UNSC Res 1906 (23 December 2009) para 13. See further measures at DRC, UNSC Res 2098 (28 March 2013) para 9.

[102] Respectively, United Nations Multidimensional Integrated Stabilization Mission in Mali (MINUSMA): Mali, UNSC Res 2100 (25 April 2013) para 16(c); Mali, UNSC Res 2164 (25 June 2014) paras 12–13(a). United Nations Multidimensional Integrated Stabilization Mission in the Central African Republic (MINUSCA): CAR, UNSC Res 2301 (26 July 2016) paras 32–33(a)(i); UNSC Res 2149 (2014) (n 26) para 30(a). MONUSCO in the DRC: DRC, UNSC Res 1925 (28 May 2010) paras 11–12(a). United Nations Mission in South Sudan (UNMISS): Reports of the Secretary-General on the Sudan and South Sudan, UNSC Res 2567 (12 March 2021) para 3(a); Reports of the Secretary-General on the Sudan, UNSC Res 1996 (8 July 2011) para 3(b). United Nations Interim Security Force for Abyei (UNISFA): Reports of the Secretary-General on the Sudan and South Sudan, UNSC Res 2469 (14 May 2019) para 12; Reports of the Secretary-General on the Sudan, UNSC Res 1990 (27 June 2011) para 3(d).

ceases.[103] Since the Balkan and Rwandan wars, the Security Council has authorised interventions with humanitarian purposes, among others, in Côte d'Ivoire and East Timor.[104] The authorisation to use force has been given to contain various escalating situations that threatened international peace and security, not necessarily directly aiming at protecting the populations against serious violations of human rights.[105]

More recently, though, the Council authorised UN action to be taken in Libya, following the civil uprising there and the Government's use of force against civilians. Security Council Resolution 1973 (2011) authorised its member states 'to take all necessary measures ... to protect civilians and civilian populated areas under threat of attack in the Libyan Arab Jamahiriya, including Benghazi'.[106] Later, the Security Council authorised French and African troops to use force to protect civilians in CAR while a sectarian civil war was escalating.[107] Soon after, it approved the European Union's request to assist the troops already deployed.[108]

To conclude, serious violations of human rights have been introduced into the UN collective security system through the interpretation of the notion of threat to the peace to encompass such violations. It is evident from the Council's practice that the focus is on serious violations of human rights as opposed to ordinary violations of human rights. It is also true that Chapter VII of the UN Charter has not so far been activated exclusively to address a situation of serious violations of human rights, but it does not seem unlikely that this might occur in the future if the Council deems it necessary. In the meantime, though, the addressing of serious violations of human rights is becoming an integral part of already established enforcement measures: both indirectly, by taking measures to contain the entire situation within which serious violations of human rights have also occurred; and directly, by imposing measures targeting serious violations of human rights.

[103] See the case of Australia's leading the operation in East Timor and France in Rwanda, Mali, and others. Chesterman, *Just War or Just Peace?* (n 97) 150–51.

[104] Respectively East Timor, UNSC Res 1264 (15 September 1999) para 3; Côte d'Ivoire, UNSC Res 1464 (4 February 2003) para 9. See also UNSC Res 929 (1994) (n 10); UNSC Res 794 (1992) (n 31) para 12 (Operation Restore Hope).

[105] See Krisch, 'Article 39' (n 36) 1272–96.

[106] The North Atlantic Treaty Organization (NATO) undertook Operation Unified Protector with the support of the League of Arab States, Qatar, and the United Arab Emirates. UNSC Res 1973 (2011) (n 18) paras 4, 6 et seq.

[107] The African Union Support Mission to the Central African Republic (MISCA) was authorised with UNSC Res 2127 (2013) (n 14) para 28(i).

[108] Letter dated 25 February 2014 from the Secretary-General addressed to the President of the Security Council (26 February 2014) S/2014/45; UNSC Res 2134 (2014) (n 15) paras 43–44.

2. Other responses to serious violations of human rights

2.1 Obligations in the law of state responsibility

Before delving into the matter of recent developments in the field of third-party countermeasures with respect to serious violations of human rights, certain remarks are reserved for the International Law Commission (ILC) Articles on State Responsibility and the so-called consequences of serious breaches of peremptory norms. They provide for a set of additional obligations, applicable to all states in cases of serious breaches of peremptory norms.[109] As already highlighted, 'serious breaches of peremptory norms' and 'serious violations of human rights', while they overlap, are not identical.[110] However, various reasons arguably justify the understanding that these obligations would also apply in cases of serious violations of human rights.

First, on the basis of the drafting history of Articles 40–41 of the Articles on State Responsibility, it was serious violations of human rights that were initially envisaged as giving rise to these particular obligations.[111] The expression 'serious breaches of peremptory norms' was introduced as a compromise, to replace the previous distinction between crimes and delicts,[112] and the new Article 40 has been described as the 'twin brother' of the former Article 19.[113]

Second, the close relationship between the breaches that are envisaged to give rise to the Article 41 obligations and serious violations of human rights is highlighted by the choice of examples provided in the ILC commentary. The ILC listed gross or systematic acts of slavery and the slave trade, genocide, and racial discrimination, torture, interference with the right to self-determination, and apartheid as examples, all of which constitute acts that would (among others) amount to serious violations of human rights.[114]

Third, the choice of the expression 'serious breaches of peremptory norms' has not gone unchallenged. The introduction of the adjective 'serious' before

[109] Articles 40–41, ARSIWA (n 1).

[110] See Section 2.1, Introduction.

[111] Article 19(3), ILC, 'Fifth report of the Special Rapporteur', Mr Roberto Ago (1976) Yb ILC, Vol II, Part Two, 75.

[112] First introduced by Roberto Ago, the second ILC Special Rapporteur on the topic of state responsibility. ibid.

[113] Eric Wyler, 'From "State Crime" to Responsibility for "Serious Breaches of Obligations under Peremptory Norms of General International Law"' (2002) 13 EJIL 1147, 1147–60 (hereinafter Wyler, 'From "State Crime"'). On history of discussion, see ILC, 'Fourth report on State responsibility by Mr James Crawford, Special Rapporteur' (2 April 2001) A/CN4/517, 2, 17–21 (hereinafter ILC, 'Fourth report by Crawford').

[114] ILC, Articles on Responsibility of States for Internationally Wrongful Acts, with commentaries (2001) Yb ILC, Vol II, Part Two, 112–13 (hereinafter ARSIWA with commentaries).

violations of peremptory norms has been rightly construed as redundant. Gaeta, while examining the gravity requirement of Article 40, points out that 'Plainly, this conclusion [that 'serious' is necessary] would be preposterous and inconsistent with the extraordinary importance of the interests protected by all rules of *jus cogens.*'[115]

Fourth, it has been argued that 'breaches of obligations owed to the international community as a whole', already appearing in Articles 48 and 54, would have been more appropriate wording.[116] Articles 48 and 54 already appear to establish more serious consequences for breaches of obligations *erga omnes* than for serious breaches of peremptory norms. Article 54 left the possibility for third states (referred to as states other than those injured) to 'take lawful measures against that State to ensure cessation of the breach' to future developments.[117]

Lastly, subsequent practice seems to favour the understanding that these obligations should apply to all violations of *erga omnes* obligations, which includes human rights obligations. The *Wall* Advisory Opinion of the International Court of Justice (ICJ) seems to favour this understanding. The Court distinguished between the obligations of the state directly responsible (Israel) and those of other, not directly injured states. While referring to obligations owed to the international community as a whole, it eventually listed the exact same obligations as Article 41. The Court relied on treaty obligations (Common Article 1 to the Geneva Conventions) and the *erga omnes* nature of Israel's obligations that were violated.[118] As mentioned earlier, serious violations of human rights constitute violations of *erga omnes* obligations—in fact, all human rights obligations should be understood as *erga omnes* obligations.[119]

Further subsequent practice will probably validate the understanding that these additional consequences do not arise only when 'serious breaches of peremptory norms' have been committed. For now, without necessarily developing general obligations of the not directly injured states, more recent treaties also in part reflect the above-mentioned additional obligations with regard to

[115] Paola Gaeta, 'The Character of the Breach' in James Crawford, Alain Pellet, and Simon Olleson (eds), *The Law of International Responsibility* (OUP 2010) 426 (hereinafter Gaeta, 'The Character of the Breach').

[116] Linos-Alexander Sicilianos, 'The Classification of Obligations and the Multilateral Dimension of the Relations of International Responsibility' (2002) 13 EJIL 1127, 1141 (hereinafter Sicilianos, 'The Classification of Obligations'); Wyler, 'From "State Crime"' (n 113) 1159.

[117] Article 54, ARSIWA with commentaries (n 114).

[118] ICJ, *Legal Consequences of the Construction of a Wall in the Occupied Palestinian Territory*, Advisory Opinion, 9 July 2004, para 159 (see also paras 148, 155–60). For a critical reflection on the position of the ICJ, see Separate Opinion of Judge Higgins, ibid paras 37–39. Separate Opinion of Judge Kooijmans, ibid paras 41–51.

[119] See Section 2.2.1, Introduction.

serious violations of human rights. For instance, the recent Arms Trade Treaty (ATT) provides that an exporting state may have an obligation to stop an arms transfer if there is an overriding risk that the arms will be used, among other things, to commit or facilitate a serious violation of human rights.[120]

The Articles on State Responsibility provide for three intertwining obligations construed as the consequences of a serious breach of a peremptory norm.[121] States that are not injured have, first, a duty to co-operate to bring to an end any serious breach of peremptory norms[122] and, second, a duty of abstention. The latter duty is twofold, including a duty not to recognise as lawful a situation created by a serious breach and a duty not to render aid or assistance in maintaining that situation.[123] In a nutshell, these are consequences that primarily aim at ensuring that the internationally wrongful acts are brought to an end. They are necessary in order to secure the performance of the subsequent obligations of cessation and reparation. As such, they also reflect the obligations that arise in cases of serious violations of human rights.

The duty of abstention has been described as a logical consequence of internationally wrongful acts.[124] For instance, in the case of human rights, other states are obliged to respect and ensure respect for human rights on the basis of the treaties to which they are parties; therefore they are also compelled to abstain from facilitating the commission of serious violations of human rights. For the duty to co-operate, the ILC recognised that it could materialise both in the framework of a competent international organisation, in particular the UN, and as non-institutionalised co-operation. However, it left open the question whether it included a positive duty of co-operation.[125] As a result, it has been difficult to pinpoint the added value of the Article 41 inclusion, particularly with regard to the UN, as the duty to co-operate derives from its already established obligations.[126]

In addition, the obligation of non-recognition remains a well-established principle in international law and closely related to human rights.[127] The principle of non-recognition took shape following the events in South Rhodesia and the

[120] Article 7, Arms Trade Treaty (adopted 2 April 2013), UNGA Res 67/234.
[121] Article 41(1), ARSIWA (n 1).
[122] Article 41(1), ARSIWA (n 1).
[123] Article 41(2), ibid.
[124] Article 41, ILC, Draft Articles on the Law of Treaties with commentaries (1966) YbILC, Vol II, 115.
[125] Article 41, ARSIWA with commentaries (n 114) 114, para 3.
[126] Andrea Gattini, 'A Return Ticket to "Communitarisme", Please' (2002) 13 EJIL 1181 (hereinafter Gattini, 'A Return Ticket').
[127] Linos-Alexander Sicilianos, *The Human Dimension of International Law: Interplay of General International Law and Human Rights* (Nomiki Bibliothiki Group 2010) 248–54 (hereinafter Sicilianos, *The Human Dimension of International Law*).

racist regime of Ian Smith.[128] It was then fully established in the process of recognition of the states that emerged out of the dissolution of the former Yugoslav republic.[129] Various examples of non-recognition in practice relate to the outcomes of illegal acts of war, including the Turkish invasion of the northern part of Cyprus and the Iraqi declaration of Kuwait's annexation.[130] Yet it is difficult to imagine a scenario where a state today would publicly recognise the legality of an act amounting to a serious violation of human rights.

How far this obligation goes is not clear. Article 41 'refers to the obligation of collective non-recognition by the international community as a whole of the legality of situations resulting directly from serious breaches' of peremptory norms.[131] Does the obligation of non-recognition entail an obligation, for instance, not to recognise a government that rose to power by committing serious violations of human rights? Many may be ready to say yes; yet in practice, it is not as straightforward. The final decision of non-recognition is still a political one. While there was a decision to overthrow the Gaddafi regime in Libya,[132] the violations of the Syrian regime have not led to the same result. Furthermore, the obligation of non-recognition would not extend to the non-recognition of official acts that facilitate the life of the population living under the specific government.[133] Decisions on recognition may not be of a legal character, but they underline the centrality of serious violations of human rights and their potential regulatory significance in the future of the international legal order.[134] Undoubtedly, the inclusion of these additional consequences in the Articles on State Responsibility had a significant symbolic value—albeit limited practical significance.[135] In the meantime, the most prominent ongoing development in the law of state responsibility with regard to serious violations of human rights is found outside the scope of these obligations.

[128] ICJ, *Legal Consequences for States of the Continued Presence of South Africa in Namibia (South West Africa) notwithstanding Security Council Resolution 276 (1970)*, Advisory Opinion, 21 June 1971, para 133 (hereinafter *Namibia Advisory Opinion*).

[129] See Sicilianos, *The Human Dimension of International Law* (n 127) 248–54.

[130] ARSIWA with commentaries (n 114) 114.

[131] ibid.

[132] Many governments had withdrawn their recognition of the (until then) official Government of Libya by the time NATO intervened in Libya, which eventually resulted in the overthrow of the Gaddafi regime.

[133] This was settled in the Namibia case. *Namibia Advisory Opinion* (n 128) para 125.

[134] On Kosovo, see Christian Tomuschat, 'Recognition of New States—The Case of Premature Recognition' in Peter Hilpold (ed), *Kosovo and International Law: The ICJ Advisory Opinion of 22 July 2010* (Martinus Nijhoff Publishers 2012) 45.

[135] Gaeta, 'The Character of the Breach' (n 115) 426.

2.2 Third-party countermeasures

Over the past two decades at least, there has been a cautiously but steadily increasing practice indicating that more and more international bodies and states—alone or collectively—feel entitled to resort to what will be referred to here as third-party countermeasures. Their measures aim, among other things, to put pressure on another state to cease serious violations of human rights. They act even in the absence of a treaty-based or other legal ground to justify such measures. As a result, such measures appear prima facie unlawful as an unjustified interference in domestic affairs.[136] These 'measures' are separate from Security Council action, as they are taken without its authorisation.[137] Also, they are not countermeasures as traditionally understood in public international law.[138] In these cases, international organisations and states cannot be understood as directly injured parties[139] but act primarily as agents to promote the interests of the international community.[140]

The possibility—and not the obligation—for states to intervene to protect humanity against the failures and breaches of other states is a relatively new concept, especially when compared to the underlying concept of countermeasures.[141] In 1989, the Institute of International Law pointed the finger at the formalisation of this possibility. In its resolution on the principle of internal affairs of states, it concluded that all states have an *erga omnes* obligation to respond to human rights violations, and a parallel legal interest in protecting universal

[136] See Christian J Tams and Alessandra Asteriti, '*Erga Omnes*, *Jus Cogens* and Their Impact on the Law of State Responsibility' in Malcolm Evans and Panos Koutrakos (eds), *The International Responsibility of the European Union; European and International Perspectives* (Hart Publishing 2013) 172–73; Denis Alland, 'Countermeasures of General Interest' (2002) 13 EJIL 1221, 1226 (hereinafter Alland, 'Countermeasures'); Pierre-Marie Dupuy, 'Observations sur la pratique récente des "sanctions" de l'illicite' (1983) 87 RGDIP 505, 505ff (hereinafter Dupuy, 'Observations'); Michael Akehurst, 'Reprisals by Third States' (1970) 44 BYIL 1.

[137] Martin Dawidowicz, 'Third-Party Countermeasures: Observations on a Controversial Concept' in Christine Chinkin and Freya Baetens (eds), *Sovereignty, Statehood and State Responsibility: Essays in Honour of James Crawford* (CUP 2015) 355 (hereinafter Dawidowicz, 'Third-Party Countermeasures').

[138] Bilateral countermeasures are not discussed here, even though measures taken by one state for the ill-treatment of its own nationals by another state could also be understood as a response to serious violation of human rights. 'Retorsions'—i.e. unfriendly acts in response to an injurious act by another state—are also excluded. On the definition and conditions for adopting countermeasures, see Articles 49–53, ARSIWA (n 1).

[139] Article 49(1), ibid.

[140] On Schelle's theory (that in certain instances, states act as agents of the international community (*dédoublement fonctionnel*)), see Antonio Cassese, 'Remarks on Scelle's Theory of "Role Splitting" (dédoublement fonctionnel) in International Law' (1990) 1 EJIL 210, 210–31.

[141] Countermeasures were long before recognised in practice. See ICJ, *Gabčíkovo-Nagymaros Project (Hungary/Slovakia)*, Judgment, 25 September 1997; *Naulilaa case (Portugal v Germany)*, 31 July 1928 (1949) II RIAA 1011.

human rights.[142] This matter occupied the ILC discussions from the very beginning of the state responsibility project until its very last year.[143] Eventually, the last Special Rapporteur, Crawford, attempted to introduce a provision that expressly allowed third-party countermeasures and failed.[144] The wording of Article 54 of the ILC Articles on State Responsibility neither allows nor prohibits the possibility for states not directly injured to take countermeasures against violations of *erga omnes* obligations.[145] The commentary 'leaves the resolution of the matter to the further development of international law'.[146]

The topic of 'third-party countermeasures' is one marked by legal controversy.[147] Apart from debating whether such measures are permitted under international law, there is neither a common terminology nor a common definition to describe those measures that entities, other than the directly injured, increasingly take on behalf of the international community. These 'measures' present several distinctive elements: they are in breach of international obligations strictly speaking;[148] they are meant to protect communitarian values; they can be taken by a plurality of states upon a decision or recommendation of an international organisation, or independently by a state (alone or as a group); in neither case is there a directly injured party; their alleged legal basis varies; and also, when taken within the auspices of an international organisation, they may be taken against member states or against non-members. So far, depending on where the emphasis is put, a varied term and definition is adopted.

In his in-depth study, Dawidowicz identified no fewer than eight different denominations: collective countermeasures, third-party countermeasures,

[142] Resolution on the Protection of Human Rights and the Principle of Non-Intervention in Internal Affairs of States, International Law Institute (13 September 1989) 63 AIDI 338 (1989).

[143] ILC, 'Fourth report by Crawford' (n 113); ILC, 'Third report on State responsibility by Mr James Crawford, Special Rapporteur' (15 March 2000) A/CN.4/507 (hereinafter ILC, 'Third report by Crawford'); ILC, 'Seventh report on State responsibility by Mr Gaetano Arangio-Ruiz, Special Rapporteur' (24 May 1995) A/CN4/469 and Add1–2, 9, paras 70–138; ILC, 'Fourth report on the content, forms and degrees of international responsibility (Part 2 of the draft articles) by Mr Willem Riphagen, Special Rapporteur' (1983) A/CN4/366 and Add1 & Add1/Corr1, para 65. See also, for brief accounts of the main objections, Gattini, 'A Return Ticket' (n 126) 1181–84; Pierre Klein, 'Responsibility for Serious Breaches of Obligations Deriving from Peremptory Norms of International Law and United Nations Law' (2002) 13 EJIL 1241, 1241–43.

[144] In the initial proposal, Article 54(2) recognised that states should be entitled to act at least in situations where the breach was 'gross, well-attested, systematic and continuing'. ILC, 'Fourth report by Crawford' (n 113) 17–18.

[145] Article 54, ARSIWA (n 1).

[146] ARSIWA with commentaries (n 114) 139.

[147] Martin Dawidowicz, *Third-Party Countermeasures in International Law* (CUP 2017) 1–35; Alain Pellet and Alina Miron, 'Sanctions' in Wolfrum Rüdiger (ed), *Max Planck Encyclopedia of Public International Law from Professor Rüdiger Wolfrum* (OUP 2013).

[148] See Declaration on Principles of International Law concerning Friendly Relations and Co-operation among States in accordance with the Charter of the United Nations, UNGA Res 2625(XXV) (24 October 1970).

third-state countermeasures, countermeasures of general interest, multilateral sanctions, multilateral countermeasures, solidarity measures, and countermeasures *omnium*.[149] Cassese, for instance, puts emphasis on the decision-making process, that is the decision taken by an international organisation independently of whether the measures target member states or non-members. He refers to them as 'sanctions', meaning 'centralized countermeasures' that are '(1) in breach of international obligations, (2) intend to respond to an internationally wrongful act of another State, (3) are taken jointly by a plurality of States upon decision or recommendation of an international organization'.[150] The European Union refers to 'sanctions', but also to 'restrictive measures' and 'autonomous sanctions' to denote such action.[151] In 2000, Crawford referred to such measures under the rubric of 'collective countermeasures' to describe the enforcement of 'multilateral obligations'. The collective aspect also covered responses by one state as they were taken for the collective interest.[152]

In this book, the term 'sanction' is reserved for measures taken by international organisations within the agreed legal framework against their member states—that is the UN Security Council or other international organisation measures against their own members operating within the respective treaty frameworks.[153] Apart from the UN, most international organisations have explicit powers to impose internal sanctions against disobedient member states. For instance, the European Union may impose fines if member states do not comply with judgments of the Court of Justice of the European Union or with prescribed measures to reduce their government deficits.[154] Lastly, any other coercive 'measures' adopted 'by a not directly injured entity [state

[149] Martin Dawidowicz, 'Public Law Enforcement without Public Law Safeguards? An Analysis of State Practice on Third-Party Countermeasures and Their Relationship to the UN Security Council' (2007) 77 BYIL 333, 333 (hereinafter Dawidowicz, 'Public Law Enforcement').

[150] Antonio Cassese, *International Law* (2nd edn, OUP 2005) 311.

[151] Council of the European Union, Regulation (EU) No 2020/1998 of 7 December 2020 concerning restrictive measures against serious human rights violations and abuses (7 December 2020) OJ L 410I; Council of the European Union, 'Guidelines on implementation and evaluation of restrictive measrues (sanctions) in the framework of the EU common foreign and security policy' (4 May 2018) 5664/18 (hereinafter EU Sanctions Guidelines).

[152] ILC, 'Third report by Crawford' (n 143) para 386.

[153] This approach was already adopted by the ILC in 1979. ILC, 'Report of the International Law Commission on the work of its thirty-first session' (14 May–3 August 1979) A/34/10, YbILC, Vol II (1979) 121. See also George Abi-Saab, 'The Concept of Sanction in International Law' in Vera Gowlland-Debbas and George Abi-Saab (eds), *United Nations Sanctions and International Law* (Kluwer 2001). For the opposite view, see Mortimer NS Sellers, 'Economic Sanctions and Human Rights Violations' in Laura Picchio Forlati and Linos-Alexander Sicilianos (eds), *Economic Sanctions in International Law* (The Centre for Studies and Research in International Law and International Relations, The Hague Academy of International Law 2004) 481–82.

[154] Articles 260, 126(11), EU, Consolidated versions of the Treaty on European Union and the Treaty on the Functioning of the European Union (TFEU) (signed on 26 October 2012) OJ C 326/47 (2016).

or international organisation] in defence of a public interest [here serious violations of human rights] and not otherwise justified in international law' are understood as third-party countermeasures.[155]

2.2.1 Third-party non-forcible countermeasures in response to human rights violations in practice

One of the first forms of response to serious violations of human rights was the curbing of, or the threat to curb, development assistance to or economic cooperation with states suspected of being responsible for such violations. For instance, during the 1991 Yugoslav war, the European Union had decided to first suspend and soon after denounce the Co-operation Agreement with the former Socialist Federal Republic of Yugoslavia.[156] Such responses initially found no basis in the treaties; the agreements that set the conditions for providing assistance, like the Lomé Agreements, did not include human rights clauses.[157] As a result, the legal validity of suspending treaty clauses on the basis of human rights violations could be questioned. A 'more formal' solution was found as early as the 1980s by introducing a human rights condition into the treaties. The 2000 Cotonou Agreement, for instance, in Article 96, explicitly recognises the right of the European Union to take appropriate measures—including the possibility of suspending the Agreement—if a state 'fails to fulfil an obligation stemming from respect for human rights, democratic principles and the rule of law'.[158] Therefore, such practices can no longer be understood as third-party countermeasures.

Nonetheless, there are also other third-party countermeasures—targeting other economic and financial privileges, either sectoral or individual—that have been adopted as a response to serious violations of human rights. These still cannot be justified by treaty clauses.[159] Nonetheless, states increasingly formalise their practices in that regard. The 2020 EU Global Human Rights Sanctions regime further formalised the practice of the European Union that was in place already in 2003.[160] The regime is similar to the US Global

[155] Dawidowicz, 'Public Law Enforcement' (n 149) 333.

[156] Council of the European Union, Regulation (EEC) No 3300/91 suspending the trade concessions provided for by the Co-operation Agreement between the European Economic Community and the Socialist Federal Republic of Yugoslavia (15 November 1991) OJ L 315/01.

[157] Lorand Bartels, 'Human Rights Provisions in Economic Partnership Agreements in Light of the Expiry of the Cotonou Agreement in 2020' (EU Publications, 2017) <https://www.europarl.europa.eu/thinktank/en/document.html?reference = EXPO_STU(2017)578011> accessed 19 August 2021.

[158] Partnership agreement between the members of the African, Caribbean and Pacific Group of States of the one part, and the European Community and its Member States: The Cotonou agreement, European Union (signed on 23 June 2000) OJ L 195/46 (2000).

[159] On forcible coercive measures, see Section 2.2.2.

[160] First adopted by the Council in 2003, it has been reviewed and updated in 2005, 2009, 2012, and 2017. EU Sanctions Guidelines (n 151). Council of the European Union, 'Sanctions: how and when the

Magnitsky Human Rights Accountability Act[161] and the UK's Global Human Rights Sanctions Regulations 2020,[162] while smaller countries, such as Switzerland, also have sanctions regimes in place that are also designed to operate outside the scope of UN Security Council authorisation.[163] The number of states resorting to such measures keeps growing. The European Union, the United States, and other Western states, initially at the forefront of these developments, are no longer alone. African and Arab states also increasingly feel entitled to impose third-party countermeasures.

Third-party countermeasures aimed at forcing the cessation of serious violations of human rights were almost automatically taken against Syria and Libya without waiting for the authorisation or recommendation of the Security Council. In the case of Libya, states had already frozen Gaddafi's accounts days before the Security Council officially imposed its sanctions.[164] In Syria, early on, in the absence of any agreement before the Security Council, several states imposed third-party countermeasures against the Assad regime in response to its ongoing brutal repression and violation of human rights.[165] Apart from the Arab League (of which Syria was member),[166] Australia, Canada, the European Union, Japan, Switzerland, and the United States have also taken measures.[167] With regard to the situation in Syria, the United States further set up a sanctions regime in 2019 in response to Turkish military action. It targeted Turkey mainly in relation to its activities in Syria.[168] Among other justifications, it

EU adopts restrictive measures', <https://www.consilium.europa.eu/en/policies/sanctions/> accessed 22 April 2021.

161 US Department of the Treasury's Office of Foreign Assets Control (OFAC), 'Sanctions Programs and Country Information' <https://home.treasury.gov/policy-issues/financial-sanctions/sanctions-programs-and-country-information> accessed 22 April 2021.

162 UK Foreign, Commonwealth & Development Office, 'UK Sanctions Relating to Global Human Rights' (6 July 2020) <https://www.gov.uk/government/collections/uk-global-human-rights-sanctions> accessed 22 April 2021.

163 Article 1, Loi fédérale sur l'application de sanctions internationales (Loi sur les embargos, LEmb) (22 March 2002) RS 946.231.

164 Martin Dawidowicz, 'State Responsibility: The General Part' (2016) 29 QIL 3, 5–6 (hereinafter Dawidowicz, 'State Responsibility').

165 Notably, EU measures, Council of Europe, Decision (CFSP) 2021/855 amending Decision 2013/255/CFSP concerning restrictive measures against Syria (27 May 2021) OJ L 188/90 (28 May 2021); Council of Europe, Decision 2013/255/CFSP concerning restrictive measures against Syria (31 May 2013) OJ L 147/14 (1 June 2013); Council of Europe, Decision 2011/273/CFSP concerning restrictive measures against Syria (9 May 2011) OJ L 121/11 (10 May 2011). For an overview of EU measures into force, see 'EU Sanctions Map', <https://www.sanctionsmap.eu/#/main> accessed 19 August 2021 (hereinafter 'EU Sanctions Map').

166 The Arab League suspended Syria's participation in November 2011.

167 For an analysis of measures against Syria, see Dawidowicz, 'Third-Party Countermeasures' (n 137) 348–50.

168 US, Blocking Property and Suspending Entry of Certain Persons Contributing to the Situation in Syria, Executive Order 13894 (14 October 2019) Federal Register Vol 84, No 201 (17 October

provided for the sanctioning of actions that threaten the peace, security, stability, or territorial integrity of Syria, and of persons or entities involved in serious human rights abuses.[169] By August 2021, the European Union had active sanctions regimes in place in relation to 33 countries with regard to situations in which they were involved within their territory or others, such as the Ukraine in 2014[170] and Belarus in 2021.[171]

Indicative of the acceptance of third-party countermeasures is that the majority of states tend not to contest the legality of peaceful coercive measures when imposed.[172] On the contrary, they occasionally even commend them. Indeed, on a few occasions, even the General Assembly and the Security Council have commended third-party countermeasures. For instance, the UN Security Council expressed its support to the African leaders who had previously decided to unilaterally impose a trade embargo on Burundi.[173] Also, the UN General Assembly had played an active role in supporting and even ordering unilateral measures taken against South Africa, pending the Security Council Action.[174]

Notably, the majority of the recorded third-party countermeasures concern situations where serious violations of human rights have taken place. In one of the most recent studies on third-party countermeasures, Dawidowicz examined specific instances of such measures taken since 1945 and the potential legal basis on which they could be justified. He argued that in the absence of any other legal basis, such practices should be understood as an emerging—if not established—*faculté* or right of not directly injured states to impose peaceful third-party countermeasures in defence of a public interest.[175] In fourteen of the twenty-two instances examined in his study, the occurrence of

2019) <https://home.treasury.gov/system/files/126/13894.pdf> accessed 20 August 2021 (hereinafter US, Sanctions Regime Turkey).

[169] ibid.

[170] Council of Europe, Decision 2014/145/CFSP concerning restrictive measures in respect of actions undermining or threatening the territorial integrity, sovereignty and independence of Ukraine (17 March 2014) OJ L 78/16.

[171] Council of Europe, Decision (CFSP) 2021/1001 amending Decision 2012/642/CFSP concerning restrictive measures in view of the situation in Belarus (21 June 2021) OJ L 219I/67. For an overview of EU measures into force, see 'EU Sanctions Map' (n 165).

[172] Dawidowicz, 'Public Law Enforcement' (n 149) 410–12.

[173] See Burundi, UNSC Res 1072 (30 August 1996) para 2.

[174] Policies of apartheid of the Government of South Africa, UNGA Res 36/172 (17 December 1981); Policies of apartheid of the Government of South Africa, UNGA Res 35/206 (16 December 1980); Policies of apartheid of the Government of South Africa, UNGA Res 34/93 (12 December 1979).

[175] Dawidowicz, 'Public Law Enforcement' (n 149) 333ff. See also Christian J Tams, *Enforcing Obligations* Erga Omnes *in International Law* (CUP 2005) (hereinafter Tams, *Enforcing Obligations*); Giorgio Gaja, 'Second Report on Obligations *Erga Omnes* in International Law' (2005) 71 AIDI 189, 199–200; ARSIWA with commentaries (n 114) 138.

serious violations of human rights was the public interest on the basis of which third-party countermeasures were taken.[176] This is not to argue that the practice of third-party countermeasures is limited to serious violations of human rights. Dawidowicz is correct to speak of 'public interest'. But the fact that practice around such measures is predominantly focused on serious violations of human rights corroborates the focus on this category of breaches here.

2.2.1.1 The gravity threshold for third-party countermeasures

Such practices have been developing around serious violations of human rights—and not all human rights violations—as a category encompassing certain human rights violations that, by their nature, constitute serious breaches of *erga omnes* obligations of international law.[177] It is indeed difficult to establish this point normatively, as there is no linguistic consistency in practice. The EU regime, though, explicitly restricts individual sanctions to serious human rights violations and abuses.[178] In addition, when looking into the practice, so far third-party countermeasures have been adopted only when there has been a well-founded belief that serious violations of human rights are being committed.[179]

There has been no objection with regard to the fact that serious violations of human rights have been committed in situations where third-party countermeasures have been recorded, such as in Libya, Syria, the CAR, and Burundi. This understanding flows factually from looking at the situations on the ground. In addition, states will usually ascertain the existence of serious

[176] Including the following instances: Developing countries against South Africa regarding the apartheid regime (1960–64); EC member states against Greece for fundamental human rights violations during the dictatorship (1967–70); the US and EC member states against Uganda for its gross and systematic violations of fundamental rights committed by Idi Amin regime (1971–78); EC member states and France against the CAR for serious violations of human rights during Bokassa's dictatorial reign (1979); EC and Economic Community of West African States (ECOWAS) member states against Liberia after a bloody military coup (1980); Western countries against South Africa for apartheid practices (1985–86); the US against Panama to end human rights abuses and restore democracy (1988); the US and European and Commonwealth countries against Nigeria for General Abacha's policy of serious human rights violations (1995); African states against Burundi when former military ruler Pierre Buyoya assumed power in the aftermath of a bloody civil war (1996); EC member states against the Federal Republic of Yugoslavia in response to the humanitarian crisis in Kosovo (1998); US against Sudan for supporting rebels in Uganda, but also for committing serious human rights violations, including slavery (1997–2005); European countries and the US against Burma (Myanmar) in response to serious human rights violations (1997–2005); Miscellaneous countries against Zimbabwe as serious human rights violations continued regarding its policy of land redistribution (2002–17); EC member states and the US against Belarus in reaction to a flawed referendum and the deterioration of the human rights situation (2004–06). Dawidowicz, 'Public Law Enforcement' (n 149) 350–98.

[177] Articles 40–41, 48, 54, ARSIWA (n 1).

[178] Council of the European Union, Decision (CFSP) 2020/1999 concerning restrictive measures against serious human rights violations and abuses (7 December 2020) OJ L 410I/13 (7 December 2020) (hereinafter Council of EU, Decision 2020/1999).

[179] Dawidowicz, 'Third-Party Countermeasures' (n 137) 361.

violations of human rights in concert with other states, and through a deliberative process of multilateral diplomacy. The recorded instances of third-party countermeasures have been adopted in the face of situations that have been 'widely acknowledged' by various international sources, including the UN Security Council, the UN General Assembly, the UN Human Rights Council, and other regional bodies. Gaja, in his report with respect to third-party countermeasures, had concluded that 'countermeasures may be taken by States other than those injured only if there is widespread acknowledgment within the international community of the existence of a breach'.[180]

Indeed, the ILC, in Article 54 of the Articles on State Responsibility, did not introduce a gravity threshold when referring to lawful measures taken as a response to violations of obligations owed to the international community as a whole. However, this approach does not seem to be followed either by practice or by scholars. No scholar who has delved into the matter and argued in support of such measures has even suggested the opposite, i.e. that third-party measures by not directly injured states can be accepted on a lower threshold.[181] Lastly, there is also a utilitarian argument favouring this understanding. The use of third-party coercive measures entails both diplomatic and financial costs for those states that resort to them—irrespective of any ulterior motives—thus they will opt to use this possibility in the most extreme and blatant cases of serious violations.

In summary, the threshold for adopting third-party countermeasures is very similar to the Security Council threshold. Similarly to the Security Council, other international organisations and states have used serious violations of human rights to factually describe a situation and strengthen a political decision by the use of legal language. The decision to adopt third-party countermeasures is political, following a careful calculation of the positive and negative

[180] Giorgio Gaja, 'First Report on Obligations *Erga Omnes* in International Law' (2005) 71 AIDI 119, 148.

[181] Notably, Christian Hillgruber, 'The Right of Third States to Take Countermeasures' in Christian Tomuschat and Jean-Marc Thouvenin (eds), *The Fundamental Rules of the International Legal Order: 'Jus Cogens' and Obligations 'Erga Omnes'* (Martinus Nijhoff Publishers 2006) 268; Tams, *Enforcing Obligations* (n 175) 248; James Crawford, *The International Law Commission's Articles on State Responsibility: Introduction, Text and Commentaries* (CUP 2002) 24; Sicilianos, 'The Classification of Obligations' (n 116) 1140–41; ILC, 'Third report by Crawford' (n 143) 404–06; Christian Dominicé, 'The International Responsibility of States for Breach of Multilateral Obligations' (1999) 10 EJIL 353, 360–61; Jochen A Frowein, 'Reactions by Not Directly Affected States to Breaches of Public International Law' (1994) 248 RCADI 345, 400–01. See also Theodor Meron, 'International Law in the Age of Human Rights: General Course on Public International Law' (2003) 301 RCADI 9, 296; Alland, 'Countermeasures' (n 136) 1221; Martti Koskenniemi, 'Solidarity Measures: State Responsibility as a New International Order?' (2001) 72 BYIL 337, 337; Michel Virally, 'Panorama Du Droit International Contemporain: Cours Général de Droit International Public' (1983) 183 RCADI 9, 223–24; Dupuy, 'Observations' (n 136) 509.

implications on multiple levels (diplomatic and economic) that a decision to adopt such measures will have for the state that imposes them. In that respect, the system remains partial and selective. There is no automatic consequence following the assertion that serious violations of human rights have been committed. However, each political decision is motivated by and based on the occurrence of serious violations of human rights and not just any human rights violation.

2.2.1.2 The type of third-party countermeasures

The sanctions adopted vary depending on their objectives and the circumstances in a particular context. However, they appear overall to deploy, similarly to the UN Security Council measures,[182] a combination of sectoral and individual targeted measures, differentiating even within the same context. The unilateral coercive measures imposed often include, among others, arms embargoes, flight bans, asset freezing, and travel bans.[183]

For instance, the 2020 EU Global Human Rights Sanctions Regime comprises three distinct types of measures to be taken against natural or legal persons, entities, or bodies. In particular, it provides for the prohibition of listed individuals from entering into or transiting through the EU region (travel ban or visa), the prohibition of providing funding to listed individuals or entities, and for the freezing of funds and assets.[184] The EU sanctions may further involve sectoral sanctions, including 'arms embargoes, embargoes on equipment that might be used for internal repression, other export restrictions, import restrictions, and flight bans'.[185] They may also impose a ban on the provision of financial services and investment, as well as, increasingly, 'sectoral bans or measures to prevent the misuse of equipment, technology or software for monitoring and interception of the Internet or of other forms of communication'.[186]

Among many examples, the European Union imposed an extensive range of economic and financial countermeasures, both individual and product-specific, against Burundi in order to put pressure on all parties to cease the serious violations of human rights that occurred following the pre-election unrest in 2015.[187] At the moment the decision was adopted, there was no UN Security

[182] See Section 1.4.

[183] For various measures adopted from the mid-20th century to the early 21st century, see Dawidowicz, 'Public Law Enforcement' (n 149).

[184] Articles 2–3, Council of EU, Decision 2020/1999 (n 178).

[185] EU Sanctions Guidelines (n 151) para 14.

[186] ibid.

[187] Articles 1(1)(b)–2(1)(b), Council of the European Union, Decision 2015/1763/CFSP concerning restrictive measures in view of the situation in Burundi (1 October 2015) OJ L 257 (2 October 2015) 37.

Council resolution on the matter. The EU decision imposed travel bans and for the freezing of assets of, among others, persons responsible for serious violations of human rights.

In the case of Libya, states froze Gaddafi's accounts early on.[188] Similarly, the European Union imposed third-party countermeasures against Zimbabwe in 2002 over electoral fraud and serious human rights abuses, which included initially an arms embargo on Zimbabwe and a travel ban on members of its Government. It later added an asset freeze and a prohibition on making funds available, restrictions on admission, and restrictions on equipment used for internal repression.[189] By February 2021, the European Union had gradually eased the measures and suspended the restrictions for all remaining listed natural persons with the exception of one listed entity.[190]

The sanctions regimes can be very focused, with limited extraterritorial effects. For instance, the US sanctions regime against Turkey is very US focused, with limited extraterritorial effects. Most importantly, in relation to interaction with designated entities and persons, it has provided for: the blocking of property and other interests in the United States; a US visa ban (but not a general travel ban); a prohibition on US persons' (citizens, residents, those who are in the United States) engaging in financial transactions with designated persons; and a ban on foreign financial institutions' facilitating financial transactions.[191]

These are just a few indicative examples. In all these situations, the adoption of third-party countermeasures by states without any direct interest (in the traditional bilateral sense) was justified not on the basis of a treaty, but on the basis of the gravity of the human rights situation in question.

2.2.1.3 *Serious violations of human rights as a condition for third-party countermeasures*

Unlike the Security Council, which has interpreted the notion of a threat to the peace to encompass serious violations of human rights, the states adopting third-party countermeasures against non-member states without the Council's authorisation do not locate their basis in a treaty mandate. Therefore, these measures appear to be prima facie unlawful under international law. The gravity of human rights violations can be a condition that permits certain

[188] Dawidowicz, 'State Responsibility' (n 164) 5–6.

[189] See Council of the European Union, Decision 2011/101/CFSP concerning restrictive measures against Zimbabwe (15 February 2011) OJ L 42/6 (16 February 2011).

[190] See Council of the European Union, Decision (CFSP) 2021/258 amending Decision 2011/101/CFSP concerning restrictive measures in view of the situation in Zimbabwe (18 February 2021) OJ L 58/51 (19 February 2021).

[191] US, Sanctions Regime Turkey (n 168).

unilateral actions to be taken, but it cannot be the legal basis that authorises and provides all necessary justification and conditions for taking such unilateral action. Asserting the importance of certain norms alone is not sufficient to defy the established legal system that provides that countermeasures can be taken only by a directly injured state.[192]

Human rights issues today concern the international community as a whole.[193] Arguably, solidarity measures should be reserved to a collective, centralised, multilateral mechanism with general law enforcement powers, representing the entire international community.[194] In the absence of an effective and representative body that can impose such measures, the calls for effective enforcement action and the lack of alternatives have been put forward as justifications for 'unilateral' action, irrespective of any ulterior motives that individual states may have.[195] Public international law as it stands may not explicitly allow third-party countermeasures, but it does not prohibit them either.[196] It leaves open the question of future developments under customary law.[197] Practice seems to be developing towards the permissiveness of third-party countermeasures rather than their prohibition. The main objections regarding the legality of third-party countermeasures have not focused on the legal basis for imposing them as such; the main concerns instead (but justifiably) relate to due process guarantees.[198]

This development in practice does not necessarily describe the development of an entirely new legal rule. It does not suffice to provide a legal basis for adopting such third-party countermeasures. Having a legal interest is not a sufficient legal basis.[199] Arguably, the logical consequence should be that subsequent practice has amended the already existing rules on countermeasures to allow not directly injured states to adopt (third-party) countermeasures as recognised in Article 22 of the ILC Articles on State Responsibility.[200] It provides

[192] Michael Byers, 'Conceptualising the Relationship between *Jus Cogens* and *Erga Omnes* Rules' (1997) 66 Nordic JIL 211, 212–13 (hereinafter Byers, 'Conceptualising the Relationship').

[193] Karin Oellers-Frahm, 'Comment: The *Erga Omnes* Applicability of Human Rights' (1992) 30 Archiv des Völkerrechts 28.

[194] Antonio Cassese, 'A Plea for a Global Community Grounded in a Core of Human Rights' in Antonio Cassese (ed), *Realizing Utopia: The Future of International Law* (OUP 2012) 136.

[195] Byers, 'Conceptualising the Relationship' (n 192) 213–14. Karl Josef Partsch, 'Reprisals' in Rudolf Bernhardt (ed), *Encyclopedia of Public International Law*, Vol IV (North-Holland 2002) 202; Christian Tomuschat, 'Obligations Arising for States without or against Their Will' (1993) 241 RCADI 195, 365.

[196] PCIJ, *SS 'Lotus' (France v Turkey)*, Series A, No 10, 7 September 1927.

[197] ICJ, *North Sea Continental Shelf (Federal Republic of Germany v Denmark and the Netherlands)*, 20 February 1969.

[198] On the debate, see Vera Gowlland-Debbas, 'Security Council Enforcement Action and Issues of State Responsibility' (1994) 43 ICLQ 55, 73–74.

[199] ICJ, *East Timor (Portugal v Australia)*, 30 June 1995, para 29. See also Christine Chinkin, 'The East Timor Case (Portugal v Australia)' (1996) 45 ICLQ 712, 721–22.

[200] ARSIWA (n 1).

for a legal basis that precludes the wrongfulness of an act reserved to the directly injured state that can now be understood to apply to not directly injured states as well. Articles 49 and following prescribe the procedural and substantive limitations of countermeasures.[201]

It follows, then, that states not directly injured that adopt—unilaterally or collectively—third-party countermeasures should subscribe to the rules and conditions that apply to traditional bilateral countermeasures. Following the model of the ILC Articles on State Responsibility, third-party countermeasures in response to serious violations of human rights should, among other things, be 'taken in such way as to permit the resumption of performance of the obligations in question'.[202] In addition, they should not affect the obligation to refrain from the threat or use of force; the obligations regarding the protection of fundamental human rights; the obligations of a humanitarian character prohibiting reprisals; and other obligations under peremptory norms of general international law.[203]

It is more challenging to apply Article 51 of the Articles on State Responsibility, which requires that countermeasures be 'commensurate with the injury suffered, taking into account the gravity of the internationally wrongful act and the rights in question'.[204] The expectation is that the injury suffered will be measured on the basis of the effects that the violation had on the injured state. However, the rules on proportionality are not rigid. Proportionality is measured by approximation, and not only in quantitative terms, taking into account the quality of the character of the rights in question.[205]

There is one additional condition that has been put forward as a requirement for justifying countermeasures: their legality is conditioned by the lack of alternative measures, and more specifically by the lack of action taken by the Security Council.[206] However, as Dawidowicz demonstrated, states have on several occasions imposed third-party countermeasures against serious violations of human rights independently and alongside any action authorised by the Security Council.[207] This raises concerns with respect to their relationship

[201] ibid.
[202] Article 49, ibid.
[203] Article 50, ibid.
[204] Article 51, ibid.
[205] ARSIWA with commentaries (n 114) 134–35.
[206] Alland, 'Countermeasures' (n 136) 1226; Bruno Simma, 'International Crimes: Injury and Countermeasures, Comments on Part 2 of the ILC Work on State Responsibility' in Antonio Cassese, Joseph HH Weiler, and Marina Spinedi (eds), *International Crimes of State: A Critical Analysis of the ILC's Draft Article 19 on State Responsibility* (Walter de Gruyter 1989) 312.
[207] Dawidowicz, 'Public Law Enforcement' (n 149) 416–17.

to the UN sanctions system.[208] While the unilateral third-party countermeasures practices continue to expand, the interpretation and specificities of the conditions for resorting to third-party countermeasures would need to be refined.

2.2.2 Forcible third-party coercive measures (humanitarian intervention)

States not directly injured by serious violations of human rights may be increasingly permitted to adopt third-party 'peaceful' countermeasures. However, they are still not entitled to resort to the threat or use of force with the intention of preventing or ending serious violations of human rights, in the absence of an explicit UN Security Council authorisation.[209]

Various international organisations adopt measures to constrain and contain escalating situations within their regions—including NATO, the African Union, and ECOWAS. They always claim to operate with Security Council's approval and not in defiance of it.[210] The 2002 Constitutive Act of the African Union appears to allow its member states to collectively intervene in humanitarian emergencies without explicitly requiring the UN Security Council's authorisation.[211] However, as it envisages a cumbersome activation procedure, there is little expectation that will operate outside the UN Security Council's remit. The Peace and Security Council is supposed to recommend action to the Assembly of the African Union, which is authorised to refer its authority on a specific case back to the Council upon achieving a two-thirds majority.[212] At least two African Union peace missions have been conducted with the consent of the state concerned, one in Burundi and one in Darfur.[213]

[208] See Alexander Orakhelashvili, 'The Impact of Unilateral EU Economic Sanctions on the UN Collective Security Framework: The Cases of Iran and Syria' in Ali Z Marossi and Marisa R Bassett (eds), *Economic Sanctions under International Law: Unilateralism, Multilateralism, Legitimacy, and Consequences* (Springer 2015) 20.

[209] Notably, Allen E Buchanan, *Human Rights, Legitimacy, and the Use of Force* (OUP 2010); Christine Gray, *International Law and the Use of Force* (4th edn, OUP 2018) 32ff (hereinafter Gray, *International Law and the Use of Force*); Philip Alston and Euan Macdonald (eds), *Human Rights, Intervention, and the Use of Force* (OUP 2008); David Kennedy, *The Dark Sides of Virtue: Reassessing International Humanitarianism* (Princeton University Press 2005); Orford, *Reading Humanitarian Intervention* (n 97). See Section 1.4.2.3.

[210] Articles 53 and 54, UN Charter (n 12). On regional organisations' practices, see Gray, *International Law and the Use of Force* (n 209) 387ff.

[211] Article 4(h), Constitutive Act of the African Union, Lomé (adopted 7 November 2000). See Ben Kioko, 'The Right of Intervention under the African Union's Constitutive Act: From Non-Interference to Non-Intervention' (2003) 85 IRRC 807, 817.

[212] Articles 4(j) and 7(e), Protocol Relating to the Establishment of the Peace and Security Council of the African Union (adopted 09 July 2002). For an in-depth and careful analysis of Article 4(h), see Dan Kuwali and Frans Viljoen (eds), *Africa and the Responsibility to Protect: Article 4(h) of the African Union Constitutive Act* (Routledge 2014).

[213] Paul D Williams, 'Military Responses to Mass Killing: The African Union Mission in Sudan' (2006) 13 Int'sl Peacekeeping 168.

Outside treaty obligations, any attempt to establish a legal entitlement to humanitarian intervention has relied on the importance of the values attacked. Most of the attempts to defend the legality of humanitarian intervention—putting aside their differences, even those opposing such a possibility—agree that any such intervention could only conceivably be justified for protection against 'gross and systematic human rights violations';[214] 'gross and egregious breaches of human rights involving loss of life of hundreds or thousands of innocent people, and amounting to crimes against humanity';[215] 'massive violations of human rights and rights of ethnic minorities';[216] and 'on-going or imminent large-scale deprivations of the most fundamental human rights'.[217] There have been some attempts to justify humanitarian intervention on expansive interpretations of the UN Charter, again in cases of serious violations of human rights of a massive and systematic character.[218] However, to justify a forcible intervention, states need to circumvent the UN Charter's explicit and absolute prohibition of the use of force.[219]

When analysing NATO's intervention as a response to the situation in Kosovo, Cassese first concluded that the Kosovo intervention was prima facie illegal because it lacked Security Council authorisation. He then relied on the principle of protection of human rights and their *erga omnes* nature as obligations owed to the international community as a whole, to eventually justify NATO's right to humanitarian intervention only for cases of serious violations of human rights.[220] Such a development would ultimately assert serious violations of human rights in the international legal order as a separate legal notion,

[214] Among many, Ciarán Burke, *An Equitable Framework for Humanitarian Intervention* (Hart Publishing 2013) 326 (hereinafter Burke, *An Equitable Framework*); Franck, *Recourse to Force* (n 54) 135ff; Linos-Alexandre Sicilianos, *Les réactions décentralisées à l'illicite: Des contre-mesures à la légitime défense* (LGDJ 1990) 479–81; Richard B Lillich, 'Forcible Self-Help by States to Protect Human Rights International Procedures to Protect Human Rights: A Symposium' (1967) 53 Iowa L Rev 325, 347–48 (opposed to a strict classification) (hereinafter Lillich, 'Forcible Self-Help'); Antoine Rougier, 'La theorie de l'intervention d'humanité' (1910) 17 RGDIP 468, 524 (situations of extreme gravity).

[215] Antonio Cassese, '*Ex Iniuria Ius Oritur*: Are We Moving towards International Legitimation of Forcible Humanitarian Countermeasures in the World Community?' (1999) 10 EJIL 23, 26 (hereinafter Cassese, '*Ex Iniuria Ius Oritur*').

[216] Bruno Simma, 'NATO, the UN and the Use of Force: Legal Aspects' (1999) 10 EJIL 1, 2 (hereinafter Simma, 'NATO, the UN and the Use of Force').

[217] Jean-Pierre L Fonteyne, 'The Customary International Law Doctrine of Humanitarian Intervention: Its Current Validity under the UN Charter' (1973) 4 Cal W Intl LJ 203, 258ff.

[218] See W Michael Reisman, 'A Humanitarian Intervention to Protect the Ibos' in Richard B Lillich (ed), *Humanitarian Intervention and the United Nations* (University Press of Virginia 1973); Lillich, 'Forcible Self-Help' (n 214) 333.

[219] Article 2(4), (use of force prohibition), 42 (Security Council authorisation) and 51 (self-defence), UN Charter (n 12). On absolute character of prohibition see, ICJ, *Military and Paramilitary Activities in and against Nicaragua (Nicaragua v United States of America)*, Merits, 27 June 1986 (hereinafter *Nicaragua v US*).

[220] Cassese, '*Ex Iniuria Ius Oritur*' (n 215) 24, 26. See also Simma, 'NATO, the UN and the Use of Force' (n 216) 2.

generating rights and obligations outside and beyond the existing treaty or customary law regimes.[221] However, the lack of supporting practice and the lack of agreement on the procedural aspects of it point towards a continued prohibition of humanitarian intervention in international law.

Despite the numerous attempts to construct a persuasive legal argument that humanitarian intervention is permissible in specific circumstances, state practice has not caught up with the scholarship.[222] The United Kingdom is the only state to have made an official statement enumerating the international law conditions under which the state is entitled to resort to humanitarian intervention.[223] The ICJ, in the specific case of the US military activities in Nicaragua, rejected the possibility.[224] Attempts to establish a 'right' to humanitarian intervention have tended to be driven by an instinctive feeling of responsibility towards those who suffer rather than actual state practice.[225]

All attempts so far have failed to convincingly construct a legal regime that would allow humanitarian intervention and introduce safeguards against the risks for abuse.[226] The most acclaimed example of humanitarian intervention in contemporary history—NATO's bombing campaign in Kosovo, in support of the repressed ethnic Albanian population in the region—is also the most contested. Even Cassese, who initially argued that a right to humanitarian intervention was based in customary international law, shortly after retracted his argument.[227] For the moment, it seems that the potential negative impact following an intervention, and the costly risks attached to military intervention,

[221] On the debate regarding the use humanitarian intervention to restore democratic rule, see Erika de Wet, 'The Modern Practice of Intervention by Invitation in Africa and Its Implications for the Prohibition of the Use of Force' (2015) 26 EJIL 979.

[222] For a full overview of arguments, see Burke, *An Equitable Framework* (n 214) 6–59. An additional reading on humanitarian intervention by Orford, ignored by Burke, draws on feminist and post-colonial theories of subjectivity and identification to unpack understandings embedded in the international community that reinforce the need to consider recourse to a humanitarian intervention as a solution. Anne Orford, 'Muscular Humanitarianism: Reading the Narratives of the New Interventionism' (1999) 10 EJIL 679.

[223] 'Chemical Weapon Use by Syrian Regime: UK Government Legal Position (Policy Paper)' (29 August 2013) <https://www.gov.uk/government/publications/chemical-weapon-use-by-syrian-regime-uk-government-legal-position/chemical-weapon-use-by-syrian-regime-uk-government-legal-position-html-version> accessed 20 August 2021.

[224] *Nicaragua v US* (n 219) para 268. Franck, *Recourse to Force* (n 54) 187.

[225] Franck, *Recourse to Force* (n 54) 187. Corten, 'Human Rights and Collective Security' (n 35) 134. Similarly, see Burke, *An Equitable Framework* (n 214) 57.

[226] Nicholas J Wheeler, *Saving Strangers: Humanitarian Intervention in International Society* (OUP 2003) 31. Schachter also, while he adhered to the notion of humanitarian intervention, rejected the notion due to the risk of abuse. Oscar Schachter, 'The Right of States to Use Armed Force International Law' (1983) 82 Mich L Rev 1620, 1629; H Scott Fairley, 'State Actors, Humanitarian Intervention and International Law: Reopening Pandora's Box' (1980) 10 Ga J Intl & Comp L 29. Cassese suggested a list of criteria. Cassese, '*Ex Iniuria Ius Oritur*' (n 215) 27.

[227] Antonio Cassese, 'A Follow-up: Forcible Humanitarian Countermeasures and *Opinio Necessitatis*' (1999) 10 EJIL 791.

continues to impede such development.[228] The last concerted attempt to reframe the debate on humanitarian intervention in order to establish a right to intervene (if necessary unilaterally) has been the concept of 'responsibility to protect'. Initially, this was an attempt to rebrand 'humanitarian intervention'.

3. Responsibility to protect

In order for any discussion on serious violations of human rights to be complete, the 'responsibility to protect' discourse cannot be ignored. The idea of 'responsibility to protect', introduced as a concept in 2001[229] and further shaped in 2005,[230] cuts through this entire book. It has generated some of the most influential debates from the beginning of the twenty-first century to the present time.[231] Multiple actors have used the notion to justify, but also condemn, international action or inaction in numerous humanitarian crises around the globe, including in: Darfur, Kenya, Georgia, Myanmar, Gaza, Sri Lanka, the DRC, North Korea, Côte d'Ivoire, Libya Syria, Yemen, and others.[232]

As such, there is a direct relation between the gradually built 'regime' around serious violations of human rights and the emergence of the concept of responsibility to protect, both constituting expressions of the same movement in the international legal order. The initial intention of the International Commission on Intervention and State Sovereignty (ICISS) was to present a holistic approach to deal with a situation where a population is suffering serious harm. It underlined the primary responsibility of the host state, but also set out the circumstances in which international society should assume responsibility for preventing, halting, and rebuilding after humanitarian emergencies. 'Responsibility to protect' has certainly motivated various developments. Especially within the United Nations, responsibility to protect has enabled and facilitated inter-sectional collaboration and cross-fertilisation.[233]

[228] Chesterman, *Just War or Just Peace?* (n 97) 231; Franck, *Recourse to Force* (n 54) 191. Orford's encouragement to move beyond military intervention encapsulates similar reservations: Orford, *Reading Humanitarian Intervention* (n 97).

[229] ICISS, 'The responsibility to Protect: Report of the International Commission on Intervention and State Sovereignty', IDRC (2001) <https://www.idrc.ca/en/book/responsibility-protect-report-international-commission-intervention-and-state-sovereignty> accessed 20 August 2021 (hereinafter ICISS Report).

[230] 2005 Outcome Document (n 45) paras 138–39.

[231] There is an ever-increasing list of publications on responsibility to protect. See, e.g., Alex Bellamy and Tim Dunne (eds), *The Oxford Handbook of the Responsibility to Protect* (OUP 2016); SFDI, *La responsabilité de protéger, Colloque de Nanterre* (Pedone 2008).

[232] Alex J Bellamy, 'The Responsibility to Protect—Five Years On' (2010) 24 Eth & Int A 143.

[233] Carsten Stahn, 'Responsibility to Protect: Political Rhetoric or Emerging Legal Norm?' (2007) 101 AJIL 99, 118 (hereinafter Stahn, 'Responsibility to Protect').

It could have evolved to encompass the regime on serious violations of human rights. Notwithstanding its powerful influence, though, responsibility to protect has not been able to fulfil this role, and it is not only its alleged threshold that stands in the way.

3.1 The threshold discrepancy

The responsibility to protect threshold was from the very beginning set too high. In the 2005 Outcome Document, states opted instead for enumerating four international crimes: genocide, war crimes, crimes against humanity, and ethnic cleansing. This was welcomed as a more practical and legally sound approach.[234] Apart from ethnic cleansing,[235] they had all already been included and defined in various international treaties, the most recent of which was the 1998 ICC Statute.[236] The suggestion that massive human rights violations be included was overlooked, on the understanding that the crimes were more specific.[237]

The chosen terminology was still unfortunate. The states chose to use individual criminal responsibility terminology to deal with state responsibility matters. The reference to crimes instead of human rights violations points towards individuals (as perpetrators or victims) rather than states. In addition, international crimes have strict definitions, as prescribed by the principle of legality in criminal justice.[238] As a result, their invocation in the context of mobilising the international community outside a judicial framework either makes the threshold unnecessarily rigid, or jeopardises the deliberation of criminal justice.[239]

Nonetheless, the differences between the thresholds for responsibility to protect and serious violations of human rights are not the only reason why responsibility to protect is not a suitable framing regarding serious violations of

[234] Mindia Vashakmadze, 'Responsibility to Protect' in Bruno Simma and others (eds), *The Charter of the United Nations: A Commentary* (3rd edn, OUP 2012) (hereinafter Vashakmadze, 'Responsibility to Protect').

[235] On a definition of ethnic cleansing, see Final Report of the Commission of Experts Established pursuant to Security Council Resolution 780 (1992) (27 May 1994) S/1994/674, para 129.

[236] Articles 5–8, ICC Statute (n 17).

[237] Alex J Bellamy, 'Whither the Responsibility to Protect? Humanitarian Intervention and the 2005 World Summit' (2006) 20 Eth & Int A 143, 165.

[238] Antonio Cassese and Paola Gaeta, *Cassese's International Criminal Law* (3rd edn, OUP 2013) 22–36.

[239] Serena K Sharma and Jennifer M Welsh (eds), *The Responsibility to Prevent: Overcoming the Challenges of Atrocity Prevention* (OUP 2015) 391 (hereinafter Sharma and Welsh, *The Responsibility to Prevent*).

human rights. In any case, the threshold could have evolved. This became apparent during the concerted attempt to operationalise one aspect of responsibility to protect—the responsibility to prevent.[240] The suggested definition to be used to assess whether a situation gives rise to responsibility to prevent includes a larger range of acts of violence, focusing more on the factual description of the acts than on criminal terminology.[241]

3.2 The open-ended scope

The concept of responsibility to protect has undergone considerable transformations since its inception, and in more than one direction, to the point where it is materially impossible to pin down exactly what it describes—whose responsibility and to do what. While it was first and foremost associated with the right to humanitarian intervention,[242] the 2005 Outcome Document, which is regarded as the most authoritative source of the responsibility to protect, excluded that possibility.[243] The 2005 Outcome Document just reaffirmed the already established primary responsibility of each state 'to protect its *own* populations from genocide, war crimes, ethnic cleansing and crimes against humanity'.[244] It emphasised the duty to prevent such crimes.[245] It then underlined the responsibility of the international community *to help to protect* populations through the United Nations against those four core crimes, and declared that states were prepared to take collective action through the Security Council.[246]

As a result, responsibility to protect was redirected to exclusively focus on the 'secondary' responsibility of the state concerned. It does not address the question of the possible direct responsibility of a state for these crimes; it only underlines the primary responsibility to protect the populations from such acts, and the residual responsibility of the international community, including international organisations and states, to help protect them.[247] Protection in

[240] Lindsey N Kingston, 'Protecting the World's Most Persecuted: The Responsibility to Protect and Burma's Rohingya Minority' (2015) 19 IJHR 1163.

[241] Sharma and Welsh, *The Responsibility to Prevent* (n 239) 372–73.

[242] The ICISS had more broadly attempted to introduce a concept of 'shared responsibility' between the sovereign state and the international community. ICISS Report (n 229).

[243] 2005 Outcome Document (n 45) para 139.

[244] ibid para 138.

[245] ibid para 138.

[246] ibid para 139.

[247] Heidarali Teimouri, 'Protecting While Not Being Responsible: The Case of Syria and Responsibility to Protect' (2015) 19 IJHR 1279.

that sense includes the criminal prosecution of the individuals responsible for these crimes, overshadowing the responsibility of the state itself for the commission of such crimes.

In the meantime, the literature has moved past humanitarian intervention to include under responsibility to protect any form of response from international organisations and towards human rights more broadly.[248] The UN Secretary-General tried to operationalise the concept and established two special advisors to assist in the process.[249] The most influential direction so far has been the focus on the prevention of the four core crimes, in an attempt to reinforce a general duty to prevent beyond the 1948 Genocide Convention.[250] However, the existence of a legal duty to prevent applying to all four crimes has yet to be established.[251]

3.3 The indeterminate nature

Irrespective of the intention of states in 2005, responsibility to protect entered the contemporary political discourse and influenced its direction.[252] However, its legal status remains highly controversial. It has been described, among other things, as: a political concept, which adds nothing to the legal debate;[253] a political concept based on existing international law;[254] as an emerging legal norm;[255] as reflecting certain underlying principles of international law;[256] as soft

[248] Gentian Zyberi (ed), *An Institutional Approach to the Responsibility to Protect* (CUP 2013).

[249] 'Report of the Secretary-General, Implementing the Responsibility to Protect' (2009) A/63/677; Secretary-General appointed the Special Adviser for the Responsibility to Protect (2008) SG/A/1120.

[250] Louise Arbour, 'The Responsibility to Protect as a Duty of Care in International Law and Practice' (2008) 34 Rev Intl Stud 445 450–51.

[251] Roland Paris, 'The "Responsibility to Protect" and the Structural Problems of Preventive Humanitarian Intervention' (2014) 21 International Peacekeeping 569; Vashakmadze, 'Responsibility to Protect' (n 234) 1222.

[252] See the influential work of Anne Orford, *International Authority and the Responsibility to Protect* (CUP 2011).

[253] Stahn, 'Responsibility to Protect' (n 233) 120; Laurence Boisson de Chazournes and Luigi Condorelli, 'De la "responsabilité de protéger", ou d'une nouvelle parure pour une notion déjà bien établie' (2006) 1 RGDIP 11, 13.

[254] Edward C Luck, 'The Responsibility to Protect: Growing Pains or Early Promise?' (2010) 24 Eth & Int A 349, 363. Similar but slightly varied opinion by Vashakmadze, 'Responsibility to Protect' (n 234) 1230.

[255] Anne Peters, 'The Responsibility to Protect: Spelling out the Hard Legal Consequences for the UN Security Council and Its Members' in Ulrich Fastenrath and others (eds), *From Bilateralism to Community Interest: Essays in Honour of Bruno Simma* (OUP 2011) 304 (hereinafter Peters, 'The Responsibility to Protect').

[256] Laurence Boisson de Chazournes, 'Responsibility to Protect: Reflecting Solidarity?' in Rüdiger Wolfrum and Chie Kojima (eds), *Solidarity: A Structural Principle of International Law* (Springer 2010) 109.

law;[257] as well as an expression of the obligation to prevent core crimes.[258]

Any attempt to assert the legal validity of responsibility to protect has mainly rested on already established treaties and obligations.[259] However, all these treaties, while containing crucial legal obligations, still create an 'uneven and complex' picture.[260] The elements that comprise the so-called responsibility to protect have diverging legal pedigrees.[261] First, they do not all contain the same obligations. Second, not all states are parties to these treaties. Third, these treaties establish rights and obligations within the jurisdiction of states. Even if they could be used as proof of the primary responsibility of the territorial state to protect its own population, they are not sufficient to establish the residual responsibility of other states or the United Nations acting as agents of the international community.[262]

Responsibility to protect could be seen as an attempt to unify multiple different rights and obligations under one comprehensive framework. However, the states showed in 2005 that they had no intention of establishing new legal obligations or a framework to systematically and consistently address humanitarian situations.[263] As such, the concept thus has little normative value. The Security Council's subsequent references to responsibility to protect reinforce this understanding, underlining the primary responsibility of the territorial state.[264] Despite its promising title, the concept did not introduce any responsibilities.

3.4 The misleading effects of a powerful brand name

Responsibility to protect as a political concept grounded on various international law principles is not problematic as such. For a primitive legal order such as the international one, this outright general commitment of states as a

[257] Jennifer M Welsh and Maria Banda, 'International Law and the Responsibility to Protect: Clarifying or Expanding States' Responsibilities Special Issue: R2P and International Law' (2010) 2 Global Responsibility to Protect 213, 230.

[258] Sandra Szurek, 'Responsibilité de proteger, nature de l'obligation et responsibilité international' in SFDI (ed), *La responsibilité de protéger* (Pedone 2008) 98–100.

[259] For instance, ICC Statute (n 17); Convention on the Prevention and Punishment of the Crime of Genocide (adopted 9 December 1948) 78 UNTS 277; International Covenant on Civil and Political Rights (adopted in 1966); International Covenant on Economic, Social and Cultural Rights (adopted in 1966).

[260] In the words of Vashakmadze, 'Responsibility to Protect' (n 234) 1222–30.

[261] ibid 1229–30.

[262] Peters, 'The Responsibility to Protect' (n 255) 303.

[263] Shraga, 'The Security Council and Human Rights' (n 23) 24.

[264] UNSC Res 1973 (2011) (n 18) Preamble, para 5; Protection of civilians in armed conflict, UNSC Res 1674 (28 April 2006) para 4.

whole to work together to ensure the protection of populations against international crimes carries a strong—albeit symbolic—value.[265] Nevertheless, the terminology used proved to be misleading, and to a certain extent it damaged more than assisted the debate.[266]

The expression 'responsibility to protect' implies that someone is responsible for taking action to protect those in danger, but the concept was not followed by the conditions and means for such action. Regular invocation of the responsibility to protect through the Security Council may have increased pressure on the Security Council members to take action,[267] but it has also increased the expectation that political bodies of the international community will react.[268] In that respect, it reinforced rather than decreased the general feeling of disappointment and dissolution as regards the international community's reactions to humanitarian emergencies.

The ICISS relied heavily on the idea that changing the permissive authority (a possibility) to an affirmative obligation (a duty) would challenge the status quo, establishing a duty of the Security Council to react and to legitimise unilateral action in the event that the former was blocked.[269] However, the simple change of terminology was not sufficient to shift the legal order already in place. States embraced an abstract responsibility to protect without any solid commitments and specific considerations regarding the content of this so-called responsibility.[270]

To conclude, the responsibility to protect, even as a framework that reinforces the normative power of existing legal rules and principles, is significant. It facilitated the mobilisation of political pressure on the United Nations to take action in extreme circumstances. It did not generate legal obligations. However, beyond that, it is not the appropriate framework for describing the special regime around serious violations of human rights. Their thresholds differ: the focus of responsibility to protect remains the primary responsibility of the state, and what exactly its responsibility entails remains vague. The argument is not that states do not have a responsibility to protect the individuals

[265] Peter Hilpold, 'From Humanitarian Intervention to Responsibility to Protect: Making Utopia True?' in Ulrich Fastenrath and others (eds), *From Bilateralism to Community Interest: Essays in Honour of Bruno Simma* (OUP 2011) 470.

[266] For a critical view, José E Alvarez, 'The Schizophrenias of R2P' in Philip Alston and Euan Macdonald (eds), *Human Rights, Intervention, and the Use of Force* (OUP 2008).

[267] Vashakmadze, 'Responsibility to Protect' (n 234) 1210.

[268] Thomas G Weiss, 'The Sunset of Humanitarian Intervention? The Responsibility to Protect in a Unipolar Era' (2004) 35 Security Dialogue 135, 148.

[269] Peters, 'The Responsibility to Protect' (n 255) 307.

[270] Simon Chesterman, '"Leading from Behind": The Responsibility to Protect, the Obama Doctrine, and Humanitarian Intervention after Libya' (2011) 25 Eth & Int A 279, 279.

under their jurisdiction, but that such responsibility is deduced from the ratified human rights treaties and customary human rights rules and is not limited to a specific set of international crimes. Undoubtedly there are elements present in both structures that reflect the current direction the international system is taking. Both constitute attempts to organise the international community's responses to violations that are of great importance to the community as a whole, and both present a similar tendency to divert from the primary responsibility of the state apparatus for these violations towards looking at its secondary responsibility to prevent, cease, and remedy such violations.

4. Enforcement in pursuit of the common purpose

The last ILC Special Rapporteur on the matter of state responsibility reached the conclusion that the '[o]ld structures of bilateral state responsibility [have been proved] plainly inadequate to deal with gross violations of human rights and humanitarian law, let alone situations threatening the survival of states and peoples'.[271] The international legal order continues to be predominantly characterised by bilateral relations between equal sovereign states and lacking a central regulatory authority. Yet the existing structures have been evolving to gradually include serious violations of human rights under their auspices. In the absence of a legitimate centralised enforcer, responses to serious violations of human rights aimed at ensuring that such breaches cease have been proliferating within and outside the UN collective security system.

On the one hand, serious violations of human rights have become one of the keys able to open the door of Chapter VII of the UN Charter—that is Article 39. On the other hand, states—alone or collectively—have permitted themselves to take peaceful countermeasures, without being the directly injured party, to respond to similar situations. The two systems—collective security and state responsibility—still differ in the nature of the relations they create, as well as in their legal basis for action. First, the Security Council creates vertical relations where states are obliged to follow its decisions,[272] while countermeasures create horizontal ones—no state can oblige another state to take unilateral action as a response to serious violations of human rights. Second, before the Security Council, serious violations of human rights have been incorporated under the notion of 'threat to the peace'. Outside the UN Charter system,

[271] ILC, 'Third report by Crawford' (n 143) para 411.
[272] Article 25, UN Charter (n 12).

serious violations of human rights have become an autonomous condition that justifies third-party countermeasures' being taken by the not directly injured states.

Nonetheless, the two mechanisms, which were separated by the ILC,[273] have irreversibly converged with regard to their target and purpose when it comes to serious violations of human rights. Measures taken under Chapter VII of the UN Charter, as well as third-party countermeasures, have both responded to serious violations of human rights, with the aim of coercing the responsible parties to comply with their international law obligations and cease those violations and abuses.[274] These measures are taken through political decision-making processes, often selectively in light of political considerations and calculations, but their adoption is influenced by the legal assessment of a situation where allegedly serious violations of human rights have been committed. Serious violations of human rights constitute the internationally wrongful acts that have irreversibly penetrated and reshaped both the UN collective security model and the legal regime regulating countermeasures under the law on state responsibility.

As a result of their convergence in relation to certain responses, each system seems to have been increasingly borrowing elements from the other, to the point where the lines between the two begin to blur. For instance, with regard to the conditions for adopting countermeasures, the UN Security Council has been increasingly expected to comply with requirements that have been central in the assessment of the legality of countermeasures, such as the conditions of temporariness and proportionality.[275] Similarly to countermeasures, it has been expected to take into consideration grave and systematic violations caused by the sanctions imposed upon its authorisation.[276] Lastly, the non-forcible coercive measures unilaterally adopted by the not directly injured states against serious violations of human rights appear to be very similar to the UN sanctions authorised by the Security Council. They mainly involve some sectoral sanctions and individual sanctions, to force those responsible to cease serious violations of human rights. However, the UN Security Council can further order the use of force, but unilateral forcible coercive measures, that is humanitarian intervention, are still not permitted.

[273] Article 59, ARSIWA (n 1).

[274] Sicilianos, 'Sanctions institutionnelles' (n 2) 61ff.

[275] Article 50(1)(b), ARSIWA (n 1).

[276] On the limits of Security Council's powers and the associated question of its judicial control, see Antonios Tzanakopoulos, *Disobeying the Security Council: Countermeasures against Wrongful Sanctions* (OUP 2011); de Wet, *The Chapter VII Powers* (n 36).

These practices together construct the second operative component of the special regime around serious violations of human rights, the enforcement component. So far as these measures are taken in order to oblige those responsible to respect specific legal norms, they acquire an enforcement role.[277] Still, this is a selective regime that will respond only to certain situations where serious violations of human rights have occurred and not to all situations. Neither the UN Security Council nor states unilaterally have an obligation to take measures when serious violations of human rights occur—they are entitled to do so. It is doubtful whether legally rigid rules obliging them to act could ever be desirable in the current state of affairs and under the current formation of the Security Council. The Security Council cannot as currently constituted punish or control all 'public law' violations of the international legal order, nor should the United Nations assume the responsibility for doing so without dramatic institutional reform.[278]

However, elements of the enforcement component of this emerging special regime are increasingly acting in concert with other elements in this regime. Particularly, the Security Council is increasingly consulting the opinions and recommendations of independent expert bodies, such as the UN High Commissioner for Refugees, the OHCHR, and even organisations such as the International Committee of the Red Cross, when making decisions on the measures to be adopted in the face of serious violations of human rights.[279] As a result of these meetings, known as 'Arria formula' meetings, its approach is influenced and shaped by their reports and their understanding of serious violations of human rights.[280]

In this framework, the directly injured state seems to disappear under other actors. A state would be considered to be directly injured when its own nationals are the victims of serious violations of human rights—or any human rights violation for that matter.[281] As long as there is a directly injured state, that state retains all the rights the directly injured state has, including the right to impose countermeasures. All the measures discussed above—i.e. sanctions and third-party countermeasures— may be taken in parallel and next to the countermeasures taken by the directly injured state.[282] However, in the context

[277] Krisch, 'Introduction to Chapter VII' (n 59) 1249.

[278] ILC, 'First report on State responsibility, by Mr James Crawford, Special Rapporteur' (1998) A/CN4/490 and Add1–7, paras 76(e), 97–101.

[279] See Bertrand G Ramcharan, 'Coordination with Other UN Organs' in Stagno Ugarte and Genser (eds), *The United Nations Security Council* (n 63).

[280] Ramcharan, *The Security Council* (n 6) 84–85.

[281] See ILC, Draft Articles on Diplomatic Protection (2006) A/61/10.

[282] See Articles 28ff, ARSIWA (n 1).

of serious violations of human rights, indeed more often than not, there is no directly injured state—as the violations often occur within one state and are committed by that state—or there may be many.[283]

Yet still the reality is that the current enforcement mechanisms tend to focus on individual rather than state responsibility for serious violations of human rights. When adopting the sanctions and the third-party countermeasures, they will still condemn the state for committing serious violations of human rights and, depending on the context, increasingly will opt for condemning the acts of all those responsible. The UN Security Council and the states unilaterally will call on the responsible authorities and/or all parties to cease those violations and abuses. However, beyond condemnations, the direct responsibility of the state increasingly becomes almost irrelevant.

The notion of responsibility to protect in the end has focused on the responsibility of the state to protect the populations under its jurisdiction and the residual responsibility of the international community to help it in the process. It does not really envisage the most regularly occurring scenario, where the state responsible for protecting those populations may be the very same that commits violations against them. It rather focuses on the criminal responsibility of the individuals, not the potential 'aggravated' responsibility of the state. There is no aim beyond the cessation of the violations. There is no consideration of how to hold states to account for failure to meet their own responsibility. This becomes also evident when one looks at the remedial component of the special regime on serious violations of human rights in Chapter 4.

[283] On the use of diplomatic protection to protect gross violations of human rights, see Menno T Kamminga, *Inter-State Accountability for Violations of Human Rights* (University of Pennsylvania Press 1992).

4
The remedial component

So far, the special regime has included in part the international community's 'soft interventions' in response to serious violations of human rights, mainly through 'naming and shaming' techniques, documentation, and reporting of such violations with a limited normative impact (the monitoring component, Chapter 2). In addition, states, either through the UN collective security system or unilaterally, have been increasingly justifying 'enforcement' measures against those states or non-state armed groups responsible for the occurrence of serious violations of human rights (enforcement measures, Chapter 3). In parallel, a third component has emerged, comprising redress procedures specific to serious violations of human rights. On the one hand, there are judicial procedures targeting only serious violations of human rights. On the other hand, certain developments in international human rights law indicate that the incidence of certain forms of remedies has not remained unaffected by the seriousness of certain human rights violations.

These remedies do not entail separate aggravated consequences for the responsible state as a result of the commission of serious violations of human rights and other serious violations of obligations owed to the international community as a whole.[1] For instance, practice so far seems to exclude punitive awards[2]—also referred to as exemplary, penal, aggravated, or multiple damages—from the remedies owed by the state responsible for serious violations of human rights law.[3] International and regional courts have thus far either avoided pronouncing on or explicitly rejected the existence of punitive

[1] Christian J Tams and Alessandra Asteriti, '*Erga Omnes, Jus Cogens* and Their Impact on the Law of State Responsibility' in Malcolm Evans and Panos Koutrakos (eds), *The International Responsibility of the European Union; European and International Perspectives* (Hart Publishing 2013) 178–79. See also Christian J Tams, 'Do Serious Breaches Give Rise to Any Specific Obligations of the Responsible State?' (2002) 13 EJIL 1161, 1166–70 (hereinafter Tams, 'Do Serious Breaches').

[2] They would involve the payment of additional damages in addition to the actual (compensatory) damages, in situations when the wrongdoer behaved in a malicious, oppressive, abusive, or wicked manner.

[3] See ILC, Articles on Responsibility of States for Internationally Wrongful Acts, with commentaries (2001) Yb ILC, Vol II, Part Two, 99, para 4, 107, para 8 (hereinafter 'ARSIWA with commentaries'). Questioning the viability and validity of punitive damages in international law more broadly, see Stephan Wittich, 'Punitive Damages' in James Crawford, Alain Pellet, and Simon Olleson (eds), *The Law of International Responsibility* (OUP 2010) (hereinafter Wittich, 'Punitive Damages') 667.

Serious Violations of Human Rights. Ilia Siatitsa, Oxford University Press. © Ilia Siatitsa 2022.
DOI: 10.1093/oso/9780192863041.003.0005

damages under international law.[4] Beyond punitive damages, various suggestions have been put forward without finding wide support. The 'particular consequences' introduced in the ILC Articles on State Responsibility regulate the obligations of all states when serious breaches of peremptory norms have been committed.[5] They do not encompass the aggravated responsibility of the wrongdoing state.

Beyond punitive damages, the obligation to accept international assessment has been suggested as a consequence of serious breaches of peremptory norms. However, states responsible for serious violations of human rights are under increasing political pressure to accept such external assessments rather than a legal obligation.[6]

Lastly, another measure that could possibly transform into a legal consequence of the perpetration of serious violations of human rights is the suspension of membership of international organisations. The suspensions of Libya in 2011[7] and Russia in 2014[8] are the only two recent examples.[9] Yet suspension of membership seems rather to be used as a form of sanction, decided at a political level to put pressure on the wrongdoing state to cease its violations.[10]

The focus hereinafter is on any legal consequences reserved for serious violations of human rights as a separate category of human rights violations. It

[4] Notably, IACtHR, *Massacres of El Mozote and nearby Places v El Salvador* (Merits, reparations and costs) 25 October 2012, para 208 (hereinafter *Massacres of El Mozote v El Salvador*); ICJ, *Application of the Convention on the Prevention and Punishment of the Crime of Genocide (Bosnia and Herzegovina v Serbia and Montenegro)*, 26 February 2007, paras 459–70; ECtHR, *Akdivar and others v Turkey (Article 50)* (GC), App no 21893/93, 1 April 1998, para 38. See analysis in Dinah Shelton, *Remedies in International Human Rights Law* (3rd edn, OUP 2015) 402–20 (hereinafter Shelton, *Remedies*). For an opposing view see Hélène Tigroudja, 'Violations de droits de l'homme et engagement de la "responsabilité aggravée" de l'état: Quelle contribution du Droit international des droits de l'homme au droit international de la responsabilité?' in *L'homme et le droit, En hommage au Professeur Jean-François Flauss* (Pedone 2014); Antônio Augusto Cançado Trindade, 'Complementarity between State Responsibility and Individual Responsibility for Grave Violations of Human Rights: The Crime of State Revisited' in Maurizio Ragazzi (ed), *International Responsibility Today, Essays in Memory of Oscar Schachter* (Martinus Nijhoff Publishers 2005).

[5] Articles 40–41, Articles on Responsibility of States for Internationally Wrongful Acts, UNGA Res 56/83 (12 December 2001) (hereinafter 'ARSIWA'). See Section 2.1, Chapter 3.

[6] The UN Human Rights Council has established inquiry mechanisms in Syria, the Democratic People's Republic of Korea (North Korea), and Eritrea without the countries' consent, but they have conducted their investigations outside the territory of the respective state. See Chapter 2.

[7] The implications of the current events in Libya and the Arab position, Cairo, League of Arab States Res 7360 (12 March 2011); Suspension of the rights of membership of the Libyan Arab Jamahiriya in the Human Rights Council, UNGA Res 65/265 (1 March 2011).

[8] Reconsideration on substantive grounds of the previously ratified credentials of the Russian delegation, PACE Resolution 1990 (21 March 2014).

[9] The only similar example that preceded the Libyan case was when the Committee of Ministers was about to decide to expel Greece from the Council of Europe, but Greece left in 1969 before any such decision was taken and re-joined after 1974.

[10] Notably, the UN General Assembly rushed to restore Libya's membership of the Human Rights Council when Libya began co-operating. Restoration of the rights of membership of Libya in the Human Rights Council, UNGA Res 66/11 (18 November 2011) 111.

is not an exhaustive analysis of the legal consequences of human rights violation. The core construction of remedies in international human rights law, as built on the basis of the general law of state responsibility,[11] has also developed elements specific to violations of human rights, for instance the obligation to investigate.[12] Therefore, a state that commits a serious violation of human rights is liable, as for violation of any other human rights, to cease that act if it is continuing; to offer appropriate assurances and guarantees of non-repetition, if circumstances so require; and to make full reparation for the injury caused by the internationally wrongful act, including restitution, compensation, and satisfaction.[13] To the extent that legal consequences with regard to serious violations of human rights do not depart from the generally applicable regime of state responsibility and international human rights law, they are not discussed here. Even though general public international law has yet to develop a fully-fledged special regime entailing separate aggravated consequences, developments in international human rights law indicate the consolidation of practices reserved only for instances of serious violations of human rights. These practices form the last operative component of the special regime.

1. Instruments specific to serious violations of human rights

1.1 The Basic Principles and Guidelines

Adopted in 2005, the Basic Principles and Guidelines' starting point and apparent primary focus encompass the provision of remedies and reparation to the victims of gross violations of human rights and serious violations of international humanitarian law. In that sense, they could be understood as reasserting the separate position of serious violations of human rights. However, in essence, they have largely reaffirmed the general reparations regime applying today to *any* human rights violation.[14] This is due to the period and the circumstances during which they were built and negotiated.

[11] Malgosia Fitzmaurice, 'Interpretation of Human Rights Treaties' in Dinah Shelton (ed), *The Oxford Handbook of International Human Rights Law* (OUP 2014).

[12] On the duty to investigate, see Alastair Mowbray, 'Duties of Investigation Under the European Convention on Human Rights' (2002) 51 ICLQ 437.

[13] Articles 29–31, 34–39, ARSIWA (n 5). See relevant chapters in James Crawford, Alain Pellet, and Simon Olleson (eds), *The Law of International Responsibility* (OUP 2010).

[14] Principle 8, Basic Principles and Guidelines on the Right to a Remedy and Reparation for Victims of Gross Violations of International Human Rights Law and Serious Violations of International Humanitarian Law, UNGA Res 60/147, Annex (16 December 2005) (hereinafter Basic Principles and Guidelines).

The Basic Principles and Guidelines emerged out of a growing response to victims' rights in the late 1980s and early 1990s, and call for more coherence between the already existing norms.[15] At the time the mandate was created, the practice around remedies in international human rights law had yet to develop.[16] At that time, even referring to the right to a remedy was considered revolutionary.[17] The Inter-American Court of Human Rights (hereinafter IACtHR or Inter-American Court) issued its first decision on merits in 1988.[18] The jurisprudence of the European Court of Human Rights (hereinafter ECtHR or European Court) proliferated after the amendment in 1998 that allowed individuals to submit applications directly to the Court.[19] In this context, the gravity of violations was used once more to push the boundaries of international human rights law to expand established norms. The inclusion of the qualifiers 'gross' and 'serious' was a result of compromise to ensure the endorsement of all states.[20] Neither of the two Special Rapporteurs, first van Boven and then Bassiouni, really believed that they were building a regime restricted to certain human rights violations.[21]

As a result, the Basic Principles and Guidelines consolidated and reproduced the generally applicable forms of reparations.[22] They did not identify additional or special consequences reflecting the aggravating responsibility of the state or special remedies for the victims. Yet certain elements recognised

[15] See Ellen Desmet, 'The UN Basic Principles and Guidelines on the Right to a Remedy and Reparation: A Landmark or Window-Dressing? An Analysis with Special Attention to the Situation of Indigenous People' (2008) 24 SAJHR 71, 74 (hereinafter Desmet, 'The UN Basic Principles').

[16] Compensation for victims of gross violations of human rights, Sub-Commission on Prevention of Discrimination and Protection of Minorities Resolution 1989/13 (31 August 1989) E/CN4/Sub2/RES/1989/13.

[17] Theo van Boven, 'Victims' Rights to a Remedy and Reparation: The New United Nations Principles and Guidelines' in Carla Ferstman, Mariana Goetz, and Alan Stephens (eds), *Reparations for Victims of Genocide, War Crimes and Crimes Against Humanity: Systems in Place and Systems in the Making* (Martinus Nijhoff Publishers 2009) 32.

[18] IACtHR, *Velásquez-Rodriguez v Honduras* (Merits), 29 July 1988 (hereinafter *Velásquez-Rodriguez v Honduras* (Merits)).

[19] Protocol No 11 to the Convention for the Protection of Human Rights and Fundamental Freedoms, restructuring the control machinery established thereby (adopted 11 May 1994) ETS No 155 (hereinafter Protocol 11, ECHR).

[20] Dinah Shelton, 'The United Nations Principles and Guidelines on Reparations: Context and Contents' in Koen de Feyter and others (eds), *Out of the Ashes: Reparation for Victims of Gross and Systematic Human Rights Violations* (Intersentia 2005) 20.

[21] See 'Final report submitted by Mr Theo van Boven, Special Rapporteur: Study concerning the right to restitution, compensation and rehabilitation for victims of gross violations of human rights and fundamental freedoms' (2 July 1993) E/CN.4/Sub.2/1993/8, para 137 (Principle 1); 'Final report of the Special Rapporteur, Mr M. Cherif Bassiouni, submitted in accordance with Commission resolution 1999/33: The right to restitution, compensation and rehabilitation for victims of gross violations of human rights and fundamental freedoms' (18 January 2000) E/CN4/2000/62, draft Principle 11.

[22] That is restitution, compensation, rehabilitation, satisfaction, and guarantees of non-repetition. See Principles 18–23, Basic Principles and Guidelines (n 14).

that the gravity of violations can still influence the incidence of remedies that can be tailored to serious violations of human rights.

First, Principle 15 reaffirmed that '[r]eparation should be proportional to the gravity of the violations and the harm suffered'.[23] Without introducing a new form, this is an express recognition that remedies should reflect the different degrees of victims' suffering. Second, certain possible forms of satisfaction are commonly associated with remedying serious violations of human rights and not *any* human rights violation. Principle 22 lists among others: '[t]he search for the whereabouts of the disappeared, for the identities of the children abducted, and for the bodies of those killed'; '[p]ublic apology, including acknowledgement of the facts and acceptance of responsibility'; and '[c]ommemorations and tributes to the victims'.[24] Subsequent practice has mostly attributed such remedies to victims of serious violations of human rights rather than any violation.[25]

Indeed, the Basic Principles and Guidelines did not build an entire special regime around serious violations of human rights. The final version of the Basic Principles and Guidelines can be used as a reference for the overall general regime on remedies and reparations in international human rights law.[26] However, they did consolidate the main principles governing the right to a remedy, set the basis for distinguishing between categories of violations of human rights, and have been instrumental in the development of subsequent practices.

1.2 Mass claims processes

Since the 1980s, mechanisms of all shapes and sizes have been put into place *post facto* to process (among others) mass claims for reparations from victims of serious violations of human rights. These mass claims processes have developed in an a*d hoc* and haphazard manner, and any decision to establish any such a mechanism is primarily and mostly a political decision, not the automatic consequence of a legal obligation.[27] However, elements of gravity,

[23] Principle 15, ibid.
[24] Principle 22, ibid.
[25] See Section 3.
[26] CCPR Committee, General Comment 31, The Nature of the General Legal Obligation Imposed on States Parties to the Covenant (26 May 2004) CCPR/C/21/Rev1/Add 13, paras 15–17.
[27] Jaime E Malamud-Goti and Lucas Sebastian Grosman, 'Reparations and Civil Litigation: Compensation for Human Rights Violations in Transitional Democracies' in Pablo De Greiff (ed), *The Handbook of Reparations* (OUP 2008) 541–43 (hereinafter Malamud-Goti and Grosman, 'Reparations and Civil Litigation').

including the sheer number of violations, have been their main trigger. They are a result of the recognition that the regular judicial mechanisms (even if still in place) would be unable to treat vast numbers of claims and that their gravity requires some form of response.[28] Despite their primarily non-judicial and administrative character, the recurrent recourse to such mechanisms reinforces the centrality of serious violations of human rights within the modern international law system.[29]

1.2.1 Types of mass claims processes

There are major contextual, legal, political, philosophical, and economic differences among the various mass claims processes that have been established over the years.[30] Yet they can be divided into three broadly defined categories with regard to their remedial roles.

The first category of mass claims procedures comprises the so-called 'international mass reparations processes'. These are procedures established following an inter-state agreement or process, such as the Iran–US Claims Tribunal in 1981 or the United Nations (UN) Compensation Commission in 1991.[31] The principal aim of these administrative bodies is to bring financial relief to victims.[32] For instance, the UN Compensation Commission (also known as the UNCC) was established in 1991 as a subsidiary organ of the UN Security Council, to process claims and pay compensation for losses resulting from Iraq's unlawful invasion and occupation of Kuwait.[33] The UNCC received and processed more than 2.6 million claims, primarily from victims of serious violations of human rights.[34] However, the Commission's mandate was restricted to material damage. It simplified the process by setting fixed amounts depending on predetermined types of loss, such as serious personal injury or the death of a family member.[35]

[28] ibid 541.

[29] This aspect of the mass claims mechanisms has been addressed in Chapter 3.

[30] Arturo J Carrillo and Jason Palmer, 'Transnational Mass Claim Processes (TMCPs) in International Law and Practice' (2010) 28 BJIL 343, 404 (hereinafter Carrillo and Palmer, 'Transnational Mass Claim Processes').

[31] ibid 343.

[32] Ibid.

[33] Iraq's legal responsibility and liability was predetermined by the UNSC Res 687 (3 April1991). Subsequent resolution created the UN Compensation Fund and the UN Compensation Commission. UNSC Res 692 (20 May 1991).

[34] UNCC, 'The Claims' <http://www.uncc.ch/claims> accessed 20 September 2021. See further Norbert Wühler, 'The United Nations Compensation Commission' in Albrecht Randelzhofer and Christian Tomuschat (eds), *State Responsibility and the Individual: Reparation in Instances of Grave Violations of Human Rights* (Martinus Nijhoff Publishers 1999) 214.

[35] Compensation for successful claims in this category was set at US$2,500 for individuals and up to US$10,000 for families. UNCC, 'Category B' <http://www.uncc.ch/category-b> accessed 20 September

In parallel, the last few decades have witnessed the proliferation of the 'transitional justice claims processes'. They have been primarily established at the national level with the aim of redressing gross violations of human rights involving thousands of victims of internal conflicts and/or political repression.[36] In the transitional justice context, the remedial responses (planning or awards) have mainly been delegated to specific mechanisms, namely the truth and reconciliation commissions.[37] At least the truth commissions, established in Burundi, Chile, Kenya, Liberia, Morocco, Peru, South Africa, South Korea, Timor Leste, and Tunisia, had some kind of 'victim redress function'.[38] Most of these commissions' mandates were limited to designing the reparations programmes. States may (or may not) subsequently introduce claims processes.[39] Only few commissions have been responsible for implementing such programmes. One of the most notable exceptions is the Truth and Dignity Commission in Tunisia.[40]

Lastly, there have been instances where a government has directly adopted laws establishing administrative compensation programmes for gross violations of human rights. A characteristic example is the two reparations laws in Hungary, which were enacted to provide compensation for unlawful seizures of properties by the state and instances of deprivation of life and liberty between 11 March 1939 and 23 October 1989.[41] Under the Human Rights Violations Act, victims or their heirs could, within a specific deadline, submit requests to receive compensation for past human rights abuses. Compensation awards were calculated on the basis of pre-established sums, depending upon the nature of the violations suffered and the identities of the victims' successors.[42]

2021. See particularly Governing Council of the UNCC, Decision 3(1991) on Personal Injury and Mental Pain and Anguish (18 October 1991).

[36] Carrillo and Palmer, 'Transnational Mass Claim Processes' (n 30) 344.

[37] See Section 4, Chapter 3.

[38] 'Report of the Special Rapporteur on the promotion of truth, justice, reparation and guarantees of non-recurrence, Pablo de Greiff' (28 August 2013) A/HRC/24/42, 13, para 43 (hereinafter 'Report on the promotion of truth' (2013)). See also Priscilla B Hayner, *Unspeakable Truths: Transitional Justice and the Challenge of Truth Commissions* (Routledge 2011) 163–202 (hereinafter Hayner, *Unspeakable Truths*).

[39] See María José Guembe, 'Economic Reparations for Grave Human Rights Violations: The Argentine Experience' in Pablo De Greiff (ed), *The Handbook of Reparations* (OUP 2008) (hereinafter Guembe, 'Economic Reparations'); Elizabeth Lira, 'The Reparations Policy for Human Rights Violations in Chile' in Pablo De Greiff (ed), *The Handbook of Reparations* (OUP 2008).

[40] 'Report on the promotion of truth' (2013) (n 38) 13–14, para 44.

[41] Respectively, Act No XXV of 1991 on Partial Compensation for Damages Unlawfully Caused by the State to Properties Owned by Citizens in the Interest of Settling Ownership Relations (1991), 2 Hungarian Rules of Law in Force 1127 (No 16, 1991); and Act XXXII of 1992 on Compensation to Persons Unlawfully Deprived of their Lives or Liberty for Political Reasons (1992). See Carrillo and Palmer, 'Transnational Mass Claim Processes' (n 30) 374–76.

[42] Carrillo and Palmer, 'Transnational Mass Claim Processes' (n 30) 375–76.

All in all, aside from their differences, the above-mentioned procedures have as a primary (or occasionally secondary) function redress for the victims. They are mandated either to award compensation directly or to design reparation programmes adapted to the situation in the country within which they operate. The reparations schemes they introduce vary considerably depending on the particular circumstances, including the political and economic conditions in a specific moment of consideration.[43] What is of interest here is whether and to what extent they diverge from the general regime on remedies applicable to all human rights violations.[44]

1.2.2 Remedies in the mass claim processes

The primary focus of every mass claim programme has been the victims and ensuring they receive some kind of remedy for the harm they suffered. The mass claim processes do not, though, establish a general obligation to provide remedies to all victims of serious violations of human rights.[45] No additional, special, or aggravated consequences against the wrongdoers (and to be more specific the wrongdoing state) have been developed from these mechanisms.[46] Certain schemes have mostly focused on individual victims and rely on the classic notion of reparation of direct benefits, either through specific financial support or through direct services.[47] For instance, the UNCC and Hungary claims provided only financial compensation to victims.[48] The amount of compensation is determined in advance, usually depending on the type of injury and often restricted to a few enumerated violations based on the patterns of behaviour relevant to the historical situation they are addressing. For instance, in Argentina, the reparations programme initially covered only victims of forced disappearances and extrajudicial executions, being later extended to include

[43] Carrillo and Palmer, 'Transnational Mass Claim Processes' (n 30) 410–412. On a detailed overview of these reparation programmes see Rachelle Kouassi, 'Programmes de Réparations, Justice Transitionnelle et Droit International: Analyse à La Lumière Du Droit Individuel à Réparation' (University of Geneva, 2017).

[44] On 'general regime on remedies in international human rights law', see Shelton, *Remedies* (n 4).

[45] On the obligation to provide reparation, see Riccardo Pisillo-Mazzeschi, 'International Obligations to Provide for Reparation Claims?' in Albrecht Randelzhofer and Christian Tomuschat (eds), *State Responsibility and the Individual: Reparation in Instances of Grave Violations of Human Rights* (Martinus Nijhoff Publishers 1999).

[46] Setting aside the increasing role of such commissions in assisting the prosecution of international crimes. See the more recent example in Tunisia. Truth and Dignity Commission of Tunisia, 'The Final Comprehensive Report, Executive Summary' (May 2019) <http://www.ivd.tn/rapport/doc/TDC_executive_summary_report.pdf> accessed 11 October 2021.

[47] Hayner, *Unspeakable Truths* (n 38) 165.

[48] On the amounts of awards, see Pablo De Greiff, 'Reparations Efforts in International Perspective: What Compensation Contributes to the Achievement of Imperfect Justice' in Erik Doxtader and Charles Villa-Vicencio (eds), *To Repair the Irreparable: Reparation and Reconstruction in South Africa* (David Philip Publishers 2004). See further Section 2.3.

victims of unlawful detention.[49] In Hungary, the Human Rights Violations Act covered loss of life and liberty, and the amount awarded for deprivation of liberty was determined on the basis of the number of days or months of detention.[50]

Increasingly, though, transitional justice reparation schemes tend to promote a diverse range of measures, putting less and less emphasis on monetary compensation and moving towards non-conventional forms of redress, such as education vouchers or other collective benefits, including memorials and legislative rehabilitation.[51] Peru, among others, opted for providing health and educational benefits to the Andean communities.[52] The approach of mass claims processes to remedies does not radically depart from that of the general regime applicable to all human rights violations. The remedies can still be categorised as forms of satisfaction or guarantees of non-repetition. The Final Report of the Commission for Reception, Truth, and Reconciliation for Timor-Leste, for instance, eventually listed the forms of reparations that have been accepted to apply to any kind of human rights violation.[53] However, it further suggested collective and symbolic measures. The latter 'might include memorialisation, commemoration ceremonies, exhumations and reburials or marking and honouring of mass graves'.

Therefore there are certain remedial awards recurrently granted to victims of serious violations of human rights.[54] These primarily include: (i) symbolic measures, individual or collective; (ii) service or benefits packages, including medical, educational, and housing assistance; and (iii) individual grants or monetary compensation.[55] Yet they should be understood as informing the incidence of existing forms of remedies rather than new types of remedies.

[49] Guembe, 'Economic Reparations' (n 39) 21–54.

[50] Carrillo and Palmer, 'Transnational Mass Claim Processes' (n 30) 372–77.

[51] ibid 407–08; See also Brandon Hamber, 'The Dilemmas of Reparations: In Search of a Process-Driven Approach' in Koen de Feyter and others (eds), *Out of the Ashes: Reparation for Victims of Gross and Systematic Human Rights Violations* (Intersentia 2005).

[52] Carrillo and Palmer, 'Transnational Mass Claim Processes' (n 30) 397 (fn 413 in particular). This becomes evident when looking into the practice of the two permanent regional human rights courts in Section 3.

[53] Namely, compensation, restitution, rehabilitation, restoration, establishment of truth, and reassurance of non-repetition. Commission for Reception, Truth, and Reconciliation (Comissão de Acolhimento, Verdade e Reconciliação de Timor-Leste, CAVR), 'Chega! Final Report of the Commission for Reception, Truth and Reconciliation in Timor-Leste (East Timor)', Part 11, Chapter 12 (2006) 37.

[54] ibid 40, para 12.7.

[55] Pablo De Greiff, 'Justice and Reparations' in Pablo De Greiff (ed), *The Handbook of Reparations* (OUP 2008) 467–71 (hereinafter De Greiff, 'Justice and Reparations'); Ruti G Teitel, *Transitional Justice* (OUP 2002) 146.

They largely fall within the requirements for satisfaction and guarantees of non-repetition.[56]

The practices of mass claims processes challenge the traditional notion of full reparation.[57] First, by providing fixed amounts of compensation, they depart from the understanding that suffering should be 'calculated' individually for each victim. Second, the increasing recourse to alternative methods of compensation also challenges the conventional understanding of what could be considered as a form of remedy. They provide for a large margin of appreciation to determine the substance of the right to reparation.[58] The principle of practical justice is central to the functioning of mass claims processes.[59] The often realistic and practical programmes and/or the recommendations reinforce the relative nature of a promising legal right to reparation. Mass claims processes constitute a reminder of 'how difficult it is to "repair" the harm of horrendous, violent crimes, committed against a seemingly uncountable number of victims'.[60]

While examining the right to reparation of victims of gross violations of human rights, Rombouts and others have suggested that the right to reparation may be subject to limitations, and that it would be possible to use the general formula on limitations found under other rights in human rights treaties as a guide for determining the legality of such limitations. According to this understanding, limitations to the right to a full remedy would be accepted only if they are pursuing a legitimate aim and are deemed necessary and proportionate—a balance between the interests of the individual victims and the legitimate aim.[61] Eventually such a suggestion might merit further consideration, especially for cases of serious violations of human rights. A rigid system of full reparation for such violations would be inconceivable.[62]

[56] On collective measures, see Section 2.3.3.

[57] On notion of full reparation see, PCIJ, *The Factory at Chorzów*, Judgment on merits, 13 September 1928, 47 (hereinafter *Chorzów* case).

[58] Carrillo and Palmer, 'Transnational Mass Claim Processes' (n 30) 407. See also Richard Falk, 'Reparations, International Law, and Global Justice: A New Frontier' in Pablo De Greiff (ed), *The Handbook of Reparations* (OUP 2008) 492.

[59] See Hans Das, 'The Concept of Mass Claims and the Specificity of Mass Claims Resolution' in The International Bureau of the Permanent Court of Arbitration (ed), *Redressing Injustices Through Mass Claims Processes: Innovative Responses to Unique Challenges* (OUP 2006) 10; Christian Tomuschat, 'Individual Reparation Claims in Instances of Grave Human Rights Violations: The Position under General International Law' in Albrecht Randelzhofer and Christian Tomuschat (eds), *State Responsibility and the Individual: Reparation in Instances of Grave Violations of Human Rights* (Martinus Nijhoff Publishers 1999) 20 (hereinafter Tomuschat, 'Individual Reparation Claims').

[60] Hayner, *Unspeakable Truths* (n 38) 164.

[61] Heidy Rombouts, Pietro Sardaro, and Stef Vandeginste, 'The Right to Reparation for Victims of Gross and Systematic Violations of Human Rights' in Koen de Feyter and others (eds), *Out of the Ashes: Reparation for Victims of Gross and Systematic Human Rights Violations* (Intersentia 2005) 453 (hereinafter Rombouts, Sardaro and Vandeginste, 'The Right to Reparation').

[62] Tomuschat, 'Individual Reparation Claims' (n 59) 25.

However, the lack of a common formula on reparations among mass claims processes, although welcome as adapted to each context,[63] reduces even more the power of their influence to introduce an elaborate calculation process.[64] Still, despite the administrative character of the distribution mechanisms and the non-binding, recommendatory nature of the truth and reconciliation commissions' reports, their practice eventually informs that of the judicial organs, which may actually provide for a stronger remedial framework in the future.

2. Adjudicating serious violations of human rights

None of the regional human rights courts was created to deal specifically with serious violations of human rights.[65] There is no explicit reference to serious violations of human rights in either the European or the American convention. The same partly applies to the African text.[66] At the same time, there is no provision preventing the courts from using gravity qualifications. They are authorised to examine any type of violation—serious or otherwise—covered by the material scope of the human rights treaties falling within each court's jurisdiction. In the end, all the human rights courts have been confronted with cases of serious violations of human rights. Serious violations of human rights have found their way into the courts' jurisprudence through different avenues: individual petitions, the special procedure of the African Court, and, increasingly, inter-state applications.

In the face of serious violations of human rights, they all need to overcome various partially common obstacles. From a procedural point of view, for instance, judicial justice is suited to examining individual cases; thus, the courts' rules of procedure and terms of reference are not necessarily apt to facilitate the examination of multiple instances of serious violations that have occurred on a large scale or systematically.[67] From a substantive point of view, the different

[63] In most cases, the programme actually developed is much more limited than the recommendations of the commissions. Hayner, *Unspeakable Truths* (n 38) 163.

[64] See Carrillo and Palmer, 'Transnational Mass Claim Processes' (n 30) 403, 406; Malamud-Goti and Grosman, 'Reparations and Civil Litigation' (n 27) 540.

[65] See Lutz Oette, 'Bringing Justice to Victims? Responses of Regional and International Human Rights Courts and Treaty Bodies to Mass Violations' in Carla Ferstman, Mariana Goetz, and Alan Stephens (eds), *Reparations for Victims of Genocide, War Crimes and Crimes Against Humanity: Systems in Place and Systems in the Making* (Martinus Nijhoff Publishers 2009) (hereinafter Oette, 'Bringing Justice to Victims?').

[66] It does contain a reference to grave or massive violations in Article 58. African Charter on Human and Peoples' Rights ('Banjul Charter') OAU (adopted 27 June 1981). See further Chapter 2.

[67] On concerns regarding regional courts suitability and capability to deal with serious violations of a systematic or widespread character, see Menno T Kamminga, 'Is the European Convention on Human Rights Sufficiently Equipped to Cope with Gross and Systematic Violations?' (1994) 12 NQHR 153,

degrees of harm need to be taken into account, especially when deciding on possible reparations.[68] Each has reacted differently depending on various factors, including the regional particularities and the discretion they enjoyed. Their practice may be described as empirical and haphazard for now, but repetition and recurrent recourse allows for a more systematic overview.

Their jurisprudence has been evolving towards a clearer separation between serious violations of human rights and other violations. By invoking 'serious violation of human rights' in their jurisprudence to underline the gravity of a violation, human rights courts introduced this category of violations into the adjudication of human rights. The focus here will be particularly on the two more active regional courts, the European Court and the Inter-American Court.[69]

2.1 Introducing serious violations of human rights into jurisprudence

2.1.1 Individual complaints remain the primary vehicle for examining serious violations of human rights

Human rights courts have primarily dealt with cases of serious violations of human rights through individual applications from the victims.[70] The Inter-American Court and the European Court have each at various times been called upon by the victims to examine cases of serious violations of human rights. Yet each had a different point of departure for reasons relating to their mandates and procedures, as well as the historical and political contexts within which they operate.

161–62 (hereinafter Kamminga, 'Is the European Convention on Human Rights Sufficiently Equipped'); Aisling Reidy, Françoise Hampson, and Kevin Boyle, 'Gross Violations of Human Rights: Invoking the European Convention on Human Rights in the Case of Turkey' (1997) 15 NQHR 161, 162–63 (hereinafter Reidy, Hampson, and Boyle, 'Gross Violations of Human Rights').

[68] See Section 2.3.

[69] The African Court's decisions are still limited. For instance, ACtHPR, *Ayants droits de feus Norbert Zongo et al & Le Mouvement Burkinabé des Droits de l'Homme et des Peuples c Burkina Faso*, App No 013/2011, Case on reparations, 5 June 2015 (hereinafter *Zongo ao v Burkina Faso* (Reparations)). The practice of the UN human rights treaty bodies regarding the distinction between serious and other human rights violations—under their quasi-judicial function when reviewing individual complaints—is scarce. For most of the UN treaty bodies, the occurrence of serious violations of human rights allows them to initiate an urgent inquiry procedure (see Chapter 2).

[70] They have no competence to examine human rights violations on their own initiative. Articles 33–34, European Convention for the Protection of Human Rights and Fundamental Freedoms (as amended by subsequent protocols), 4 November 1950, CETS No 5, Council of Europe (hereinafter ECHR); Article 41, International Covenant on Civil and Political Rights (adopted 16 December 1966) 999 UNTS 171; Article 5, Protocol to the African Charter on Human and Peoples' Rights on the Establishment of the African Court on Human and Peoples' Rights (adopted 10 June 1998) OAU (hereinafter 1998 Protocol to the African Charter).

2.1.1.1 Cases of serious violations in the Latin-American context

The Inter-American Court was the first international judicial organ to systematically differentiate between serious and other violations of human rights.[71] It is also the only court to have referred to 'serious violation of human rights' as a distinct legal concept with specific consequences.[72] Notably, in a 2011 judgment it concluded:

> [T]he Court deems that any human rights violation involves a level of severity by its own nature, because it implies a breach of certain State obligations to respect and guarantee the rights and freedoms for people. However, this should not be confused with what the Court throughout its jurisprudence has deemed to be *'serious violations of human rights' which*, as is clear from the provisions above (supra para 117), *have their own connotation and consequences . . .*[73]

Various reasons explain why the Inter-American Court considered it necessary to embrace this distinction.

First, the Court began operating in 1979,[74] amidst the overthrow of brutal dictatorships in Latin America. Most countries in the region had been suffering from long periods of political instability, authoritarian regimes, and devastating conflicts. The Inter-American Court has been called upon to examine numerous cases of massacres, extrajudicial killings, enforced disappearances, and ill-treatment in Honduras, Suriname, Colombia, Ecuador, Guatemala, Peru, Uruguay, Mexico, Chile, Venezuela, Bolivia, the Dominican Republic, Paraguay, Nicaragua, and elsewhere.

In this historical and political environment, the Court faced from the very beginning several cases of extreme gravity. The majority of the early cases before the Court revealed the immense suffering of the victims and their relatives, by violations that were perpetrated systematically by state officials and that often involved large numbers of victims. Its first judgment concerned the practice of involuntary disappearances, carried out or tolerated by officials

[71] See IACtHR, *Gelman v Uruguay* (Merits and reparations), 24 February 2011, paras 99, 243 (hereinafter *Gelman v Uruguay*).

[72] IACtHR, *Vera et al v Ecuador* (Preliminary objections, merits, reparations and costs), 19 May 2011, paras 117–18 (hereinafter *Vera et al v Ecuador*). Repeated in IACtHR, *Vélez Restrepo and family v Colombia* (Preliminary objection, merits, reparations and costs), 3 September 2012, para 282 (hereinafter *Vélez Restrepo and family v Colombia*).

[73] *Vera et al v Ecuador* (n 72) para 118 (emphasis added).

[74] American Convention on Human Rights ('Pact of San José'), San José, Costa Rica (adopted 22 November 1969) Organization of American States (OAS) (hereinafter ACHR).

between 1981 and 1984 in Honduras.[75] This was followed by a case concerning horrendous events in Suriname, for which the Government did not even try to contest its responsibility. *Aloeboetoe et al v Suriname* dealt with the disappearance, ill-treatment, and extrajudicial killings of numerous victims suspected of being members of a guerrilla commando group,[76] by the state's armed forces.[77]

Second, the Inter-American Court was established twenty years after the European Court. It did not exercise its contentious jurisdiction until 1986 and issued its first judgment on the merits in 1988.[78] By that time the human rights debate had already been flourishing, influencing the newly established Court's jurisprudence. The discussions with regard to a hierarchy among human rights, as well as in general international law, but also the debate regarding *erga omnes* obligations had already emerged.[79] In the meantime, the UN political bodies were already using such expressions of gravity to expand their competences and justify extraordinary measures.[80] In the same period, the transitional justice movement started developing as a response to gross violations of human rights.[81]

Lastly, Article 63 of the American Convention is framed quite broadly, allowing a certain flexibility to the Court with respect to the remedial measures it can order.[82] In addition, the American Convention does not provide for a strong follow-up mechanism.[83] As a result, the Court has felt compelled to be more explicit and has used its power extensively from the very beginning. In this context, the notion of serious violations of human rights has been used as a vehicle for expanding the forms of remedies awarded to the victims.

[75] *Velásquez-Rodriguez v Honduras* (Merits) (n 18) para 147. Followed by IACtHR, *Godínez-Cruz v Honduras* (Merits), 20 January 1989; IACtHR, *Fairén-Garbi and Solís-Corrales v Honduras* (Merits), 15 March 1989.

[76] The 'Jungle Commando', formally known as the Suriname National Liberation Army.

[77] The *Aloeboetoe* case concerned more than twenty unarmed men who were beaten and humiliated by the soldiers who detained them. Afterwards, seven of them were driven 30 km away from the detention facility, where they were shot and killed, with the exception of one survivor who was found alive. IACtHR, *Aloeboetoe et al v Suriname* (Merits), 4 December 1991 (hereinafter *Aloeboetoe et al v Suriname* (Merits)).

[78] *Velásquez-Rodriguez v Honduras (Merits)* (n 18).

[79] See Chapter 2.

[80] See Chapter 3.

[81] For a history of transitional justice, see Teitel, *Transitional Justice* (n 55).

[82] Article 63, ACHR (n 74) provides that where a right or freedom protected by the Convention is violated, the injured party shall be ensured the enjoyment of that right and freedom, and the consequences of the violation shall be remedied and compensation paid to the injured party.

[83] Unlike the European system, where the Committee of Ministers supervises the execution of the Court's judgments (Article 46, ECHR (n 70), the American Convention does not explicitly recognise the political organ of the OAS as responsible for supervising the implementation of the Court's judgments.

2.1.1.2 Individual complaints in the European continent

On the other side of the Atlantic, the European Court has been more cautious in its use of gravity qualifiers. This also relates to the context in which it operates. First, the political and historical conditions in states parties to the European Convention, especially at the beginning, were very different from the scenarios in the American context. There were (mainly) stable democracies with elaborate and (almost) fully functioning legal systems, at least up until the 1990s when new conflicts broke out and with the exception of the situations in Northern Ireland and Greece.[84]

Second, international human rights law was at a rudimentary stage when the European Commission and Court began functioning. The European Convention was adopted two years after the 1948 Universal Declaration of Human Rights, and international human rights law was just starting to develop. At that time, criticising states for the treatment of their own nationals within their borders was rare. Even though they voluntarily submitted themselves to the European system of supervision, a decision by the Commission or the Court recognising a violation of the Convention was perceived almost as causing 'offence' to the state concerned.[85]

Third, the European Court was given much less room for manoeuvre regarding the form of remedies it could grant. In the 1940s, the drafters of the Convention considered that recognition of a violation by the European Court was a sufficient guide for states as to the most appropriate means to remedy the situation.[86] It was left exclusively to the Committee of Ministers to follow up and supervise the execution of the Court's judgments.[87] Until recently, the European Court was only making monetary awards as just satisfaction, and only if deemed necessary. Initially, it rejected any request to order more than compensatory awards.[88]

Lastly, due to the active role of the Committee of Ministers in the Council of Europe, the measures taken by the European states are not as easily discernible as those ordered by the Inter-American Court, whose remedial measures are

[84] See ECtHR, *Ireland v UK*, App no 5310/71, 18 January 1978; EComHR, *Denmark, Norway, Sweden, & Netherlands v Greece*, App nos 3321–3323, 3344/67, Decision, Yearbook of the ECHR, Vol 12-I (1969), 5 November 1969 (hereinafter *The Greek Case*).

[85] On the gradual evolution of the system, see Linos-Alexander Sicilianos, 'The Involvement of the European Court of Human Rights in the Implementation of its Judgments: Recent Developments under Article 46 ECHR' (2014) 32 NQHR 235, 235–36 (hereinafter Sicilianos, 'The Involvement of the European Court').

[86] Shelton, *Remedies* (n 4) 285–97.

[87] Article 46, ECHR (n 70).

[88] Among others, ECtHR, *Campbell and Cosans v UK*, App nos 7511/76; 7743/76, Just satisfaction, 22 March 1983, para 16. See further Section 2.2.3.

explicitly enumerated in the latter's judgments. As a result, not much attention has been given to the measures taken by those states convicted following the European Court's judgments on the guidance of the Committee of Ministers. Many of these measures are, however, increasingly reported in detail in the resolutions and reports of the Committee of Ministers.[89]

Various developments in the 1990s had a significant impact on the cases that reached the European Court. Many countries of Central and Eastern Europe acceded to the Council of Europe around that time altering as a result the composition of the Court.[90] In addition, the 1998 reform allowed individual victims to bring cases directly before the Court, including those of serious violations of human rights.[91] Cases from Turkey, Russia, Turkey, Ukraine, Romania, and Italy occupy a large part of the Court's workload.[92] Finally, new civil and inter-state conflicts that broke out within the borders of the Council of Europe led to a substantial increase in individual complaints for serious violations of human rights.[93] Multiple cases concerning the systematic practice of enforced disappearances in Russia continue to be submitted,[94] as well as torture cases against Turkey.[95] To date, there have been over 7,000 individual complaints relating to the conflict in Ukraine that started in 2014.[96]

Faced with more and more cases of serious violations of human rights, the European Court has been increasingly invoking the gravity of the violations, and it has been expanding the forms of remedies it orders. For instance, in a case involving the ill-treatment of a member of the Kurdish minority in South East Turkey while in police custody, the European Court gave particular

[89] See, for example, CoM, 'Supervision of the execution of judgments and decisions of the European Court of Human Rights, 14th Annual Report of the Committee of Ministers', 2020, Council of Europe; CoM, 'Supervision of the execution of judgments and decisions of the European Court of Human Rights, 8th Annual Report of the Committee of Ministers' (2014) Council of Europe (hereinafter CoM, 8th Annual Report (2014)). See further 'Department for the Execution of Judgments of the European Court of Human Rights' <http://www.coe.int/web/execution> accessed 31 August 2021.

[90] Article 20, ECHR (n 70).

[91] The 1998 Protocol also terminated the activities of the European Commission of Human Rights. Protocol 11, ECHR (n 19).

[92] ECtHR, 'The ECHR in facts & figures 2020' <https://www.echr.coe.int/Pages/home.aspx?p = reports/factsfigures&c=> accessed 31 August 2021.

[93] See 'Violations by Article and by State 1959–2016, Statistics by State' <http://www.echr.coe.int/documents/stats_violation_1959_2016_eng.pdf> accessed 2 September 2021.

[94] Their systematic character was recognised in ECtHR, *Aslakhanova and others v Russia*, App nos 2944/06 and 8300/07, 50184/07, 332/08, 42509/1018 December 2012, paras 216 et seq (hereinafter *Aslakhanova ao v Russia*). On missing persons, see also ECtHR, *Varnava and others v Turkey* (GC), App nos 16064/90, 16065/90, 16066/90, 16068/90, 16069/90, 16070/90, 16071/90, 16072/90, and 16073/90, 18 September 2009 (hereinafter *Varnava ao v Turkey*).

[95] Notably, ECtHR, *İzci v Turkey*, App no 42606/05, 23 July 2013. For past cases on Turkey, see Reidy, Hampson, and Boyle, 'Gross Violations of Human Rights' (n 67) 161–73; Kamminga, 'Is the European Convention on Human Rights Sufficiently Equipped' (n 67) 155–59.

[96] ECtHR, 'Country Profile: Russia', 32 <https://www.echr.coe.int/Documents/CP_Russia_ENG.pdf> accessed 2 September 2021.

weight to the prohibition of torture and the vulnerable position of torture victims when interpreting the right to an effective remedy, underlining the obligation to conduct a thorough and effective investigation.[97] The European Court's jurisprudence is thus becoming much more elaborate in that respect. While it has avoided embracing the more outspoken normative approach of the Inter-American Court, its approach to serious violations reveals more and more common elements with regard to the incidence of remedies awarded to the victims.

2.1.2 The African system's special procedure

The youngest of the three regional courts, the African Court of Human and Peoples' Rights, drew on the experiences of other regional (and universal) human rights systems.[98] The African judicial system formally introduced an additional accelerated procedure for serious violations of human rights. On the basis of Rule 118(3), the African Commission can expeditiously seize the Court without first adopting a decision on an individual complaint (communication) submitted to it.[99] As a result, the judicial organ can treat such cases in an accelerated manner. In addition, under this procedure, the Commission can group together multiple complaints. This procedure allows the monitoring organs to shift the focus from one individual victim to an overall assessment of the situation. The formal inclusion of the notion 'serious or massive violations' in the Rules of Procedure reflects as such the evolving recognition of serious violations as a separate category of human rights violations that justifies the establishment of additional procedural avenues.

Interestingly, according to Article 5 of the 1998 Protocol to the African Charter, the African Commission can submit an application on its own motion independently of any complaints submitted, for any violation, irrespective of its gravity.[100] Such an interpretation provides the quasi-judicial organ of the African system with a similar power to trigger the judicial process similarly as states. This prerogative of the Commission was confirmed by the African Court in its 2017 judgment, where the Court, on the basis of the 1998 Protocol and its

[97] ECtHR, *Aksoy v Turkey* (GC), App no 21987/93, 18 December 1996, para 98 (hereinafter *Aksoy v Turkey* (GC)). ECtHR, *Aydin v Turkey*, App no 57/1996/676/866, 25 September 1997, para 103.

[98] It started operating in 2006 almost fifty years after the European Court. The 2008 Protocol is meant to replace the previous Protocols. With only eight ratifications up to June 2020, it has yet to enter into force. (African Union, Protocol on the Statute of the African Court of Justice and Human Rights, 1 July 2008.)

[99] Rule 118(3), 2010 Rules of Procedure of the African Commission.

[100] Article 5(1), 1998 Protocol to the African Charter (n 70).

own Rules of Procedure, recognised that the Commission may submit applications to the Court independently of their serious or massive character.[101]

The African Commission has submitted at least three complaints to the African Court claiming that serious and massive violations had been committed. The first application was against Libya, for serious and massive violations that occurred during the 2011 conflict in that country.[102] Later on, it submitted another complaint against Libya with regard to the incommunicado detention and conditions of detention of Saif al-Islam Gaddafi (second son of the former Libyan leader Muammar Gaddafi).[103] In 2012, it also submitted a complaint against Kenya regarding the arbitrary forced evictions of indigenous communities from their lands, threatening their very existence.[104] The Court's judgments on the merits for the second and third applications do not appear to take the gravity of violations into consideration.[105] In the Libya judgment, the Court explicitly acknowledged that '[i]ncommunicado detention constitutes in itself a gross violation of human rights'.[106]

However, this does not preclude that gravity will be taken into account when the Court pronounces on reparations in cases. The numerous situations of extreme violence and armed conflict that continue to unfold in many countries on the African continent provide a clear indication of the types of cases that, in slow progression, will reach the African Court. The judicial system, whose terms of reference already allow it to embrace the distinction between serious and other violations of the African Charter, could in time further influence the evolution of the special regime around serious violations of human rights.

[101] The Court invoked Articles 3(1) and 5(1), 1998 Protocol to the African Charter (n 70), which do not provide for any additional conditions. ACtHPR, *African Commission on Human and Peoples' Rights v The Republic of Kenya*, App No 006/2012, Judgment on merits, 26 May 2017, para 53 (hereinafter *AComHPR v Kenya* (Merits)).

[102] The Court adopted a decision on provisional measures, but it was obliged to discontinue the case on the merits because the applicant (the African Commission) failed to pursue its Application. ACtHPR, *African Commission on Human and Peoples' Rights v Great Socialist People's Libyan Arab Jamahiriya*, App No 004/2011, Order on discontinuance of proceedings, 15 March 2013; ACtHPR, *African Commission on Human and Peoples' Rights v Great Socialist People's Libyan Arab Jamahiriya*, App No 004/2011, Order for provisional measures, 25 March 2011.

[103] ACtHPR, *African Commission on Human and Peoples' Rights v Libya*, App No 002/2013, Judgment on merits, 3 June 2016 (hereinafter *AComHPR v Libya* (Merits)); ACtHPR, *African Commission on Human and Peoples' Rights v Libya*, App No 002/2013, Order for provisional measures, 15 March 2013.

[104] *AComHPR v Kenya* (Merits) (n 101); ACtHPR, *African Commission on Human and Peoples' Rights v The Republic of Kenya*, App No 006/2012, Order of provisional measures, 15 March 2013.

[105] *AComHPR v Kenya* (Merits) (n 101); *AComHPR v Libya* (Merits) (n 103).

[106] *AComHPR v Libya* (Merits) (n 103) para 84.

2.1.3 Inter-state applications as a form of collective application

Next to individual applications, inter-state complaints are becoming (or at least could become) a key avenue by which widespread and aggravated human rights violations are brought before judicial bodies, but so far mainly within the European system.[107] Even though Article 33 of the European Convention does not limit inter-state complaints to serious violations of human rights, to date, most of the applications have referred only situations of gravity and scale.[108] The marginally increasing recourse to this option is in line with the purpose of inter-state complaints, initially introduced as a collective guarantee of all protected rights.[109]

The renowned *Greek* case before the European Commission on Human Rights is the uncontested example of inter-state applications' being used to defend serious violations of human rights. The initial application was submitted by a number of 'not directly interested' member states, namely Denmark, Norway, Sweden, and The Netherlands, against the brutal dictatorship that was established after the military coup d'état in Greece in 1967. As a result of this application, the Commission published a cataclysmic report condemning serious violations of human rights committed by the junta.[110] By that time, though, Greece had left the Council of Europe, only to re-join after the fall of the dictatorship in 1974. As a result, the case never reached the Court. Similarly, there was an inter-state application against Turkey for the horrendous torture practices after the 1980 coup. The friendly settlement that followed the application unfortunately diminished its impact.[111] The most positive outcome was that Turkey recognised the right of individuals to bring complaints, which has led to numerous complaints against Turkey ever since.[112]

Apart from these two cases, all other inter-state complaints have been submitted by the state whose nationals were primarily attacked, hence bringing

[107] At least two complaints have been filed before the Inter-American Commission: IAComHR, *Franklin Guillermo Aisalla Molina (Ecuador v Colombia)*, Case 12.779, Decision to archive, Report No 96/13, 4 November 2013; IAComHR, *Nicaragua v Costa Rica*, Inter-state Case 01/06, Report No 11/07, 8 March 2007. On the various reasons for their limited use, see Søren C Prebensen, 'Inter-State Complaints Under Treaty Provisions – The Experience Under The European Convention On Human Rights' in Alfred Zayas and others (eds), *International Human Rights Monitoring Mechanisms* (Brill, 2009) 459.

[108] One exception was the case of EComHR, *Austria v Italy*, App no 788/60, Decision, 11 January 1961.

[109] Linos-Alexander Sicilianos, 'La Cour européenne des droits de l'homme face à l'Europe en crise' (2016) 105 RTDH 5, 33–34.

[110] *The Greek Case* (n 84); EComHR, *Denmark, Norway, Sweden, & Netherlands v Greece* (The Greek Case), App nos 3321–3323, 3344/67, Decision, Yearbook of the ECHR, Vol 12-II (1969), 5 November 1969.

[111] EComHR, *France, Norway, Denmark, Sweden, Netherlands v Turkey*, App nos 9940–9944/82, Decision, 6 December 1983.

[112] Kamminga, 'Is the European Convention on Human Rights Sufficiently Equipped' (n 67)158–59.

it closer to diplomatic protection. This does not altogether eliminate the legal significance of these applications as means of judicial enforcement regarding serious violations of human rights. Notably, an important number of the atrocities committed during the Troubles in Northern Ireland were brought before the European Court through the *Ireland v The United Kingdom* judicial proceedings.[113]

Similarly, the *Cyprus v Turkey* case, relating to human rights violations committed in Northern Cyprus following the Turkish occupation in 1974, constitutes a pivotal example of the potential influence of inter-state applications. The 2001 judgment of the European Court on the merits was followed in 2014 by the first ever judgment on reparations after an inter-state complaint.[114] The Court declared that it was possible to request reparation on behalf of the victims under Article 41 of the Convention.[115]After Cyprus's applications, inter-state applications have been used closer to the date of the conflict, particularly but not only by smaller states against Russia.

Georgia submitted its first application against Russia amid the escalation of political tensions that led to the conflict in August 2008. The 2007 application concerned the arrest, detention, and collective expulsion of Georgian nationals in the autumn of 2006.[116] Georgia lodged the second application only a few days after the beginning of the 2008 conflict,[117] and two more applications in 2009 and 2018.[118] The two first judgments of the Grand Chamber of the European Court found Russia responsible for numerous serious violations of human rights.[119] Ukraine, for its part, has filed multiple applications against Russia in relation to the events in Crimea and the developments in the eastern regions of Ukraine, from the outset of the 2014 conflict.[120] However, the

[113] ibid 156.

[114] ECtHR, *Cyprus v Turkey* (GC), App no 25781/94, Just satisfaction, 12 May 2014 (hereinafter *Cyprus v Turkey* (GC) (Just satisfaction)); ECtHR, *Cyprus v Turkey* (GC), App no 25781/94, 10 May 2001.

[115] *Cyprus v Turkey* (GC) (Just satisfaction) (n 114) paras 39–47. For further information on this case, see Section 3.3.

[116] ECtHR, *Georgia v Russia (I)* (GC), App no 13255/07, Merits, 14 July 2014 (hereinafter *Georgia v Russia (I)* (Merits)). The war officially started on 9 August 2008. Georgia submitted an application on 11 August 2008, asking the Court to order interim measures. It lodged the formal application as it stands now on 9 February 2009.

[117] ECtHR, *Georgia v Russia (II)* (GC), App no 38263/08, Merits, 21 January 2021 (hereinafter *Georgia v Russia (II)* (Merits)).

[118] The 2009 case was struck out at the request of the Georgian Government. ECtHR, *Georgia v Russia (IV)*, App no 39611/18, lodged on 22 August 2018; ECtHR, *Georgia v Russia (III)*, App no 61186/09, Decision, 16 March 2010.

[119] *Georgia v Russia (II)* (Merits) (n 117); *Georgia v Russia (I)* (Merits) (n 116).

[120] The various applications have been merged or struck out by the Court in the process. At the time of writing, two cases were pending before the Grand Chamber: *Ukraine v Russia (re Crimea)* (GC), App nos 20958/14 and 38334/18, Decision, 16 December 2020; *Ukraine and the Netherlands v Russia (re Eastern Ukraine)* (GC), App nos 8019/16, 43800/14, and 28525/20, Decision to join the case, 27

Netherlands has also filed an application against Russia regarding the events in eastern Ukraine in 2020.[121]

Undeniably, the inter-state complaints are intertwined with the political interests of the states that bring them. In 2021, Russia lodged its own application against Ukraine alleging an administrative practice in Ukraine of, among other things, killings, abductions, and forced displacement. It also included a complaint that Ukraine was responsible for the deaths of those on board Malaysia Airlines Flight MH17 because it failed to close its airspace.[122]

Yet the political motives of the applicants cannot diminish the significance of inter-state procedures as an effective and authoritative mechanism for resolving cases of serious violations of human rights (with respect to obligations towards the victims). Judicial questions are often inextricably linked to political issues, and vice versa. Human rights matters are never devoid of political nuances; their fulfilment more often than not comes down to the political choices of each government.[123] When submitting an inter-state application concerning human rights violations against its own nationals, the applicant state is acting both as an injured state and as a member of the group of states towards which the collective interest of the protection of human rights is owed.[124]

The challenge regarding these inter-state complaints is not the political motives of the applicants as such, but the fact that these applications are ultimately linked to legal questions addressed by other international law branches. For instance, the *Ukraine v Russia* cases, with the recent annexation of Crimea by Russia, are closely connected to other legal aspects of the conflict, such as the question of the legality of the use of force and questions of control over Crimea. These are questions associated with the overall resolution of the conflict, possibly far beyond the human rights Court's mandate.[125] Similar concerns relate

November 2020, Press release ECHR 354 (2020) 4 December 2020 (hereinafter *Ukraine and the Netherlands v Russia (re Eastern Ukraine)* (GC), Press Release). Two other cases were pending before a Chamber: *Ukraine v Russia (IX)*, App no 10691/21, lodged on 19 February 2021, Press release ECHR 069 (2021) 23 February 2021; *Ukraine v Russia (VIII)*, App no 55855/18, lodged on 29 November 2018, Press Release ECHR 421 (2018) 4 December 2018.

[121] *Ukraine and the Netherlands v Russia (re Eastern Ukraine)* (GC), Press Release (n 120).

[122] *Russia v Ukraine*, App no 36958/21, lodged on 22 July 2021, Press Release ECHR 240 (2021) 23 July 2021.

[123] See ICJ, *Legality of the Threat or Use of Nuclear Weapons*, Advisory Opinion, 8 July 1996, 73–74, para 16.

[124] Articles 42, 48(1)(a), ARSIWA (n 5). On the inter-state cases, as a form of *actio popularis*, see Rüdiger Wolfrum, 'Enforcing Community Interests Through International Dispute Settlement: Reality or Utopia?' in Ulrich Fastenrath and others (eds), *From Bilateralism to Community Interest: Essays in Honour of Bruno Simma* (OUP 2011) 1140.

[125] Kamminga, 'Is the European Convention on Human Rights Sufficiently Equipped' (n 67) 161. The Court's Registrar has highlighted the inadequacy of the Court to deal with situations of a certain scale that are closely related to conflict resolutions. Speech by Erik Fribergh, Presentation to the 3rd

to three inter-state cases that followed the hostilities that took place between Armenia and Azerbaijan from 27 September 2020 to 10 November 2020 (before the entry into force of a ceasefire agreement).[126] While these cases contain allegations of widespread violations of the Convention, they are also clearly intertwined in the geopolitical battle. Each complaint has been lodged by another state involved in the conflict. Armenia, Azerbaijan, and Turkey have each filed one complaint.[127]

2.2 Procedural adjustments to gravity in the European system

Beyond the special procedure provided by the African Charter,[128] no procedures were explicitly introduced into the human rights treaties to take into account the gravity of violations before the courts. Yet the European human rights system has been gradually amending or updating its rules of procedure, incorporating in the process the gravity of the violations. Neither the Inter-American Court nor the African Court has so far amended its procedures in a similar manner. These institutional changes, both in the review of applications and the supervision of execution of judgments systems, have been introduced less as responses to serious violations than as solutions to the ever-increasing number of applications the European Court faces.[129] Nevertheless, these amendments have ultimately created tools addressing serious violations of human rights and facilitating access to remedies for victims of those violations.[130]

2.2.1 Amending the Rules of Procedure

There have been two major amendments to the Rules of Procedure of the European Court that, while primarily aimed at tackling the sheer number of

meeting by the Registrar of the European Court of Human Rights, Drafting Group 'F' on the Reform of the Court (GT-GDR-F), Committee of Experts on the Reform of the Court (DH-GDR), Steering Committee for Human Rights (CDDH) (24 September 2014) GT-GDR-F(2014)021 4.

[126] ECtHR, *Armenia v Azerbaijan*, App no 42521/20, lodged on 27 September 2020; ECtHR, *Armenia v Turkey*, App no 43517/20, lodged on 4 October 2020; ECtHR, *Azerbaijan v Armenia*, App no 47319/20, lodged on 27 October 2020. On 9 March 2021, the Chamber to which the two of these inter-state applications had been allocated relinquished jurisdiction in favour of the Grand Chamber of the Court. See, for information on all three, ECtHR, Press Release, ECHR 145 (2021) 12 May 2021.

[127] See cases listed above n 126.

[128] See Section 2.1.2.

[129] ECtHR, Factsheet—Pilot Judgments, Press Unit, July 2021.

[130] These modifications relate primarily to individual applications, as inter-state applications are always examined in priority. ECtHR, Rule 51(1), Rules of the Court, 1 August 2021 (hereinafter ECtHR, Rules of the Court).

applications, incorporate in the process the gravity of violations: (i) the pilot judgment process; and (ii) the Court's priority policy.

The pilot judgment process constitutes a vehicle for addressing 'repetitive' cases before the European Court, revealing underlying structural problems that may or may not amount to serious violations of human rights.[131] When the Court decides to examine a set of repetitive cases under the pilot judgment process, it pronounces only upon one leading case and defers consideration of all other similar pending cases until the government in question takes measures to remedy the situation.[132] The primary purpose of the procedure is to ensure faster redress for a broader range of victims directly at the domestic level, while facilitating the workload of the Court.[133] The leading criterion for seizing this process is quantitative ('repetitive' cases) rather than qualitative.[134] The pilot process is nevertheless becoming a tool for addressing instances of serious violations of human rights that present both qualitative and quantitative elements.[135]

First, when deciding to activate the pilot process, the Court groups together a series of cases on its own initiative. As such, it partly lifts the burden from the victims to prove the existence of an administrative practice (that is a systematic practice). Before, the Court required detailed evidence from individual victims to prove the existence of an administrative practice.[136] For instance, under the pilot procedure, in *Kaverzin v Ukraine*, the Court underlined that the previous judgments proved the recurring nature of the problem, since they revealed similar facts regarding when and how torture occurred and the reluctance of the prosecution to investigate those cases.[137] This is already a step away

[131] Rule 61(1) ECtHR, Rules of the Court (n 130). Introduced by ministerial resolution: Committee of Ministers Res(2004)3 on judgments revealing an underlying systemic problem 114th Session (12 May 2004).

[132] Rule 61, ECtHR, Rules of the Court (n 130). The way the leading case is chosen remains unclear, though. The details of the pilot procedure are gradually being formed. The number of previously received cases required in order to enter the pilot process is not specified.

[133] ECtHR, *Kurić and others v Slovenia* (GC), App no 26828/06, 12 March 2014, paras 133–34. See Antoine Buyse, 'The Pilot Judgment Procedure at the European Court of Human Rights: Possibilities and Challenges' [2009] 'European Court of Human Rights, 50 Years', Special issue, Nomiko Vima [Greek Law Journal] 78, 84–86.

[134] Quantity does not necessarily amount to a serious violation. See Chapter 1.

[135] See Dilek's critical analysis of the suitability of the pilot judgments system for addressing gross and systematic violations. Kurban Dilek, 'Forsaking Individual Justice: The Implications of the European Court of Human Rights' Pilot Judgment Procedure for Victims of Gross and Systematic Violations' (2016) 16 HR L Rev 731, 731–69 (hereinafter Dilek, 'Forsaking Individual Justice').

[136] See, the *Aksoy* and *Kurt* cases, where the Court considered they did not provide sufficient evidence to conclude that there was an administrative practice: *Aksoy v Turkey* (GC) (n 97); ECtHR, *Kurt v Turkey* (GC), App no 15/1997/799/1002, 25 May 1998. See also Reidy, Hampson, and Boyle, 'Gross Violations of Human Rights' (n 67) 171.

[137] ECtHR, *Kaverzin v Ukraine*, App no 23893/03, 15 May 2012, paras 172–80.

from the traditional delivery of justice, where the victim bears the burden of convincing the Court of the gravity of the situation the victim faced. In cases of serious violations of human rights of a systematic character the state apparatus is often organised to conceal any such practices and, as a result, the evidence of each individual victim's suffering. Lifting the burden from the victims of serious violations of human rights may prove crucial for ensuring they receive redress.

Moreover, the Court continues to take into account in the process the substantive gravity of the violations (qualitative assessment) once deciding whether to adjourn ('freeze') the grouped cases or not.[138] Under the pilot process, once it recognises that there is an administrative practice, it may decide to still examine each case individually. One of the main criteria justifying the Court's discretionary power is the gravity of the violations before it. The Court therefore formally recognises that certain violations are too serious to be left without individual redress too.[139]

In addition, outside the pilot judgment process, as of 2009 the European Court takes into account 'the *importance* and *urgency* of the issues raised' when 'determining the order in which cases are to be dealt with'.[140] Before the 2009 amendment, the Court had examined all applications before it in the chronological order of their submission. Only exceptionally and rarely were cases dealt with in an expedited manner.[141] Thereafter, the Court officially adopted a 'priority policy', setting the criteria to determine the order in which cases are examined.[142] The amendment was introduced in 2017 to ensure that cases of a certain importance were not neglected under the constantly growing pile of pending cases.[143] Serious violations are found at the core of this procedural adjustment and treated in priority.

First, the Court examines urgent cases involving situations where: the life or health of the applicant is at risk; the applicant is deprived of liberty as a direct consequence of the alleged violation of their Convention rights; or there are other circumstances linked to the personal or family situation of the applicant,

138 Rule 61(6)(a), ECtHR, Rules of Court (n 134).

139 Notably, *Aslakhanova ao v Russia* (n 94).

140 Rule 41, ECtHR, Rules of Court (n 134) (emphasis added).

141 Among the few, ECtHR, *Siddik Aslan and others v Turkey*, App no 75307/01, 18 November 2005, para 81 (advanced age and ill-treatment of applicant in detention); ECtHR, *Mouisel v France*, App no 67263/01, 14 November 2002, para 4 (continuing detention of applicant suffering from cancer); ECtHR, *Papon v France*, App no 54210/00, 25 July 2002 (advanced age and ill-treatment of applicant in detention); ECtHR, *Soering v UK*, App no 14038/88, 7 July 1989 (extradition to a country, potentially facing a very long period of time spent on death row).

142 ECtHR, The Court's Priority Policy, June 2009 (as amended 22 May 2017) (hereinafter ECtHR, The Court's Priority Policy).

143 Speech by Erik Fribergh, Presentation by the Registrar of the ECtHR (n 125).

particularly the well-being of a child.[144] Then applications presenting in particular a structural or endemic situation, or applications raising an important question of general interest are examined.[145] They are followed by any case relating to violations of the rights listed as 'core' rights of the Convention (Articles 2 (right to life), 3 (prohibition of torture, inhuman and degrading treatment) and 5(1) (protection of liberty)), and cases revealing systemic problems will be examined in priority to others.[146]

The priority policy may not refer to serious violations of human rights per se. However, the categories introduced result in the prioritisation of both isolated cases of serious violations of human rights and situations of a certain scale (caused by either systemic deficiencies of the system or other reasons). The joint implementation of the pilot judgment process and the priority policy will eventually bring cases of serious violations of human rights (presenting all the defining elements of gravity)[147] to the top of the list of pending cases before the European Court.

2.2.2 Enhancing the supervision of judgments mechanism

Similarly to the Court's Rules of Procedure, the gravity of human rights violations has also been introduced into the process of the execution of the European Court's judgments with the aim of making the system more efficient. The supervision of the execution of decisions evidently does not concern only cases of serious violations of human rights; nonetheless, serious violations of human rights have been gradually occupying a central place in the increasingly elaborate supervision system, which today involves political, judicial, and administrative actors.[148] The Committee of Ministers, the political organ of Council of Europe, is still the primary organ in charge of supervising the execution of the European Court's judgments. It is, though, assisted not only by an implementation division, but also by the Court and the Parliamentary Assembly.[149]

[144] These are cases also qualifying for interim measures under Rule 39, ECtHR, Rules of Court (n 134). ECtHR, The Court's Priority Policy (n 142).

[145] ECtHR, The Court's Priority Policy (n 142).

[146] ibid.

[147] See Chapter 1.

[148] Elisabeth Lambert Abdelgawad, 'L'exécution des arrêts de la Cour européenne des droits de l'homme (2014)' (2015) 104 RTDH 965, 985 (hereinafter Lambert Abdelgawad, 'L'exécution des arrêts (2014)').

[149] Article 46(2), ECHR (n 70). Lambert Abdelgawad, 'L'exécution des arrêts (2014)' (n 148) 975. See also Elisabeth Lambert Abdelgawad, 'La Convention européenne des droits de l'homme: Exécution des arrêts de la Cour européenne' in Maya Hertig and Michel Hottelier (eds), *Introduction aux droits de l'homme* (Schulthess 2014); David Harris and others, *Harris, O'Boyle & Warbrick: Law of the European Convention on Human Rights* (3rd edn, OUP 2014) 180–99 (hereinafter *Harris, O'Boyle & Warbrick*).

In 2011, the Committee of Ministers established a twin-track system to supervise the execution of judgments. The majority of cases are scrutinised under the standard procedure, but the most important ones are classified under the enhanced procedure.[150] Priority under the enhanced procedure is to be given to those cases in which the Court has identified a systemic problem, but not to the detriment of those cases where the violation has caused grave consequences for the injured party—describing, essentially, serious violations of human rights.[151] Pilot judgments, individual cases of an urgent nature, cases revealing complex systemic problems, as well as inter-state complaints, are all examined under the enhanced procedure.[152] Cases that concern violations of right to life and ill-treatment by security forces, poor detention conditions, detention rights, cases concerning expulsions, house evictions of vulnerable groups, and violations relating to abortion and domestic violence are followed under the enhanced procedure.[153]

Even before this amendment, the Committee of Ministers had adopted unprecedented resolutions in cases where the Court had found serious violations of the Convention, particularly in relation to violations of the right to life and prohibition of torture. The Committee adopted resolutions with strong condemnatory language in such cases, and specific measures have been demanded.[154] For instance, it adopted multiple interim resolutions with respect to the use of force by security forces in Turkey resulting, among other things, in the deaths and or disappearance of the applicants' next-of-kin. It exerted pressure for measures to be taken to improve the situation and closely followed, in many consecutive resolutions, the steps taken by Turkey.[155]

In parallel, potentially the most significant development, also enhancing the protection of individuals against serious violations, has been the active

[150] Supervision of the execution of judgments and decisions of the European Court of Human Rights: implementation of the Interlaken Action Plan–Modalities for a twin-track supervision system—Document prepared by the Department for the Execution of Judgments of the European Court of Human Rights (DG-HL) (6 September 2010) CM/Inf/DH(2010)37E; CoM, 'Supervision of the execution of judgments and decisions of the ECtHR, Annual Report of the Committee of Ministers 2011', Council of Europe, 18–21 (hereinafter CoM, Annual Report 2011). See also Elisabeth Lambert Abdelgawad, 'L'exécution des arrêts de la Cour européenne des droits de l'homme (2011)' (2012) 92 RTDH 861, 863ff.

[151] Rules 4(1) and (2), Committee of Ministers, Rules of Procedure.

[152] CoM, Annual Report 2011 (n 150) 18–21.

[153] CoM, 8th Annual Report (2014) (n 89) 40.

[154] Execution of the judgments of the European Court of Human Rights of cases concerning the Actions of the security forces in Turkey–Progress achieved and outstanding issues, Council of Europe, Interim Resolution CM/ResDH(2008)69 (18 September 2008).

[155] See Philip Leach, *Taking a Case to the European Court of Human Rights* (3rd edn, OUP 2011) 101.

involvement of the European Court in the execution of its judgments.[156] Over the past few years, the European Court has exceptionally suggested and occasionally even ordered the state in question to take certain general or specific measures.[157] For instance, in the *Ilaşçu* case, the Committee of Ministers had adopted five interim resolutions demanding measures to be taken to respect the Court's ruling that had found that the victims were unlawfully detained. However, it was the new decision by the Court that eventually led to the release of the two last detainees.[158]

This practice is not limited to instances of serious violations of human rights, but the gravity of the violation is often a motivating factor.[159] As a result, the Court has not hesitated to suggest certain urgent corrective measures pending the implementation of broader reforms. For instance, the *Aslakhanova* case involved the systematic practice of enforced disappearances amounting to serious violations in Russia. After invoking both the scope and the nature of violations involved, the Court first declared that it was not in a position to order the full range of necessary measures.[160] It then went on to order urgent measures to ensure effective investigations into already disappeared persons, until further measures could be taken to eliminate the practice of enforced disappearances. It also imposed a deadline for Russia to submit a plan containing concrete measures for the elimination of such practices.[161]

The European Court has so far decided to 'intervene' in the implementation process for pilot and quasi pilot judgments, and only exceptionally for other isolated cases.[162] The Court has ordered measures 'where the very nature of the violation found was such as to leave no real choice between measures capable of remedying it'.[163] For instance, it requested the state to release an unlawfully detained individual.[164] It remains a progressively developing trend, but it

[156] ECtHR, *Scozzari and Giunta v Italy* (GC), App nos 39221/98 and 41963/98, 13 July 2000, paras 249–50; ECtHR, *Assanidze v Georgia* (GC), App no 71503/01, 8 April 2004, para 202 (hereinafter *Assanidze v Georgia* (GC)).

[157] Elisabeth Lambert Abdelgawad, 'L'exécution des arrêts de la Cour européenne des droits de l'homme (2012)' (2013) 95 RTDH 635, 644.

[158] For a detailed account of the resolutions, see Lambert Abdelgawad, 'L'exécution des arrêts (2014)' (n 148) 971, 979. See also *Harris, O'Boyle & Warbrick* (n 149) 191–94.

[159] Notably, *Gluhaković v Croatia*, App no 21188/09, 12 April 2011, para 89.

[160] *Aslakhanova ao v Russia* (n 94) paras 220–21.

[161] ibid.

[162] Article 46, ECHR (n 70). For an analysis on the possible legal basis, see Sicilianos, 'The Involvement of the European Court' (n 85) 253–60.

[163] *Assanidze v Georgia* (GC) (n 156) para 202.

[164] Among others, ECtHR, *Benzer and others v Turkey*, App no 23502/06, 12 November 2013, para 217 (hereinafter *Benzer ao v Turkey*); ECtHR, *MSS v Belgium and Greece* (GC), App no 30696/09, 21 January 2011, para 399; ECtHR, *Abuyeva and others v Russia*, App no 27065/05, 2 December 2010, para 237 (hereinafter *Abuyeva ao v Russia*).

seems so far that the more serious the violations, the more probable the Court's involvement becomes. The main cases that have so far prompted the Court to indicate, or even prescribe, individual measures to be taken by the respondent state have concerned violations of the right to life, the prohibition of torture, and unlawful detention.[165]

To sum up, these recent practices reveal the significance and utility of the gravity dichotomy, while avoiding making official pronouncements on an artificial hierarchical superiority of certain rights.[166] These amendments illustrate the more practical (functional) approach of the European system compared, for instance, to the purely normative approach utilised in the American system.[167] In parallel, though, they constitute evidence of the increasing tendency of the human rights courts to distinguish a specific category of human rights violations—the serious ones—and adjust their procedures to take account of this distinction. All these modifications embrace gravity at a meta-level to achieve a delicate balance between efficient judicial procedures and ensuring in parallel that serious violations of human rights are appropriately protected and not overlooked; serious violations of human rights are eventually found at the centre of the new procedures.

2.3 Influencing the incidence of forms of remedies

The various human rights treaties provide little guidance with regard to the remedies that should be made available to the victims of violations of their human rights obligations.[168] The European Convention stipulates that the European Court can, if necessary, 'afford just satisfaction to the injured party' and provides for a wide margin of appreciation to the responsible state to remedy the situation.[169] The American Convention allows the Court to order measures to remedy a violation and pay fair compensation to the injured party.[170] The youngest instrument, the Statute of the African Court, authorises

[165] Sicilianos, 'The Involvement of the European Court' (n 85) 248.
[166] See Section 1.1.1.3 .
[167] For an extensive analysis of the execution of regional courts' judgments, see Anne-Catherine Fortas, *La surveillance de l'exécution des arrêts et décisions des Cours Européenne et Interaméricaine des droits de l'homme* (Pedone 2015). On the importance of the collaboration between judicial and political mechanisms for another Convention, see Ilia Maria Siatitsa, 'The Evolution of the Monitoring Mechanism of the Framework Convention for the Protection of National Minorities; Cooperation of Independent and Political Bodies in the Interest of Effectiveness' (2010) 63 Revue Hellénique de Droit International 771, 771–93.
[168] On the right to reparation, see Rombouts, Sardaro, and Vandeginste, 'The Right to Reparation' (n 61) 345–503.
[169] Articles 41, 46, ECHR (n 70).
[170] Article 63(1), ACHR (n 74).

the Court to order any measures necessary to remedy the breach, including granting fair compensation.[171]

Yet when it comes to awarding reparations, the human rights bodies have been compelled to express in some way the gradation in the degree of suffering of the victims in relation to the harm they suffered.[172] None of the forms of remedies ordered by the European Court and the Inter-American Court are new. The general categories of forms of remedy remain the same—cessation, guarantees of non-repetition, reparations, including compensation and satisfaction—but their incidence has been tailored towards serious violations of human rights.[173]

2.3.1 Reflecting aggravation in monetary awards

2.3.1.1 Awards for non-pecuniary damage even in the absence of victim's request

Compensation remains the most common form of remedy for all violations of human rights, not only the serious ones.[174] Beyond providing pecuniary damages for the loss suffered (actual and expected), damages for non-pecuniary loss are recurrently awarded in cases of serious violations of human rights. This does not imply that awards for non-pecuniary damage are made only in cases of serious violations of human rights, but there is a higher probability given that the gravity of violation is taken into account in the process. Also, the amount and conditions for awarding damages for non-pecuniary losses are influenced by the degree of gravity of the violations.

While awards for non-pecuniary damage are not subjected to a precise calculation, a monetary award has to be adequate and proportionate to the degree of suffering of the victim, which is impacted by the gravity of the violation.[175] Human rights courts rely on the principle of equity to calculate the compensation, which

> involves flexibility and an objective consideration of what is just, fair and reasonable *in all the circumstances of the case*, including *not only the position of the applicant* but *the overall context in which the breach occurred*. [The Court's]

[171] Article 45, 1998 Protocol to the African Charter (n 70).

[172] Rombouts, Sardaro, and Vandeginste, 'The Right to Reparation' (n 61) 370.

[173] IACtHR, *Osorio Rivera and Family Members v Peru* (Preliminary objections, merits, reparations and costs), 26 November 2013, para 235 (hereinafter *Osorio Rivera ao v Peru*); ECtHR, *Papamichalopoulos and others v Greece*, App no 14556/89, Just satisfaction, 31 November 1995, para 36.

[174] Oette, 'Bringing Justice to Victims?' (n 65) 233. For a critical approach regarding compensation as the main form of reparation, see Dilek, 'Forsaking Individual Justice' (n 135) 755–59.

[175] IACtHR, *La Cantuta v Peru* (Merits, reparations and costs), 29 November 2006, para 202 (hereinafter *La Cantuta v Peru*); IACtHR, *Goiburú et al v Paraguay* (Merits, reparations and costs), 22 September 2006, para 143. Found in the *Chorzów* case (n 57) 47.

> non-pecuniary awards serve to give recognition to the fact that moral damage occurred as a result of *a breach of a fundamental human right* and *reflect in the broadest of terms the severity of the damage.*[176]

The severity of the violation is a critical factor when calculating an award for non-pecuniary damage before the European Court.[177] This has also been repeatedly supported in the Inter-American Court's practice.[178] Time and again, serious violations of human rights have resulted in increased amounts of compensation for non-pecuniary damage.[179]

Both the Inter-American and the European Courts rely on a presumption of suffering in such cases.[180] The Inter-American Court considers that injury to moral well-being is self-evident in cases of cruel, inhuman, or degrading treatment, extrajudicial execution, forcible disappearance, or arbitrary detention.[181] Additionally, the European Court has been exceptionally departing from its principle that it would not make an award non-pecuniary damage if the applicant did not make such a request.[182] It has established that serious violations of the Convention may justify an award of just satisfaction, even in the absence of a claim properly made.[183]

[176] *Varnava ao v Turkey* (n 94) para 224 (emphasis added). More recently, ECtHR, *Tagayeva and others v Russia*, App no 26562/07 and six other applications, 13 April 2017, para 645 (hereinafter *Tagayeva ao v Russia*) (the seriousness of the damages caused). Similarly, IACtHR, *Velásquez-Rodríguez v Honduras* (Reparations and costs) 21 July 1989, para 27 (hereinafter *Velásquez-Rodríguez v Honduras* (Reparations and costs)); *Zongo ao v Burkina Faso* (Reparations) (n 69) para 61. See further Rombouts, Sardaro, and Vandeginste, 'The Right to Reparation' (n 61) 388.

[177] Notably, *Abdulkhanov v Russia*, App no 35012/10, 6 July 2021, para 126; *Moustahi v France*, App no 9347/14, 25 June 2020, para 174. See further Szilvia Altwicker-Hamori, Tilmann Altwicker, and Anne Peters, 'Measuring Violations of Human Rights: An Empirical Analysis of Awards in Respect of Non-Pecuniary Damage Under the European Convention on Human Rights' (2016) 76 Zeitschrift für ausländisches öffentliches Recht und Völkerrecht/Heidelberg Journal of International Law 1.

[178] Jo M Pasqualucci, *The Practice and Procedure of the Inter-American Court of Human Rights* (2nd edn, CUP 2014) 238 (hereinafter Pasqualucci, *The Practice and Procedure*); Ludovic Hennebel, *La Convention américaine des droits de l'homme: mécanismes de protection et étendue des droits et libertés* (Bruylant 2007) 291.

[179] Similarly CCPR Committee, *Wilson v The Philippines*, Comm No 868/1999, Views, 30 October 2003, para 9. On non-pecuniary damages, see Pasqualucci, *The Practice and Procedure* (n 178) 235.

[180] IACtHR, *Myrna Mack Chang v Guatemala* (Merits, reparations and costs) 25 November 2003, para 260 (hereinafter *Myrna Mack Chang v Guatemala*); IACtHR, *'White Van' (Paniagua-Morales et al) v Guatemala* (Reparations and costs) 25 May 2001, para 105; IACtHR, *Castillo-Páez v Peru* (Reparations and costs), 27 November 1998, para 84 (hereinafter *Castillo-Páez v Peru*).

[181] Among others, *Vera Vera et al v Ecuador* (n 72) para 136; IACtHR, *Chitay Nech et al v Guatemala* (Preliminary objections, merits, reparations, and costs), 25 May 2010, para 276; IACtHR, *Vélez Loor v Panama* (Preliminary objections, merits, reparations and costs) 23 November 2010, para 313 (hereinafter *Vélez Loor v Panama*); IACtHR, *La Rochela Massacre v Colombia* (Merits, reparations, and costs) 11 May 2007, para 256 (hereinafter *La Rochela Massacre v Colombia*).

[182] Notably, ECtHR, *Adzhigitova and Others v Russia*, App nos 40165/07 and 2593/08, 22 June 2021, para 285.

[183] Notably ECtHR, *Borodin v Russia*, App no 41867/04, 6 November 2012, para 166 (hereinafter *Borodin v Russia*). For a critique on this approach, see Octavian Ichim, *Just Satisfaction under the European Convention on Human Rights* (CUP 2014) 123.

In the *Nagmetov* case, the European Court spelled out the criteria and principles upon which, in exceptional circumstances (rare, as mentioned by the Court), it may decide to make an award for non-pecuniary damage even in the absence of a claim by the applicants:

> 69. The Court previously found it necessary, in *rare* cases, to make a monetary award in respect of non-pecuniary damage, *even where no such claim had been made* or where the claim was belated, taking into account the *exceptional circumstances of the cases*, for instance the *absolute or fundamental character of the right or freedom violated*
>
> . .
>
> 81. Where the Court envisages of its own motion a just-satisfaction award on account of non-pecuniary damage, it is appropriate to take into account the *particular gravity* and the *particular impact of the violation* of the Convention (for instance, *on account of its nature or degree*), which, for example, *significantly harmed* the moral well-being of the applicant, otherwise seriously affected his or her life or livelihood or caused another particularly significant disadvantage . . ., and, as it may be pertinent in the particular circumstances of a given case, the overall context in which the breach occurred.[184]

The rare cases in which the Court made an award for non-pecuniary damage absent the applicant's request have so far concerned the violation of a right of fundamental importance, such as torture.[185]

2.3.1.2 Contemplating higher awards as a form of 'aggravated' damages

Beyond compensatory awards directly reflecting the harm suffered, high monetary awards could (or should) arguably be understood as a form of aggravated damages. Aggravated damages are mostly equated to punitive damages in international law.[186] However, aggravated damages could be understood to

[184] ECtHR, *Nagmetov v Russia* (GC), App no 35589/08, 30 March 2017, paras 49–92. See also, *Varnava ao v Turkey* (n 94) para 224

[185] *Borodin v Russia* (n 183) para 166; ECtHR, *Chudun v Russia*, App no 20641/04, 21 June 2011, para 129; ECtHR, *Crabtree v the Czech Republic*, App no 41116/04, 25 February 2010, para 60; ECtHR, *Kats and Others v Ukraine*, App no 29971/04, 18 December 2008, para 149; ECtHR, *Rusu v Austria*, App no 34082/02, 2 October 2008, para 62; ECtHR, *Nadrosov v Russia*, App no 9297/02, 31 July 2008, para 54; ECtHR, *Chember v Russia*, App no 7188/03, 3 July 2008, para 77; ECtHR, *Babushkin v Russia*, App no 67253/01, 18 October 2007, para 62; ECtHR, *Igor Ivanov v Russia*, App no 34000/02, 7 June 2007, paras 50–51; ECtHR, *Davtyan v Georgia*, App no 73241/01, 27 July 2006, para 71; ECtHR, *Mayzit v Russia*, App no 63378/00, 20 January 2005, para 88; ECtHR, *Bursuc v Romania*, App no 42066/98, 12 October 2004, para 124.

[186] Nina HB Jørgensen, *The Responsibility of States for International Crimes* (OUP 2000) 186 (hereinafter Jørgensen, *The Responsibility of States*).

describe 'damages on an increased scale awarded to the injured party over and above the actual economic, financial or other material loss, where the wrong done was aggravated by reprehensible conduct on the part of the wrongdoing party'.[187] The exclusion of punitive damages as a consequence of serious violations of human right may not automatically discount the existence of 'aggravated' damages for serious violations of human rights[188]—albeit the evidence for the award of aggravated damages as distinct from the award of just satisfaction for non-pecuniary damages appears slim in practice.

Crawford (the last ILC Special Rapporteur on state responsibility) suggested maintaining the distinction between punitive and aggravated damages. He understood aggravated damages as 'damages reflecting the gravity of the injury', either as a form of compensation or as a form of satisfaction.[189] The references to both punitive and aggravated damages were eventually deleted from the final text of the State responsibility Articles, because most members regarded aggravated and punitive damages as similar.[190] If aggravated damages were to be accepted as a special, distinct form of compensation,[191] they would be a direct consequence of serious violations of human rights.

The degree of suffering in instances of serious violations of human rights is in most cases impossible to quantify. Therefore, almost any amount awarded to the victims would be to a degree arbitrarily calculated and insufficient. The principle of full reparation cannot fully apply in cases of serious violations of human rights. The irreparable harm suffered, the often high number of victims, as well as the societal injury make any claim for full reparation impossible.[192] In numerous cases, the Inter-American Court has not hesitated to award exceptionally high amounts of compensation for non-pecuniary damage that could be justified as aggravated damages.[193]

However, while imposing aggravated damages may appear as a fair response to serious violations of human rights, similar reservations to those raised for punitive damages would apply here as well. From the very beginning, supporters of punitive damages were ready to accept that punishing the wrongdoing state

[187] Wittich, 'Punitive Damages' (n 3) 667–68; Tams, 'Do Serious Breaches' (n 1) 1166–67.
[188] Both courts repeatedly excluded punitive damages, see n 4.
[189] ILC, 'Third report on State responsibility by Mr James Crawford, Special Rapporteur', 15 March 2000, para 190. See also Tams, 'Do Serious Breaches' (n 1) 1166–67.
[190] Wittich, 'Punitive Damages' (n 3) 673.
[191] An accepted distinction in several common law jurisdictions, including the United Kingdom, Canada, and Australia. Wittich, 'Punitive Damages' (n 3) 667; Rombouts, Sardaro, and Vandeginste, 'The Right to Reparation' (n 61) 390.
[192] Rombouts, Sardaro, and Vandeginste, 'The Right to Reparation' (n 61) 459.
[193] For a critique, see Hayner, *Unspeakable Truths* (n 38) 173–75.

would inevitably also punish the entire society of that state.[194] Often the direct victims of serious violations of human rights are also members of the same society that is to be blamed for these violations. As a result, it appears that the payment of the aggravated or punitive awards would also burden the victims of those same violations for which remedies are awarded. Also, if the courts award punitive damages to each victim before them, there is the risk that the responsible state will be punished multiple times for the same offence.[195]

Furthermore, if the regional human rights courts were to develop a practice of awarding aggravated damages as a result of serious violations of human rights, this could be disruptive of transitional justice reparation programmes.[196] This was made apparent in the case of Peru. The Peruvian Government established various reparation programmes following the recommendations of the Truth and Reconciliation Commission, including both individual and collective awards. It had provided almost US$38 million, from 2007 to 2009, to individual reparations programmes, to be distributed equally among the victims.[197] However, a parallel process before the Inter-American Court of Human Rights complicated the implementation of these programmes. The cases concerned instances of torture and disappearances, already covered by the national reparation programmes. The resulting awards made by the Court could go as high as US$200,000, to be paid by the state to each victim. In the *Barrios Altos* case, each victim was awarded US$175,000 in total, and one was awarded US$250,000.[198] These sums could never be paid to the approximately 69,000 direct victims identified by the Truth and Reconciliation Commission. They would have arguably have consumed the entire annual budget of Peru.[199] Further collaboration and co-ordination among the various bodies could prevent such instances.

However, an alternative approach to monetary compensation for serious violations of human rights involving large number of victims could be given more weight, that is, a departure from the calculation of individual amounts of compensation and the awarding at judicial level of 'alternative' monetary

[194] See analysis in Jørgensen, *The Responsibility of States* (n 186) 168–72; Pasqualucci, *The Practice and Procedure* (n 178) 272–74.

[195] Shelton, *Remedies* (n 4) 402ff.

[196] See Section 1.2.

[197] Hayner, *Unspeakable Truths* (n 38) 175.

[198] IACtHR, *Barrios Altos v Peru* (Reparations and costs), 30 November 2001. See also *Castillo-Páez v Peru* (n 180). See further Arturo J Carrillo, 'Justice in Context: The Relevance of Inter-American Human Rights Law and Practice to Repairing the Past' in Pablo De Greiff (ed), *The Handbook of Reparations* (OUP 2008).

[199] De Greiff, 'Justice and Reparations' (n 55) 456–57. See also Malamud-Goti and Grosman, 'Reparations and Civil Litigation' (n 27) 539–59.

awards that take into account the collective and aggravating aspects of certain situations.

2.3.1.3 Surpassing the individualistic approach to reparations

When serious violations of human rights occur on a massive scale, they often leave behind numerous victims who suffered in equal measure degrees of harm that cannot really be quantified, fully restored, or fully compensated. Such instances have been demanding the (at least partial) re-examination of traditional forms of remedies, including monetary compensation, that focus primarily on each individual victim. The human rights courts' response has so far been inconsistent and, as a result, inconclusive in that respect.

Only sporadically has the Inter-American Court awarded collective monetary compensation instead of individual compensation. For instance, in certain cases relating to the illegal expropriation of indigenous peoples' lands on which their entire existence depends, it awarded lump sums to each community as a whole for non-material damage.[200] These sums were to be deposited in community development funds created and established for the benefit of the members of the particular community in their traditional territory, to finance educational, housing, agricultural, and health projects.

By recognising the community as a whole to be the injured party, and awarding collective sums, the Court appeared to partially bypass the constraints of individualistic conceptions of remedies. Technically, though, it remained within the confines of the individualistic model. In these cases, almost all the members of the respective communities were listed as direct victims.[201] Eventually, the Inter-American Court hesitated to award compensation to the entire Maroon community as argued for by the Inter-American Commission.[202] The latter invoked the preponderant collective dimension and the close ties of each victim to their family, village community, and tribe. The Court dismissed the argument, concluding as follows:

[200] IACtHR, *Saramaka People v Suriname* (Preliminary objections, merits, reparations, and costs) 28 November 2007, para 201 (hereinafter *Saramaka People v Suriname*); IACtHR, *Sawhoyamaxa Indigenous Community v Paraguay* (Merits, reparations and costs) 29 March 2006, para 224 (hereinafter *Sawhoyamaxa Indigenous Community v Paraguay*); IACtHR, *Yakye Axa Indigenous Community v Paraguay* (Merits, reparations and costs) 17 June 2005, para 205 (hereinafter *Yakye Axa Indigenous Community v Paraguay*).

[201] *Saramaka People v Suriname* (n 200) paras 188–89; *Sawhoyamaxa Indigenous Community v Paraguay* (n 200) para 204; *Yakye Axa Indigenous Community v Paraguay* (n 200) para 189.

[202] IACtHR, *Aloeboetoe et al v Suriname* (Reparations and costs), 10 November 1993, paras 18–19, 84–85.

> In practice, the obligation to pay moral compensation does not extend to such communities, nor to the State in which the victim participated; these are redressed by the enforcement of the system of laws. If in some exceptional case such compensation has ever been granted, it would have been to a community that suffered direct damages.[203]

In another case, however, the Inter-American Court once again pushed the boundaries of the bilateral model between the applicant and the state. It requested the state to pay individual reparations not only to the applicants, but also to other victims who were not parties to the judicial process. Specifically, in the *Mapiripan Massacre* case, involving the massacre or disappearance of at least forty-nine civilians, the Court indicated that victims who were not identified in the process could claim reparations within twenty-four months after the publication of the judgment.[204]

The European Court so far appears to have adopted an individualistic approach. For instance, even for the pilot judgment process, which by design allows the Court to group together similar cases and pronounce on only one leading case, it has declared that it will not adjudicate similar cases when they involve serious violations.[205] However, a recent in-depth analysis of the Court's awards in cases of violations of the right to life or the prohibition of torture suggests that the Court does take into account the individual victim's vulnerability and the impact of the violation when calculating damages.[206] In the meantime, though, when it comes to inter-state applications, the European Court appears to depart, at least partially, from the individualistic approach to reparations.

The *Cyprus v Turkey* case constitutes the first case in history where an international court awarded compensation to hundreds of victims through an inter-state procedure. The European Court awarded a lump sum of €90 million, taking into account the number of victims. It awarded in total 'EUR 30,000,000 for non-pecuniary damage suffered by the surviving relatives of the missing persons, and EUR 60,000,000 for non-pecuniary damage suffered by the enclaved residents of Karpas peninsula'.[207] It ordered Cyprus to distribute the

[203] ibid paras 83. See also Rombouts, Sardaro, and Vandeginste, 'The Right to Reparation' (n 61) 391–392.

[204] IACtHR, *"Mapiripán Massacre" v Colombia* (Merits, reparations and costs) 15 September 2005, paras 257(b), 289.

[205] The pilot judgment process assumes that the adjourned cases will be remedied by the measures taken at the national level following the decision on the pilot (leading) case.

[206] Veronika Fikfak, 'Non-Pecuniary Damages before the European Court of Human Rights: Forget the Victim; It's All about the State' (2020) 33 LJIL 335, 352.

[207] *Cyprus v Turkey* (GC) (Just satisfaction) (n 114) paras 47, 58.

sum evenly among all the victims listed in the judgment. The Court reaffirmed its approach in the first *Georgia v Russia* case.[208]

These global sum awards as such challenge the individualistic approach to reparations, which is deeply embedded in the calculation of damages. The premise is that the acts committed on the victims produce in them distinct forms and different degrees of fear, suffering, anxiety, humiliation, and degradation, and feelings of inferiority, insecurity, frustration, and helplessness.[209] By awarding either an aggregate amount or the same amount to all victims, the presumption appears to switch in the opposite direction.

The ultimate diversion from the individualistic approach towards monetary awards was the *Srebrenica* case before the Human Rights Chamber for Bosnia and Herzegovina. The Chamber, while recognising the forty-nine applicants' individual suffering, did not award any individual damages to them.[210] Instead, it made a collective monetary award to benefit all family members of those persons missing from Srebrenica (not only the applicants), and ordered the Republic of Serbia to make a lump sum contribution of 4 million convertible marks (approximately €2.10 million) to the Foundation of the Srebrenica-Potocari Memorial and Cemetery.[211]

The idea of monetary damages awarded to a collective as a whole—whether a community or a group of victims in a specific situation—directly conflicts with the individualistic conception of remedies in international human rights law. Traditionally, protection and remedies are owed separately to each individual victim.[212] However, these situations highlight the deficiencies of the individualistic model in awarding reparations not only for indigenous and minority groups, but also in situations of massive violations. Scholars have been warning about the risks of a decrease in the relevance of human rights and the absurdity of results using the individual approach.[213] While the practice around monetary awards evolves relatively slowly, there are other forms of reparation that have been increasingly awarded in cases of serious violations of human rights that indicate a more holistic response to such instances.

[208] ECtHR, *Georgia v Russia (I)* (GC), App no 13255/07, Judgment on just satisfaction, 31 January 2019.

[209] IACtHR, *Miguel Castro-Castro Prison v Peru* (Merits, reparations and costs) 25 November 2006, para 410 (hereinafter *Miguel Castro-Castro Prison v Peru*).

[210] Human Rights Chamber for Bosnia and Herzegovina, *Selimović & others v the Republika Srpska ('the Srebrenica case')*, 7 March 2003, para 218.

[211] ibid paras 214–17.

[212] Rombouts, Sardaro, and Vandeginste, 'The Right to Reparation' (n 61) 390–91. For arguments for and against, see Desmet, 'The UN Basic Principles' (n 15) 85–89.

[213] Oette, 'Bringing Justice to Victims?' (n 65) 236; Desmet, 'The UN Basic Principles' (n 15) 88–89; Rombouts, Sardaro, and Vandeginste, 'The Right to Reparation' (n 61) 460.

2.3.2 Individual and general measures addressing serious violations

In addition to compensation, the responsible state may have to order individual and or general measures to remedy a human rights violation. For instance, the courts may respectively request the release of an unlawfully detained person, or demand legal reforms and capacity-building measures. Again, such measures are not ordered exclusively in cases of serious violations of human rights. They have been applied both to a case of prolonged unlawful detention and to an individual case of unlawful confiscation of property. The measures ordered vary considerably, depending on the particular circumstances and the context of each case. Notwithstanding, the serious character of each violation shapes the form of the measures ordered. Serious violations of human rights have pushed the human rights tribunals to become more engaged and creative.

From early on the Inter-American Court did not hesitate to request individual forms of remedy, adapted to the unique circumstances of each case of serious violations of human rights. For instance, it ordered Peru to pay the educational expenses and training of the daughter of a disappeared whose fate had yet to be determined.[214] Similarly, it has ordered a state to implement a suitable programme of psychosocial care for members of victims' families.[215] Its European counterpart was initially more reluctant to order specific individual measures.

In the past, the responsible state would be left to choose the most appropriate measures under the supervision of the Committee of Ministers, which controlled the implementation of those measures. For example, in the cases concerning the destruction of Kurdish villages, neither of the supervisory organs (Committee of Ministers or Court) ordered Turkey to fund the restoration of those villages it had destroyed.[216] However, increasingly both the European Court and the Committee of Ministers are becoming more explicit and demanding regarding the measures a state must adopt following a judicial determination that serious violations of human rights have been committed.[217] More recently, the Court has not hesitated to request specific measures to be taken by the responsible governments to ensure that they comply with the

[214] IACtHR, *Gómez-Palomino v Peru* (Merits, reparations and costs) 22 November 2005, para 148.

[215] *Osorio Rivera ao v Peru* (n 173) para 253; IACtHR, *Serrano-Cruz Sisters v El Salvador* (Merits, reparations and costs) 1 March 2005, paras 197 et seq (hereinafter *Serrano-Cruz Sisters v El Salvador*).

[216] ECtHR, *Selçuk and Asker v Turkey*, App no 12/1997/796/998–999, 24 April 1998, paras 123–25. Similar conclusions were reached in other cases, such as *Varnava ao v Turkey* (n 94) para 222.

[217] There are three avenues through which the individual and general measures can be adopted in the European system, following a court judgment, i.e.: (i) by the state; (ii) then by the Committee of Ministers; and (iii) exceptionally, by the Court. See Section 2.2.2. On the other hand, in the other two regional systems, the Courts are primarily responsible for specifying the measures to be taken. Article 63(1), ACHR (n 74); Article 45, 1998 Protocol to the African Charter (n 70).

Court's ruling. For example, it requested specific measures to be taken by Russia to determine the fate of victims of enforced disappearances in its territory.[218] Along with general measures to ensure the non-repetition of systematic enforced disappearance practices, the Committee of Ministers has also been persistent with regard to the individual measures to be taken to ensure that the fate of disappeared is determined.[219]

In *Mamazhonov*, which related to the failure of the authorities to take preventive measures against the risk of disappearance of a person extradited to Uzbekistan, the Court applied Article 46 of the ECHR and ordered Russia to take general measures to prevent a recurrent problem and improve domestic remedies for extradition and expulsion cases.[220] Similarly, it ordered the Government, responsible for facilitating extraordinary renditions, to 'take tangible remedial measures with a view to protecting the applicant against the existing risks to his life and health in a foreign jurisdiction'.[221] The Court applied the same principle both when the United Kingdom transferred a prisoner to Iraqi authorities and when the applicant was transferred to Tajikistan by Russia.[222]

In parallel, general measures for addressing situations of serious violations of human rights are ordered regularly.[223] Such measures would include modifications to criminal legislation, with the aim of introducing provisions concerning certain serious violations, and capacity-building measures, such as the training of public officials. One of the most well-known examples has been the determination by the Inter-American Court that unconditional amnesty laws in several Latin-American countries were invalid and that all the legislation should be re-written.[224] However, other measures have also been ordered. In

[218] *Aslakhanova ao v Russia* (n 94) para 238.

[219] Department for the Execution of Judgments of the ECHR, *Khashiyev and Akayeva v Russia*, App no 57942/00, <http://hudoc.exec.coe.int/eng?i = 004-9> accessed 2 September 2021.

[220] ECtHR, *Mamazhonov v Russia*, App no 17239/13, 23 October 2014, paras 229, 233, 237.

[221] ECtHR, *Al Nashiri v Poland*, App no 28761/11, 24 July 2014, paras 586–89 (hereinafter *Al Nashiri v Poland*). Other cases where the Court ordered individual measures include: *Benzer ao v Turkey* (n 164) paras 214–19; ECtHR, *Nihayet Arıcı and others v Turkey*, App nos 24604/04 and 16855/05, 23 October 2012; ECtHR, *Ilaşcu and others v Moldova and Russia*, App no 48787/99, 8 July 2004, para 490. See more recently, on an order to investigate, *Abuyeva ao v Russia* (n 164) paras 240–43. Also *Assanidze v Georgia* (GC) (n 156) paras 202–03. On the Court's individual measures, see further, Sicilianos, 'The Involvement of the European Court' (n 85).

[222] Respectively, ECtHR, *Al-Saadoon and Mufdhi v UK*, App no 61498/08, 2 March 2010, paras 170–71; ECtHR, *Savriddin Dzurayev v Russia*, App no 71386/10, 25 April 2013, paras 254–55.

[223] Among others, IACtHR, *Gomes Lund et al ('Guerrilha Do Araguaia') v Brazil* (Preliminary objections, merits, reparations and costs), 24 November 2010, paras 286–87 (hereinafter *Gomes Lund et al v Brazil*); IACtHR, *Trujillo-Oroza v Bolivia* (Reparations and costs) 27 February 2002, para 98 (hereinafter *Trujillo-Oroza v Bolivia*).

[224] *Massacres of El Mozote v El Salvador* (n 4) para 283; *Gelman v Uruguay* (n 71) para 241; *Gomes Lund et al v Brazil* (n 223) para 174; IACtHR, *Almonacid-Arellano et al v Chile* (Preliminary objections, merits, reparations and costs), 26 September 2006, para 114 (hereinafter *Almonacid-Arellano et al v*

Gelman v Uruguay, a case concerning the disappearance of a pregnant woman, the Court also ordered Uruguay to train judicial authorities in the investigation of disappearance cases.[225] Further, in the *Fernandez Ortega* case, where soldiers had raped an indigenous woman, Mexico was ordered to train not only the police but also judicial and prosecutorial authorities, and healthcare personnel, in the diligent investigation of cases of sexual abuse of women that included a gender and ethnicity perspective.[226]

The European Court has repeatedly affirmed that it 'is not in a position to order the exact general and individual measures to be implemented ... in order to comply with the judgment'.[227] However, in the *Aslakhanova* case, it went into some detail regarding the measures it considered necessary for Russia to redress the systemic failure to investigate disappearances, pending the adoption of measures to tackle the overall problem of disappearances in the Northern Caucasus. It requested, among other things, the creation of a high-level body in charge of solving disappearances in the region, the allocation of specific and adequate resources for conducting investigations, and the provision of funds to compensate the victims.[228] Furthermore, the reforms ordered included modifications to the rules on responsibility for detainees, access to records of passage of service vehicles, and unlimited access by investigators to the relevant data of the military and security agencies to ensure that effective and independent investigations are conducted.[229] The Committee of Ministers has welcomed the Court's involvement and included these measures in its report, and it went into further detail to explain the general measures necessary to address the overall problem.[230]

Subsequent judgments indicate that the Court intends to continue suggesting measures under Article 46 of the Convention. Indicatively, in *Tagayeva*

Chile); *Myrna Mack Chang v Guatemala* (n 180) para 153; IACtHR, *Barrios Altos v Peru* (Merits), 14 May 2001, para 41; *Velásquez-Rodriguez v Honduras (Merits)* (n 18) para 165.

225 Among others, *Gelman v Uruguay* (n 71) para 278; *La Rochela Massacre v Colombia* (n 181) para 303; IACtHR, *The Ituango Massacres v Colombia* (Preliminary objections, merits, reparations and costs), 1 July 2006, para 409 (hereinafter *Ituango Massacres v Colombia*). See also *Osorio Rivera ao v Peru* (n 173) para 272.

226 Notably, IACtHR, *Fernández Ortega et al v Mexico* (Preliminary objections, merits, reparations and costs), 30 August 2010, paras 259–60.

227 *Aslakhanova ao v Russia* (n 94) paras 220–22. See, in contrast, where it did order individual measures but also quoted previous case law in which it had refused to order measures: *Abuyeva ao v Russia* (n 164) paras 240–43.

228 *Aslakhanova ao v Russia* (n 94)paras 225–28.

229 ibid paras 229–37.

230 The leading case is *Khashiyev v Russia*. See Section 2.2.1.

case, the Court suggested various measures that could be taken to remedy the situation:

> In the Court's view, the above found violations should be addressed *by a variety of both individual and general measures* consisting of appropriate responses by the State institutions, aimed at drawing lessons from the past, raising awareness of the applicable legal and operational standards and deterring new violations of a similar nature. Such measures could include further *recourse to non-judicial means of collecting information and establishing the truth, public acknowledgement and condemnation of violations of the right to life in the course of security operations, and greater dissemination of information and better training for police, military and security personnel in order to ensure strict compliance with the relevant international legal standards.*[231]

In another case, it requested the responsible government 'to bring the reform of legislation and/or practice forward, in order to ensure that domestic criminal procedure complies with the requirements of Article 5'.[232]

In a case concerning detention conditions, the Court also recommended various provisional measures that the government could take. The Court underlined that in view of the significant and urgent nature of the problem identified and the fundamental nature of the rights in question, general measures had to be implemented within a reasonable time. The Romanian Government was ordered to provide a precise timetable for introducing the appropriate measures within six months.[233] Among other things, the Court encouraged the Government to reduce the prison population by making use of a wider range of penalties as an alternative to detention and by relaxing the conditions for waiving the imposition of a sentence.[234] Additionally, it encouraged the introduction of a specific compensatory remedy, such as reduced prison sentence explicitly granted to afford redress for the violation of Article 3 of the Convention.[235]

The individual and general measures are not ordered exclusively for serious violations of human rights. However, the gravity of the violations has pushed the Courts, even the European Court, to become more involved and more

[231] *Tagayeva ao v Russia* (n 176) para 640. See also, ECtHR, *Abakarova v Russia*, App no 16664/07, 15 October 2015, para 112.
[232] ECtHR, *Ignatov v Ukraine*, App no 40583/15, 15 December 2016, para 53.
[233] ECtHR, *Rezmiveş and others v Romania*, App nos 1467/12, 39516/13, 48231/13, and 68191/13, 25 April 2017, para 126.
[234] ibid paras 112–20.
[235] ibid paras 121–26.

outspoken with regard to the measures the state responsible for serious violations of human rights should implement. It is not unlikely that the European Court will limit its involvement to cases presenting violations of human rights of a certain gravity. Their impact will often go beyond the reparation of the individual applicants who brought the case before the Court, as they also aim at ensuring the non-occurrence of similar violations or rectifying a systemic problem. Nonetheless, it is not easy to categorise these measures. Some may be construed as measures contributing to the cessation of violation, or as guarantees of non-repetition. As they directly aim at restoring and remedying the situation created by a serious violation, they should be distinguished from 'symbolic awards'.

2.3.3 Symbolic and collective awards

In addition, but directly linked to the gravity of violations, alternative forms of satisfaction and guarantees of non-repetition have been increasingly awarded to victims of serious violations of human rights.[236] Described as 'symbolic awards', they are primarily granted in cases where the suffering caused is not quantifiable due to its grave nature, as well as where there is a large number of victims; essentially, cases of serious violations of human rights where it is materially impossible to provide a full remedy to each victim.[237] There is no 'one-size-fits-all' definition of them, nor an exhaustive list of symbolic awards; they adapt to the specificities of each case.[238]

The Inter-American Court recurrently awards symbolic remedies in cases of serious violations of human rights. For instance, in a case of the assassination of an environmental activist, where there were strong indications that the state had been involved, the Court asked the governmental authorities to implement a national campaign to educate the population about the work of public activists and their contributions.[239] In other cases, the Court has ordered the states concerned to, among other things: make public acts to acknowledge their responsibility;[240] publicly apologise to victims of enforced disappearance;[241] or

[236] Arguing that symbolic satisfaction measures are attached to grave breaches of international law, see Alain Pellet, 'Can a State Commit a Crime? Definitely, Yes!' (1999) 10 EJIL 425, 431.

[237] See Tomuschat, 'Individual Reparation Claims' (n 59) 1–26.

[238] For a brief overview of the challenges the reparation of mass violations of human rights presents, see Oette, 'Bringing Justice to Victims?' (n 65) 217–42.

[239] IACtHR, *Kawas Fernández v Honduras* (Merits, reparations and costs) 3 April 2009, Operative para 14 (hereinafter *Kawas Fernández v Honduras*).

[240] *Myrna Mack Chang v Guatemala* (n 180) para 278; *Kawas Fernández v Honduras* (n 239) para 202.

[241] *The Ituango Massacres v Colombia* (n 225) para 406. See also *Osorio Rivera ao v Peru* (n 173) para 261; *Serrano-Cruz Sisters v El Salvador* (n 215) para 194; *Myrna Mack Chang v Guatemala* (n 180) para 278; IACtHR, *Juan Humberto Sánchez v Honduras* (Preliminary objections, merits, reparations and

publish and disseminate judgments.[242] It has also requested measures to commemorate the victims or events, such as building monuments[243] or naming streets and schools after victims.[244]

The Inter-American Court has also occasionally awarded sums to be used for improving the living conditions of entire communities that have suffered violations, and not only those of the applicants. For instance, in the *Plan Sanchez Massacre* case, which dealt with one of 600 recorded massacres in Guatemala, the Court decided that, given that the victims were all members of the Mayan people, it should also grant reparations to the community as a whole,[245] even though it refused to recognise the entire community as a victim and award damages.[246] It explicitly distinguished monetary awards for non-pecuniary damage and symbolic awards. In cases of indigenous people's land where the Court awarded a lump sum, the community was considered to be the injured party and the members of the community were listed.[247]

According to the Inter-American Court, these collective measures were necessary, 'owing to the *extreme gravity of the facts* and the *collective nature* of the damage produced'.[248] It ordered the state—as a form of satisfaction—to

costs) 7 June 2003, para 188; IACtHR, *Cantoral-Benavides v Peru* (Reparations and costs) 3 December 2001, para 81.

[242] IACtHR, *Manuel Cepeda Vargas v Colombia* (Preliminary objections, merits, reparations and costs), 26 May 2010, para 220 (hereinafter *Manuel Cepeda Vargas v Colombia*); *Kawas Fernández v Honduras* (n 239) para 199; IACtHR, *Radilla-Pacheco v Mexico* (Preliminary objections, merits, reparations and costs), 23 November 2009, para 350. See also *Osorio Rivera ao v Peru* (n 173) para 257; *Serrano-Cruz Sisters v El Salvador* (n 215) para 195.

[243] IACtHR, *Contreras et al v El Salvador* (Merits, reparations and costs), 31 August 2011, paras 209–10 (documentary); *Kawas Fernández v Honduras* (n 239) para 206 (monument); IACtHR, *Moiwana Community v Suriname* (Preliminary objections, merits, reparations and costs) 15 June 2005, para 225 (massacre site). See also *Castillo-Páez v Peru* (n 180) paras 94–95; IACtHR, *Godínez-Cruz v Honduras* (Reparations and costs), 21 July 1989, para 30.

[244] IACtHR, *Gómez-Paquiyauri Brothers v Peru*, 8 July 2004, para 236; IACtHR, *Huilca-Tecse v Peru* (Merits, reparations and costs) 3 March 2005, para 103(4) (create a university course in victim's name); IACtHR, *The 'Street Children' (Villagrán-Morales et al) v Guatemala* (Reparations and costs), 26 May 2001, paras 103, 115(7) (national commemoration day). See also *Serrano-Cruz Sisters v El Salvador* (n 215) para 196 (commemoration day dedicated to disappeared children); *Myrna Mack Chang v Guatemala* (n 180) para 286; *Trujillo-Oroza v Bolivia* (n 223) para 122. Some of these awards have also been described as having been made to compensate damage to the victim's life plan. Pasqualucci, *The Practice and Procedure* (n 178) 270.

[245] IACtHR, *Plan de Sánchez Massacre v Guatemala* (Reparations), 19 November 2004 (hereinafter *Plan de Sánchez Massacre v Guatemala* (Reparations)) paras 49(15), 86.

[246] ibid para 62.

[247] *Saramaka People v Suriname* (n 200) paras 188–89, 201; *Sawhoyamaxa Indigenous Community v Paraguay* (n 200) paras 204, 224; *Yakye Axa Indigenous Community v Paraguay* (n 200) paras 189, 205.

[248] *Plan de Sánchez Massacre v Guatemala* (Reparations) (n 245) para 93 (emphasis added). Repeated in, IACtHR, *'Las Dos Erres' Massacre v Guatemala* (Preliminary objection, merits, reparations and costs) 24 November 2009, para 226 (hereinafter *'Las Dos Erres' Massacre v Guatemala*); *The Ituango Massacres v Colombia* (n 225) para 385; IACtHR, *Pueblo Bello Massacre v Colombia* (Merits, reparations and costs) 31 January 2006, para 256.

relocate funds and resources to improve the educational and health services of certain communities, or to build new houses.[249] Monetary symbolic awards have been mostly complementary to other awards. In other cases, the Court also asked a state to create a DNA database to assist in the research carried out by families looking for their children who had been forcibly taken and adopted by others.[250]

Similarly, the International Criminal Court (ICC), in the *Katanga* case, ordered individual symbolic awards of US$250 to each individual. However, in addition, it made 'an award for collective reparations designed to benefit each victim, in the form of support for housing, support for an income-generating activity, support for education and psychological support'.[251] The ICC adopted a 'collective reparations with individualised components' approach.[252] While it insisted that collective awards should still focus on individual victims to the extent possible, the case highlights the limits of full reparation of each individual victim in cases of serious violations of human rights.

The European Court, for its part, has so far refrained from ordering any symbolic awards. In those rare instances where it has ordered something resembling a symbolic award, it was in monetary form, such as awarding only €1 in compensation in the *Vaney v France* case.[253] The choice of monetary awards as symbolic awards is problematic, as it implies that a state can buy injustice despite the inalienable nature of the rights concerned.

Symbolic monetary compensation on its own seems to reduce the notion of human rights to 'a series of propositions assuring the payment of money to the victims'.[254] The text of the European Convention could allow for a broader interpretation regarding the type of measures the Court can order. It refers to 'just satisfaction',[255] which may include an acknowledgment of the breach, an expression of regret, a formal apology, or any other 'appropriate modality'.[256]

[249] *Plan de Sánchez Massacre v Guatemala* (Reparations) (n 245) paras 105, 109–11; See also *The Ituango Massacres v Colombia* (n 225) para 407; *Aloeboetoe et al v Suriname* (Merits) (n 77) para 96.

[250] *'Las Dos Erres' Massacre v Guatemala* (n 248) paras 271–74; *Serrano-Cruz Sisters v El Salvador* (n 215) paras 189–91.

[251] ICC, *The Prosecutor v Germain Katanga*, Order on reparations, ICC-01/04-01/07, 24 March 2017, para 306.

[252] ICC, *The Prosecutor v Bosco Ntaganda*, Order on reparations, ICC-01/04-02/06, 8 March 2021, para 186. Initially set out in ICC, *The Prosecutor v Thomas Lubanga Dyilo*, Judgment on the appeals against the 'Decision establishing the principles and procedures to be applied to reparations' of 7 August 2012 with amended order for reparations (Annex A) and public annexes 1 and 2, Appeals Chamber, Decision, 3 March 2015, ICC-01/04-01/06-3129.

[253] ECtHR, *Vaney v France*, App no 53946/00, 30 November 2004, para 57.

[254] Shelton, *Remedies* (n 4) 400. Quoting Owen Fiss, *The Civil Rights Injunction* (Indiana University Press 1979), 75.

[255] Article 41, ECHR (n 70).

[256] Article 37, ARSIWA (n 5); Principle 22, Basic Principles and Guidelines (n 14).

Therefore, it may be that the more the Court gets involved in the execution of its judgments, the more it will probably try to find ways to accommodate the irreparable character of serious violations of human rights. In the process, it may eventually embrace and recognise the importance of symbolic awards. Already, following the Court's judgments, under the supervision of the Committee of Ministers, several states have adopted measures that have a collective impact.[257]

Such measures do not aim at restoring the situation for or compensating the victims.[258] They complement and strengthen the remedies awarded to victims who have suffered irreparable harm.[259] An issue of concern regarding such awards, which also relates to general measures, is that there is a risk of undermining the welfare duties of the state. Guarantees of non-repetition in human rights law are also the measures a state should take to effectively protect human rights—that is, the states' positive obligations to protect and fulfil human rights. However, it is difficult to imagine what kind of remedies could not be simultaneously constructed as positive human rights law obligations to ensure respect. Their lines inevitably blur.

Similarly to collective monetary awards and general measures, symbolic and collective awards habitually bypass the strict bilateral relationship between the parties to the judicial proceedings.[260] They often have an impact on victims that were not party to the case and on societies at large. In some cases involving massacres and large-scale violations, the Inter-American Court has ordered the state to invest in measures that will benefit an entire community, comprising almost a form of 'collective' reparation.[261] The reach of such measures goes beyond restoration of the reputation and memory of the victims,[262] to inform the general population.[263] They represent tangible proof of the state's determination that there will be no repetition of the violations. Symbolic awards also serve as a means to restore the faith of the population in the official state.

[257] See Section 2.3.1.

[258] On symbolic awards as a supplementary form of remedy: Rombouts, Sardaro, and Vandeginste, 'The Right to Reparation' (n 61) 464–65.

[259] In the law of state responsibility, see Articles 30 and 37, ARSIWA with commentaries (n 3) 88–91, 105–06.

[260] For an in-depth analysis of the tensions between collective and individual awards, see Diana Odier-Contreras Garduno, *Collective Reparations: Tensions and Dilemmas Between Collective Reparations and the Individual Right to Receive Reparations* (Intersentia 2018).

[261] For criticism regarding the lack of a collective perspective in the Basic Principles and Guidelines, see Desmet, 'The UN Basic Principles' (n 15) 100–01.

[262] *Vélez Loor v Panama* (n 181) para 266; IACtHR, *Tiu Tojín v Guatemala* (Merits, reparations and costs) 26 November 2008, para 108; *Plan de Sánchez Massacre v Guatemala* (Reparations) (n 245) para 104.

[263] On concerns regarding the unintended impact on the architecture of the society in which they are ordered, see Rombouts, Sardaro, and Vandeginste, 'The Right to Reparation' (n 61) 461.

They become a symbolic promise to society as a whole that these violations will never occur again—a guarantee of non-repetition to the entire society.[264]

2.3.4 Gravity justifying additional rights to the victims

Last but not least, a particular development specific to serious violations of human rights is the emergence of additional rights for the victims of such violations. The gravity of violations has given rise to two additional rights for the victims: the right to truth[265] and, arguably, the right to 'access to criminal justice'.[266] Neither of these rights is explicitly recognised in the human rights conventions. They were gradually constructed out of various remedial practices relating to serious violations of human rights and following a combined reading of different human rights provisions. They have, though, almost acquired an autonomous standing (at least one of the two), giving rise to direct corresponding obligations for the state concerned.

The right to truth emerged as a direct result of the principle of effective protection of specific rights included in the human rights conventions, particularly the right to life and the prohibition of torture.[267] 'Knowing this individual truth was also the indispensable basis for measures to repair ... '[268] It has emerged as a consequence of the occurrence of certain serious violations of human rights and not any human rights violation.[269] A violation of the right to property, for instance, would not automatically give rise as such to the right to know the truth about the whereabouts of the lost property. For the relatives, it is understood as a form of satisfaction to know the truth regarding the circumstances of an enforced disappearance or the death of their loved ones.[270] Recognised as 'a

[264] Shelton, *Remedies* (n 4) 61.

[265] See Concurring Opinion of Judge Diego García-Sayán, *Massacres of El Mozote v El Salvador* (n 4). See also *Barrios Altos v Peru* (Reparations and costs) (n 198).

[266] In one of the first cases before it, the IACtHR recognised that victims have a right to have the violations investigated and those responsible prosecuted and punished: *Velásquez-Rodríguez v Honduras* (Reparations and costs) (n 176) paras 32–33. Also, among others, *Gelman v Uruguay* (n 71) para 255; *Gomes Lund et al v Brazil* (n 223) para 256; *Manuel Cepeda Vargas v Colombia* (n 242) para 216; *Miguel Castro-Castro Prison v Peru* (n 209) para 404; *Trujillo-Oroza v Bolivia* (n 223) para 111.

[267] Article 24(2), International Convention for the Protection of All Persons from Enforced Disappearance (adopted 20 December 2006) 2716 UNTS 3. Also Principle 2, 'The inalienable right to the truth', 'Updated set of principles for the protection and promotion of human rights through action to combat impunity, Addendum, Report of the independent expert to update the Set of principles to combat impunity, Diane Orentlicher' (8 February 2005).

[268] 'Report of the Chilean National Commission on Truth and Reconciliation' (1993) University of Notre Dame Press, Vol I/II, 28.

[269] Yasmin Naqvi, 'The Right to the Truth in International Law: Fact or Fiction?' (2006) 88 IRRC 245, 249.

[270] IACtHR, *Las Palmeras v Colombia* (Reparations and costs) 26 November 2002, para 77; IACtHR, *Neira-Alegría et al v Peru* (Reparations and Costs), 19 September 1996, para 69.

component of reparation in its own right' by all human rights judicial bodies, its impact also bypasses the bilateral relations of the judicial proceedings.[271]

Interestingly, in *Al Nashiri v Poland*, the European Court highlighted that

> where allegations of *serious human rights violations* are involved in the investigation, *the right to the truth* regarding the relevant circumstances of the case does *not belong solely to the victim* of the crime and [their] family *but also to other victims of similar violations and the general public*, who have the right to know what has happened.[272]

The right to 'access to criminal justice' is also closely related to the right to truth; it ensures the investigation and clarification of past events and provides, if necessary, for the prosecution of the perpetrators. It has also emerged out of case law that addressed instances of serious violations of human rights. Based on Articles 8 (right to fair trial), 25 (right to judicial protection) and 1(1) (obligation to respect rights) of the American Convention, the Inter-American Court concluded that the state has an obligation to facilitate victims' access to criminal proceedings.[273] The European Court has provided a similar interpretation of Article 13 (right to a remedy) of the ECHR, read in conjunction with Articles 2 (the right to life) and 3 (prohibition of torture) and taking into account Article 1 (states should ensure the effective protection of all the Convention rights).[274] It requires states to take steps to ensure victims' access to criminal proceedings.[275] The Human Rights Committee has adopted a similar approach.[276]

Access to criminal proceedings in human rights law is broader than victims' access to trial proceedings. It includes the opportunity for the victims to provide information that could open an investigation and to be informed about the progress of the proceedings that could possibly lead to

[271] See ECtHR, *Nasr and Ghali v Italy*, App no 44883/09, 23 February 2016, para 265; *Nashiri v Poland* (n 221) para 495; ECtHR, *Husayn (Abu Zubaydah) v Poland*, App no 7511/13, 24 July 2014, para 489 (hereinafter *Husayn (Abu Zubaydah) v Poland*); ECtHR, *El-Masri v The Former Yugoslav Republic of Macedonia* (GC), App no 39630/09, 13 December 2012, para 191; *Miguel Castro-Castro Prison v Peru* (n 209) para 440; AComHPR, *Malawi African Association and others v Mauritania*, Comm 54/91, 61/91, 98/93, 164/97, 196/97, 210/98, 11 May 2000, 13th ACHPR AAR Annex V (1999–2000).

[272] *Al Nashiri v Poland* (n 221) para 495 (emphasis added).

[273] *Barrios Altos v Peru* (Merits) (n 224) para 41.

[274] *Aksoy v Turkey* (GC) (n 97) para 98; ECtHR, *McCann and Others v UK* (GC), App no 18984/91, 27 September 1995, para 161.

[275] *Tagayeva ao v Russia* (n 176) paras 496, 539, 623–27.

[276] CCPR Committee, *Bautista d Arellana v Colombia*, Comm No 563/1993, Views, 27 October 1995, para 8.6; CCPR Committee, *Mojica v Dominican Republic*, Comm No 449/1991, Views, 10 August 1994, para 6.

trial.[277] The right to access to criminal justice could be understood as occupying the other side of the coin to what is described as the obligation to prosecute the perpetrators of international crimes.[278] Nonetheless, the emergence of a general obligation to prosecute under human rights law has been contested. Specific treaties explicitly provide for such obligation, but not as a right of the victims.[279]

The reference to an obligation to prosecute creates false expectations that the perpetrators will be prosecuted. The state has at most an obligation to conduct an effective investigation, capable of potentially leading to the prosecution of the alleged perpetrators. However, an effective investigation may be inconclusive; it does not guarantee a prosecution, and even a prosecution does not guarantee that the individual will be found guilty of all charges.[280] It is more accurate to refer to a broader right to 'access to criminal justice', which requires authorities to take measures to ensure that victims have access to judicial means, while taking into account the circumstances of a particular situation.

Various closely connected due-process obligations may flow from these two rights—the right to truth and the right to access to criminal justice—depending on the circumstances of each case. These obligations are mostly assessed against the overall situation: whether the violations occurred in a context of widespread violence, whether there is a domestic infrastructure in place, and whether the system is fully functioning. For instance, the obligation to conduct an effective investigation is closely related to the right of victims to know the truth of past serious violations of human rights and having access to criminal justice.[281] An

[277] On the obligation to prosecute, see Fernando Felipe Basch, 'The Doctrine of the Inter-American Court of Human Rights Regarding States' Duty to Punish Human Rights Violations and Its Dangers' (2007) 23 AUILR 195, 195–229.

[278] There are two substantive differences in the approaches of international criminal law and international human rights law. In the latter, the obligation arises as a remedy for the victims of serious violations of human rights, not as a direct obligation of states. In addition, in human rights courts' jurisprudence, the obligation is not limited to cases where the acts amount to international crimes. They have also recognised an obligation in isolated cases of serious violations of human rights, such as arbitrary executions or enforced disappearances.

[279] Specifically, the Geneva Conventions for grave breaches, the Convention against Torture, and the Convention on Genocide. On the obligation to prosecute from a criminal and humanitarian law perspective, see Paola Gaeta, 'The Interplay Between the Geneva Conventions and International Criminal Law' in Andrew Clapham, Paola Gaeta, and Marco Sassòli (eds), *The 1949 Geneva Conventions: A Commentary* (OUP 2015) (hereinafter Gaeta, 'The Interplay').

[280] See further 'Final Report of the ILC, The obligation to extradite or prosecute (*aut dedere aut judicare*)' (2014) Yb ILC, Vol II, Part Two; Anja Seibert-Fohr, *Prosecuting Serious Human Rights Violations* (OUP 2009); Robert Cryer, *Prosecuting International Crimes: Selectivity and the International Criminal Law Regime* (CUP 2005).

[281] Among others, ECtHR, *Akkoç v Turkey*, App nos 22947/93 and 22948/93, 10 October 2000, para 103; *Aslakhanova ao v Russia* (n 94) paras 222 et seq; *Husayn (Abu Zubaydah) v Poland* (n 271). On the dual nature of the obligation to investigate that is both a primary and a secondary obligation of a state, see Sandra Krähenmann, 'Positive Obligations in Human Rights Treaties', Thesis (Graduate Institute of

investigation can help to clarify the facts, identify the disappeared and their fate, or even verify their remains.[282] The European Court also highlighted that new investigatory steps by the Turkish authorities were necessary in order to identify and punish those responsible for bombing the applicants' villages and to end impunity.[283]

Also, it may be argued that the obligation to repeal any laws offering full amnesties or allowing statutory limitations for serious violations of human rights derives directly from these rights—the right to truth and the right to 'access to criminal justice'. Both the Inter-American Court and the European Court have concluded that unconditional amnesty laws for serious violations of human rights are inadmissible.[284] The former repeatedly pointed out

> that all amnesty provisions, provisions on prescription and the establishment of measures designed to eliminate responsibility are inadmissible, because they are intended to prevent the investigation and punishment of those responsible for serious human rights violations . . .[285]

Similarly, in a more recent case before the European Court, where the applicant complained that their right not to be tried twice for the same crime (*ne bis in idem*) had been violated, the Court found that there was no violation of the applicant's rights, underlining

> that granting amnesty in respect of the killing and ill-treatment of civilians would run contrary to the State's obligations under Articles 2 and 3 of the Convention since it would hamper the investigation of such acts and necessarily lead to impunity for those responsible.[286]

International and Development Studies, 2012); Michel Hottelier, 'La nécessaire complémentarité des droits matériels et des garanties de procédure' [2007] RTDH 573.

[282] Among others, see *Aslakhanova ao v Russia* (n 94) paras 158, 213, 238; *Gelman v Uruguay* (n 71) Operative para; *Velásquez-Rodríguez v Honduras* (Reparations and costs) (n 176) para 181.

[283] *Benzer ao v Turkey* (n 164) para 219. See also, *Abuyeva ao v Russia* (n 164) para 243.

[284] See Ilia Maria Siatitsa and Marieke Wierda, 'Principle 24: Restrictions and Other Measures Relating to Amnesty' in Frank Haldenmann and Thomas Unger (eds), *The United Nations Principles to Combat Impunity: A Commentary (Oxford Commentaries on International Law)* (OUP 2018).

[285] *Barrios Altos v Peru* (Merits) (n 224) para 41. The Inter-American Court has confronted numerous amnesty laws that were adopted after the dictatorships in Peru, Chile, Brazil, Uruguay, and others. Among others, ibid para 41; *Almonacid-Arellano et al v Chile* (n 224) paras 154–55.

[286] The case concerned a trial that was discontinued in 1996 because of an amnesty law, but it resumed years later as the law was found inadmissible. ECtHR, *Marguš v Croatia* (GC), App no 4455/10, 27 May 2014, Operative para 1. Similarly, see ECtHR, *Yeşil and Sevim v Turkey*, App no 34738/04, 5 June 2007, para 38; ECtHR, *Abdülsamet Yaman v Turkey*, App no 32446/96, 2 November 2004, para 55.

The Inter-American Court has also reiterated that 'the statute of limitation provisions … that are intended to prevent the investigation and punishment of those responsible for serious violations [of] human rights … are not admissible'.[287]

3. A victim-oriented but not individualistic approach to remedies

The preceding discussion reveals the progressive construction of the third operative component of the special regime around serious violations of human rights. On the one hand, several *ad hoc* mass claims processes have been established as a response to serious violations of human rights. On the other hand, the human rights courts increasingly recognise serious violations of human rights in their jurisprudence as a separate category of violations giving rise to specific procedures and remedies. The emergent practices may not be as ambitious as one would have hoped in the face of violations that pierce the very heart of the societal structure, leaving an indelible mark on entire communities, the victims of these violations. At the same time, though, any attempt to repair constitutes a recognition of the fundamental importance of tackling serious violations of human rights.

The various procedures through which reparations are awarded have developed as a result of attempts to find a balance between the inability of regular procedures to address such violations and the recognition that these violations are so important that they cannot be left unanswered. The *ad hoc* mass claims processes have been established due to the double recognition that it is imperative to respond to serious violations of human rights but that their massive character makes the chances of addressing them all through the regular judicial systems impossible. Similarly, even though the pilot judgment process before the European Court was introduced because of the constantly increasing workload of the Court, it is increasingly portrayed as an indispensable tool for addressing serious violations of human rights of a massive character.

On a substantive level, that is the actual reparations awarded to victims, the Courts have so far avoided systematising the reparatory measures that are

[287] *Gomes Lund et al v Brazil* (n 223) para 171. See also *Vélez Restrepo and family v Colombia* (n 72) paras 282–83; *'Las Dos Erres' Massacre v Guatemala* (n 248) para 129; *La Cantuta v Peru* (n 175) para 152.

primarily reserved for serious violations. It is the increasing recourse to certain reparatory measures that has allowed for a more coherent and systematic presentation of these practices. It may be that no new categories of reparations have been introduced for serious violations of human rights, but the incidence of different forms of reparations has nevertheless been affected. The various massive claims mechanisms put into question the right to full reparation, while higher monetary awards made through the judicial processes reflect the aggravated character of serious violations.[288] In the meantime, symbolic awards are becoming—on the American continent at least—a regular form of satisfaction and guarantees of non-repetition. The emergence and consolidation of the right to the truth directly emanates from serious violations of human rights. It is unambiguously linked to the right to reparation, even though it cannot be categorised as a form of reparation.

These practices reflect a subtle recognition of the qualitative differences between serious violations of human rights and other human rights violations. It is inherent to the notion of reparation for any harm that the remedy should be proportionate to the gravity of the infraction and the harm suffered. Hence it is inevitable that reparations for violations of human rights 'should be proportional to the gravity of the violations and the harm suffered'.[289] Yet the systematic recourse to similar forms of remedies in cases of serious violations of human rights permits the gradual emergence and solidification of certain remedial practices around this category of human rights violations and not any human rights violations.

The procedural and substantive practices described above primarily aim at ensuring that victims of serious violations of human rights receive the most just satisfaction possible after surviving irreparable traumatic experiences.[290] For instance, symbolic awards, such as memorials, are intended first and foremost to satisfy the victims by recognising what they went through and reassuring them that such violations will never be repeated. Increasingly, the remedial awards are acquiring a collective dimension surpassing the bilateral relation between victim and state before the human rights courts. Judgments are expected to have a broader impact that ensures that such violations are not repeated. However, remedies increasingly ordered as a response to serious

[288] See, for argument why the two approaches are reconcilable and complementary, Carrillo and Palmer, 'Transnational Mass Claim Processes' (n 30) 343–430.

[289] Principle 15, Basic Principles and Guidelines (n 14).

[290] Brandon Hamber, 'Repairing the Irreparable: Dealing with the Double-Binds of Making Reparations for Crimes of the Past' (2000) 5 Ethnicity and Health 215, 221.

violations of human rights, such as symbolic awards, also explicitly aim at benefiting an entire community or the society at large.[291]

The primary motivation behind all these measures remains the redress of victims. Still there is no intention to punish or in any way directly reprimand the state responsible for serious violations of human rights. Certain measures ordered in individual cases may in passing also highlight the aggravated responsibility of the state. For instance, monetary awards may be interpreted as implying aggravated damages. Similarly, symbolic awards can be considered not only as measures of satisfaction of victims, but also as broader sanctions targeting those responsible. However, their primary purpose remains the redress of the victims and not punishing the state. Also, the UN Basic Principles and Guidelines aimed at ensuring that victims of such harm were remedied to the extent possible, rather than punishing the wrongdoing state for the damage caused.[292]

Placing the victim at the centre of the 'remedial' component of the special regime around serious violations of human rights is essential, yet it does have a significant secondary effect. It displaces the state as the perpetrator of these violations. Obviously, when a court concludes that a serious violation of human rights has been committed, it is the state that is held accountable for these violations. However, the state is held accountable in order to repair, to the extent possible, the harm caused to this particular victim or group of victims. To primarily focus on the redress of victims eventually allows states to remain on the side-lines of the remedial 'events', as the remedying power not the wrongdoer.

These developments to a large extent accommodate the contemporary increasing focus around the accountability of the individual in the international legal order. Individual perpetrators, if circumstances permit, will be prosecuted for the international crimes they have committed, and individual victims will receive reparation, to the extent possible, for their suffering. Ever since the Nuremberg trials, the international community has embraced individual criminal accountability as necessary to achieve justice for at least certain serious violations of human rights, that is international crimes, highlighting the community's increasing attention to these violations. Fletcher concluded that the result of the focus on individual criminal responsibility has been an extensively articulated system of international criminal law, with no parallel

[291] Schöensteiner describes all these measures as reparations addressed to the 'society as a whole': Judith Schönsteiner, 'Dissuasive Measures and the "Society as a Whole": A Working Theory of Reparations in the Inter-American Court of Human Rights' (2007) 23 AUILR 127, 139–63.

[292] Basic Principles and Guidelines (n 14) para 3.

system to enforce state responsibility for similar violations (that is, here, serious violations of human rights).[293]

States may be composed of individuals but they are also recognised as entities; they are politically organised communities living under a single system of governance. States remain the actors at the heart of the international legal order. This is only partly reflected in this component of the special regime. The developments discussed, violating obligations owed to the international community as a whole, seldom understand the state as the perpetrator of internationally wrongful acts (once described as international crimes of states).

[293] Laurel E Fletcher, 'A Wolf in Sheep's Clothing: Transitional Justice and the Effacement of State Accountability for International Crimes' (2015) 39 FILJ 447, 460. See also, Gaeta, 'The Interplay' (n 279) 737–53.

Conclusion

The objective of this book was to demonstrate that a new special regime has formed around a specific category of human rights violations—serious violations of human rights. This special regime is understood as substantively limited to a very specific issue-area of human rights violations; where a series of monitoring mechanisms and procedures is in place to predominantly highlight, document, and record such violations; where specific measures are taken, aimed at enforcing compliance; and where certain consequences arise, focusing primarily on affording the victims of such violations a remedy. As such, this special regime is arguably comprised of at least four thinly interconnected components: the substantive, the monitoring, the enforcement, and the remedial ones, as illustrated in Figure 1.

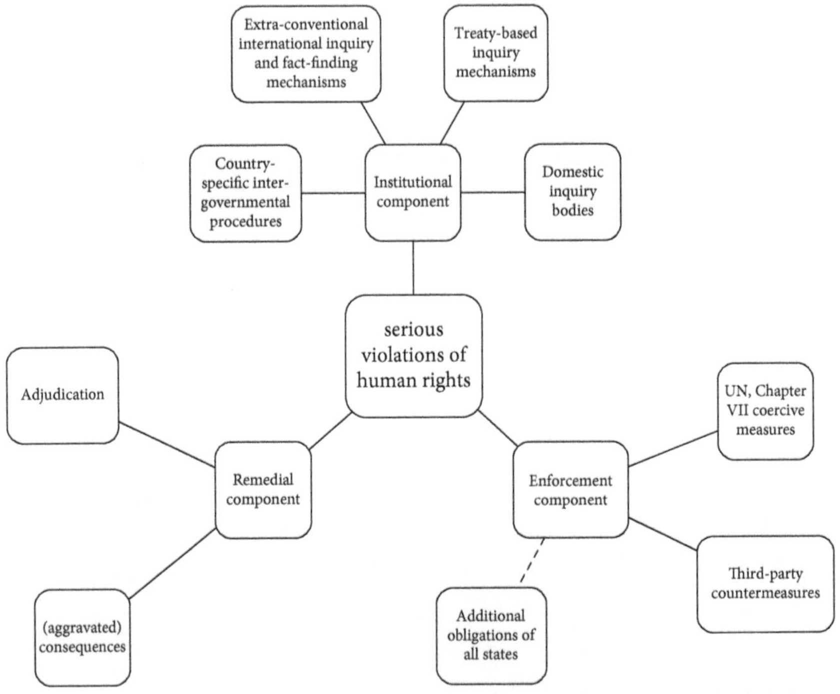

Figure 1 A visual depiction of the special regime illustrating the three operational components around the substantive component

Serious Violations of Human Rights. Ilia Siatitsa, Oxford University Press. © Ilia Siatitsa 2022.
DOI: 10.1093/oso/9780192863041.003.0006

The first component of this special regime is the specific subject-matter itself, namely the serious violations of human rights. The substantive component is the one around which all the other components of the regime operate. The interpretation of the expression, as reflected in international practice, illustrates that its use does not clash with the principles of equality and indivisibility of human rights. It does not create a hierarchy among human rights norms. On the contrary, this expression, correctly understood, allows for a unified and complementary approach to human rights norms.

The degree of gravity of certain human rights violations calls for an assessment that combines multiple factors. Gravity is not quantifiable—*x* number of violations of *y* right does not necessarily equal a serious violation of human rights. A more complicated equation is required to describe its flexibility and fluidity. Perhaps it would have been easier to construct a pyramid, at the apex of which certain specific violations would appear, such as torture and extrajudicial killings. However, this would be an artificial construction. It would have ignored the premise that different violations of different rights can eventually have the same end result, that is, causing irreparable harm to the victims.

With the expression 'serious violations of human rights' it is not necessary to agree upon such a closed list. It indicates that in specific circumstances, the violation of any right, and not only specific rights, may have an irreparable impact on the victims. For instance, violations of the right to life do not always amount to serious violations of human rights, while the violation of the right to property may amount to a serious violation in certain circumstances, albeit not as often. It is the combination of different elements present in a specific context that determines the gravity of the violation. Each element can only be considered in relation to the others elements—not autonomously. For example, the systematic burning of houses belonging to socially marginalised groups, in combination with the absence of any provisions to rectify the situation, constitutes a serious violation of human rights. Similarly, the infliction of torture is serious because of the nature of the violation and the irreparable impact on the victims, and so it goes on.

The risk with this interpretation of the expression is that it becomes subject to change, depending on future developments and the context in which it is used. However, this is also the power of this expression: it is flexible, neutral, easy to understand, and sufficiently wide. The degree of acceptance of this position is further illustrated by the increasing use of the expression as a standard in other branches of international law. Even if one fails to accept that there is a special regime forming around this expression, it is a fact that 'a serious violation of human rights' has been developing into a general standard, repeatedly called into use when it is impractical to refer to the entire human rights law regime.

Interestingly, specific branches of international law invoke serious violations of human rights and not all human rights violations. In refugee law, arms trade law, and in business and human rights, the expression has been introduced as a standard in treaty rules and guiding principles. For instance, Article 7 of the Arms Trade Treaty prohibits arms exports when there is a serious risk that the arms will be used to commit or facilitate a serious violation of human rights. Even on issues closely related to international crimes, such as the prohibition of amnesties for certain acts, the expression has often been used as the standard for prohibiting amnesties instead of international crimes. A similar development can be observed when looking at the debate around immunities and the possibility to establish certain exceptions to what acts they cover. These developments demonstrate the persistence of the distinction between serious and other human rights violations, and its gradual development into more than a qualifier—into a special category of violations triggering specific procedures and consequences.

As a result, the monitoring component of the special regime has emerged as a diverse network of special monitoring and inquiry processes. It contains various mechanisms and procedures that are set up or triggered following the occurrence of serious violations of human rights, recognising their existence, raising awareness, applying pressure, documenting, and recording those violations. Their material scope is formally or informally limited to human rights violations of certain gravity. Beyond their material scope, their formal institutional character and their means of operation, constituting primarily promotional and declaratory processes, bring them together.

The spectrum of mechanisms and procedures included therein is broad, including country-specific resolutions adopted by inter-governmental bodies (e.g. the UN General Assembly), treaty-based urgent inquiries, as well as extra-conventional inquiry procedures led by inter-governmental bodies, such as the UN Human Rights Council. In addition, a wide array of extra-conventional *ad hoc* inquiry bodies, mostly comprised of independent experts, have been regularly established as one-off responses to specific situations of serious violations of human rights. Their mandates are adapted to the particular circumstances of every case, as well as their duration, function, and composition. They can take the form of a commission of inquiry, fact-finding mission, high-level panel, special rapporteur, and truth and reconciliation commission, among others.

Ultimately, these monitoring and inquiry procedures as a whole construct a large web of procedures around serious violations of human rights. As such, they draw together the most complete public record of such violations that has ever existed in international law history. These monitoring procedures and mechanisms are often the first step of the formal mobilisation of the international community to respond to serious violations of human rights.

The next step—normatively at least, as the components of the regime do not necessarily operate in consequence in a co-ordinated manner—is the enforcement component. The second operational component includes coercive measures taken as a response to serious violations of human rights within both the UN sanctions regime and the inter-state countermeasures framework. The two forms of coercive measures—UN sanctions and third-party countermeasures—have irreversibly converged with regard to their target and purpose. The UN Security Council has interpreted the 'threat to the peace'—the key that opens Chapter VII's door—to include serious violations of human rights. As a consequence, it has ordered measures under Chapter VII of the UN Charter as a response to such violations. Next to the Security Council's measures and independently of those, states alone or collectively have been increasingly imposing countermeasures as a response to serious violations of human rights.

Apart from sharing a common purpose, the types of coercive measures taken—either as Security Council measures or as third-party countermeasures—are quite similar, including a range of sectoral and individual targeted sanctions, such as export bans and the freezing of assets. Still, though, it is only forcible coercive measures that remain the exclusive prerogative of the UN Security Council. It is only the latter that can authorise the use of force to compel the cessation of serious violations of human rights either directly or indirectly. For example, individual sanctions, such as freezing of assets, may be directly imposed on perpetrators of serious violations of human rights.

The last component of the special regime around serious violations of human rights is the remedial component. On the one hand, several *ad hoc* mass claims processes have been established as a response to serious violations of human rights. On the other hand, the human rights courts increasingly recognise serious violations of human rights in their jurisprudence as a separate category of violations giving rise to specific procedures and remedies. Their primary aim is to ensure that victims of such violations receive some form of remedy for the harm they have suffered.

Yet serious violations of human rights have not given rise to new forms of remedies. The gravity of human rights violations has rather been influencing the incidence of these forms of remedies—that is compensation, guarantees of non-repetition, and satisfaction—than providing for aggravated consequences. As a result, there are today some remedies that have been awarded first and foremost in cases of serious violations of human rights. The legal consequences specific to serious violations of human rights so far include: higher monetary awards (such as compensation for non-pecuniary losses); collective awards; symbolic awards. Beyond reparations, serious violations of human rights have been giving rise to additional rights for the victims, including the right to the truth and the right to access to criminal justice. The primary motivation behind all the adjudicative measures and remedial awards remains the redress of victims. Still, there is no intention to punish or in any way directly reprimand the state responsible for serious violations of human rights.

The regime in question is not set up by an international treaty that plainly defines the scope, the procedures, and the consequences of these violations. In fact, the various parts that compose this regime mostly emanate from already established legal regimes, at least international human rights law and the United Nations (UN) Charter regimes, as well as the general public international law regime. The aim of this research has been to bring some of the 'pieces of the puzzle' together. There are other developments in international law that could also have been arguably included as components of this special regime or other aspects related to it. For instance, the international criminal law system could be understood as part of this regime, even if it focuses on a narrower set of serious violations of human rights.

The three operational components have been examined here following an increasing degree of normativity: the narrative began in Chapter 2 with the consideration of the various non-binding monitoring and inquiry procedures, and ended in Chapter 4 with certain legal consequences to which this category of violations gives rise. One could imagine them functioning in a co-ordinated, escalated manner, where softer forms of intervention (non-binding mechanisms) are followed by enforcement measures, to be concluded by the imposition of remedies. However, the three operational components do not function in co-ordination with each other or in a sequence. Instead, and for various reasons—including procedural constraints, jurisdictional matters, political interests, and others—each of them has so far emerged and operates to a large extent independently from the others. More often than not, they do not even address the same instances of serious violations of human rights.

This is not to say that the formation of all these practices is altogether accidental. All the different parts of the components develop, influence, inspire, and get informed by the others, but beyond that—for the moment—they cannot be understood as a closed system or a clearly built structure. For instance, the UN Economic and Social Council Resolutions 1503 and 1235 initially authorised the UN Commission on Human Rights to respond to a specific instance of serious violations of human rights, and eventually influenced the instigation and development of further procedures and mechanisms. The UN Security Council will increasingly consult the reports of inquiry mechanisms before deciding to take action. However, these synergies are so far accidental and sporadic.

As Saul pointed out, while examining a different special regime, 'The existence of a specialised regime is a matter of methodology and appreciation, but also of degree.'[1] The regime may not be as 'unified, centralized or coherent as some others'.[2] Nonetheless, this book reveals a solid and continually evolving accretion of international rules and practice on serious violations of human rights, developed and serviced by competent institutions and actors. As Saul had added:

> To be sure, the regime is open-textured, fragmented, and constantly changing shape. Its relationships with other specialized regimes remain messy and are still being worked out; and the meaningful legal consequences of identifying such a regime are not always obvious.[3]

Even so, the special regime around serious violations of human rights remains distinctively normative, systemic, and institutionalised.

The characteristics of the special regime concerning serious violations of human rights are *grosso modo* typical of the international legal order to which this regime belongs; a legal system characterised by political flexibility, the dominance of individual interests and lack of formalism, as well as by the absence of a central governing body. These are features of the entire international law system.[4] As Gowlland-Debbas underlined:

> The evolution of the international legal system has included certain contradictory trends: on the one hand, a certain fragmentation and compartmentalization of international law, on the other, the construction of unifying,

[1] Ben Saul, *Research Handbook on International Law and Terrorism* (Edward Elgar 2014) x.
[2] ibid x–xi.
[3] ibid x–xi.
[4] See Alan Boyle and Christine Chinkin, *The Making of International Law* (OUP 2007) 100.

> universalizing elements—the development of what may be viewed as an international public policy or *ordre public*, leading to a hierarchization of rules due to a growing value-oriented or public-interest oriented international law.[5]

Ignoring the emergence of serious violations of human rights as a distinct category of human rights, which implies specific consequences, obliges political actors and advocates to continually underline that certain situations are unprecedented and exceptional in order to motivate and push the political organs to take action. However, contemporary history has shown that, unfortunately, such violations occur regularly, recurrently justifying 'extraordinary' measures. Therefore, more systematic attention to these practices would allow for their more coherent and constructive development. One can consider, for instance, ways to optimise the operation of the special regime as a whole. Serious violations of human rights do not call for the adoption of a special treaty but for greater awareness of their normative effects to be able to utilise the tools they provide more effectively. As the regime is still developing, it continues to progress and evolve, leaving plenty of space for further research and evaluation.

The analysis of international practice demonstrates that there is a common understanding regarding the human rights violations that would amount to serious violations. It has also shown that there is a set of rules, decision-making procedures, and consequences that revolve around this specific issue-area. This can seldom be understood as reflective of the development of customary international law. Custom in international law is understood as describing rules of behaviour that prescribe what is permitted and what is not. At best, current practice is constantly informing existing customary rules, such as the rules on countermeasures. It still rather presents the qualities of a multi-layered regime with increasing legal normativity, where certain rules may gradually be understood to have acquired a customary law function. Seldom do any of the above components appear to reflect a belief by a state (or other international) that it is under a legal obligation to behave in a certain way.

In broad terms, the current regime remains in line with the main principles and structures of the international legal order. The various mechanisms and processes have developed without defying the status quo or challenging the existing structures. In most instances, the various organs have either developed practices within their mandates, or at most expanded their mandates. For instance, the UN Security Council has interpreted its mandate, which

[5] Vera Gowlland-Debbas, 'The Security Council as Enforcer of Human Rights' in Bardo Fassbender (ed), *Securing Human Rights? Achievements and Challenges of the UN Security Council* (OUP 2011) 37.

covers 'threats to the peace', to include serious violations of human rights. Similarly, both the European Court and the Inter-American Court, in the process of examining situations of serious violations of human rights, have been adapting the already established forms of remedies to reflect the gravity of those violations.

Aspects of the regime are not limited to serious violations of human rights but cover a broader spectrum of what is described as the 'public interests' of the international community. This is particularly the case with the enforcement component. Yet this cannot be said for the totality of the regime—at least for the moment. The focus of this book has primarily been on the existence and construction of the special regime around serious violations of human rights. Therefore, it has not analysed these synergies and potential tensions.

In equal measure, the use and understanding of the expression 'serious violations of international humanitarian law' requires further attention. The notion of serious violations of international humanitarian law appears increasingly alongside serious violations of human rights in international practice. For instance, a serious violation of international humanitarian law is another condition in the Arms Trade Treaty that may be invoked to stop an arms export. The relation between the two notions was not covered here. The content and potential consequences of serious violations of international humanitarian law need to be further analysed, both on their own and in relation to serious violations of human rights. It could be the case that the same regime has emerged for both categories of violations, but this assumption remains to be answered.

Within the regime under evaluation here, serious violations of human rights have not given rise to new consequences, and certainly not aggravated consequences for the responsible state. One of the biggest gaps of the special regime around serious violations of human rights arguably remains the fact that it continues to largely divert attention from the responsible state. It has not been possible so far to develop additional aggravated consequences for the wrongdoing state under general international law. Discussions around punitive damages found no support in practice, and arguments in favour of their inclusion as automatic legal consequences of serious violations of international law are not convincing. Other potential candidates, such as the suspension of membership of an international organisation, still remain primarily political tools rather than aggravated legal consequences.

The individual perpetrators and the individual victims of serious violations of human rights are the primary objects of attention of the special regime. For instance, the enforcement measures, both UN collective measures and third-party countermeasures, are corrective measures aimed at coercing those responsible to cease such violations. They do not aim to punish the state responsible for committing or facilitating such violations (even if they can be perceived as punishment by the targeted state). These are reactive measures pending a more permanent resolution to the situation in question. Also, these coercive measures quite often today take the form of individual sanctions, rather than constraining the state as an entity responsible for the violations. Measures such as the establishment of the International Criminal Tribunals in the former Yugoslavia and Rwanda targeted individual criminal liability and not the responsibility of the state in the strict sense.

Similarly, the remedies developed aim to ensure that victims of serious violations of human rights have access to appropriate redress, rather than punishing the responsible state. Particularly, mass claims processes, through truth commissions or administrative laws, have been motivated by attempts to achieve justice for victims. These processes are set up by the state and form part of the state's reparatory mechanisms. Also, the reparations awarded by the regional human rights courts aim at ensuring that the aggravated consequences for the victims are appropriately remedied, and not that the aggravated responsibility of the state is punished. They do not, for instance, award punitive damages.

It could have been argued that this is a special regime more around international crimes than serious violations of human rights. Indeed, substantively, the two notions are overlapping; however, they are not identical. Maybe all crimes against humanity amount to serious violations of human rights, but not all serious violations of human rights need occur in the context of systematic or widespread violations. While there are texts and scholars that use the two interchangeably, there are equally texts and instances that clearly distinguish the two. In any event, it is rather better to avoid using the terminology of individual criminal responsibility to deal with state responsibility matters. The reference to crimes instead of human rights violations points towards individuals (as perpetrators or victims) rather than states.

The international community's primary focus on international crimes and individual criminal responsibility has overshadowed matters relating to state responsibility generally, and more specifically concerning serious violations of human rights. Ever since the Nuremberg trials, the focus has been on individual criminal accountability as a necessary tool to achieve justice for at least certain serious violations of human rights (that is international crimes), highlighting the community's increasing attention to these violations. Even the notion of 'responsibility to protect' has eventually been connected to international crimes. However, the result of the focus on individual criminal responsibility has been an extensively articulated system of international criminal law, which does not appear to be fully backed by a parallel system to enforce state responsibility for closely related—even though not fully overlapping—violations (that is, here, serious violations of human rights).

If anything, the special regime requires the collaboration of the state apparatus to function—irrespective of whether state officials directly contributed to the violations. The international community's reactions remain in a way secondary, albeit more active, and complementary to the responsibilities of the wrongdoing state. These developments are undoubtedly significant for the evolution and completion of the international legal order. Nonetheless, states are politically organised communities living under a single system of governance; they may be composed of individuals, but they are also recognised as entities with distinct legal personalities. As such, they remain the principal actors at the heart of the international system. This role is not sufficiently reflected in the special regime under scrutiny here.

The whole international legal order is premised on the notion of the sovereign state, but what we observe here is pushing the sovereign state to the sidelines as the system still requires their co-operation to operate. This undermines the system of state responsibility for those violations; downplays the responsibility of the state; and arguably admits to the inability of the nation state to exist as a construct with other than administrative responsibilities.

Bibliography

Books

Alston P and Knuckey S (eds), *The Transformation of Human Rights Fact-Finding* (OUP 2015)

Alston P and Macdonald E (eds), *Human Rights, Intervention, and the Use of Force* (OUP 2008)

Alston P and Mégret F (eds), *The United Nations and Human Rights: A Critical Appraisal* (2nd edn, OUP 2020)

Alvarez JE, *The Impact of International Organizations on International Law* (Brill/Nijhoff 2016)

Bailey S, *The UN Security Council and Human Rights* (Macmillan 1994)

Bartolomei ML, *Gross and Massive Violations of Human Rights in Argentina 1976–1983: An Analysis of the Procedure under ECOSOC Resolution 1503* (Juristförlaget 1994)

Beaulac S, *The Power of Language in the Making of International Law: The Word Sovereignty in Bodin and Vattel and the Myth of Westphalia* (Brill/Nijhoff 2004)

Bellamy A and Dunne T (eds), *The Oxford Handbook of the Responsibility to Protect* (OUP 2016)

Biersteker TJ, Eckert SE, and Tourinho M, *Targeted Sanctions: The Impacts and Effectiveness of United Nations Action* (CUP 2016)

Boyle A and Chinkin C, *The Making of International Law* (OUP 2007)

Buchanan AE, *Human Rights, Legitimacy, and the Use of Force* (OUP 2010)

Burke C, *An Equitable Framework for Humanitarian Intervention* (Hart Publishing 2013)

Cassese A and Gaeta P, *Cassese's International Criminal Law* (3rd edn, OUP 2013)

Chesterman S, *Just War or Just Peace?: Humanitarian Intervention and International Law* (OUP 2002)

Chesterman S, Johnstone I, and Malone DM, *Law and Practice of the United Nations* (2nd edn, OUP 2016)

Clapham A, *Human Rights Obligations of Non-State Actors* (OUP 2006)

Clapham A, *Brierly's Law of Nations: An Introduction to the Role of International Law in International Relations* (7th edn, OUP 2012)

Clapham A and Bourke J, *The Promotion and Protection of All Human Rights is a Legitimate Concern of the International Community* (The Graduate Institute of International Studies 1999)

Clapham A and others (eds), *The Arms Trade Treaty: A Commentary* (OUP 2016)

Conforti B and Focarelli C, *The Law and Practice of the United Nations* (5th edn, Brill/Nijhoff 2016)

Cortright D and Lopez GA, *Smart Sanctions: Targeting Economic Statecraft* (Rowman & Littlefield 2002)

Crawford J, *The International Law Commission's Articles on State Responsibility: Introduction, Text and Commentaries* (CUP 2002)

Cryer R, *Prosecuting International Crimes: Selectivity and the International Criminal Law Regime* (CUP 2005)

Dawidowicz M, *Third-Party Countermeasures in International Law* (CUP 2017)

De Wet E, *The Chapter VII Powers of the United Nations Security Council* (Hart Publishing 2004)

Doswald-Beck L, *Human Rights in Times of Conflict and Terrorism* (OUP 2011)

Egan S, *The UN Human Rights Treaty System: Law and Procedure* (Bloomsbury Professional 2011)

Evans C, *The Right to Reparation in International Law for Victims of Armed Conflict* (CUP 2012)

Fortas A-C, *La surveillance de l'exécution des arrêts et décisions des Cours Européenne et Interaméricaine des droits de l'homme* (Pedone 2015)

Fortin K, *The Accountability of Armed Groups under Human Rights Law* (OUP 2017)

Franck TM, *Fairness in International Law and Institutions* (OUP 1998)

Franck TM, *Recourse to Force: State Action against Threats and Armed Attacks* (CUP 2002)

Gaer FD and Broecker CL (eds), *The United Nations High Commissioner for Human Rights: Conscience for the World* (Martinus Nijhoff Publishers 2014)

Gray C, *International Law and the Use of Force* (4th edn, OUP 2018)

Harris D, O'Boyle M, Bates E, and Buckley C, *Harris, O'Boyle & Warbrick: Law of the European Convention on Human Rights* (3rd edn, OUP 2014)

Hayner PB, *Unspeakable Truths: Transitional Justice and the Challenge of Truth Commissions* (Routledge 2011)

Henderson C (ed), *Commissions of Inquiry: Problems and Prospects* (Hart Publishing 2017)

Hennebel L, *La Convention américaine des droits de l'homme: mécanismes de protection et étendue des droits et libertés* (Bruylant 2007)

Higgins R, *The Development of International Law Through the Political Organs of the United Nations* (OUP 1963)

Higgins R, *Problems and Process: International Law and How We Use It* (Clarendon Press 1994)

Ichim O, *Just Satisfaction under the European Convention on Human Rights* (CUP 2014)

Ingelse C, *United Nations Committee Against Torture: An Assessment* (Kluwer 2001)

Jennings R and Watts A (eds), *Oppenheim's International Law*, Vol 1: *Peace* (9th edn, Longman 1992)

Jørgensen NHB, *The Responsibility of States for International Crimes* (OUP 2000)

Kamminga MT, *Inter-State Accountability for Violations of Human Rights* (University of Pennsylvania Press 1992)

Katayanagi M, *Human Rights Functions of United Nations Peacekeeping Operations* (Martinus Nijhoff Publishers 2002)

Kennedy D, *The Dark Sides of Virtue: Reassessing International Humanitarianism* (Princeton University Press 2005)

Kolb R, *Peremptory International Law*—Jus Cogens: *A General Inventory* (Hart Publishing 2015)

Krause C and Scheinin M, *International Protection of Human Rights: A Textbook* (2nd edn, Åbo Akademi University 2012)

Kuwali D and Viljoen F (eds), *Africa and the Responsibility to Protect: Article 4(h) of the African Union Constitutive Act* (Routledge 2014)

Lattanzi F, *Garanzie dei diritti dell'uomo nel diritto internazionale generale* (Dott A Giuffrè Editore 1983)

Leach P, *Taking a Case to the European Court of Human Rights* (3rd edn, OUP 2011)

Lempinen M, *Challenges Facing the System of Special Procedures of the United Nations Commission on Human Rights* (Institute for Human Rights—Åbo Akademi University 2001)
Lempinen M, *The United Nations Commission on Human Rights and the Different Treatment of Governments: An Inseparable Part of Promoting and Encouraging Respect for Human Rights?* (Åbo Akademis Förlag—Åbo Akademi University Press 2005)
Medina Quiroga C, *The Battle of Human Rights: Gross, Systematic Violations and the Inter-American System* (Kluwer 1988)
Meron T, *The Humanization of International Law* (Martinus Nijhoff Publishers 2006)
Moelle MP, *The International Responsibility of International Organisations: Cooperation in Peacekeeping Operations* (CUP 2017)
Murray R and Long D, *The Implementation of the Findings of the African Commission on Human and Peoples' Rights* (CUP 2015)
Nowak M and McArthur E, *The United Nations Convention Against Torture: A Commentary* (OUP 2008)
O'Flaherty M, *Human Rights and the UN: Practice Before the Treaty Bodies* (Kluwer 2002)
Ochoa JC, *The Rights of Victims in Criminal Justice Proceedings for Serious Human Rights Violations* (Martinus Nijhoff Publishers 2013)
Odier-Contreras Garduno D, *Collective Reparations: Tensions and Dilemmas Between Collective Reparations and the Individual Right to Receive Reparations* (Intersentia 2018)
Orakhelashvili A, *Peremptory Norms in International Law* (OUP 2006)
Orford A, *Reading Humanitarian Intervention Human Rights and the Use of Force in International Law* (CUP 2003)
Orford A, *International Authority and the Responsibility to Protect* (CUP 2011)
Ouguergouz F, *The African Charter on Human and Peoples' Rights, A Comprehensive Agenda for Human Dignity and Sustainable Democracy in Africa* (Martinus Nijhoff Publishers 2003)
Owen Fiss Q, *The Civil Rights Injunction* (Indiana University Press 1979)
Pasqualucci JM, *The Practice and Procedure of the Inter-American Court of Human Rights* (2nd edn, CUP 2014)
Pazartzi F, *Criminal Repression in International Law. International Criminal Justice in Modern Times* (Sakkoulas 2007) (in Greek)
Picchio Forlati L and Sicilianos L-A (eds), *Economic Sanctions in International Law* (The Centre for Studies and Research in International Law and International Relations, The Hague Academy of International Law 2004)
Ragazzi M, *The Concept of International Obligations* Erga Omnes (OUP 2000)
Ramcharan BG, *The Security Council and the Protection of Human Rights* (Martinus Nijhoff Publishers 2002)
Ramcharan BG, *The UN Human Rights Council* (Routledge 2011)
Rieter E, *Preventing Irreparable Harm, Provisional Measures in International Human Rights Adjudication* (Intersentia 2010)
Saul B, *Research Handbook on International Law and Terrorism* (Edward Elgar 2014)
Scelle G, *Précis de droit des gens, principes et systématique*, Vol I (Dalloz 1932)
Seibert-Fohr A, *Prosecuting Serious Human Rights Violations* (OUP 2009)
Seiderman I, *Hierarchy in International Law: The Human Rights Dimension* (Intersentia 2001)
SFDI, *La responsabilité de protéger, Colloque de Nanterre* (Pedone 2008)
Sharma SK and Welsh JM (eds), *The Responsibility to Prevent: Overcoming the Challenges of Atrocity Prevention* (OUP 2015)
Shaw M, *International Law* (8th edn, CUP 2017)

Shelton D, *Remedies in International Human Rights Law* (3rd edn, OUP 2015)
Sicilianos L-A, *Les réactions décentralisées à l'illicite: Des contre-mesures à la légitime défense* (LGDJ 1990)
Sicilianos L-A, *The Human Dimension of International Law: Interplay of General International Law and Human Rights* (Nomiki Bibliothiki Group 2010)
Sloan J, *The Militarisation of Peacekeeping in the Twenty-First Century* (Hart Publishing 2011)
Stahn C, *The Law and Practice of International Territorial Administration: Versailles to Iraq and Beyond* (CUP 2008)
Sunga L, *Individual Responsibility in International Law for Serious Human Rights Violations* (Martinus Nijhoff Publishers 1992)
Tams CJ, *Enforcing Obligations* Erga Omnes *in International Law* (CUP 2005)
Teitel RG, *Transitional Justice* (OUP 2002)
Tomaševski K, *Responding to Human Rights Violations: 1946–1999* (Martinus Nijhoff Publishers 2000)
Tzanakopoulos A, *Disobeying the Security Council: Countermeasures against Wrongful Sanctions* (OUP 2011)
Umozurike O, *The African Charter on Human and Peoples' Rights* (Martinus Nijhoff Publishers 1997)
Vandenhole W, *The Procedures Before the UN Human Rights Treaty Bodies: Divergence or Convergence?* (Intersentia 2004)
Viljoen F, *International Human Rights Law in Africa* (2nd edn, OUP 2012)
Villalpando S, *L'émergence de la communauté internationale dans la responsabilité des états* (PUF 2005)
von Einsiedel S, Malone DM, and Stagno Ugarte B (eds), *The UN Security Council in the 21st Century* (Lynne Rienner Publishers 2015)
Wheeler NJ, *Saving Strangers: Humanitarian Intervention in International Society* (OUP 2003)
Zyberi G (ed), *An Institutional Approach to the Responsibility to Protect* (CUP 2013)

Contributions to edited volumes

Abi-Saab G, 'The Concept of Sanction in International Law' in Gowlland-Debbas V and Abi-Saab G (eds), *United Nations Sanctions and International Law* (Kluwer 2001) 29–41
Alston P, 'The Commission on Human Rights' in Alston P (ed), *The United Nations and Human Rights: A Critical Appraisal* (OUP 1992) 126–210
Alvarez JE, 'The Schizophrenias of R2P' in Alston P and Macdonald E (eds), *Human Rights, Intervention, and the Use of Force* (OUP 2008) 275–84
Antonopoulos K, 'The Definition of Crimes against Humanity' in Koufa K and Pazartzi F (eds), *International Criminal Justice as an Enforcement Mechanism for International Law* (Sakkoulas 2007) 241–68
Bailey S, 'The Security Council' in Alston P (ed), *The United Nations and Human Rights: A Critical Appraisal* (Clarendon 1992) 304–36
Baldwin-Pask T and Scannella P, 'The Unfinished Business of a Special Procedures System' in Bassiouni MC and Schabas WA (eds), *New Challenges for the UN Human Rights Machinery: What Future for the UN Treaty Body System and the Human Rights Council Procedures?* (Intersentia 2011) 419–78

Bhuta N, 'The Role International Actors Other Than States Can Play in the New World Order' in Cassese A (ed), *Realizing Utopia: The Future of International Law* (OUP 2012) 61–75

Bianchi A, 'State Responsibility and Criminal Liability of Individuals' in Cassese A (ed), *The Oxford Companion to International Criminal Justice* (OUP 2009) 16–24

Boisson de Chazournes L, 'Responsibility to Protect: Reflecting Solidarity?' in Wolfrum R and Kojima C (eds), *Solidarity: A Structural Principle of International Law* (Springer 2010) 93–122

Brahm E, 'Judging Truth: The Contributions of Truth Commissions in Post-Conflict Environments' in Shawki N and Cox M (eds), *Negotiating Sovereignty and Human Rights; Actors and Issues in Contemporary Human Rights Politics* (Ashgate 2009) 119–38

Brooks R, 'Civilians and Armed Conflict' in Stagno Ugarte B and Genser J (eds), *The United Nations Security Council in the Age of Human Rights* (CUP 2014) 35–67

Brownlie I, 'Comment' in Cassese A and Weiler J (eds), *Change and Stability in International Law-Making* (Walter de Gruyter 1988) 108–10

Buergenthal T, 'Codifications and Implementation of International Human Rights' in Henkin A (ed), *Human Dignity, The Internationalization of Human Rights* (Aspen Institute for Humanistic Studies 1979) 15–21

Cadelo V, 'Truth and Reconciliation Commissions' in Pons N and Djukic D (eds), *Companion of International Humanitarian Law: Lexicon* (Brill 2018) 701–02

Cançado Trindade AA, 'Complementarity between State Responsibility and Individual Responsibility for Grave Violations of Human Rights: The Crime of State Revisited' in Ragazzi M (ed), *International Responsibility Today, Essays in Memory of Oscar Schachter* (Martinus Nijhoff Publishers 2005) 253–69

Carrillo AJ, 'Justice in Context: The Relevance of Inter-American Human Rights Law and Practice to Repairing the Past' in De Greiff P (ed), *The Handbook of Reparations* (OUP 2008) 504–38

Cassese A, 'The General Assembly: Historical Perspective 1945–1989' in Alston P (ed), *The United Nations and Human Rights: A Critical Appraisal* (CUP 1992) 25–54

Cassese A, 'A Plea for a Global Community Grounded in a Core of Human Rights' in Cassese A (ed), *Realizing Utopia: The Future of International Law* (OUP 2012) 136–43

Cismas I, 'The Intersection of Economic, Social, and Cultural Rights and Civil and Political Rights' in Riedel E, Giacca G, and Golay C (eds), *Economic, Social, and Cultural Rights in International Law: Contemporary Issues and Challenges* (OUP 2014) 448–72

Clapham A, 'The Complex Relationship between the 1949 Geneva Conventions and International Human Rights Law' in Clapham A, Gaeta P, and Sassòli M (eds), *The 1949 Geneva Conventions: A Commentary* (OUP 2015) 701–35

Clapham A, 'Non-State Actors' in Moeckli D and others (eds), *International Human Rights Law* (3rd edn, OUP 2018) 557–79

Clapham A, 'The General Assembly' in Alston P and Mégret F (eds), *The United Nations and Human Rights: A Critical Appraisal* (2nd edn, OUP 2020) 99–129

Corten O, 'Human Rights and Collective Security: Is There an Emerging Right of Humanitarian Intervention?' in Alston P and Macdonald E (eds), *Human Rights, Intervention, and the Use of Force* (OUP 2008) 87–137

Cortright D, Lopez GA, and Gerber-Stellingwerf L, 'Sanctions' in Weiss TG and Daws S (eds), *The Oxford Handbook on the United Nations* (OUP 2009) 349–69

Crawford J, 'Responsibility for Breaches of Communitarian Norms: An Appraisal of Article 48 of the ILC Articles on Responsibility of States for Internationally Wrongful Acts' in

Fastenrath U and others (eds), *From Bilateralism to Community Interest: Essays in Honour of Bruno Simma* (OUP 2011) 224–40

Darcy S, 'Laying the Foundations: Commissions of Inquiry and the Development of International Law' in Henderson C (ed), *Commissions of Inquiry: Problems and Prospects* (Hart Publishing 2017) 231–56

Das H, 'The Concept of Mass Claims and the Specificity of Mass Claims Resolution' in The International Bureau of the Permanent Court of Arbitration (ed), *Redressing Injustices Through Mass Claims Processes: Innovative Responses to Unique Challenges* (OUP 2006) 3–11

Dawidowicz M, 'Third-Party Countermeasures: Observations on a Controversial Concept' in Chinkin C and Baetens F (eds), *Sovereignty, Statehood and State Responsibility: Essays in Honour of James Crawford* (CUP 2015) 340–62

de Frouville O, 'Les organes subsidiaires de la commission des droits de l'homme des Nations Unies, Rapport Général' in Decaux E (ed), *Les Nations Unies et les droits de l'homme: enjeux et défis d'une réforme* (Pedone 2006) 171–99

de Frouville O, 'Building a Universal System for the Protection of Human Rights: The Way Forward' in Bassiouni MC and Schabas WA (eds), *New Challenges for the UN Human Rights Machinery: What Future for the UN Treaty Body System and the Human Rights Council Procedures?* (Intersentia 2011) 241–66

De Greiff P, 'Justice and Reparations' in De Greiff P (ed), *The Handbook of Reparations* (OUP 2008) 451–77

De Greiff P, 'Reparations Efforts in International Perspective: What Compensation Contributes to the Achievement of Imperfect Justice' in Doxtader E and Villa-Vicencio C (eds), *To Repair the Irreparable: Reparation and Reconstruction in South Africa* (David Philip Publishers 2004) 321–58

De La Vega C and Lewis TN, 'Peer Review in the Mix: How the UPR Transforms Human Rights Discourse' in Bassiouni MC and Schabas WA (eds), *New Challenges for the UN Human Rights Machinery: What Future for the UN Treaty Body System and the Human Rights Council Procedures?* (Intersentia 2011) 451–77

Falk R, 'Reparations, International Law, and Global Justice: A New Frontier' in De Greiff P (ed), *The Handbook of Reparations* (OUP 2008) 478–503

Fichtelberg A, 'Transitional Justice and the End of Impunity: Hybrid Tribunals' in Lawther C, Moffett L, and Jacobs D (eds), *Research Handbook on Transitional Justice* (Edward Elgar 2017) 328–41

Gaeta P, 'The Character of the Breach' in Crawford J, Pellet A, and Olleson S (eds), *The Law of International Responsibility* (OUP 2010) 421–26

Gaeta P, 'The Interplay Between the Geneva Conventions and International Criminal Law' in Clapham A, Gaeta P, and Sassòli M (eds), *The 1949 Geneva Conventions: A Commentary* (OUP 2015) 737–53

Gowlland-Debbas V, 'The Security Council as Enforcer of Human Rights' in Fassbender B (ed), *Securing Human Rights? Achievements and Challenges of the UN Security Council* (OUP 2011) 36–73

Gowlland-Debbas V and Gaggioli G, 'The Relationship between International Human Rights and Humanitarian Law: An Overview' in Kolb R and Gaggioli G (eds), *Research Handbook on Human Rights and Humanitarian Law* (Edward Elgar Publishing 2013) 77–103

Grace R, 'Lessons from Two Regional Missions: Fact-Finding in Georgia and South Sudan' in Henderson C (ed), *Commissions of Inquiry: Problems and Prospects* (Hart Publishing 2017) 65–87

Guembe MJ, 'Economic Reparations for Grave Human Rights Violations: The Argentine Experience' in De Greiff P (ed), *The Handbook of Reparations* (OUP 2008) 21–54

Hamber B, 'The Dilemmas of Reparations: In Search of a Process-Driven Approach' in de Feyter K and others (eds), *Out of the Ashes: Reparation for Victims of Gross and Systematic Human Rights Violations* (Intersentia 2005) 135–50

Heller JK, 'Situational Gravity Under the Rome Statute' in Stahn C and van den Herik L (eds), *Future Perspectives on International Criminal Justice* (Asser 2010) 227–53

Hertig Randall M, 'The History of International Human Rights Law' in Kolb R and Gaggioli G (eds), *Research Handbook on Human Rights and Humanitarian Law* (Edward Elgar Publishing 2013) 3–34

Hillgruber C, 'The Right of Third States to Take Countermeasures' in Tomuschat C and Thouvenin J-M (eds), *The Fundamental Rules of the International Legal Order:* 'Jus Cogens' *and Obligations* 'Erga Omnes' (Martinus Nijhoff Publishers 2006) 265–94

Hilpold P, 'From Humanitarian Intervention to Responsibility to Protect: Making Utopia True?' in Fastenrath U and others (eds), *From Bilateralism to Community Interest: Essays in Honour of Bruno Simma* (OUP 2011) 462–76

Katayanagi M, 'UN Peacekeeping and Human Rights' in Stagno Ugarte B and Genser J (eds), *The United Nations Security Council in the Age of Human Rights* (CUP 2014) 123–53

Krisch N, 'Article 39' in Simma Band others (eds), *The Charter of the United Nations: A Commentary* (3rd edn, OUP 2012) 1272–96

Krisch N, 'Article 41' in Simma B and others (eds), *The Charter of the United Nations: A Commentary* (3rd edn, OUP 2012) 1305–29

Krisch N, 'Introduction to Chapter VII: The General Framework' in Simma B and others (eds), *The Charter of the United Nations: A Commentary* (3rd edn, OUP 2012) 1237–71

Lambert Abdelgawad E, 'La Convention européenne des droits de l'homme: Exécution des arrêts de la Cour européenne' in Hertig M and Hottelier M (eds), *Introduction aux droits de l'homme* (Schulthess 2014) 427–39

Lawther C, 'Transitional Justice and Truth Commissions' in Lawther C, Moffett L, and Jacobs D (eds), *Research Handbook on Transitional Justice* (Edward Elgar 2017) 328–41

Lira E, 'The Reparations Policy for Human Rights Violations in Chile' in De Greiff P (ed), *The Handbook of Reparations* (OUP 2008) 55–101

Lopez GA, 'Enforcing Human Rights through Economic Sanctions' in Shelton D (ed), *The Oxford Handbook of International Human Rights Law* (OUP 2014) 772–93

Malamud-Goti JE and Grosman LS, 'Reparations and Civil Litigation: Compensation for Human Rights Violations in Transitional Democracies' in De Greiff P (ed), *The Handbook of Reparations* (OUP 2008) 539–59

Nolte G, 'Article 2(7)' in Simma B and others (eds), *The Charter of the United Nations: A Commentary* (3rd edn, OUP 2012) 280–312

Oette L, 'Bringing Justice to Victims? Responses of Regional and International Human Rights Courts and Treaty Bodies to Mass Violations' in Ferstman C, Goetz M, and Stephens A (eds), *Reparations for Victims of Genocide, War Crimes and Crimes Against Humanity: Systems in Place and Systems in the Making* (Martinus Nijhoff Publishers 2009) 217–42

Orakhelashvili A, 'The Impact of Unilateral EU Economic Sanctions on the UN Collective Security Framework: The Cases of Iran and Syria' in Marossi AZ and Bassett MR (eds), *Economic Sanctions under International Law: Unilateralism, Multilateralism, Legitimacy, and Consequences* (Springer 2015) 3–21

Partsch KJ, 'Reprisals' in Bernhardt R (ed), *Encyclopedia of public international law*, Vol IV (North-Holland 2002) 200

Pellet A and Miron A, 'Sanctions' in Wolfrum Rüdiger (ed), *Max Planck Encyclopedia of Public International Law from Professor Rüdiger Wolfrum* (OUP 2013)

Peters A, 'The Responsibility to Protect: Spelling out the Hard Legal Consequences for the UN Security Council and Its Members' in Fastenrath U and others (eds), *From Bilateralism to Community Interest: Essays in Honour of Bruno Simma* (OUP 2011) 297–325

Pisillo-Mazzeschi R, 'International Obligations to Provide for Reparation Claims?' in Randelzhofer A and Tomuschat C (eds), *State Responsibility and the Individual: Reparation in Instances of Grave Violations of Human Rights* (Martinus Nijhoff Publishers 1999) 149–72

Prebensen SC, 'Inter-State Complaints Under Treaty Provisions—The Experience Under The European Convention On Human Rights' in Zayas A and others (eds), *International Human Rights Monitoring Mechanisms* (Brill 2009) 439–64

Quiroga Medina C, 'The Inter-American System for the Protection of Human Rights' in Krause C and Scheinin M (eds), *International Protection of Human Rights: A Textbook* (2nd edn, Åbo Akademi University, Institute for Human Rights 2012) 519–49

Ramcharan BG, 'Coordination with Other UN Organs' in Stagno Ugarte B and Genser J (eds), *The United Nations Security Council in the Age of Human Rights* (CUP 2014) 154–70

Rechetov Y, 'International Responsibility for Violations of Human Rights' in Cassese A (ed), *UN Law Fundamental Rights: Two Topics in International Law* (Sijthoff & Noordhoff 1979) 237–48

Reisman WM, 'A Humanitarian Intervention to Protect the Ibos' in Lillich RB (ed), *Humanitarian Intervention and the United Nations* (University Press of Virginia 1973) 167–95

Rodley N, 'The United Nations Human Rights Council, Its Special Procedures, and Its Relationship with the Treaty Bodies: Complementarity or Competition?' in Boyle K (ed), *New Institutions for Human Rights Protection* (OUP 2010) 49–73

Rodley N, 'Integrity of the Person' in Moeckli D, Shah S, and Sivakumaran S (eds), *International Human Rights Law* (3rd ed, OUP 2018) 165–85

Rombouts H, Sardaro P, and Vandeginste S, 'The Right to Reparation for Victims of Gross and Systematic Violations of Human Rights' in de Feyter K and others (eds), *Out of the Ashes: Reparation for Victims of Gross and Systematic Human Rights Violations* (Intersentia 2005) 345–503

Salmon J, 'Les obligations quantitatives et l'illicéité' in Boisson de Chazournes L and Gowlland-Debbas V (eds), *L'ordre Juridique international, un système en quête d'équité et d'universalité/The International Legal System in Quest of Equity and Universality, Liber Amicorum Georges Abi-Saab* (Martinus Nijhoff Publishers 2001) 305–25

Schabas W, 'Accountability for International Crimes—Special Tribunals and Referrals to the International Criminal Court' in Stagno Ugarte B and Genser J (eds), *The United Nations Security Council in the Age of Human Rights* (CUP 2014) 173–94

Scheinin M, 'Core Rights and Obligations' in Shelton D (ed), *The Oxford Handbook of International Human Rights Law* (OUP 2014) 527–40

Schmalenbach K, 'Article 53, Treaties Conflicting with a Peremptory Norm of General International Law ("*Jus Cogens*")' in Dörr O and Schmalenbach K (eds), *Vienna Convention on the Law of Treaties: A Commentary* (Springer 2011) 897–942

Sellers MNS, 'Economic Sanctions and Human Rights Violations' in Picchio Forlati L and Sicilianos L-A (eds), *Economic Sanctions in International Law* (The Centre for Studies and Research in International Law and International Relations, The Hague Academy of International Law 2004) 477–526

Shalev C, 'State Reporting and the Convention on the Elimination of All Forms of Discrimination Against Women' in Bayefsky AF (ed), *The UN Human Rights Treaty System in the 21st Century* (Kluwer 2000) 23–34

Shelton D, 'The United Nations Principles and Guidelines on Reparations: Context and Contents' in de Feyter K and others (eds), *Out of the Ashes: Reparation for Victims of Gross and Systematic Human Rights Violations* (Intersentia 2005) 11–34

Shraga D, 'The Security Council and Human Rights—From Discretion to Promote to Obligation to Protect' in Fassbender B (ed), *Securing Human Rights?: Achievements and Challenges of the UN Security Council* (OUP 2011) 8–35

Siatitsa IM and Wierda M, 'Principle 24: Restrictions and Other Measures Relating to Amnesty' in Haldenmann F and Unger T (eds), *The United Nations Principles to Combat Impunity: A Commentary (Oxford Commentaries on International Law)* (OUP 2018) 258–69

Sicilianos L-A, 'Sanctions institutionnelles et contre-mesures: Tendances recentes' in Picchio Forlati L and Sicilianos L-A (eds), *Economic Sanctions in International Law* (The Centre for Studies and Research in International Law and International Relations, The Hague Academy of International Law 2004) 3–98

Simma B, 'International Crimes: Injury and Countermeasures, Comments on Part 2 of the ILC Work on State Responsibility' in Cassese A, Weiler JHH, and Spinedi M (eds), *International Crimes of State: A Critical Analysis of the ILC's Draft Article 19 on State Responsibility* (Walter de Gruyter 1989) 283–315

Sivakumaran S, 'Impact on the Structure of International Obligations' in Kamminga MT and Scheinin M (eds), *The Impact of Human Rights Law on General International Law* (OUP 2009) 133–50

Sob P, 'Article 58' in Kampto M (ed), *La Charte africaine des droits de l'homme et des peuples et le protocole y relatif portant création de la Cour africaine des droits de l'homme: Commentaire article par article* (Bruylant 2011) 1069–86

Sobers OH, 'The Inter-American System of Human Rights' in Zyberi G and Mason K (eds), *An Institutional Approach to the Responsibility to Protect* (CUP 2013) 459–80

Stagno Ugarte B and Genser J, 'Evolution of the Security Council's Engagement on Human Rights' in Stagno Ugarte B and Genser J (eds), *The United Nations Security Council in the Age of Human Rights* (CUP 2014) 3–31

Sunga L S, 'What Should Be the UN Human Rights Council's Role in Investigating Genocide, War Crimes and Crimes against Humanity?' in Bassiouni MC and Schabas WA (eds), *New Challenges for the UN Human Rights Machinery: What Future for the UN Treaty Body System and the Human Rights Council Procedures?* (Intersentia 2011) 319–49

Szurek S, 'Responsibilité de proteger, nature de l'obligation et responsibilité international' in SFDI (ed), *La responsibilité de protéger* (Pedone 2008) 91–134

Tams CJ and Asteriti A, '*Erga Omnes, Jus Cogens* and Their Impact on the Law of State Responsibility' in Evans M and Koutrakos P (eds), *The International Responsibility of the European Union; European and International Perspectives* (Hart Publishing 2013) 163–88

Tavernier T, 'L'identification des règles fondamentales, un problème résolu?' in Tomuschat C and Thouvenin J-M (eds), *The Fundamental Rules of the International Legal Order:* 'Jus Cogens' *and Obligations* 'Erga Omnes' (Martinus Nijhoff Publishers 2006) 1–20

Tigroudja H, 'Violations de droits de l'homme et engagement de la "responsabilité aggravée" de l'état: Quelle contribution du droit international des droits de l'homme au droit international de la responsabilité?' in *L'homme et le droit, En hommage au Professeur Jean-François Flauss* (Pedone 2014) 755–64

Tomuschat C, 'Individual Reparation Claims in Instances of Grave Human Rights Violations: The Position under General International Law' in Randelzhofer A and Tomuschat C (eds), *State Responsibility and the Individual: Reparation in Instances of Grave Violations of Human Rights* (Martinus Nijhoff Publishers 1999) 1–26

Tomuschat C, 'Recognition of New States—The Case of Premature Recognition' in Hilpold P (ed), *Kosovo and International Law: The ICJ Advisory Opinion of 22 July 2010* (Martinus Nijhoff Publishers 2012) 31–45

van Boven T, 'Prevention, Early-Warning and Urgent Procedures; a New Approach by the Committee on the Elimination of Racial Discrimination' in de Waart PJIM, Denters E, and Schrijver N (eds), *Reflections on International Law from the Low Countries in Honour of Paul de Waart* (Martinus Nijhoff Publishers 1998) 165–82

van Boven T, 'Victims' Rights to a Remedy and Reparation: The New United Nations Principles and Guidelines' in Ferstman C, Goetz M, and Stephens A (eds), *Reparations for Victims of Genocide, War Crimes and Crimes Against Humanity: Systems in Place and Systems in the Making* (Martinus Nijhoff Publishers 2009) 19–40

van Boven T, 'Categories of Rights' in Moeckli D, Sangeeta S, and Sivakumaran S (eds), *International Human Rights Law* (3rd edn, OUP 2018) 135–47

Vashakmadze M, 'Responsibility to Protect' in Simma B and others (eds), *The Charter of the United Nations: A Commentary* (3rd edn, OUP 2012) 1201–36

Viljoen F, 'The African System of Human Rights' in Zyberi G and Mason K (eds), *An Institutional Approach to the Responsibility to Protect* (CUP 2013) 481–508

Weschler J, 'Acting on Human Rights' in von Einsiedel S and others (eds), *The UN Security Council in the 21st Century* (Lynne Rienner Publishers 2015) 259–75

Wittich S, 'Punitive Damages' in Crawford J, Pellet A, and Olleson S (eds), *The Law of International Responsibility* (OUP 2010) 667–75

Wolfrum R, 'Enforcing Community Interests Through International Dispute Settlement: Reality or Utopia?' in Fastenrath Uand others (eds), *From Bilateralism to Community Interest: Essays in Honour of Bruno Simma* (OUP 2011) 1132–45

Wühler N, 'The United Nations Compensation Commission' in Randelzhofer A and Tomuschat C (eds), *State Responsibility and the Individual: Reparation in Instances of Grave Violations of Human Rights* (Martinus Nijhoff Publishers 1999) 213–30

Wyler E and Papaux Al, 'The Different Forms of Reparation: Satisfaction' in Crawford J, Pellet A, and Olleson S (eds), *The Law of International Responsibility* (OUP 2010) 623–38

Articles in periodicals

Abbott K and Snidal D, 'Hard and Soft Law in International Governance' (2000) 54 International Organization 421–46

Abi-Saab G, 'The Uses of Article 19' (1999) 10 EJIL 339–51

Akehurst M, 'Reprisals by Third States' (1970) 44 BYIL 1–18

Albertson Fineman M, 'The Vulnerable Subject: Anchoring Equality in the Human Condition' (2008) 20 Yale J L Fem 1–23

Alland D, 'Countermeasures of General Interest' (2002) 13 EJIL 1221–39

Altwicker-Hamori S, Altwicker T, and Peters A, 'Measuring Violations of Human Rights: An Empirical Analysis of Awards in Respect of Non-Pecuniary Damage Under the European Convention on Human Rights' (2016) 76 Zeitschrift für ausländisches öffentliches Recht und Völkerrecht/Heidelberg Journal of International Law 1–51

Arbour L, 'The Responsibility to Protect as a Duty of Care in International Law and Practice' (2008) 34 Rev Intl Stud 445–58

Arcari M, 'Responsabilité de l'État pour violations graves du droit international et système de securité collective des Nations Unies' (2005) 21 Anuario de Derecho Internacional 415–48

Aznar-Gómez MJ, 'A Decade of Human Rights Protection by the UN Security Council: A Sketch of Deregulation?' (2002) 13 EJIL 223–41

Basch FF, 'The Doctrine of the Inter-American Court of Human Rights Regarding States' Duty to Punish Human Rights Violations and Its Dangers' (2007) 23 AUILR 195–229

Bellal A, 'Building Respect for the Rule of Law in Violent Contexts: The Office of the High Commissioner for Human Rights' Experience and Approach' (2014) 96 IRRC 881–900

Bellamy AJ and Williams PD, 'Whither the Responsibility to Protect? Humanitarian Intervention and the 2005 World Summit' (2006) 20 Eth & Int A 143–69

Bellamy AJ and Williams PD, 'The Responsibility to Protect—Five Years On' (2010) 24 Eth & Int A 143–69

Bellamy AJ and Williams PD, 'Libya and the Responsibility to Protect: The Exception and the Norm' (2011) 25 Eth & Int A 263–69

Bianchi A, 'Human Rights and the Magic of Jus Cogens' (2008) 19 EJIL 491–508

Boisson de Chazournes L and Condorelli L, 'De la "responsabilité de protéger", ou d'une nouvelle parure pour une notion déjà bien établie' (2006) 1 RGDIP 11–18

Buyse A, 'The Pilot Judgment Procedure at the European Court of Human Rights: Possibilities and Challenges' (2009) 'European Court of Human Rights, 50 Years', Special issue, Nomiko Vima [Greek Law Journal] 78–90

Byers M, 'Conceptualising the Relationship between Jus Cogens and Erga Omnes Rules' (1997) 66 NJIL 211–39

Cançado Trindade AA, 'The Domestic Jurisdiction of States in the Practice of the United Nations and Regional Organisations' (1976) 25 ICLQ 715–65

Carrillo AJ and Palmer J, 'Transnational Mass Claim Processes (TMCPs) in International Law and Practice' (2010) 28 Ber JIL 343–430

Cassese A, 'Remarks on Scelle's Theory of "Role Splitting" (dédoublement fonctionnel) in International Law' (1990) 1 EJIL 210–31

Cassese A, 'A Follow-up: Forcible Humanitarian Countermeasures and *Opinio Necessitatis*' (1999) 10 EJIL 791–99

Cassese A, '*Ex Iniuria Ius Oritur*: Are We Moving towards International Legitimation of Forcible Humanitarian Countermeasures in the World Community?' (1999) 10 EJIL 23–30

Chapman AR and Carbonetti B, 'Human Rights Protections for Vulnerable and Disadvantaged Groups: The Contributions of the UN Committee on Economic, Social and Cultural Rights' (2011) 33 HRQ 682–732

Chesterman S, '"Leading from Behind": The Responsibility to Protect, the Obama Doctrine, and Humanitarian Intervention after Libya' (2011) 25 Eth & Int A 279–85

Clapham A, 'Human Rights Obligations of Non-State Actors in Conflict Situations' (2006) 88 IRRC 491–523

Dawidowicz M, 'Public Law Enforcement without Public Law Safeguards? An Analysis of State Practice on Third-Party Countermeasures and Their Relationship to the UN Security Council' (2007) 77 BYIL 333–418

Dawidowicz M, 'State Responsibility: The General Part' (2016) 29 QIL 3–15

de Gouttes R, 'La Convention Internationale et Le Comité Des Nations Unies Sur l'élimination de La Discrimination Raciale' (1996) 28 RTDH 515–39 de Gouttes R, 'Le rôle du Comité des Nations Unies pour l'élimination de la discrimination raciale' (2001) 46 RTDH 567–84

de Wet E, 'The Modern Practice of Intervention by Invitation in Africa and Its Implications for the Prohibition of the Use of Force' (2015) 26 EJIL 979–98

Desmet E, 'The UN Basic Principles and Guidelines on the Right to a Remedy and Reparation: A Landmark or Window-Dressing? An Analysis with Special Attention to the Situation of Indigenous People' (2008) 24 SAJHR 71–103

Dilek K, 'Forsaking Individual Justice: The Implications of the European Court of Human Rights' Pilot Judgment Procedure for Victims of Gross and Systematic Violations' (2016) 16 HR L Rev 731–69

Dominicé C, 'The International Responsibility of States for Breach of Multilateral Obligations' (1999) 10 EJIL 353–63

Donnelly J, 'International Human Rights: A Regime Analysis' (1986) 40 International Organisation 599–642

Donnelly J, 'The Emerging International Regime Against Torture' (1986) 33 NILR 1–23

Doswald-Beck L, 'The Right to Life in Armed Conflict: Does International Humanitarian Law Provide All the Answers?' (2006) 88 IRRC 881–904

Droege C, 'Elective Affinities? Human Rights and Humanitarian Law' (2008) 90 IRRC 501–48

Dupuy P-M, 'Observations sur la pratique récente des "sanctions" de l'illicite' (1983) 87 RGDIP 505–48

Ermacora F, 'Procedures to Deal with Human Rights Violations: A Hopeful Start in the United Nations?' (1974) 7 HRJ 670–89

Fairley HS, 'State Actors, Humanitarian Intervention and International Law: Reopening Pandora's Box' (1980) 10 Ga J Intl & Comp L 29–63

Fikfak V, 'Non-Pecuniary Damages before the European Court of Human Rights: Forget the Victim; It's All about the State' (2020) 33 Leiden Journal of International Law 335–69

Fletcher LE, 'A Wolf in Sheep's Clothing: Transitional Justice and the Effacement of State Accountability for International Crimes' (2015) 39 FILJ 447–531

Focarelli C, 'Promotional Jus Cogens: A Critical Appraisal of Jus Cogens' Legal Effects' (2008) 77 NJIL 429–60

Fonteyne J-PL, 'The Customary International Law Doctrine of Humanitarian Intervention: Its Current Validity under the UN Charter' (1973) 4 Cal W Intl LJ 203–70

Gaja G, 'Réflexions sur le rôle du Conseil de sécurité dans le nouvel ordre mondial. A propos des rapports entre maintien de la paix et crimes internationaux des états"' (1993) 97 RGDIP 297–320

Gattini A, 'A Return Ticket to "Communitarisme", Please' (2002) 13 EJIL 1181–99

Gonzales TD, 'The Political Sources of Procedural Debates in the United Nations: Structural Impediments to Implementation of Human Rights' (1980) 13 NYUJILP 427–72

Gowlland-Debbas V, 'Security Council Enforcement Action and Issues of State Responsibility' (1994) 43 ICLQ 55–98

Green JF, 'Changing Approaches to Human Rights: The United Nations, 1954 and 1974' (1977) 12 TILJ 223–38

Gutter J, 'Special Procedures and the Human Rights Council: Achievements and Challenges Ahead' (2007) 7 HR L Rev 93–107

Haeck Y and Burbano Herrera C, 'Interim Measures in the Case Law of the European Court of Human Rights' (2003) 21 NQHR 625–75

Hamber B, 'Repairing the Irreparable: Dealing with the Double-Binds of Making Reparations for Crimes of the Past' (2000) 5 Ethnicity and Health 215–26

Hasenclever A, Mayer P, and Rittberger V, 'Integrating Theories of International Regimes' (2000) 26 Rev Intl Stud 3–33
Hayner PB, 'Truth Commissions: A Schematic Overview' (2006) 88 IRRC 295–310
Higgins R, 'The Place of International Law in the Settlement of Disputes by the Security Council' (1970) 64 AJIL 1–18
Hottelier M, 'La nécessaire complémentarité des droits matériels et des garanties de procédure' (2007) RTDH 573, 573–86
Kamminga MT, 'The Thematic Procedures of the UN Commission on Human Rights' (1987) 34 NILR 299–323
Kamminga MT, 'Is the European Convention on Human Rights Sufficiently Equipped to Cope with Gross and Systematic Violations?' (1994) 12 NQHR 153–64
Kingston LN, 'Protecting the World's Most Persecuted: The Responsibility to Protect and Burma's Rohingya Minority' (2015) 19 IJHR 1163–70
Kioko B, 'The Right of Intervention under the African Union's Constitutive Act: From Non-Interference to Non-Intervention' (2003) 85 IRRC 807–25
Klein P, 'Responsibility for Serious Breaches of Obligations Deriving from Peremptory Norms of International Law and United Nations Law' (2002) 13 EJIL 1241–55
Kolb R, 'La structure constitutionnelle du droit international public' (2001) 39 CYIL 69–114
Kolb R, 'Du domaine reserve—Réflexions sur la théorie du domaine réservé' (2006) 113 RGDIP 597–629
Koskenniemi M, 'The Police in the Temple Order, Justice and the UN: A Dialectical View' (1995) 6 EJIL 325–48
Koskenniemi M, 'The Pull of the Mainstream' (1989) 88 Mich L Rev 1946–62
Koskenniemi M, 'Solidarity Measures: State Responsibility as a New International Order?' (2001) 72 BYIL 337–56
Krasner SD, 'Structural Causes and Regime Consequences: Regimes as Intervening Variables' (1982) 36 International Organization 185–205
Lambert Abdelgawad E, 'L'exécution des arrêts de la Cour européenne des droits de l'homme (2011)' (2012) 92 RTDH 861–86
Lambert Abdelgawad E, 'L'exécution des arrêts de la Cour européenne des droits de l'homme (2012)' (2013) 95 RTDH 635–52
Lambert Abdelgawad E, 'L'exécution des arrêts de la Cour européenne des droits de l'homme (2014)' (2015) 104 RTDH 965–85
Le Mon CJ and Taylor RS, 'Security Council Action in the Name of Human Rights: From Rhodesia to the Congo' (2003) 10 UC Dav J Int L & Pol 197–228
Lillich RB, 'Forcible Self-Help by States to Protect Human Rights International Procedures to Protect Human Rights: A Symposium' (1967) 53 Iowa L Rev 325–51
Luck EC, 'The Responsibility to Protect: Growing Pains or Early Promise?' (2010) 24 Eth & Int A 349–65
Mégret F, 'International Judges and Experts' Impartiality and the Problem of Past Declarations' (2011) 10 The Law and Practice of International Courts and Tribunals 31–66
Meron T, 'On a Hierarchy of International Human Rights' (1986) 80 AJIL 1–23
Morowa Al HE, 'Vulnerability as a Concept of International Human Rights Law' (2003) 6 J Intl Rel Dev 139–55
Mowbray A, 'Duties of Investigation Under the European Convention on Human Rights' (2002) 51 ICLQ 437–48
Naqvi Y, 'The Right to the Truth in International Law: Fact or Fiction?' (2006) 88 IRRC 245–73

Nollkaemper A, 'Systemic Effects of International Responsibility for International Crimes' (2010) 8 San Cl J Intl L 313–52

Nowak M, 'The Right to Reparation of Victims of Gross Human Rights Violations' (2001) 7(1) HR Dev C YB 275–308

Oellers-Frahm K, 'Comment: The Erga Omnes Applicability of Human Rights' (1992) 30 Archiv des Völkerrechts 28–37

Orakhelashvili A, 'The Legal Basis of the United Nations Peace-Keeping Operations' (2002) 43 Va J Intl L 485–524

Orford A, 'Muscular Humanitarianism: Reading the Narratives of the New Interventionism' (1999) 10 EJIL 679–711

Österdahl I, 'The Exception as the Rule: Lawmaking on Force and Human Rights by the UN Security Council' (2005) 10 JC & SL 1–20

Palmisano G, 'Les causes d'aggravation de la responsabilité des etats et la distinction entre "crimes" et "delits" internationaux' (1994) 98 RGDIP 629–73

Paris R, 'The "Responsibility to Protect" and the Structural Problems of Preventive Humanitarian Intervention' (2014) 21 Int'l Peacekeeping 569–603

Pellet A, 'Can a State Commit a Crime? Definitely, Yes!' (1999) 10 EJIL 425–34

Peroni L and Timmer A, 'Vulnerable Groups: The Promise of an Emerging Concept in European Human Rights Convention Law' (2013) 11 ICON 1056–85

Reidy A, Hampson F, and Boyle K, 'Gross Violations of Human Rights: Invoking the European Convention on Human Rights in the Case of Turkey' (1997) 15 NQHR 161–73

Reisman WM, 'International Lawmaking: A Process of Communication' (1981) 75 ASILP 101–20

Rougier A, 'La theorie de l'intervention d'humanité' (1910) 17 RGDIP 468–526

Schachter O, 'Human Dignity as a Normative Concept' (1983) 77 AJIL 848–54

Schachter O, 'The Right of States to Use Armed Force International Law' (1983) 82 Mich L Rev 1620–46

Schönsteiner J, 'Dissuasive Measures and the "Society as a Whole": A Working Theory of Reparations in the Inter-American Court of Human Rights' (2007) 23 AUILR 127–64

Siatitsa IM, 'The Evolution of the Monitoring Mechanism of the Framework Convention for the Protection of National Minorities; Cooperation of Independent and Political Bodies in the Interest of Effectiveness' (2010) 63 Revue Hellénique de Droit International 771–93

Siatitsa IM, '"A Serious Violation of International Human Rights Law"—An Attempt to Clarify a Crucial Provision of the Arms Trade Treaty' (2015) 5 EJHR 606–30

Siatitsa IM and Titberidze M, 'Human Rights in Armed Conflict: Ten Years of Affirmative State Practice within United Nations Resolutions' (2012) 3 JIHLS 233–62

Sicilianos L-A, 'The Classification of Obligations and the Multilateral Dimension of the Relations of International Responsibility' (2002) 13 EJIL 1127–45

Sicilianos L-A, 'L' influence des droits de l'homme sur la structure du droit international, première partie: la hiérarchisation de l'ordre juridique international' (2012) 117 RGDIP 5–30

Sicilianos L-A, 'L' influence des droits de l'homme sur la structure du droit international, deuxième partie: Les consequences structurelles de la hierarchisation' (2012) 117 RGDIP 241–74

Sicilianos L-A, 'The Involvement of the European Court of Human Rights in the Implementation of Its Judgments: Recent Developments under Article 46 ECHR' (2014) 32 NQHR 235–63

Sicilianos L-A, 'La Cour européenne des droits de l'homme face à l'Europe en crise' (2016) 105 RTDH 5–42

Simma B, 'NATO, the UN and the Use of Force: Legal Aspects' (1999) 10 EJIL 1–22

Simma B and Alston P, 'The Sources of Human Rights Law: Custom, *Jus Cogens*, and General Principles' (1988) 12 Aust YB IL 82–108

Stahn C, 'Responsibility to Protect: Political Rhetoric or Emerging Legal Norm?' (2007) 101 AJIL 99–120

Stultz N, 'The Apartheid Issue at the General Assembly: Stalemate or Gathering Storm?' (1987) 86 African Affairs 25–45

Tams CJ, 'Do Serious Breaches Give Rise to Any Specific Obligations of the Responsible State?' (2002) 13 EJIL 1161–80

Tardu ME, 'United Nations Response to Gross Violations of Human Rights: The 1503 Procedure' (1980) 20 Sant Cl LR 559–601

Teimouri H, 'Protecting While Not Being Responsible: The Case of Syria and Responsibility to Protect' (2015) 19 IJHR 1279–89

Teraya K, 'Emerging Hierarchy in International Human Rights and Beyond: From the Perspective of Non-Derogable Rights' (2001) 12 EJIL 917–41

Thirlway H, 'The Law and Procedure of the International Court of Justice 1960–1989, Part One' (1990) 60 BYIL 1–157

Tolley H, 'The Concealed Crack in the Citadel: The United Nations Commission on Human Rights' Response to Confidential Communications' (1984) 6 HRQ 420–62

Truscan I, 'Considerations of Vulnerability: From Principles to Action in the Cases Law of the European Court of Human Rights' (2013) 36 Retfærd Årgang [Nordic Journal of Law and Justice] 64–83

van den Herik L, 'An Inquiry into the Role of Commissions of Inquiry in International Law: Navigating the Tensions between Fact-Finding and Application of International Law' (2014) 13 CJIL 507–37

Villalpando S, 'The Legal Dimension of the International Community: How Community Interests Are Protected in International Law' (2010) 21 EJIL 387–419

Weil P, 'Towards Relative Normativity in International Law' (1983) 77 AJIL 413–42

Weiss TG, 'The Sunset of Humanitarian Intervention? The Responsibility to Protect in a Unipolar Era' (2004) 35 Security Dialogue 135–53

Welsh JM and Banda M, 'International Law and the Responsibility to Protect: Clarifying or Expanding States' Responsibilities Special Issue: R2P and International Law' (2010) 2 Global Responsibility to Protect 213–31

Wyler E, 'From "State Crime" to Responsibility for "Serious Breaches of Obligations under Peremptory Norms of General International Law"' (2002) 13 EJIL 1147–60

Theses

Brugere A-L, 'La "menace contre la paix" dans la pratique du Conseil de sécurité des Nations Unies: réflexions sur un concept de droit international' (University of Geneva 2013)

Kouassi R, 'Programmes de réparations, justice transitionnelle et droit international: analyse à la lumière du droit individuel à réparation' (Thesis, University of Geneva 2017)

Krähenmann S, 'Positive Obligations in Human Rights Treaties' (Thesis, Graduate Institute of International and Development Studies 2012)

Collected Courses of the Hague Academy of International Law (RCADI)

Cançado Trindade AA, 'International Law for Humankind: Towards a New *Jus Gentium* (I): General Course on Public International Law' (2005) 316 RCADI 9

Crawford J, 'Multilateral Rights and Obligations in International Law' (2006) 319 RCADI 325

Frowein JA, 'Reactions by Not Directly Affected States to Breaches of Public International Law' (1994) 248 RCADI 345

Gaja G, '*Jus Cogens* beyond the Vienna Convention' (1981) 172 RCADI 271

Gaja G, 'The Protection of General Interests in the International Community: General Course on Public International Law' (2013) 364 RCADI 9

Meron T, 'International Law in the Age of Human Rights: General Course on Public International Law' (2003) 301 RCADI 9

Reisman WM, 'The Quest for World Order and Human Dignity in the Twenty-First Century: Constitutive Process and Individual Commitment' (2012) 351 RCADI 9

Sicilianos L-A, 'Entre multilatéralisme et unilatéralisme: L'autorisation par le Conseil de sécurité de recourir à la force' (2009) 339 RCADI 9

Simma B, 'From Bilateralism to Community Interest in International Law' (1994) 254 RCADI 217

Tomuschat C, 'Obligations Arising for States without or against Their Will' (1993) 241 RCADI 195

Virally M, 'Panorama du droit international contemporain: Cours Général de Droit International Public' (1983) 183 RCADI 9

Williams PD, 'Military Responses to Mass Killing: The African Union Mission in Sudan' (2006) 13 Int'l Peacekeeping 168

Online sources

Akande D and Tonkin H, 'International Commissions of Inquiry: A New Form of Adjudication?' <https://www.ejiltalk.org/international-commissions-of-inquiry-a-new-form-of-adjudication/> accessed 12 August 2021

Amnesty International, 'Turkey accused of gross human rights violations in Gezi Park protests', 2 October 2013 <https://www.amnesty.org/en/latest/news/2013/10/turkey-accused-gross-human-rights-violations-gezi-park-protests/> accessed 16 September 2021

Bartels L, 'Human Rights Provisions in Economic Partnership Agreements in Light of the Expiry of the Cotonou Agreement in 2020' (EU Publications 2017) <https://www.europarl.europa.eu/thinktank/en/document.html?reference=EXPO_STU(2017)578011> accessed 19 August 2021

Bellal A, 'Human Rights Obligations of Armed Non-State Actors: An Exploration of the Practice of the UN Human Rights Council', Geneva Academy of International Humanitarian Law and Human Rights (2016) <https://www.geneva-academy.ch/joomlatools-files/docman-files/InBrief7_web.pdf> accessed 16 September 2021

Boutruche T, 'Selecting and Applying Legal Lenses in Monitoring, Reporting, and Fact-Finding Missions' (SSRN 2013) SSRN ID 2337437, 31–32 <http://papers.ssrn.com/abstract=2337437>

Byman D, 'Do Targeted Killings Work?' (2006) 85 Foreign Affairs <https://www.foreignaffairs.com/articles/israel/2006-03-01/do-targeted-killings-work> accessed 9 October 2021

International Committee of the Red Cross (ICRC), 'Article 1: Respect for the Convention' in *Commentary on the First Geneva Convention: Convention (I) for the Amelioration of the Condition of the Wounded and Sick in Armed Forces in the Field* (2nd edn, 2016) <https://ihl-databases.icrc.org/ihl/full/GCI-commentary> accessed 11 October 2021

Leach P, Paraskeva C, and Uzelac G, 'International Human Rights & Fact-Finding; An Analysis of the Fact-Finding Missions Conducted by the European Commission and Court of Human Rights', Report by the Human Rights and Social Justice Research Institute at London Metropolitan University (2009) <http://www.academia.edu/1315823/INTERNATIONAL_HUMAN_RIGHTS_and_FACT-FINDING> accessed 11 October 2021

Mégret F and others, 'Human Dignity: A Special Focus on Vulnerable Groups, Protecting Dignity', Panel on Human Dignity (2014) <https://www.graduateinstitute.ch/sites/internet/files/2020-11/HumanDignity_Megret.pdf> accessed 11 October 2021

Index

For the benefit of digital users, indexed terms that span two pages (e.g., 52–53) may, on occasion, appear on only one of those pages.